THE POLITICS OF ETHNICITY:
INDIGENOUS PEOPLES
IN LATIN AMERICAN STATES

Edited by
David Maybury-Lewis

Published by Harvard University
David Rockefeller Center for Latin American Studies

Distributed by Harvard University Press
Cambridge, Massachusetts
London, England

Library of Congress Cataloging-in-Publication Data

The politics of ethnicity: indigenous peoples in Latin American states / edited by David Maybury-Lewis.
 p. cm. — (David Rockefeller Center series on Latin American studies, Harvard University)
 Includes bibliographical references and index
 ISBN 0-674-00964-9
 1. Indians of South America—Government relations. 2. Indians—Government relations.
3. Indians—Politics and government. 4. Indians—Ethnic identity. I. Maybury-Lewis,
David. II. Series.

F2230.1.G68 P65 2002
323.1'19708—dc2l
                                                        2002073938

*This book is dedicated to the native
peoples of the Americas, who have
fought for five centuries for the right to
be themselves, and to their
organizations, whose continuing
struggle is an inspiration to us all.*

Contents

Section I: **Mexico and Central America**

Section II: **The Colombian War Zone**

Section III: **The Andean Countries**

Section IV: **Lowland South American Countries**

List of Maps

Contributors to this Volume

Bartholomew Dean is Assistant Professor of Anthropology at the University of Kansas. Dean's research and publications have emphasized the kinship, politics, material culture, cosmology, and human rights of Peruvian Amazonia's indigenous peoples. In 1995, he and his wife Michelle McKinley cofounded the Amazonian Peoples' Resources Initiative. Dean is also a founding member of the Graduate program in Amazonian Studies at the Universidad Nacional Mayor de San Marcos where he has been a visiting professor of Anthropology since 1999. He currently serves as the Contributing Editor for Lowland South American Ethnology for the U.S. Library of Congress' *Handbook of Latin American Studies*. He was awarded the Royal Anthropological Institute's Fellowship in Urgent Anthropology, 1998–1999. Dean coedited *At the Risk of Being Heard: Identity, Indigenous Rights & Postcolonial States* and is currently completing a monograph entitled *Ambivalent Exchanges: Urarina Society, Cosmos & History in Peruvian Amazonia*.

Paul H. Gelles, an Associate Professor of Anthropology at the University of California at Riverside, has carried out research on different aspects of highland society in the central and southern Peruvian Andes. He is author of numerous articles as well as the book, *Water and Power in Highland Peru: The Cultural Politics of Irrigation and Development*. He is also the cotranslator of a widely used text, *Andean Lives,* and the coproducer of the award-winning film, *Transnational Fiesta*.

Bret Gustafson, Assistant Professor of Anthropology at Washington University in St. Louis, received his PhD in Anthropology from Harvard University in 2002 for research on the relationship between state bilingual education reform and Guarani political mobilization in southeastern Bolivia. His next project will examine the politics of natural gas exploitation and pipeline development in the Guarani region.

James Howe, Professor of Anthropology at the Massachusetts Institute of Technology, has worked in Panama since 1970. He is the author of *The Kuna Gathering: Contemporary Village Politics in Panama, A People Who Would Not Kneel: Panama, the United States, and the San Blas Kuna,* and numerous articles and reports.

Jean Jackson is Professor and Head of Anthropology in the Anthropology Program at the Massachusetts Institute of Technology. She has carried out fieldwork in Mexico, Guatemala and in the Vaupés region in southeastern Colombia. Her earlier Latin American research interests included small-scale societies, kinship and marriage, and anthropological linguistics; more recently they have been concerned with gender and the indigenous movement. She published *The Fish People: Linguistic Exogamy and Tukanoan Identity in Northwest Amazonia* (Cambridge University Press) in 1983. *Indigenous Movements, Self-Representation and the State in Latin America*, co-edited with Kay B. Warren, was published by the University of Texas Press in 2002. An ethnography based on research in the United States, *"Camp Pain": Talking with Chronic Pain Patients*, appeared in 2000, University of Pennsylvania Press.

Jerome M. Levi, an Associate Professor of Anthropology and Chair of Latin American Studies at Carleton College in Northfield, Minnesota, has conducted research in Mexico among the Tarahumara of Chihuahua and Tzotzil of Chiapas as well as in the southwestern U.S. among the Navajo and Yuman peoples in the borderlands. His work has focused on religion, material culture, and interethnic relations. He has prepared Congressional testimony on indigenous land rights, was a recent Fellow at the University of Chicago's Globalization Project, and in 2001 was awarded a Technos International Fellowship to Japan by the Tanaka Ikueikai Educational Trust. A contributor to *The Oxford Encyclopedia of Mesoamerican Cultures*, he is the author of numerous articles and co-editor of a new book, *At the Risk of Being Heard: Identity, Indigenous Rights, and Postcolonial States.*

Theodore Macdonald is the Associate Director for the *Program on Nonviolent Sanctions and Cultural Survival* at the Weatherhead Center for International Affairs, Harvard University, and a Research Associate at the Peabody Museum of Anthropology, Harvard University. Since 1974 he has been conducting research in Ecuador's Upper Amazon region and, as Projects Director for Cultural Survival (1979–1995), worked with many of the region's indigenous organizations, social movements, development projects, and conflicts. His most recent book, *Ethnicity and Culture Among New "Neighbors": The Runa of Ecuador's Amazon Region,* chronicles much of that period.

David Maybury-Lewis is the Edward C. Henderson Professor of Anthropology at Harvard University. He has done fieldwork in Brazil and written extensively about indigenous affairs in the Americas and elsewhere. He and his wife founded Cultural Survival.

María Clemencia Ramírez is a Senior Researcher at Instituto Colombiano de Antropología e Historia, and Professor of Anthropology at Universidad de los Andes, Bogotá (Colombia). Since 1975 she has carried out research on different topics (ethnohistory, ethnology, politics of identity, state formation, social movements and violence) in the Amazon Region of Colombia and specifically in the Putumayo department; this area of southern Colombia, where the armed forces, guerillas, paramilitaries and drug traffickers are all active, is scarred by severe conflict. She is author of various articles as well as the books *Entre el estado y la guerrilla: identidad y ciudadanía en el movimiento de los campesinos cocaleros del Putumayo* and *Frontera fluida entre Andes piedemonte y selva: el caso del Valle de Sibundoy, siglos XVI–XVIII*. She is also co-author of the book *Atlas cultural de la Amazonia Colombiana: la construcción del territorio en el siglo XX*.

Richard Reed is Associate Professor of Anthropology at Trinity University. His research focuses on indigenous groups in Paraguay, western Brazil and northern Argentina. He is the author of numerous articles as well as two recent books, *Prophets of Agroforestry* and *Forest Dwellers, Forest Protectors: Indigenous Models of International Development*.

Jennifer Schirmer is a Research Professor in Oslo and an Affiliate of PONSACS (Program on Nonviolent Sanctions and Cultural Survival) at Harvard University. She has written extensively on Guatemala, including her book *The Guatemalan Military Project: A Violence Called Democracy,* based on ten years of research. Currently she is conducting research on Guatemala, supported by a grant from the John D. and Catherine T. MacArthur Foundation.

Preface and Acknowledgments

David Maybury-Lewis

For more than five centuries the nations of the Americas have insisted that their indigenous populations should abandon their ethnicity and blend into the mainstream. In recent years this has begun to change. Country after country has formally declared itself pluriethnic and announced that its indigenous peoples were welcome to maintain their ethnic identities.

In the spring of 2000 David Maybury-Lewis took advantage of a special opportunity to convene a conference in Cambridge, Massachusetts to discuss this phenomenon. The opportunity arose because a large number of scholars specializing in indigenous affairs in Latin America were already in the Cambridge area. Seven of them (Bret Gustafson, James Howe, Jean Jackson, Theodore Macdonald Jr., David Maybury-Lewis, María Clemencia Ramírez and Jennifer Schirmer) were able to attend the conference. They were joined by four others (Bartholomew Dean, Paul Gelles, Jerome Levi and Richard Reed) who came to Cambridge for the meeting. In this way we could gather, at modest cost, an unusually wide range of expertise, covering most of Latin America, though the conference could not and did not attempt to be encyclopedic. Jerome Levi and Jennifer Schirmer discussed Mexico and Central America, showing the contrast in indigenous policies in that region. Jean Jackson and María Clemencia Ramírez dealt with the Colombian war zone which, as James Howe showed, has also seriously affected Panama. Theodore Macdonald Jr. (Ecuador), Bartholomew Dean (lowland Peru), Paul Gelles (highland Peru) and Bret Gustafson (Bolivia) dealt with the Andean countries. Finally, Richard Reed (Paraguay) and David Maybury-Lewis (Brazil) talked about lowland South America.

The major omission in this volume is of the Southern Cone countries (Argentina and Chile). We hope to discuss them at a follow-up conference on *Manifest Destinies and Indigenous Peoples,* which will focus on large, "continental" countries with sparse indigenous populations such as Argentina, Chile, Brazil, the USA and Canada. That conference will focus on the histories of ethnic cleansing, justified by theories of entitlement, which have characterized the relations between invaders and indigenous peoples in those countries.

This book, by contrast, presents those cases where the relations between states and their indigenous populations have become part of contemporary rethinkings of the states themselves. This volume consists of papers, now edited for publication, that were first presented at the Cambridge conference on indigenous peoples in Latin American states in the spring of 2000.

We are deeply grateful to Jorge Domínguez and James Cooney who arranged funding for the conference through the Weatherhead Center for International Affairs at Harvard University. We are also grateful for the collaboration, both during and after the conference, of the David Rockefeller Center for Latin American Studies (DRCLAS), of the Program on Nonviolent Sanctions and Cultural Survival (PONSACS) and the Department of Anthropology, all of Harvard University. It was the efforts of Amanda Flohr in particular that ensured the smooth running of the conference. Finally, we wish to acknowledge the inspiration and collaboration of Cultural Survival, an organization that does not allow indigenous issues to disappear from the world's agenda.

We have been able to move this volume quickly from conference to publication thanks to the help received from the United States Institute of Peace (USIP) in Washington, D.C. The USIP appointed David Maybury-Lewis to a Senior Fellowship in the first half of 2001, during which time he was able, among other things, to do much of the editing of this book. In this he was ably assisted by Heather Staley in Washington and Linda Ordogh in Cambridge. We also wish to express our deepest gratitude to June Carolyn Erlick, our editor, who believed in this book and gave us constant help with it. In conclusion, we owe an immense debt of gratitude to Jennifer Soroko for her superlative work in preparing the manuscript for publication just as she was due to depart for the Pacific.

Introduction

David Maybury-Lewis

The traditional, in some cases centuries-old, relations between states and indigenous peoples in Latin America are now changing, or at the very least being rediscussed. States that once insisted that their indigenous populations should abandon their ethnicities and assimilate have now proclaimed themselves pluriethnic (Mexico, Colombia, Ecuador, Bolivia). In some states, indigenous protests have attracted support from other sectors of society (Mexico, Ecuador) and led to a rethinking of the nature and future of the nations concerned. Such rethinking is complicated in many states by the fact that it is being carried out in the midst of civil wars and/or conflicts related to the drug trade (Colombia, Peru, Bolivia, and even Panama). In other states indigenous peoples are trying to find a new relationship to the state in the aftermath of long and bitter conflict (Guatemala). In yet other states (Brazil, Paraguay) dramatic social changes are affecting the circumstances of indigenous peoples, while their governments drag their feet on issues of indigenous rights. Meanwhile the international indigenous movement, with its representation at the United Nations in Geneva, keeps these issues on the agenda of a world that would probably just as soon forget them. This is, therefore, a good moment to take stock of the unprecedented changes taking place throughout the hemisphere in order to understand, through comparative analysis, why the relations between indigenous peoples and states play out in such different ways in different countries.

In his paper on Mexico, Jay Levi stresses the variety of distinct relationships that indigenous peoples maintain with the Mexican state, using the Tarahumara and the Maya of Chiapas as his two prime examples. He points out that Maya leaders in Chiapas had become an indigenous elite, benefiting from the patronage of the PRI, the party that governed Mexico from the revolution until the election of President Vicente Fox in 2000. He goes on to analyze the internal schisms among both the Maya and the Tarahumara and to consider how these and similar phenomena elsewhere in Mexico relate to the nation's formal declaration (by the constitutional amendment of 1990) that it is pluricultural. This pluriculturalism represents a dramatic break with Mexico's traditional *indigenismo*, through which the nation took the

lead in developing programs that would persuade and assist indigenous peoples to assimilate to the mainstream mestizo culture. Yet it is
not clear what the new pluriculturalism actually means and what its
practical effects will be. What is clear is that the Zapatista challenge to
the Mexican state has evoked considerable sympathy from Indians and
non-Indians throughout Mexico who believe that a reorientation of
the state's relationship to the nation's people is much to be desired.
Meanwhile, an argument is raging over what kinds of *pueblos* will have
their rights guaranteed under the new constitution, since the word
pueblo can mean a town, a community, or a people. In any case, indigenous rights and their implications are now recognized to be at the
center of Mexico's sense of itself as a modern nation.

Jennifer Schirmer's chapter provides a sharp contrast to Levi's. She
shows how the military feel that they too are creating a new Guatemala,
but they are doing so by "disciplining the Indians like children." Their
technique during the civil war was to create a culture of fear and complicity among the Maya. The Indians were forced to fight against other
Indians, thus implicating them in the horrors being perpetrated by the
army, and turning the conflict from a war of the army versus revolutionaries into one of Indians versus Indians. Those communities that
refused to do the army's bidding were those marked down for annihilation. The army is thus seeking to reinvent the Maya of Guatemala as
a people bereft of history, of memory, and above all of agency in their
own affairs.

The Kuna Indians of Panama have long been considered the prime
example of an indigenous people that has succeeded in protecting its
lands and its way of life and controlling its own affairs locally. James
Howe's paper shows that, nevertheless, all is not roses for the Kuna.
They have been helped by long experience of negotiations with outsiders, whether these were English buccaneers or Colombians interested in Kuna resources. Meanwhile Panama has been disarmed again
and again in its history, so that the Kuna, protected by their marginality, did not have to deal with a powerful and assertive state. In recent
years the self-confident Kuna have found themselves entangled in drug
smuggling and afflicted by the corruption that comes with engagement
in electoral politics. Even their prized development organization (PE-
MASKY), which has been a magnet for funds from pro-indigenous organizations, failed to meet its primary objectives and, at the time of its
greatest fame, had already begun to fall apart. The Kuna are thus discovering the difficulties and discontents of development programming

at the same time as they are struggling to avoid the violence that keeps spilling over the frontier from Colombia.

Next, Jean Jackson and María Clemencia Ramírez present two papers on Colombia, the vortex of South American violence. Both writers stress that Colombia has made an effort, as can be seen in the constitution of 1991, to give indigenous peoples a place in the nation that does not depend on their abandoning their own cultures. This new policy toward indigenous minorities was intended to symbolize the new Colombia, but it faces innumerable obstacles. In 1998 the government of Colombia ceded control of parts of its territory to revolutionary movements in an unsuccessful effort to make peace with them. Even where the government did not formally cede control of territory, it occasionally lost it. Meanwhile the endemic violence, involving government forces, paramilitaries, revolutionaries, and drug dealers (who may be tied to any or all of the above) makes it difficult to reorganize the state and bring indigenous peoples into a new Colombia that has yet to be born.

Jackson notes that seats are reserved nationally for indigenous deputies and senators and that they have been filled, yet she concludes that indigenous gains have so far been largely symbolic. Ramírez focuses on the complex negotiations of local identity that are taking place as a result of the new policies. She shows how it is now advantageous in rural areas of the country to be able to claim indigenous status. As a result, groups are emerging and claiming to be indigenous on the basis of their "distinct traditions." Alternatively, other rural groups are demanding that they be recognized as ethnic minorities, with all the rights that should accrue to them, even though they are *not* indigenous. In this connection, Ramírez refers to her own fieldwork, where she documented the struggles of coca cultivators in Colombia's far south. These are people who are insisting that the national government negotiate with them and help them to move out of coca production (at present the only viable option open to them) and into alternative economic activities. The government continues to insist, however, that the coca growers are criminals, with whom they cannot and will not negotiate. Instead the official policy remains that of fumigating their crops (and not only their coca fields) and forcing them to emigrate and do something else. Since the coca growers are already refugees from the violence in other parts of the country, the government's policy is unlikely to be successful. Sadly, it is not likely to be changed either, since it is strongly supported by the United States, which continues to insist that

Colombia must get tough on anybody and everybody involved in the drug trade.

Next Ted Macdonald offers an explanation of the dramatic events that have recently taken place among the indigenous peoples of Ecuador. President Jamil Mahuad was ousted in a coup in January 2000 and for a few hours the country was governed by a triumvirate, including one military and one indigenous representative. Although the triumvirate resigned before the end of the day, it made history in that it elevated an indigenous leader to the presidency of Ecuador for the first time. Macdonald traces the development of Indian assertiveness in Ecuador from the indigenous federations that were launched in the nation's Amazonian regions in the 1970s. He discusses the indigenous uprisings (really stoppages) during which the Indians have blocked the roads and brought the country to a halt more than once. These uprisings were remarkable in that they brought the Amazonian and the Andean indigenous groups together, elicited considerable sympathy for the indigenous cause among the general public, and did not provoke a military response. On the contrary, the army has also been willing to negotiate and even form alliances with indigenous peoples, as the history of the brief triumvirate demonstrates. Macdonald argues that the indigenous protests in Ecuador, like the Zapatista uprising in Mexico, have elicited sympathy among the general public who see their indigenous compatriots as taking the lead in redefining Ecuadorian democracy and the Ecuadorian state.

Next, Bartholomew Dean and Paul Gelles analyze the other major arena of South American violence: Peru. Both writers note that the populist regime of General Velasco Alvarado (1968–1980) had immense influence, particularly among indigenous peoples, who still consider Velasco a hero. However, Velasco tried to abolish Indian-ness and to improve the lot of the masses by transforming them into a prosperous peasantry. This has complicated Peru's efforts to become a pluriethnic country, which it has now proclaimed itself to be. Dean argues that official pluriethnicity has had little effect in the Amazon regions, other than to promote a backlash against indigenous rights. Indigenous groups in Peru's Amazon regions are more affected by the continuous fighting involving the military, a variety of different insurgent groups, and the drug dealers. In addition to these, the Indians must also confront the enterprises that invade their territories in search of resources, with the connivance of the government.

Gelles points out that the indigenous peoples of Andean Peru, who make up the bulk of the nation's population, have likewise been severely affected by civil conflicts, neoliberal economic policies, and repression, especially during the last years of the Fujimori regime. In sum, Peru contrasts with two of its neighbors, Ecuador and Bolivia, where channels of participation in national life have been recently opened up for indigenous people. This has not happened in Peru.

The process by which Bolivia is striving to live up to its redefinition of itself as a multiethnic country is described by Bret Gustafson. The Bolivian revolution of the 1950s, like the reformist movement in Peru in the 1970s, was intended to improve the lot of the peasantry and to ignore their ethnicity. However, there is now a tendency in Bolivia for *asuntos campesinos* (peasant affairs) to be redefined as *asuntos etnicos* (ethnic affairs). Ethnic affairs become indigenous affairs in the Bolivian Amazon. They are thought to have to do with *pueblos originarios* (first nations) in the Highlands. The indigenous peoples of the highlands have traditionally been more revolutionary toward the central government, while the lowlanders were more accommodating, especially when the lowlands were a major coca producing area. Recently, however, the highland/lowland divide has been bridged by the indigenous marches on La Paz that involved meetings in the capital between highland and lowland representatives to present their grievances jointly to the government. The first of these marches took place in 1991, making Bolivian Indians the pioneers in this type of protest. The Bolivian government has opened up channels of participation that enable indigenous peoples to take part in municipal politics, but it is not yet clear what effect this will have at the national level. Meanwhile, Gustafson indicates that there is currently a virulent backlash in Bolivia against the policies that seek to redefine the relationship between the nation's indigenous peoples and its state.

In the next chapter, Richard Reed shows that Paraguay has proclaimed itself a pluriethnic nation, but has done little to implement new policies that would alter and perhaps improve the situation of its indigenous peoples. Reed suggests in his paper that the country's small indigenous population (only about 2 percent of the national total) is somewhat worse off now that democracy has replaced the long dictatorship of General Stroessner. Previously, Paraguay's native peoples defended themselves by attaching themselves to powerful patrons—landowners, political bosses, missionaries, Mennonites, or the institutions of the government's own indigenist bureaucracy. Most of the patrons disappeared after the fall of Stroessner and were replaced by a variety of parties and interest groups that had little interest in indigenous peoples. The indigenous peoples discovered that foreign foundations and environmentalists were fickle allies and that there was no obvious way for them to defend their interests via party politics. The indigenous peoples of Paraguay are therefore making the discovery that the native peoples across the border in Argentina have already made, namely that oligarchic certainties, however unjust they may be at times, are often preferable to democratic uncertainties.

Finally, David Maybury-Lewis stresses the fact that there are comparatively few Indians in Brazil. They make up only a fraction of one percent of the nation's population. They have received a great deal of press attention, both nationally and internationally, because of the "winning of the west" (Brazilian style) that took place under the military dictatorship (1964–1985), when Brazil was accused of committing genocide against its indigenous populations. This was a surprising accusation, because Brazil had always prided itself on following the precepts of its explorer-hero Candido da Silva Rondon, who founded the Brazilian Service for the Protection of Indians (SPI) in 1911, with its proud motto "Die if need be, but never kill." Note that the motto and the SPI itself assumed that indigenous affairs were a matter of "pacifying" (their word) wild natives in the backlands. Nevertheless, the legislation guaranteeing indigenous peoples the rights to their lands and cultures was amazingly liberal for those times. The SPI was supposed to enforce it but was generally too weak and too underfunded to do so. To the extent that Brazil's indigenous populations were protected at all, it was more as a result of their remoteness than of the efforts of the SPI. When the military regime decided to open up the interior of the country and to encourage development in the Amazonian regions, the consequences were predictably harsh for indigenous peoples and others such as smallholders who were held to "stand in the way of progress." It was the killings and expropriations that accompanied the advancing frontier of settlement in the 1960s and 1970s that prompted an international outcry, together with accusations of genocide. The Brazilian government responded by abolishing the SPI and replacing it with the National Indian Foundation (FUNAI). FUNAI has, however, been caught on the horns of the same dilemma that proved too much for the SPI. It is an agency supposed to protect indigenous rights, but which does not have either the funds or the political support to do battle with those who infringe on those rights. Meanwhile the violence endemic in the countryside against the poor, the landless, and even against small-holders is also frequently visited on indigenous peoples.

Nevertheless, indigenous peoples have been fighting back, with support from the Catholic church, from national and international pro-indigenous organizations and, above all, from the plethora of indigenous groups that have been organizing all over the country. Yet indigenous peoples are still physically attacked by anti-Indian elements in the backlands and politically attacked by those who argue that indigenous peoples and their demands destabilize the state, stand in the way of development, and undermine the security of the nation's frontiers.

In his concluding chapter, Maybury-Lewis discusses conflicting ideas about ethnicity and indigenous peoples and how they are affected by the wars and violence that plague many countries of Latin America. He contrasts the differing indigenist traditions of Mexico, Peru, and Brazil. Mexico has for nearly a century pioneered policies intended to help its indigenous peoples assimilate into the mestizo state. Peruvian writers and politicians, such as Mariátegui and Haya de la Torre, argued that indigenous peoples would lead processes of change that would constitute an American revolution. Brazil, following Rondon, claimed to be able to befriend its remote indigenous peoples and help them to assimilate into a society that was in theory built on racial intermingling without prejudice. None of these policies worked. Indigenous people did not assimilate in Mexico, nor did they lead the revolution in Peru, nor were they won over by kindness in Brazil. Instead, Mexico has made a dramatic about-face and is experimenting with a policy that will tolerate locally autonomous indigenous cultures within the state. Peru is in theory adopting similar policies, but in practice has done little to implement them. Brazil, on the other hand, still refuses to adopt any policy that recognizes its indigenous peoples as nations within the state.

These outcomes derive from the different strategies of nation building employed by the countries concerned. Among the countries with large indigenous populations, Mexico has always striven to incorporate its native populations, in marked contrast to Guatemala and Peru, which have tried to keep them subordinated and marginalized. What is remarkable is that so many countries in the Americas are, after five centuries of refusal, willing at last to experiment with the idea that their indigenous peoples can maintain their own cultures without, as a result, being treated as second-class citizens or, worse still, being considered as outsiders within the state. All the states discussed in this volume have declared themselves multiethnic, with the exception of Brazil and Panama, and Panama has in fact implemented regimes of local autonomy for its indigenous peoples. It is especially noteworthy that Ecuador, which was traditionally a conservative country as far as its indigenous policies were concerned, and Bolivia, which is demographically the most "Indian" country in the Americas, have both taken the lead in recognizing the right of their indigenous populations to be different and given them opportunities to participate in national life at the same time. Furthermore, in these two countries, as in Mexico, the new policies are part of a national debate concerning the redefinition of the state and of the meaning of citizenship within it.

A similar redefinition has been set in motion in Colombia, where indigenous municipalities were formally established and made part of the table of organization of the state. Unfortunately, Colombia's long-running civil war, which has lately been drawing new groups into the hostilities, serves to undermine these new initiatives, as it does so much else in that unhappy country. The violence in Colombia is perhaps more intense and more widespread than in other Latin American countries, but it is by no means unique. In fact, it is a sad commentary on the current state of affairs in Latin America that Mexico, which is officially battling the Zapatista insurgency, seems relatively peaceful when compared not only to Colombia but also to the recent violence in Guatemala or Peru.

Finally, it is significant that this rethinking of the nature of the state and of the definition of citizenship within it is being undertaken in the countries with comparatively large indigenous populations. It is being resisted in countries with small indigenous minorities, of which Brazil is the classic example. This volume concludes by exploring that paradox.

SECTION

I

Mexico and Central America

1

A New Dawn or a Cycle Restored? Regional Dynamics and Cultural Politics in Indigenous Mexico, 1978–2001[1]

Jerome M. Levi

As the North American Free Trade Agreement (NAFTA) went into effect January 1, 1994, Maya Indians captured seven municipalities in the southern state of Chiapas, thus forcing a globalizing Mexico to focus on its long ignored indigenous question. Landless Maya and other peasants emerged as rebel insurgents, members of the Zapatista Army of National Liberation (EZLN), struggling for recognition and rights, for dignity, land, justice, and inclusion in a political process from which they had long been marginalized.

Nothing has been the same since in Mexico. Politics is no longer "business as usual." The July 2000 presidential victory of Vicente Fox, from the center-right National Action Party (PAN), spelled an end to 71 years of single party rule by the Institutional Revolutionary Party (PRI). The apparent reassertion of Mexican democracy signals a twenty-first century electorate tired of the PRI's monopoly on power through the party's baroque system of *caudillos*, cronyism, and corruption.[2]

Although victory went to a candidate from the right, ironically it was provoked at the opposite end of the political spectrum. If the Zapatistas cannot claim to have sparked Mexico's recent dialogue about democracy, at least they must be credited with having fanned the flames of a national debate.

Does this political opening and the historic transfer of power to an opposition political party for the first time since 1929 represent "a new dawn" for indigenous peoples, as President Fox said when he took office in December 2000 (parroting Zapatista spokesman Subcomandante Marcos)?[3] Or does it portend a renewed assault on indigenous communities in the guise of more neoliberal reforms? To answer this query, I believe that one must reject the view that relations between indigenous peoples and the state can be reduced either to a hegemonic domination from the top down or a popular struggle from the bottom up. Instead, we need to detect other social relations and identities that cut across the familiar boundaries of ethnicity, class, and region. This means moving beyond strictly *political* analyses of indigenous discourse that have narrowed our focus to post-Zapatista Chiapas in the 1990s in order to understand distinctive *cultural* processes in previous decades and in other geographical areas. Only by widening the scope of the analysis in this way, thereby comprehending the cultural construction of political agency and the historical antecedents and social diversity of indigenous Mexico, can we interpret the expansive, albeit varied, significance Zapatistas have had at both local and national levels.

Diverse Refractions of a Single Reality: Rethinking the Politics of Culture(s) in Indigenous Mexico

Much has been written about the Zapatistas, notably how they have burst onto the global scene, riveted international media on Chiapas, and moved discourse on indigenous rights from the periphery to the center of Mexican politics. Indeed, there is now a small but active industry devoted exclusively to observing, assisting, and reporting on Mexico's "indigenous cause." Journalists, anthropologists, political scientists, legal scholars, human rights activists, and documentary filmmakers among others have covered the topic.[4] Given the burgeoning amount of information, I have opted to depict the relations between indigenous peoples and the state in Mexico in broad brush strokes, a contribution necessarily of a general nature. This analysis is bolstered, however, by more than two decades of research connecting empirical data on indigenous issues in Chiapas, Chihuahua, and the nation with cultural and political analyses.

Scholars agree that the Zapatistas' emergence from the Lacandon rainforest in 1994 is virtually incomprehensible without seeing this movement in relation to the shifting patterns of peasant mobilization, organization of new Catholic and Protestant congregations, and the gradual heightening of political consciousness that had been building in Chiapas since the 1970s. Yet authors differ as to whether the opening created by the Zapatistas is better analyzed in terms of an unprecedented political space for voicing the grievances of civil society or as a new instance of familiar cultural forms that have long used opaque, hybrid identities as strategies for survival.

Neil Harvey, a political scientist, persuasively argues that the Zapatista movement represents a new form of rural protest in Mexico because the indigenous struggle became embedded in broader efforts to contest representation in government and bring about democratic elections (1998). While this is undoubtedly true, anthropologist Gary Gossen contends that in addition to comprehending the Chiapas rebellion and its aftermath as an outcome of specific political and economic pressures, the events also must be understood in terms of cultural agency. Gossen convincingly demonstrates that the Zapatista movement manifests a distinctly Mesoamerican identity (relating to the self and other, pluricultural communities, souls, and human destiny, which have all been firmly established in the course of Mesoamerican cultural history) (1999, 225–266; see also Nash 1997, 2001). The movement represents, as he puts it, "the future of an ancient idea" (1999, 243), one with a genealogy reaching as far back as the Olmec, the mother civilization of ancient Mexico.

The argument I advance in this essay draws intellectual capital from both positions. I suggest that the domain of politics in general, and particularly democracy and citizenship, must be reexamined in terms of historical constructs and social reproductions. Precisely because of its cultural foundation, Zapatista political action is not just another revolutionary struggle. Despite the communiqués of Marcos that addressed "brothers, sisters" and literally everyone in the world, the heart of Zapatismo manifests a distinctly indigenous and broadly Mesoamerican identity. This, together with the call for "democracy, liberty, and justice," causes Zapatismo to resonate with the ideas and ideals of the Mexican people. "The political" can assume its place as the conceptual cornerstone of the movement only if one admits that culture and history are the architects of "the people" and that the latter are self-conscious political actors creating spaces for the emergence of democracy through popular struggle. Zapatismo appeals to a wide sector of Mexican civil society, non-indigenous as well as indigenous, for it permits citizens to connect with modern ideals, such as democracy, as well as ancient ones, such as Mesoamerican culture. The shape of political agency is changing because the melding of the indigenous rights movement with the struggle for democracy makes sense, cultural sense, to the people of Mexico.

At the same time, an important part of this Mesoamerican identity is one that draws strength from the very diversity of the indigenous and neighboring mestizo cultures that constitute it, appositely termed *México profundo* (Bonfil Batalla 1987). The indigenous peoples of Mexico represent a staggering array of sociocultural diversity, from small bands of people numbering less than a hundred individuals, who well into the twentieth century were hunter-gatherers in the deserts of northwest Mexico (e.g., the Kiliwa in Baja California) to dense populations of indigenous peasants in the central and southern highlands, (e.g., Mexico's largest ethno-linguistic group, the nearly one and a half million Nahuatl speakers who still inhabit the home of their Aztec ancestors in the center of the country). Moreover, although indigenous peoples are stereotypically associated with rural areas, increasing numbers are now living in urban spaces. More indigenous peoples live in Mexico City than in any other place in the nation.

Ironically, state recognition of this heterogeneity is directly related to the "imagined" homogeneity caused by the spread of nationalism. Once the national map and national census were created and used as normalizing instruments in countries throughout Southeast Asia and Latin America, they soon revealed to the dominant masses of these postcolonial states the incontrovertible existence of difference— other peoples, cultures, and languages—within a country's territorial boundaries (Anderson 1983, 163–186). Yet these same instruments used so adroitly by the nation-state to promote its own hegemony also stimulate realizations among subaltern peoples regarding their positions as self-conscious ethnic groups within the nation. As such, despite their cultural and linguistic differences, these groups may share certain experiences of subordination and therefore, possibly, also certain political goals (Anderson, in press). As Stavenhagen observes, cultural heterogeneity by itself is not responsible for conflict, but ethnic differences may "erupt into violence when a state wishes to impose its own vision and attempts to eliminate or minimize the differences amongst the population through authoritarian or arbitrary measures" (2000, 11).

In the eyes of Mexican officialdom, there are 56 indigenous ethnolinguistic groups in the country. However, while this number has remained the same for decades, the groups—and how they are counted—change from year to year. According to the National Indigenist Institute (INI), there existed 56 indigenous groups in 1978 and again in 1993 (Ovalle Fernández 1978, 388, Gutiérrez 1999, map 1).

But upon closer inspection of the national maps showing the number and distribution of these peoples, one observes a less than perfect fit between the 56 listed in 1978 and those in 1993. For example, in 1978 the Pima Alto and the Pima Bajo were enumerated as different groups, just as the Chontal of Tabasco were ethnically differentiated from the Chontal of Oaxaca (the latter were designated by the ethnonym "Tequistlateco"), whereas by 1993 these distinctions had disappeared. The four groups now were counted as only two, the former being merged into a single ethnic group as Pima and the latter as Chontal. Similarly, one group listed in 1978 (Tepehua) did not appear in 1993. Conversely, three groups listed in 1993 did not appear in 1978—namely, the Tlacuate, Tlahuica, and Kakchiquel—the last, strictly speaking, are not indigenous to Mexico at all, but rather to the central highlands of Guatemala, although they now show up in Chiapas, presumably as refugees from their war-torn country.

Obviously ethnographic problems abound when a state autocratically defines ethnic groups from the top down. Here, the important point is that for decades Mexico has reified 56 as the number of indigenous peoples in the country, a number that remains constant, even if the facts periodically had to be fudged to fit the preconceived objective. It is as if the nation can accommodate this number of indigenous minorities, and hence this degree of cultural diversity, but neither more (since indigeneity is equated with poverty) nor less (since diminution might incite accusations of ethnocide). The irony is heightened because although Mexico's indigenous peoples have had this de facto recognition from government bureaucracies all along, they did not receive *de jure* recognition until the reforms to the federal constitution in 1990.

The Zapatistas realized that the movement they instigated could never be a one-size-fits-all solution for Mexico's nearly ten million indigenous people, even though marginalization was a common problem. After all, Mexico's indigenous cultures were radically different from one another, reflected in diverse settlement patterns, subsistence strategies, political organizations, social structures, religious practices, and histories of interethnic relations. Cognizant of this diversity, Zapatistas have visited indigenous peoples throughout the country since the 1994 insurgency, more to listen and learn than to promote a specific ideology. In return, indigenous groups from all parts of Mexico are aware that this cultural diversity could inform the emerging dialogue about national unity. They have therefore sent delegations to the

National Indigenous Congress (CNI) since its first meeting in Mexico City in October 1996. Not all members of the CNI are Zapatistas. Indeed, after the four Zapatista comandantes gave their historic addresses before the Mexican Congress of the Union, March 28–29, 2001, the whole CNI went in, and representatives of 45 other indigenous organizations besides the EZLN also spoke. Mexico's diverse indigenous movement works because, at a cultural level, there is a profound respect for difference, while at a political level, governance is predicated on democracy, if not always unanimity (Nash 1997, Stephen 1997). The critical point, as noted by Pablo Yanes, a prominent member of Mexico's Lawyer's Network for Indigenous Rights, is that people "who think that the indigenous issue is temporary and is only related to the Zapatista uprising are fooling themselves. On the contrary, it is a structural issue and one of national interest" (Yanes Rizo 1999, 49).

Bearing in mind that the indigenous issue is of national consequence, on the one hand, and that indigenous Mexico is extremely diverse, on the other, I compare two indigenous regions in Mexico, each highlighting different cultural constructions of indigenous political action. The first offers a general description of the conditions that led up to the 1994 emergence of the Zapatistas in Chiapas as well as a brief overview of the major events that have occurred since then in the state. I also examine the turbulent cultural politics among the Tzotzil Maya in the northern highlands that allowed the PRI to co-opt the "traditional" indigenous government in that area. The second regional case switches our attention from southeastern to northwestern Mexico. Here, I discuss a different, although equally ominous, set of local circumstances characterizing the indigenous political culture among the Tarahumara (Rarámuri) of Chihuahua, who demonstrate a different reaction to Zapatismo. Because of certain similarities, such as the incongruity of impoverished people amidst a wealth of natural resources, both Chiapas and Chihuahua played leading roles in the history of relations between indigenous peoples and the Mexican state. Yet without comprehending the significance of different constructions of cultural agency, it is impossible to understand why Chiapas gave birth to an indigenous insurgency in the 1990s whereas the Sierra Tarahumara did not.

Similarly, as long as Mexico is thought of as being geographically and politically divided between an indigenous periphery and a mestizo core, the cultural politics that animate the country will remain obscure, as Florencia Mallon noted a decade ago in her seminal article on indigenous peoples and the state in Latin America (1992). Nor shall we be able to understand why hundreds of thousands of mestizos have embraced the indigenous cause as their own without comprehending that the peasant masses in central Mexico have systematically been denied their ethnic identity as indigenous peoples (Bonfil Batalla 1987, Mallon 1992). Thus in the last part of this essay, I examine how the call for indigenous rights has become a broad national movement, with specific reference to the debates on indigenous rights and autonomy encompassed in the San Andrés Accords, the National Indigenous Congress, and the responses by the federal government.

Why Chiapas? Cultural Roots of Political Action

Why did the Zapatista movement emerge in Chiapas as opposed to some other part of Mexico?[5] Chiapas has a large indigenous population (35.2 percent of the state's population speaks an indigenous language), but Oaxaca (52.7 percent), Yucatán (52.5 percent), and Quintana Roo (36.7 percent) are states with even larger indigenous populations (Fox 1999, 26); so the sheer number of indigenous people by itself cannot explain the location of the uprising. Chiapas shares a long border with Guatemala—a small, turbulent nation marked in recent decades by a war-torn countryside, weak civilian government, strong military and, since 1987, increasingly noteworthy indigenous movements and Pan-Maya activism (Warren 1998, Schirmer, this volume). Yet it would be wrong to attribute the insurgency to Guatemalan sources. Still, given that the Chiapas uprising coincided with Mexico's entry into NAFTA, a joke made the rounds in Mexico City that "President Salinas went to bed on New Year's Eve expecting to wake up the next morning as a North American, but instead he woke up to find himself a Guatemalan" (Maybury-Lewis 1997, 19). So too, it frequently is pointed out that Chiapas was ripe for rebellion since it remained a poor and backward part of Mexico. But poor in what sense?

The state boasts prodigious natural resources (Collier 1994). From the Chiapas oil fields, 25,000,000 barrels of crude oil and over 500 billion cubic feet of gas are sucked out of the ground every day by Pemex, the government owned petroleum company (Carrigan 2001, 421). Chiapas alone supplies more than 54 percent of Mexico's hydroelectric energy from its dams on the Grijalva River (Collier 1994, 16), and 35 percent of all the coffee produced in the country (Carrigan 2001, 421).

Between 1981 and 1989, nearly seven million cubic meters of wood were extracted from Chiapas. As forests shrank, grasslands grew, along with the cattle industry. Small wonder, then, that after coffee, beef is the state's most important export (*ibid*). The situation of poor people in this rich land is summed up well by Jan Rus:

> As journalists and others have pointed out, of the Mexican states, Chiapas leads or shares with Oaxaca the lead—in such dubious categories as infant mortality, illiteracy, and percentage of houses without running water, electricity, or floors; it accounts for almost a third of the nation's unresolved agrarian reform claims; and even according to the national census, sixty percent of its workers earn less than the minimum wage of three dollars a day, forty percent less than half of that (Rus 1995, 71).

Aware of these glaring inequities, the "Salinas administration's star social program 'Solidarity' spent more money in Chiapas than in any other state, but the funds never reached needy Indian cooperatives and businesses" (Nigh 1994, 10). In any event, the aid was only a temporary measure, since indigenous peoples were not thought to have a future in the age of Mexican neoliberalism.

The Zapatistas rose in Chiapas because a unique blend of pressures and possibilities had been brewing there for decades in the highlands, the lowlands to the north, and in the eastern part of the state encompassing the vast, although ever shrinking, Lacandon rainforest, a remote and largely roadless region comprising the Mexican frontier with Guatemala. In this latter region, myriad factors incubated and eventually hatched a rebellion whose shock waves have been felt not only throughout Mexico, but around the world; these include the loss of forests, spread of grasslands, lack of agrarian reform, immigration from other states, and influx of diverse indigenous colonists from the highlands and northern lowlands combined with the growth of alternative peasant organizations, increasing presence of Protestants, Evangelicals, and Catholic catechists, development of multiethnic agrarian communities, and almost total absence of commerce and transportation (Collier 1994). Below I offer a brief outline of the history that led up to these events.

Popular rebellion and other forms of resistance have marked Chiapas since the time of the region's conquest in 1524–27 through the colonial era to the twentieth century. Without implying that either class or ethnicity are absolutely determinant factors, one can easily detect centuries of strained relations between the *ladino* (non-indigenous) elite and the indigenous peoples of Chiapas. More than anything else, the steady usurpation of indigenous land and labor has long been the single greatest source of interethnic conflict. Despite several centuries of indigenous uprisings, typically associated with new religious movements, notably the Tzeltal Revolt of 1712–13 and the 1867–70 Caste War, the regional elite did not seek to confront the exploitation that provoked the rebellions in the first place. Rather, they maneuvered in the opposite direction, endeavoring to extend their power further over the indigenous population by devising new forms of colonial and neocolonial control.

Indigenous peoples of highland Chiapas attempted to protect themselves from the economic incursions during the *Porfiriato* (1876–1910) and the clashing armies of the Revolution (1910–1920) by turning inward, tightening the ethnic boundaries of their closed corporate communities. By the mid-twentieth century, however, the PRI and regional elite had managed to undermine indigenous authority by co-opting key positions in the *cargo* system (Rus 1994)—a civil-religious hierarchy of local governance dating from colonial times. The subversion of local governance created a group of indigenous *caciques*, or political bosses, who exploited their positions in the town councils for personal gain and continued party patronage. This in turn generated growing opposition to the corruption and consolidation of power that was increasingly part of indigenous politics. New social movements, such as independent peasant organizations and Protestantism, offered alternatives that were seemingly more in keeping with familiar cultural conventions governing the moral exercise of power. Yet converts to new religions as well as political dissidents were both *expulsado* (expelled) by town leaders as "enemies of tradition." In the central highlands, particularly from Chamula, thousands were forced to flee on the basis of their involvement with Protestantism, Catholic catechists, or alternative political organizations. State and federal agencies conveniently refused to intervene in these civil disturbances, on the pretext that such affairs were internal to indigenous communities, whose "traditions" they now claimed to respect. In reality, of course, these were the very government forces, aided by the ladino oligarchy, that had already subverted indigenous power structures.

The Subversion of Indigenous Governance in the Northern Highlands

One problem in the scholarship on the emergence of Zapatismo in Chiapas is its failure to comprehend the significance of microregional dynamics, especially in the highlands (but see Cancian and Brown 1994, Collier 1997, and Rus 1994). Along the northern rim of the highlands, for example, the subversion of indigenous government played havoc in a way that differed from the central highlands. I observed this firsthand while conducting research on the relationship between political and religious power in the northern Tzotzil municipality of San Pablo Chalchihuitán (Levi 1988, Vogt 1994, 339).[6] Whereas the iron rule of town authorities could not be challenged in the PRI-stronghold of Chamula, neighboring the colonial city of San Cristóbal de las Casas, in more distant Chalchihuitán, the municipal president and his cronies had a more tenuous hold on the township. Furthermore, in Chamula the dissenting masses were the ones who were exiled, whereas in Chalchihuitán, it was high-ranking municipal authorities who had to flee for their lives. Nevertheless, by the 1980s political intolerance in Chalchihuitán led to mass expulsions as well. Part of the difference in microregional dynamics is attributable to the northern zone's distance from San Cristóbal, long the stronghold of ladino power and government control in the highlands. On the one hand this made the area more difficult for the PRI to monopolize at the grassroots level and, on the other hand, more open to alternative or egalitarian ideologies. For example, just north over the mountains from Chalchihuitán is Simojovel, a support base for the Independent Confederation of Agricultural Workers and Peasants (CIOAC), an organization with strong links to the Mexican Communist Party (Weinberg 2000, 34). To the east is Pantelhó (up the road from the cut-off to Chalchihuitán), one of the few highland areas, besides San Cristóbal, where Protestant converts were allowed to reside.[7]

Throughout the 1960s and 1970s there was bitter conflict between townsfolk and Chalchihuitán's municipal presidents. During the course of my fieldwork, I witnessed one of these tumultuous events. On October 13, 1978, after town authorities had vied for months against the municipal president and his allies for control of the town, several hundred people from all parts of the municipality converged on the town square for a rally. The town hall was stormed and a melee ensued. They demanded that the president, who had gone into hiding, pay a "fine" of 52,000 pesos—about $2,364 U.S. dollars, a substantial sum in those days for rural Tzotzil peasants. Some people were beaten and jailed. Others fled for their lives to San Cristóbal. Death threats went on for weeks and individuals carried concealed weapons to protect themselves. The president purchased a car to make quick escapes to San Cristóbal and elsewhere in the middle of the night as needed. He threatened to call in the federal army to put down the rebellion, though at the last minute he retracted the order.

The causes of this uproar were many and varied, but the gist of it began in 1965 when, in exchange for a dirt road, clinic, schools, potable water, and other improvements, the government reorganized Chalchihuitan's top political office, in spite of a faction that opposed the changes. Among other things, the opposition claimed that with the changes would come an army and "that the road would bring in soldiers"; observations that, in retrospect, were eerily prescient given the rapid militarization of the area after 1994, which indeed was facilitated by the new roads. Although from 1937 to 1939 the PRI had abolished the colonial cargo office of the "governor" (Spanish, *gobernador*, Tzotzil, *kotnerol)* throughout indigenous Chiapas and replaced it with a "municipal president" in an effort to institute Mexican constitutional forms of authority (and, of course, greater party control), in Chalchihuitán the municipal presidents acted "as if" they were the old style gobernadores until the mid-1960s. Even though in both cases the offices were occupied by indigenous men native to Chalchihuitán who, as the town's chief political officers, had the same jurisdiction over the municipality, the cultural orientations of the gobernadores and the new style municipal presidents after 1965 were diametrically opposed.

Gobernadores were appointed by *principales* (elders) who searched for someone who was *tzotz yo'onton,* or "strong of heart," someone renowned for his leadership, wisdom, and honesty, someone who could command authority as well as respect. The gobernador was not a salaried position and the cargo, literally "burden," in the civil-religious hierarchy, was relatively inexpensive despite being highly prestigious. Rather, the position was an honor bestowed in acknowledgment of a life devoted to community service through the assumption of previous cargos, work that not only was unpaid but often required the official to host costly fiestas.

By contrast, the only requirement to become municipal president after 1965 was that the candidate be a literate, Spanish-speaking man from Chalchihuitán. Most municipal presidents by this time had rejected the cargo careers that were virtual career requirements for indigenous highland males in favor of becoming *promotores bilingues* (bilingual school teachers). (Bolivia offers another view of bilingual education; see Gustafson, this volume.) Via education, these individuals promoted the national policy of *indigenismo* at the local level; essentially state-sponsored assimilation and ipso facto ethnocide.

These new presidents were regarded as people who put on airs, adopted ladino ways, and said it was "no longer their custom" to speak Tzotzil, go barefoot, or wear the native tunic. They seldom visited the municipality's *parajes* (hamlets), since these were accessible only by foot trails. Consequently, after political officials (*agentes*) were installed in the hamlets in 1974, they were frequently at odds with the top authorities in the town hall. Moreover, much of the time the new presidents were away in San Cristobal or Tuxtla Gutiérrez, the state capital, rather than attending to their duties in Chalchihuitán. Many wished to abolish the native fiestas, saying that such expenditures were wastes of money. Several wanted to tear down the crosses atop the mountain shrines and waterholes. They neither prayed nor acknowledged San Pablo, the town's patron saint, as the municipality's true authority. In fact, people were afraid some presidents would attack the images of the saints in the church. The majority of these new presidents asserted that times had changed and that power was now vested in the laws of the state, not in the saints in the church. Thus, rather than mingling with the people outside of the town hall, as was customary, they sat alone in the back reading their law books. Rather than keeping the peace through the maintenance of goodwill, they ruled by force—on one occasion showing up in town with a band of lawyers when the people refused to obey orders. With several notable exceptions, Chalchihuitán's municipal presidents after 1965 represented willing participants in a government scam. It was a takeover that decapitated the old system of limited self-rule in exchange for a new order that rewarded personal aggrandizement and split loyalties, installed bilingual culture brokers as town leaders, inexorably bound indigenous municipal government to the PRI party machinery, and openly repudiated local mores and religion.

Small wonder that the histories I collected of the seven municipal presidents who held office between 1966 and 1978 do not entirely match the official government chronology of municipal presidents who served in Chalchihuitán during this period. The latter reflects a seamless, orderly, and uneventful progression of standard three-year terms, whereas the data I gathered indicate a series of battles for control of the town, expulsions of presidents as well as townspeople, and the installation of emergency interim presidents as needed by the townspeople. In general, most of the government-backed presidents after 1965 failed miserably at maintaining order in the municipality. Some were thrust in the town jail, others were threatened with having their homes burned down, and at least one was thrown out of office in what was tantamount to a palace coup.

Chalchihuitán's political struggles in the 1970s grew into levels of extreme violence in the next decade (Burgete Cal y Mayor n.d.).[8] What has become known as "the massacre of Ts'akiuk'um"—which erupted in March 1983, leaving eleven dead and hundreds homeless as a result of expulsions—is now seared into the collective memory of Chalchihuitán. The forces that caused this event were already in place in the late 1970s, but they continued, and even intensified, in the 1980s. In essence, local caciques and their backers in the PRI increasingly controlled the presidents, along with other municipal authorities. Their reign was supported by a district attorney accused of illegally selling communal lands, a man who used Chalchihuitan's municipal police, as well as a private militia, as personal bodyguards. By the late 1980s the people of Chalchihuitán attempted to protect themselves by joining independent indigenous and peasant organizations that denounced the violation of human rights and manipulation of tradition. Organized opposition to the subversion of local governance by the corrupt regime was substantial by the early 1990s.

Given this history of repression and political intolerance, it is not surprising that ten months after the initial Zapatista insurgency, Chalchihuitán zoomed into the view of Chiapas-watchers around the world. Just as the people of Chalchihuitán had done in previous decades, on October 7, 1994, the Democratic Movement of Chalchihuitán (MODECH), aided by members of the Indigenous Organization of the Highlands of Chiapas (ORIACH), the Emiliano Zapata Peasant Organization (OCEZ), and the Party of the Democratic Revolution (PRD), stormed Chalchihuitán's town hall, forced the municipal president to resign, and demanded an audit of the money that had gone through his office.[9] But this time, rather than acting alone in a remote town unknown to people outside the highlands, they were bolstered by a national indigenous movement spearheaded by Zapatistas.

Expulsions, Popular Struggle, and the Building of Pluriethnic Communities

As the Mexican state assumed greater control over local affairs, as power increasingly was consolidated in the hands of indigenous or ladino elites, and as agriculture declined in profitability through the 1970s, the indigenous population was pressed even harder, both economically and politically (Rus, Hernández Castillo, and Mattiace 2001). Big landowners responded by shifting their plantations from cultivation to cattle production. In the jungle they continued to encroach on indigenous community land, although in the northern lowlands, most indigenous people by this time had already become *acasillados*, basically serfs, on their own ancestral lands. Meanwhile, due to an unprecedented population boom, indigenous people in the highlands were experiencing serious demographic pressures. Not surprisingly, those who opposed the alliance between the PRI and what had become a virtual reign of terror in the countryside were exiled from their densely populated communities. Consequently, from the 1960s to the 1980s, tens of thousands of indigenous villagers from all over Chiapas either voluntarily fled or were forcibly expelled from their communities of origin to start life anew as colonists in the diminishing rainforests of eastern Chiapas or the outskirts of San Cristóbal, Tuxtla Gutiérrez, Ocosingo, and Palenque.

During this period, the expulsados in San Cristóbal described themselves as beginning "a stage of resistance" (Gómez Nuñez 2000, 178). At first, they formed multiethnic indigenous organizations that fought for immigrant rights in the city. Yet by 1994 they had become a vital source of indigenous political experience, supplying support as well as key actors for the formation of the Autonomous Pluriethnic Regions (RAP) in Chiapas. Meanwhile, in the Lacandon forest, aided by Catholic catechists and Protestant community organizers, Tzotzil, Tzeltal, Chol, and Tojolobal colonists similarly transcended their old cultural and linguistic boundaries and formed new multiethnic communities, building upon similar political histories and common religious orientations. The significance of this is that these new communities in the Lacandon jungle were the very ones that gave birth to the EZLN, fertilized its ideas and collaborations, and remain the strongholds of the rebels to this day.

The development of distinctive politico-cultural identities and the restructuring of communities, which emerged in areas that were geographically and administratively peripheral to federal agencies, is of central importance in understanding the Zapatistas (Stephen 2002, in press). Although *ladino* elites essentially blocked the post-revolutionary agrarian reforms from taking place in much of Chiapas, and despite President Salinas' amendments in 1992 to Article 27 of the Mexican Constitution—which effectively ended agrarian land reform throughout the nation and opened up *ejidos* (agrarian reform communities) to neoliberal interests and privatization, the land-starved peasants organized on their own.

Since colonial times, San Cristóbal de las Casas has been the heart of ladino rule in the Chiapas highlands. But as one moved away from the city, state surveillance and official power waned. To the north and south, around Simojovel and Venustiano Carranza respectively, state presence was ambiguous and uneven until the 1994 uprising, while to the east, in the besieged Lacandon jungle, it was virtually absent. It was in these spaces that key independent peasant organizations emerged: the Independent Confederation of Agricultural Workers and Peasants (CIOAC) in Simojovel, the Emiliano Zapata Peasant Organization (OCEZ) in Venustiano Carranza, and the Union óf Ejidal Unions and United Peasant Groups of Chiapas (UU) in the Lacandon forest and the central highlands (Collier 1994, 72). The complex histories of these organizations throughout the 1970s and early 1980s reveal demands and struggles, internal conflicts and external alliances (Harvey 1998). During this period the indigenous peasants of Chiapas lost additional land due to hydroelectric dams, ranching, logging, and oil exploration. However, a national network slowly developed among independent peasant organizations, despite sometimes violent local factionalism and opposition from government sponsored groups, including local militias and the PRI-affiliated National Peasant Confederation (CNC). Over a decade of organizing had successfully raised political consciousness in the countryside. But the CIOAC, OCEZ, and UU ultimately failed to meet the needs of their constituencies, each for its own reason, although they did become bases for other independent organizations and in fact still survive. Nevertheless, for the majority of Chiapas's indigenous peasants, there still remained the dreary monotony of unrelieved land pressure, grinding poverty, and lack of voice and dignity.

The bad situation of the 1970s grew worse in the 1980s, as municipal presidents and other members of the town councils were placed directly on the state government payrolls throughout the indigenous highlands. Whereas in the previous decade bribes and kickbacks were channeled to government-backed members of the town councils in exchange for delivering votes for the PRI, in the 1980s the top town officials were now paid outright. The last shreds of respect, dignity, and honor in the cargo system were replaced by wholesale fear, *caciquismo*, and corruption. Campaigns became increasingly violent as aspirants for the top posts in the town councils fought for these positions.[10] Given the economic crises of the 1980s, salaried jobs such as these were almost unheard of in the rural districts. Over the span of several decades, leadership and the very meaning of community had changed irrevocably (Cancian 1992). Once a gerontocracy based on the assumption of onerous civil-religious burdens that entitled high-ranking men to respect and prestige as town officials after a lifetime of community service, by the late 1980s the system had been transformed into a fearsome alliance rewarding all comers who were willing to employ mafia-like tactics in order to enrich themselves at the cost of their communities.

Zapatistas in Chiapas

Into this situation of ambiguity, fear, and contradiction, there flowed an unlikely mix of ideas and people who, sensing opportunity beyond repression, ignited a new movement capable of articulating agrarian struggles in indigenous terms. The EZLN was born on November 17, 1983, during a meeting between three indigenous people and three mestizos, one of whom eventually would become the spokesman known to the world as Subcomandante Marcos. As the Zapatistas' support base slowly grew over the next few years along kin lines through the communities of the Cañadas region in the Lacandon forest, it gradually became apparent that Marcos was not converting the indigenous peasants to Marxism, Maoism, Leninism, Guevarism, or another familiar revolutionary ideology. Rather, it was Marcos himself who was being transformed by experiencing the distinctive cultural beliefs of indigenous life in "*la montaña*, that magical world inhabited by the whole of Mayan history, by the spirits of ancestors, and by Zapata himself" (Harvey 1998, 166). In turn, the political discourse that had shaped Marcos's thinking required a new idiom in this environment, "and it was found in the convergence of the Zapatistas' critical interpretation of Mexican history and the indigenous people's own stories of humiliation, exploitation, and racism" (*ibid*). By combining magical realism and a practice-based critique of globalization, with Mayan ethno-poetics and Internet savvy, Zapatistas and their allies created an inclusive social movement sometimes dubbed the world's "first post-modern revolution" (Carrigan 2001, 417; Nash 1997, 263). The merging of insurgent politics with the poignant images of Mesoamerican myth is a salient dimension of the synergistic syncretism characteristic of Marcos's Zapatista rhetoric.

The political message was novel, as was the culturally hybrid language by which it was conveyed both to new indigenous recruits in Chiapas and to viewers around the world via electronic media; so too were the tactics, structure, and goals of the EZLN. Informed by indigenous practices, the EZLN leadership was subordinate to its social base, thus inverting the classic Marxian leader-masses relationship. This is most clearly illustrated by the fact that the Zapatistas institutionalized the local custom of *mandar obedeciendo*, that is, "to govern by obeying," essentially handing political authority of the EZLN command over to the civil community (Harvey 1998, 75, Stephen 2002, 125). Zapatistas sought neither to overthrow the Mexican government nor to secede from the nation. Nor was their rebellion simply an attempt to change who was in power. Instead, it was an effort to change the very way that power and political community were constructed. The Zapatistas contested Mexico's near total disinterest in a citizenry that could not profit from neoliberal reforms. They also contested the authoritarian national rule of a fraudulent single-party government. In so doing, they generated a social awakening that transcended old labels and resonated with the deepest stirrings of all Mexicans ready to democratize the political process.

Zapatistas, along with indigenous supporters throughout the state, were literally remaking the map of Chiapas. They were redrawing municipal boundaries, building new communities, and renaming old ones. Eleven months after their initial uprising, Zapatistas declared the civil authority of thirty-eight indigenous autonomous municipalities in Chiapas. This created a series of parallel municipal governments, one of which was constitutionally recognized by the Mexican state and the others declared an autonomous administrative and territorial unit. In retaliation for undermining PRI hegemony at the local level: "the army mounts a massive invasion in Zapatista areas of influence [on February 9, 1995], implementing a strategy of low-intensity warfare (also known as civilian-targeted warfare) . . . During the next five years, over 60,000 army troops occupy nearly every corner of the state" (Hansen 2001, 448). Rather than crippling the movement, the army offensive redoubled indigenous opposition. Support for the Zapatistas continued to spread, while Zapatistas themselves constructed five new centers of resistance named *Aguascalientes*, as well as pushing further into the jungles of eastern Chiapas. Growing counterinsurgency had escalated the ongoing war in Chiapas "in which 1,500 people have been killed, most by state security forces or paramilitaries" (Hernández Navarro 1998a, 7).

By the late 1990s, major events were taking place again in the Chiapas highlands, particularly in the northern area. Chalchihuitán, located in a heavily militarized conflict zone, was at the eye of the storm. To the southwest is the autonomous municipality of San Andrés Larráinzar—renamed *San Andrés Sakam Ch'en de los Pobres* in an act that simultaneously politicizes and indigenizes the former place name into a part-Spanish, part-Tzotzil toponym, which translates as "Saint Andrew Bright Cave of the Poor."[11] This is where the historic San Andrés Accords on indigenous autonomy and cultural rights were signed between the EZLN and the government on February 16, 1996. Immediately south of Chalchihuitán is the constitutional municipality of Chenalhó, where Acteal, site of the infamous massacre, is located. Here, forty-five Tztozil civilians—mostly women and children belonging to The Bees of Civil Society, a church-based organization explicitly rejecting armed struggle as a vehicle for change—were shot in the back and killed by PRI-supported paramilitaries as they prayed for peace in a chapel on December 22, 1997. To the north and west of Chalchihuitán is the autonomous municipality of El Bosque, which was invaded by federal forces in late spring of 1998, leaving a number of dead and wounded. EZLN insurgent troops fought back at one point when civilians came under direct attack; this is the only time the EZLN has broken its cease-fire since it was declared in January 1994.[12] In the adjacent mountains to the southeast of Chalchihuitán is the autonomous center of Polhó. More than 12,000 refugees fled there after the Acteal massacre, when they were forced out of their communities at gunpoint by paramilitary troops and the federal army in the greater Chenalhó and Pantelhó areas.

The concentration of refugees in Polhó quickly turned it into the most important pro-Zapatista civilian community in the highlands (after Oventic).[13] In view of this and given Polhó's proximity to Chalchihuitán, it is not surprising that Chalchihuitán itself finally was invaded in May 2000 by the elite Federal Preventative Police (FPF), together with reinforcements from the federal army and the infamous judicial police (Angeles 2000).[14] The following month eleven army trucks with an estimated 200 soldiers arrived in town.[15] Residents of Chalchihuitán publicly denounced both incursions as recently instituted army tactics enabling soldiers to enter peaceful communities on trumped-up charges in order to increase surveillance and militarization around neighboring Zapatista support bases.[16]

By June 2000, with the Mexican presidential election only a few weeks away, there was widespread fear that a final military solution to the problems in Chiapas would soon be imposed, especially if the PRI candidate, Francisco Labastida, won the election. Labastida's position on the indigenous struggle in Chiapas was clear. Having already increased militarization throughout the state as interior minister, he maintained that enough time had been wasted and existing law should be applied—in other words, a military rather than a democratic solution would be the likely outcome if the EZLN did not lay down its arms. However, Fox came to power, not Labastida, and Mexico's policy on the indigenous struggle went to the legislature rather than the army.

Indigenous Struggles outside Chiapas: Strife in the Sierra Tarahumara

With Chiapas dominating the headlines, less is known about the rising tide of indigenous struggles that has been occurring all over Mexico in the last decade (Weinberg 2000). The Yaqui in the northern state of Sonora, renowned for their nineteenth-century resistance against the takeover of their rich farmlands by the Mexican state, have recently called for autonomy. Struggles for indigenous autonomy have also arisen in Oaxaca and Guerrero. Supporting the San Andrés Accords, Huichol (Wixárika) of Nayarit and Jalisco have denounced the expropriation of 64,000 hectares of their land by encroaching ranchers. Indigenous peoples whose territorial boundaries are bisected by the U.S.-Mexican border—such as the Kumeyaay of southern California and the Kumiai of northern Baja California, Mexico—have organized binational summits to discuss ways of maintaining family ties, cultural integrity, and common environmental concerns despite growing impediments to the flow of people and ideas across "the line."

EZLN is not the only organization of rural rebellion that has attracted indigenous people. In the mountains of Guerrero, the Insurgent People's Revolutionary Army (ERPI) had become by the late 1990s a notable guerrilla organization outside Chiapas that involved indigenous recruits. On June 7, 1998, an ERPI guerilla unit was ambushed by the federal army in the Mixtec community of El Charco,

Guerrero. "In all, seven civilians and four guerrillas were killed in El Charco. Five others were wounded. More than two dozen people, mostly indigenous Mixtecos, were taken prisoner" (Paulson 2000, 26).

Suffering in the Sierra Tarahumara: Drought, Deforestation, and Drug Wars

Shifting attention from southeastern to northwestern Mexico, a different set of local circumstances characterizes cultural politics among the Rarámuri (as the Tarahumara call themselves) in the Sierra Tarahumara of Chihuahua (Levi 2001), and hence a different reaction to Zapatismo, although there also exist certain similarities with the situation in Chiapas.[17] The comparison of Chiapas with Chihuahua is extremely instructive for politico-economic as well as culturally historical reasons. Just as the indigenous revolts in the Chiapas highlands of 1712–13 and 1867–70 were sparked by millenarian movements, the indigenous rebellions in the Sierra Tarahumara likewise have had important religious overtones, from the Tepehuan Revolt of 1616–18 and the early Rarámuri rebellions of the 1690s to the uprising at Santa Ynez in 1918. Similarly, from 1876 to 1910, under the dictatorship of Porfirio Díaz, "[t]he far northern and southern states (Chihuahua, Coahuila, Nuevo Leon, Tamaulipas, Campeche, Yucatan, and Chiapas) consistently refused to pay any attention to the constitutional prohibition on debt peonage" (Adams 1967, 476). Consequently, peasant and indigenous groups in these frontier zones entered the twentieth century as the poorest and most exploited people in Mexico. By the mid-twentieth century, however, Mexico recognized its need to reach out to them, the nation's most marginalized peoples. Hence, in 1951 INI established the first of its more than seventy regional Coordinating Centers in San Cristobál de las Casas, Chiapas, for the Tzeltal and Tzotzil peoples (Aguirre Beltrán et al. 1976, 44). A year later, the second INI regional Coordinating Center was established for the Rarámuri in Guachochi, Chihuahua, in the heart of the Sierra Tarahumara (Plancarte 1954, 96). For all these reasons, contemporary indigenous struggles in the highlands of Chiapas and the highlands of Chihuahua beg for comparison.

The Rarámuri number around 60,000 (Stefani, Urteaga, and González 1994, 18). This alone makes the group demographically noteworthy, since in northern Mexico indigenous peoples, with the exceptions of the Yaqui and Mayo, tend to have small populations. Rarámuri now share their territory, however, with about three times as many mestizos who dominate the region politically and economically.

The Rarámuri's homeland encompasses approximately 35,000 square kilometers in the southwestern portion of the state of Chihuahua, comprising a rugged region of the Sierra Madre Occidental range commonly referred to as the Sierra Tarahumara. One of the most spectacularly corrugated landscapes in North America, it is characterized by mile-deep *barrancas* (gorges) and serpentine canyons. This terrain offered refuge to Rarámuri who fled there after they rebelled against the expropriation of their best lands by Spaniards in a series of bellicose uprisings in the seventeenth century. But the very inaccessibility and geographical isolation of this region, which had safeguarded Rarámuri for centuries, in recent years has attracted elements that are now jeopardizing Rarámuri lives and security. Today, the Sierra Tarahumara is besieged by some of the most terrifying forces in the country.

Local variations have caused some places to be more susceptible to specific problems than others, but, generally speaking, four components come together in the Sierra Tarahumara to make it a site of suffering, urgency, and concern. First, the timber industry has brought roads and deforestation to even remote corners of the Sierra. Second, Rarámuri lands have been colonized to grow narcotics. Third, in order to combat the latter, federal troops and judicial police have heavily militarized the Sierra Tarahumara. Fourth, the region recently experienced the worst drought in living memory. The Rarámuri are caught between these forces, over which they exercise virtually no control. Given the way these factors are interrelated and the inescapable violence, uncertainty, and fear they generate, the Rarámuri's anguish is especially poignant.

The pine forests of the Sierra Tarahumara have allowed Chihuahua to become Mexico's leading producer of wood. Although a source of revenue, the logging industry has also been a major source of conflict for the Rarámuri, who too often have been cheated in the removal of their timber. Conservationists managed to stall a World Bank loan worth $45.5 million dollars to Mexico for the development of the massive Sierra Madre Forestry Project. After NAFTA went into effect in 1994, however, "it became apparent that the World Bank loan, which was still on hold, was simply the tip of a rather large iceberg" (Raat and Janacek 1996, 146). The rapacious deforestation of the Rarámuri's homeland, therefore, continues unabated. Although the region was virtually inaccessible until the Chihuahua al Pacifico Railway pierced the heart of the Sierra Tarahumara in the 1960s, nowadays the once isolated region can be reached via a major road-building project known as the *Gran Visíon*, a highway system totaling 911 kilometers around the Sierra Tarahumara (González Rodríguez 1985, 20). Still, much of the Sierra is accessible only by foot, horseback, or bush plane, especially in the rough canyon country to the southwest, bordering the state of Sinaloa.

Logging and roads have paved the way for the most notorious incursion into the Sierra Tarahumara in recent years, namely the penetration of the area by the Sinaloa and Chihuahua drug cartels. Seizure of Rarámuri lands for illegal logging or to grow marijuana and opium poppies, locally known as *chutama*, has been reported in media ranging from *The New York Times* to *The Los Angeles Times*, from *National Geographic* to network television, not to mention its frequent coverage in the Mexican press.[18] Environmental and human rights activists advocating on behalf of the Rarámuri have been attacked, outspoken indigenous leaders killed, and some logging companies have allegedly been operated as fronts for laundering profits from illicit crops (Weinberg 2000, 323–341). Replicating the term for the opium zone in the highlands of Myanmar, Laos, and Thailand, the mountainous region where the states of Chihuahua, Sinaloa, and Durrango come together is now known as Mexico's "Golden Triangle," and the Sierra Tarahumara is its center. Examining the relationship between drug cultivation and the escalating violence in the Sierra Tarahumara, Alvarado Licón, in his book *La Tarahumara: una tierra herida*, documents that with barely five percent of Chihuahua's population, the eight municipalities in the Sierra accounted for nearly twenty percent of all homicides in the state between 1978 and 1981 (1996, 69). He argues that the disproportionately high levels of violence in the Sierra in part are attributable to the fact that the municipal authorities there are unable, or unwilling, to resolve these drug-related conflicts. According to officials in the western municipality of Batopilas, much of which is located in roadless gorges, the firearms used most are the 9 millimeter pistol, the .38 super, and the *cuerno de chivo* or "goat horn," the local term for an AK-47 (Turati 2001). These weapons would be intimidating enough to anyone, let alone Rarámuri equipped with only bows and arrows.

While many have rightly attributed the escalating conflicts in the Sierra to the drug business, they have not appreciated how this culture of violence builds on a preexisting social and historical template. Ethnohistorical works make clear that the mestizos of Chihuahua's Sierra developed a distinctive culture based on what Alonso refers to as "the social organization of warfare" (1995, 21–50). This part of Mexico's northern frontier was settled by tough *serranos*, armed peasants who repelled Apache depredations in the eighteenth and early nineteenth centuries and revolted against the Mexican nation-state when it tried to incorporate them in the late nineteenth and early twentieth centuries. Their current resistance to government anti-narcotics forces, including the federal army, is thus part of a long tradition of armed struggle constitutive of their self-identity as a ruggedly independent people, a people who for centuries have defined themselves as a militarized peasantry.

Although as early as the 1950s federal troops occasionally searched for the clandestine cultivation of opium poppies in the western Sierra Tarahumara, along the nearly inaccesible Chihuahua-Sinaloa border (Plancarte 1954, 37), it was not until the late 1970s that the army arrived en masse to launch Operation Condor, its first big counter-narcotics campaign in the Sierra Tarahumara. "Troops tortured and raped Indians, but never caught up with the Fontes gang" (Weinberg 2000, 329), the reigning family of the most powerful drug cartel in Chihuahua. Military patrols, road blockades, army bases, and civilian searches continued to be a routine part of life in the Sierra through the 1980s, but in the 1990s the army's growing presence and intimidation of indigenous people prompted protests from local priests, human rights organizations, and the Bishop of the Tarahumara, José Luis Dibildox (Alvarez 1998). By the late 1990s, American-made Humvees plied the roads and unmarked black helicopters thundered overhead. Seemingly everyone but the Rarámuri were armed with semiautomatic weapons. According to Heliodoro Juárez González, president of the National Commission on Human Rights for the State of Chihuahua (CNDH), whom I interviewed in April 1997, Rarámuri are displaced not only because they are physically pushed off their lands, but because their labor and farms are forcibly co-opted for the purposes of cultivation. When federal troops or state police arrive, Rarámuri are the ones who are arrested or beaten.[19] Caught between narco-terrorism on the one hand and the army on the other, it is not surprising that many Rarámuri are abandoning their homes.[20]

The Rarámuri's problems, however, have not been solely confined to encroachments on their lands. Even the heavens seem to have abandoned them in recent years. During the last decade, the Sierra began suffering through the worst drought in forty years. Many Rarámuri blamed the drought on the wholesale logging that was robbing the mountains of their pine forests, reflecting their belief that pines act as the highlands' sacred sentinels that annually call the rains. In the Sierra, where Rarámuri maintain themselves as subsistence farmers, the situation was desperate. As springs dried up, livestock died, and crops withered, hunger spread among the Rarámuri. *Exelsior*, a Mexico City newspaper, reported that 240 Rarámuri died in 1996 due to complications related to malnutrition (Robles 1996a). By 1999, the severity of the drought compelled Mexico to declare Chihuahua, as well as four other northern states, disaster zones.

Unsubstantiated rumors have long circulated in the Sierra Tarahumara that both the *narcotraficantes* and the army, together with the police, were benefiting from the illicit drug trade. In late April 2001, headlines flared in the national press about how the drug cartels discovered a new way of using the government infrastructure to terrorize Rarámuri into meeting their demands for indigenous land or labor by burning schools. "In March was the latest offense against the presence of the government. In Segórachi, municipality of Urique, the nacrotraficantes burned for the second time the INI boarding school, with all the children inside, to send their message" (Turati 2001). As the Bishop of the Tarahumara recently said in an interview: "I know whole families who devote themselves to [the cultivation of drugs], and I tell them to get out, and they say to me, 'What do you want us to do, if there are no other alternatives?'" (Turati 2001). Pressed between years of drought on the one side and a drug war on the other, Rarámuri have few choices indeed. The futility, not to mention cruelty, of continuing to wage a "war on drugs," via a military solution to the problem, in zones that produce illicit crops when the causes are largely socio-economic and the casualties are largely indigenous peoples and peasants with few alternatives, is evident not only in the Sierra Tarahumara, but also in the Peruvian Amazon (see Dean, this volume) and the Putumayo region of Colombia (see Ramírez, this volume).

Rarámuri Resistance: The Cultural Construction of Political Action

According to Weinberg, "[t]he Tarahumara are besieged by violence and pushed from traditional lands by the drug mafias much as Tzotzil and Tzeltal are by the cattle oligarchy in Chiapas, far away at the other end of Mexico" (2000, 323). While this is undoubtedly true, the comparison raises the question: if their situations are so similar, why have these indigenous peoples responded so differently? That is, in view of the Rarámuri's desperate situation, why has rebellion not broken out in the Sierra Tarahumara, as it has in Chiapas? In fact, authorities as well as the general public in Chihuahua City have expressed worries that since dire poverty and automatic weapons are already in the Sierra, all that is lacking is a leader and an ideology to ignite an uprising. Ultimately they may be right, but I suggest that, in the search for reasons as to why the Rarámuri have not rebelled, we should remember to look beyond political and economic explanations. Their agency also must be accounted for in cultural terms, a dimension that is important when theorizing about indigenous mobilization.

Whereas in the highlands of Chiapas the "traditional" indigenous political community is generally isomorphic with the municipality (as embodied in the cargo system), there are multiple Rarámuri townships, each with its own civil-religious government within each municipality in the Sierra Tarahumara. Because municipal and *ejidal* boundaries do not conform to Raramuri *pueblos* (townships) and *rancherías* (dispersed hamlets), indigenous governance in the Sierra Tarahumara is not formally articulated with the political infrastructure recognized by the state, as it was in the Chiapas highlands. This reality, coupled with the fact that mestizos dominate the leadership positions in the municipalities and ejido assemblies, effectively marginalizes Rarámuri from official power structures. The compartmentalization of these two political systems has made it easy for mestizo caciques to exclude Rarámuri from their own lands. In Coloradas de la Virgen, one of the most volatile sites of narco-colonialism in the Sierra, 360 Rarámuri families "had been working the land, but only some thirty were granted access to the ejido" (Weinberg 2000, 328).

Moreover, Rarámuri society is characterized by greater social disjunction between town centers and outlying hamlets than is the case elsewhere in highland Mesoamerica, essentially producing two politico-religious subcultures (Fried 1977). In the pueblos, this authority structure is based on a Spanish colonial model, whereas in the hamlets a more indigenous organization is maintained. In some places, this distinction corresponds to the difference between *pagótame*, or baptized Rarámuri whose seats of politico-religious life are in the pueblos, and *gentiles*, non-baptized Rarámuri who have their own officials in the rancherías (Kennedy 1996; Levi 2001, 186). The loose connections between municipalities and pueblos on the one hand and pueblos and rancherías on the other, coupled with the Rarámuri's fluid social organization and dispersed settlement pattern, meant that the Mexican state could not infiltrate, and thereby subvert, indigenous

governance in the same way it had in Chiapas. In fact, the highest rank-
ing local political officials among the Rarámuri are still the indigenous
gobernadores of the pueblos, just as the Chiapas highland townships
also had gobernadores until they were replaced by municipal
presidents in 1937–39, as discussed in the previous section on
Chalchihuitán.

Given the lack of correspondence between indigenous and official
political structures in the Sierra Tarahumara, the Mexican state could
neither "assist" the scattered Rarámuri nor co-opt their politics at the
local level, as it had done in Chiapas. Another plan was needed. Thus,
in 1939 federal agencies created a "tribe-wide" political organization,
the Supreme Council of the Tarahumara (Plancarte 1954, 93), in an effort to encompass and politically represent the Rarámuri as an ethnic
group. When this "tribal council" became affiliated in 1957 with the
state sponsored National Peasant Confederation (CNC), the Rarámuri
were for the first time officially linked to the PRI. This "supreme council" and its formal political affiliations, however, mattered little to ordinary Rarámuri for the simple reason that the new "tribal" government
was at variance with Rarámuri models of group identity, which cus-
tomarily do not rise above the level of the pueblo (Kummels 2001,
76–77). To this day, many Rarámuri do not know that such an organization even exists. The Supreme Council of the Tarahumara was composed of bilingual Rarámuri culture brokers who served the paternalistic and integrationist policies of the Mexican state, rather than the
interests of the Rarámuri people whom they supposedly represented
(Stefani, Urteaga, and González 1994, 39), a situation reminiscent of
the bicultural municipal presidents in Chalchihuitán. The Rarámuri
did not participate to any significant degree in Chihuahua's independent peasant organizations or political movements, such as the Committee for Popular Defense (CDP) or the Peasant Alliance of Northwestern Chihuahua (ACNC). With the exception of a few handpicked
Rarámuri who either served in the PRI affiliated Supreme Council of
the Tarahumara or in the State Coordinating Office of the Tarahumara
(established in the 1980s by the opposition PAN in Chihuahua), Rarámuri did not consequently experience the heightening of political consciousness and grassroots organizing that had already affected thousands of indigenous peoples in Chiapas for several decades. Rather
than entering independent or state sponsored political life, Rarámuri
continued to most commonly interact with *mestizos* through individual trading relationships, phrased in terms of fictive kinship, and re-

sponded to the incursions of outsiders through acts of passive resistance, silence, secrecy, and withdrawal, as they have since their military defeats in the late seventeenth century (Kennedy 1996; Levi 1999).

However some Rarámuri have begun responding in new and dramatic ways, considering both the intensification of problems in the Sierra Tarahumara and the inspiration sparked by the example of the Zapatistas (including two Tzeltal Zapatistas who visited the Sierra in the late 1990s). More than anything else, this new political action is marked by its great diversity, which ranges from insurgent to peaceful. Since 1997 this action has included forcibly closing a sawmill in the Sierra, rioting in the state capital, entering official electoral politics as candidates at both local and national levels (ranging from Sierra ejidos to the Mexican Congress of the Union), and collaborating on a broad basis with various nongovernmental organizations (NGOs) (Levi, in press).

Today, many Rarámuri work with environmental groups, such as the Sierra Madre Alliance, Sierra Tarahumara Diversity Project, Native Seed/Search, and the Advisory Council of the Sierra Madre (CAS-MAC), whose founder was awarded the 1996 Goldman Environmental Prize for North America, the equivalent of a Nobel Prize for environmental activists. Rarámuri collaboration with the Chihuahua-based Commission for Solidarity and Defense of Human Rights (COSYD-DHAC) has enabled this organization to be a zealous watchdog for abuses committed against indigenous peoples of the Sierra. So too, outspoken Jesuit allies in the Tarahumara Diocese have been important, particularly José Luis Dibildox, Bishop of the Tarahumara, and Father Ricardo Robles, an advisor to the EZLN. Rarámuri have actively participated in the emerging national indigenous movement, participation ranging from initially sending a delegate to the first National Indigenous Forum held by Zapatistas in San Cristobal de las Casas in January 1996 (Weinberg 2000, 340), to more recently showing their support by joining the historic Zapatista caravan that entered Mexico City's Zócalo March 10, 2001 (Ramírez 2001).

There are also indications that the construction of a more inclusive collective identity, superceding older pueblo-based distinctions, may be occurring among Rarámuri in some places. For example, contemporary urban Rarámuri in Chihuahua City, a very heterogeneous group, do identify themselves as members of a generalized "Rarámuri" ethnic group, thereby transcending local differences in language and culture that used to serve as functional bases for identification in the

Sierra (Kummels 2001, 93). Significantly, in the past Rarámuri occasionally mobilized above the level of the pueblo for military campaigns. Even though these political organizations were ephemeral, it is noteworthy that these mobilizations included alliances with neighboring indigenous groups, such as the Tepehuan, and even nonindigenous people, such as mestizos or mulattos (Molinari and Merrill 1995, 16). These instances of supralocal identity formation among the Rarámuri in both the past and the present invite comparisons with the multiethnic communities in the Lacandon forest that gave birth to the EZLN.[21]

The Rarámuri's recent involvement in grassroots organizations and supralocal networks likewise has given them the confidence to express differences. "Rarámuri" in the Alta Tarahumara have begun differentiating themselves from "Rarómari" in the Baja Tarahumara (Petrich 1999). Meanwhile, both groups are also experimenting with new forums, gatherings, and interactions at the state-recognized "ethnic" level (Petrich 2000). Echoing Zapatista demands in Chiapas, some Rarámuri want the military to withdraw from indigenous territories, including their own, whereas other Rarámuri, in marked contrast to the Zapatistas, have requested the army to remain, stating that it is their only means of protection against the violence caused by the usurpation of their lands for illegal logging or the cultivation of narcotics (Petrich 1999). In general, while the fragmented topography and atomized sociopolitical organization in the Sierra Tarahumara is mirrored in the diversity of contemporary Rarámuri political action, there is no doubt that Rarámuri have joined their voices with the growing chorus of indigenous peoples who, at the first meeting of the National Indigenous Congress in October 1996, declared: "Never again a Mexico without us!"

Toward a Polymorphous National Indigenous Movement

Below I offer a snapshot of the cultural politics leading toward Mexico's current indigenous movement (Hernández Navarro 1998, Nash 2001, Stephen 2002). As Hernández Navarro put it, "Zapatismo did not 'invent' the indigenous struggle, but gave it a national dimension, stimulated its growth, [and] unified many of its currents" (1998b, 26). Previously there had been other policies and organizations that involved or concerned indigenous peoples, but primarily they had been run *for,* rather than *by,* indigenous peoples. Chief among these was *indigenismo*, a positivist state policy directed by government officials and social scientists, aimed at integrating indigenous peoples into the life of the nation by promoting economic development, education, health, nutrition, and other modernizing programs of directed change in indigenous communities. Indigenous cultures were valued as a source of folklore but regarded overall as static remnants of the mighty civilizations of precolumbian Mexico. As President Lázaro Cárdenas (1934–40) put it, "our indigenous problem is not to conserve 'Indian' for the Indian nor to indigenize Mexico, rather to Mexicanize the Indian" (Villa Rojas 1976, 12).

In 1948 the National Indigenist Institute (INI) was founded under the Secretariat of Public Education (SEP). With guidance from Alfonso Caso, Gonzalo Aguirre Beltrán, Alfonso Villa Rojas, and other prominent Mexican anthropologists, INI functioned as the official institute that promoted indigenismo. Starting in the 1960s and 1970s, however, state sponsored *indigenista* approaches to indigenous issues came under attack from Mexican anthropologists, a critique that soon was supported by indigenous intellectuals (see Gutiérrez 1999). Ten months after the EZLN uprising, in a highly symbolic act, indigenous organizations took over the INI offices in San Cristóbal, Chiapas, and transformed them into the seat of government for the Autonomous Pluriethnic Regions (RAP) (Gómez Nuñez 2000, 181). By literally turning the physical facilities of assimilation into the building of self-determination, the Zapatistas signaled their intention to drive the last nail into the coffin of indigenismo.

Indigenous mobilization in Mexico has its roots in diverse struggles to gain land or to resist poverty, but during the last quarter of the twentieth century the identity of this movement began to change. In the 1970s and 1980s, indigenous peoples in some parts of the countryside became politicized through their involvement with peasant organizations, workers' parties, and Catholic catechists. However, contrary to the predictions of both Marxists and modernization theorists, albeit for contrasting reasons, class-based interests never completely supplanted ethnicity as a basis for indigenous organization. Indigenous peoples gradually began to redefine their involvements during this period. Whereas formerly they had participated in agrarian struggles as *campesinos* (peasants), now they were increasingly organizing themselves as an ethnopolitical movement (Hernández Navarro 1998, 16). Processes of self-identification were also changing. The revalorization of indigenous ethnicity on a broad organizational scale was first evidenced in 1974, when an Indigenous Congress was convened in San Cristóbal de las Casas, Chiapas. Over the next twenty years, independent indigenous organizations continued to gain strength, despite several attempts by federal agencies, such as the CNC and INI, to co-opt the nascent movement. Indigenous organizations in Mexico, alongside others throughout the hemisphere, commemorated Columbus Day in October 1992 with demonstrations marking 500 years of resistance. Motivated by the experiences of the Zapatistas in Chiapas, yet with delegations of indigenous peoples from all over Mexico, the first National Indigenous Congress (CNI) was held on October 10–12, 1996, in Mexico City. This convention, which has continued to meet annually, marks a critical moment in the development of a sustained indigenous movement at the national level.

Nevertheless, even at the national level, the importance of taking into account the diverse cultural and historical experiences of Mexico's nearly ten million indigenous people became quite apparent in the CNI. While discussing the contentious issue of indigenous rights and autonomy at these meetings, the proposal of pluriethnic autonomous communities that had developed in Chiapas did not make sense to other peoples, such as the Yaqui of Sonora and Mixe of Oaxaca (Stephen 1997a, 30). Consequently, an alternative model was proposed, the mono-ethnic autonomous community, which better harmonized with these peoples' cultural histories (Stephen, in press). Even in Chiapas, there are different understandings of autonomy. Tojolab'al have complained that the post-1994 push for autonomy has empowered new "advisors" while displacing Tojolab'al elders and religious leaders. Similarly, when indigenous leaders of the Autonomous Pluriethnic Regions (RAP) began negotiations with the federal government, they were denounced as "capitulators" by the EZLN command, NGOs, and the intellectual middle-class for whom, according to Gómez Nuñez, " 'autonomous' meant having no relation with the government whatsoever" (2000, 184).[22]

Several years before the Zapatistas captured international attention, Mexico's indigenous communities already were becoming salient at the level of national legislation. Preceded only by Norway, Mexico was the second country in the world to ratify, on September 5, 1990, the International Labor Organization Convention (ILO) No. 169 Concerning Indigenous and Tribal Peoples in Independent Countries (Gómez 1995, 25). Although ILO 169 has been criticized for its restrictive interpretation of "self-determination" (Díaz Polanco and Sánchez 2000), Mexico's ratification of this document prompted constitutional reforms. Consequently, after superficial consultation with indigenous groups, Article 4 of the Federal Constitution was changed in 1990 to officially recognize that the "Mexican nation has a pluricultural composition, fundamentally sustained by the presence of indigenous peoples" (Estrada Martínez and González Guerra 1995, 9). This conferred vague cultural rights on indigenous peoples (such as the right to "develop" their languages, customs, and specific forms of social organization) but not political rights, other than their civil rights as individuals, which they already possessed by reason of Mexican citizenship. The reforms to Article 4 did not confer upon indigenous communities the right to self-determination or autonomy, but they did not jeopardize them either, since a people's right to self-determination is explicitly guaranteed by ILO 169 (Díaz Polanco and Sánchez 2000). Therefore both the signing of ILO 169 and the changes to Article 4 have the effect of making the Mexican government appear to the international community as though it is ratifying legislation that benefits its indigenous peoples when in fact, in a political sense, their status has not changed. Elsewhere in Latin America, a year after Mexico made its constitutional reforms to Article 4, Colombia ratified a new constitution in 1991 that recognized its indigenous peoples and granted them full citizenship, although like Mexico, the gains seem to be more symbolic than substantive (see Jackson, this volume).

The San Andrés Accords on Indigenous Rights and Culture

Four years later, the most important document in Mexico dealing with the rights of indigenous peoples was signed on February 16, 1996, in the highland Chiapas town of San Andrés Larráinzar, between representatives of the federal government and the EZLN. The importance of the cultural dimension in these negotiations and its linkage with the political aspect from an indigenous perspective is enshrined in the last word in the title by which the document is known, namely the "San Andrés Accords on Indigenous Rights and Culture." The accords, comprising four different documents, reflect the fact that in Mexico relations between indigenous peoples and the state need to be predicated on a new set of premises based on indigenous rights, cultural autonomy, land reform, and political participation. After the government had failed to move forward on the Accords signed in February, the Concord and Pacification Commission (COCOPA), a Mexican Congressional Commission that had been established to broker peace, moved into high gear. Under pledges of support from both the EZLN and the government, the COCOPA drafted a proposal to be presented to Congress in early December for the constitutional implementation of certain elements of the Accords, specifically those requiring changes or amendments to articles 4, 18, 26, 53, 73, 115 and 116 of the Federal Constitution.

Yet by 1998, the federal government still had failed to implement the Accords that its own representatives had already signed. Instead, President Zedillo submitted his own counter-initiative to congress. One difference between the COCOPA document and the PRI counter-initiative had to do with the attribution of different meanings to the word *pueblos*, which in Spanish may variously mean peoples, towns, or communities. This is significant because "peoples" have the right to *libre determinación* (self-determination), according to international legal covenants, except ILO 169, the very document most often cited as protecting the rights of indigenous peoples.[23] Thus, whereas the Accords make use of the words "*pueblos indígenas*," the government has pursued a more restrictive meaning, substituting the words "*comunidades indígenas*" in their counter-initiative. However, government fears that congressional ratification of the Accords would balkanize the country remain unfounded, because indigenous peoples seek politico-cultural autonomy within a constitutional framework rather than outright secession or laissez-faire autonomy. The latter would result in their separation from the rest of the country, whereas a central goal of the indigenous movement has been to decrease indigenous marginalization. Despite different interpretations regarding how "indigenous autonomy" would affect relationships among nation, state, and municipality as political units in Mexico (Stephen 1997a; cf. Díaz Polanco 1997), there is little doubt that the Zapatistas' call for "democracy, liberty, and justice" reached out and touched, not only the politically alienated, but a broad spectrum of Mexican civil society anxious for reform. As such, Mexico's indigenous rights movement, as spearheaded by the Zapatistas and their supporters, aligned itself with the democratic aspirations of a nation hungry for change, irrespective of party membership. Indeed, hundreds of thousands of Mexicans greeted the Zapatista caravan from Chiapas when it arrived in Mexico City to lobby for the COCOPA proposal, and when Marcos spoke in the capitol's Zócalo, he addressed the largest crowds to have gathered there since the Revolution. Significantly, Ecuador represents a similar case illustrating how non-indigenous masses have identified with indigenous protests to promote a national debate on the nature of the state (see Macdonald, this volume).

Indigenous Rights on the Road to the Presidency: The Fox Administration *in Medias Res*

What is the relationship between the indigenous movement and ethnicity in an overwhelmingly mestizo nation? Does the indigenous struggle in Chiapas and elsewhere represent the redeployment of nationalism from below (Stephen 1999a, 26) or the appropriation of indigeneity from above, given its wide support among unions, students, and the middle-class (Gutiérrez 1999, 199)? Seeking to translate these broad social stirrings and diverse cultural understandings of citizenship into an explicitly political idiom for the purposes of the July 2000 presidential race, the candidates from each of the three major parties developed platforms on indigenous rights. This meant, also for the first time in history, that indigenous rights were part of the national electoral discourse.

PRI candidate Francisco Labastida's position on the San Andrés Accords on Indigenous Rights and Culture was that he would support Zedillo's counter-initiative, but not the one the government already agreed to by signing its own treaty on indigenous rights in 1996. In contrast to the PRI's candidate, Cuauhtémoc Cárdenas, representing the opposition PRD party on the left, rejected the government's counter-initiative and supported the COCOPA proposal. Meanwhile, the right-wing PAN party made known that it would support neither the San Andrés Accords submitted by the COCOPA nor the government's counter-initiative. Instead, PAN proposed its own plan, based on a vague concept of "municipal charters," but this was taken seriously by neither the EZLN nor the government, nor apparently even by PAN's own candidate, Vicente Fox. Instead, Fox's most famous soundbite summarizing his populist position on indigenous rights was that if elected he simply would speak with Marcos and "resolve the problems in Chiapas in 15 minutes."

On November 30, 2000, the eve of Fox's inauguration, the EZLN broke five months of silence and presented him with three "goodwill" conditions for resuming dialogue: 1) Liberation of all Zapatista political prisoners; 2) demilitarization of seven Zapatista communities in Chiapas; and 3) implementation of the San Andrés Accords by way of congressional (and state) approval of the COCOPA proposal. Almost all the Zapatista prisoners were released. Five of the army encampments were gradually dismantled. In two cases, however, the land was not returned to the community, but rather held by the government and turned into "social service centers," that is, new offices for the Secretariat of Social Development (SEDESOL).

Four days after taking office on December 1, 2000, Fox presented to the national Senate the COCOPA proposal for constitutional reforms in the area of indigenous rights and culture, so as to move forward with the long-delayed implementation of the San Andrés Accords, thus keeping a campaign promise that this would be his first act in office. In order to lobby for passage of the COCOPA proposal, Zapatistas led a march from Chiapas to Mexico City on February 24, 2000. Indigenous peoples from across the country eventually joined the caravan. When they arrived in the capital on March 10, they were greeted by hundreds of thousands of Mexicans. In late April, both the House and Senate passed a radically modified version of the COCOPA proposal.

The indigenous rights law that was passed, however, was not the initiative that had been agreed upon by the COCOPA. Instead, the Congress had altered the COCOPA initiative to the point of being unrecognizable regarding the important issues of indigenous autonomy and self-determination. Specifically, the new document changed the constitutional definition of indigenous peoples from "subjects of public law" (implying rights), as the COCOPA proposal stated, to "objects of public interest." The changed wording reverses the whole meaning of indigenous agency; *subjects are active*, creative agents engaged in making their own futures, whereas *objects are passive,* inert instruments wielded by more powerful others.

Nevertheless, the altered proposal passed Congress overwhelmingly, with only the PRD and a few PRI deputies voting against it. The measure was rejected outright by the National Indigenous Congress and the EZLN; the latter severed all communication with the Fox government in April 2001. In June 2001, Fox and Central American presidents ratified "Plan Puebla Panama"—a neoliberal initiative designed to privatize and develop virtually everything from the Isthmus of Tehuantepec through Chiapas and Central America right down the to the northern tip of South America. The consequences this would likely have on the region's indigenous peoples are devastating.

In the following months, the indigenous law was approved by the requisite number of state congresses. Yet it cannot be formally entered into the constitution until the Supreme Court rules on dozens of appeals that have been filed by critics of the law regarding its validity, who claim that the revised proposal was not passed by the states with the largest indigenous populations. Nor is it in keeping with the conditions that were mutually agreed upon by the Zapatistas and the government.

By early February 2002, the indigenous rights law had bounced back into the Legislature, where the Lower House of Congress voted to revise it since it differed markedly from the COCOPA initiative. In its place, a new version of the law was presented that restored the same stipulations as in the original treaty signed by the Zapatistas and the government. Meanwhile, in early March indigenous people in the Lacandón rainforest of eastern Chiapas filed a human rights complaint in response to their violent displacement. They denounced the government's plan to open the region to natural resource exploration by multinational companies, reporting that the army had begun surrounding their communities again. As Tom Hansen aptly put it, "The Zapatista struggle continues, but with new challenges that look very much like the old challenges" (2002, 15).

Conclusion

There is no denying that much of Zapatismo is new; certainly both the media and message are. The revalorization of indigenous ethnicity, the Zapatistas' capacity for national "in-reach" and international "out-reach," the merging of indigenous issues with the desires of a citizenry demanding democracy, and the building of an independent, diverse, and truly national indigenous movement are all unprecedented changes. Yet beneath the ski masks, and within the cadences of Zapatista speeches, one can still detect the unmistakable faces and voices of *México profundo*. Zapatista orations are laced with the poetic couplets of Maya prayer, familiar semantic and syntactic parallelisms that have long denoted ritual language among the indigenous peoples of southern Mexico. The discourse on the "radicalization of democracy" is surely novel to anyone unaccustomed to the realpolitik of Mesoamerican cultures. It corresponds to the notion that tolerance and respect for cultural differences are basic to the pluralistic worldviews and multicultural environments that are the civilizational building-blocks of precolumbian Mexico. Even the spread of new religions that helped recruits transcend the limitations of their old locally based identities, such as the multiethnic Protestant and Evangelical communities that gave birth to the EZLN in the Lacandón rainforest, has its historical analogue in the messianic movements that fanned indigenous rebellions in 1712 and 1867 in the highlands of Chiapas.

It is, however, still too early to tell whether we are seeing a "new dawn" for Mexico's indigenous peoples or merely witnessing another cycle in the more ancient Mesoamerican conception of history that is predicated on recurring periods of creation and destruction. But one thing is certain: indigenous peoples have vital roles to play in Mexico's political future, and their moment has arrived. Success will depend on flexibility and the ability to mirror unity at the national level while remaining sensitive to distinctive regional, cultural, and historical experiences at the grassroots level.

Comparison of indigenous struggles in different parts of Mexico, particularly the geographical extremes of the country (i.e., frontier and border zones), is therefore instructive. Indeed, there are important parallels between the problems faced by the Tzotzil and Tzeltal in the highlands of Chiapas and the Rarámuri in the highlands of Chihuahua. Among others, these similarities include the expropriation of their best lands by outsiders and the invasion of their territories by both legal and extra-legal armed forces. The Sierra Tarahumara finds itself in the grip of narco-terrorism, while the Chiapas countryside has been terrorized by the equally illegal actions of paramilitaries. Federal troops and judicial police have invaded both regions, forcing the indigenous peoples to live under similar regimes of low-intensity warfare.

But indigenous peoples in the Chiapas highlands and the Sierra Tarahumara also manifest equally important differences in their regional dynamics and cultural politics. Perhaps the Mexican anthropologist Aguirre Beltrán best summed up these differences when he noted that the systems of indigenous government among the Rarámuri in the highlands of Chihuahua and the Tzeltal-Tzotzil in the highlands of Chiapas exhibit different levels of indigenous influence, such that the impress of Spanish colonial structures is less evident among the former than the latter (Aguirre Beltrán [1953] 1980, 66–152). Consequently, the PRI could use this colonial political infrastructure to infiltrate local indigenous government in Chiapas, until the EZLN severed the corrupt connection by stimulating the growth of autonomous indigenous municipalities. In the Sierra Tarahumara, on the other hand, local indigenous governance has never been connected effectively to organs of the state. Rarámuri pueblos already enjoyed de facto autonomy, although in reality this porous scenario only made the political marginalization and economic exploitation of the Rarámuri people easier. In an attempt to rectify this situation, federal agencies created a top down "tribe-wide" political organization. Nevertheless this fabricated ethnic identity has been of minimal importance to most Rarámuri since it was governed by a "supreme council" that deviated from local models of cultural identity and political organization. In the last decade, however, there are important signs that Rarámuri political action and modes of self-identification are changing. For instance, the Rarámuri now support the Zapatistas in some places. Overall, the scope of indigenous mobilization and the intensity of new political consciousness have historically differed in Chiapas and the Sierra Tarahumara. Finally, it must be recalled that diverse regional dynamics and their cultural politics indicate that variety exists not only *between* regions, but *within* them as well, variety not only of local circumstances, but of interests and voices too.

In sum, I have argued here that one must look beyond strictly political or economic aspects to the cultural definitions they draw on in order to understand the current indigenous situation in Mexico. Because the architects of democracy are the people and Mexicans view it through a Mesoamerican prism, mestizos have embraced the indigenous movement as their own. Although the absorption and expansion of democracy is part of a broader social transition occurring throughout the country, it cannot be forgotten that the indigenous peoples and the affirmation of their cultures are elements that provoked the initial political opening and continue to stimulate its progress. At a practical level, what this means is a greater tolerance for pluralism in both political *and* cultural domains. But the thorny question of whether the political or the cultural is more critical to understanding the emergent indigenous situation can only be solved if one concedes that in making constructive arguments about democracy, neither variable can be privileged over the other. Instead, the relationship between the political and the cultural must be seen as stubbornly dialectical.

Notes

1 I wish to thank David Maybury-Lewis for convening the Weatherhead Center's March 24–25, 2000, Working Group on Relations between Indigenous Peoples and the State in Latin America and to Evon Vogt for offering his reflections on the paper when I presented it there. Special thanks go to Jean Jackson, Joshua Paulson, and Jan Rus for reading earlier drafts of this paper and providing valuable comments and criticisms.

2 Some of the ideas in this chapter were originally developed in the author's review of *The Chiapas Rebellion: The Struggle for Land and Democracy,* by Neil Harvey (Duke University Press 1998), in the *Journal*

of Interamerican Studies and World Affairs 42, 4 (Winter 2000), pp. 151–157.

3   "Mexico's new president orders troop pullback in Chiapas," December 1, 2000; http://www.cnn.com/2000/WORLD/americas/12/01/mexico.fox.04/index.html, December 8, 2000 (website defunct).

4   For a recent list of some key sources on this subject in both English and Spanish, including books, monographs, regular journals, recent special issues, relevant web sites, and selected videos, see "CSQ Resource List: Indigenous Rights and Organizations in Mexico," Cultural Survival Quarterly 23(1):62–64, 1999.

5   Several months after the uprising, *Cultural Survival Quarterly* published the first in-depth account of the cultural, historical, and political events that precipitated the crisis, drawing on the expertise of ethnographers, several of whom had worked in Chiapas since the 1960s. See "Special Report: Why Chiapas? Eight Experts Offer Their Views," *Cultural Survival Quarterly,* Volume 18, Number 1 (Spring 1994).

6   These data were gathered in 1978 during seven months of fieldwork in San Pablo Chalchihuitán. I was one of the last students to have had the opportunity of working with Evon Z. Vogt on the Harvard Chiapas Project (Vogt 1994, 359, 437). My research focused on the relationship between political and religious power.

7   Antún Méndez Ton, personal communication, May 5, 2001

8   I am indebted to Jan Rus for giving me a copy of this document.

9   "Mexico: Chiapas Alert" http://nativenet.uthscsa.edu/archive/nl.9410/0126.html. May 12, 2000 (website defunct).

10 Antún Méndez Ton, personal communication, May 5, 2001

11 For a discussion of the cosmology and cultural politics of San Andrés Larráinzar, see Ochiai 1989.

12 Joshua Paulson, personal communication, May 11, 2000.

13 Joshua Paulson, personal communication, May 11, 2000.

14 See also, Mexico Solidarity Network, Weekly News Summary, May 8–14, 2000.

15 Denuncia de Chalchihuitan, http://www.laneta.apc.org/pipermail/enlacecivil-l/2000-June/000081.html, May 10, 2001.

16 Ibid.; *La Jornada* May 13.

17 I first visited the Sierra Tarahumara in the 1970s. I conducted ethnographic fieldwork in the summers of 1985 and 1986, and again from January 1988 to August 1989, principally in the El Cuervo district, Municipality of Batopilas. My research has focused on Rarámuri religion,

ethnicity, and economy. I made brief visits to the Sierra again in December 1994 and April 1997.

18 Felix Gehm recently produced an important documentary on this subject, "Voices of the Tarahumara," which was screened at the 2001 Sundance Festival. It includes clips on the drug problem in the Sierra which aired on network television.

19 Interview with Lic. Heliodoro Juárez González, President of the National Commission on Human Rights for the State of Chihuahua; Chihuahua City, April 4, 1997.

20 For a discussion of Rarámuri who have migrated to urban areas outside the Sierra, see Kummels 2001; Levi, in press.

21 For an interesting discussion comparing indigenous rebellions in previous centuries in Chihuahua with the 1994 Zapatista uprising in Chiapas, see Molinari and Merrill 1995.

22 The irony of this is heightened for members of the NGOs and intellectual middle classes because "many of them were professors or teachers in the university or research centers and had their wages paid by a government institution. But they did not question this" (Gómez Nuñez 2000, 184).

23 A people's right to self-determination is taken as a foundational principle in international law. In the United Nation Charter it is affirmed as "a peremptory norm" (Anaya 1996, 75). Article 3 in the Draft U.N. Declaration on the Rights of Indigenous Peoples, states: "Indigenous peoples have the right of self-determination" (Anaya 1996, 209). Yet Part 3 of Article 1 of ILO 169 calls this right into question by stating "The use of the term 'peoples' in this Convention shall not be construed as having any implications as regards the rights which may attach to the term under international law" (Anaya 1996, 169).

Works Cited

Adams, Richard

1967   "Nationalization." In Manning Nash, ed. *Social Anthropology*, Vol. 8, pp. 469–489, *Handbook of Middle American Indians*, Robert Wauchope, general ed. Austin: University of Texas Press.

Aguirre Beltrán, Gonzalo

1980   [1953]*Formas de Gobierno Indígena*. Mexico City: Instituto Nacional Indigenista.

Aguirre Beltrán, Gonzalo, Alfonso Villa Rojas, Romano D., *et al*

1976   *El Indigenismo en Acción.* Mexico City: Instituto Nacional Indigenista.

Alonso, Ana María

1995   *Thread of Blood: Colonialism, Revolution, and Gender on Mexico's Northern Frontier.* Tucson: University of Arizona Press.

Alvarado Licón, Carlos Mario

1996   *Tarahumara, Una Tierra Herida: Análisis de la Cultura de Violencia en Zonas Productoras de Estupefacientes en Sierra de Chihuahua.* Chihuahua: Talleres Gráficos de Estado de Chihuahua

Alvarez, Jaime

1998   Pide Obispo de Tarahumara Frenar Excesos de la Milicia. *El Diario de Chihuahua.* 31 August.

Anaya, S. James

1996   *Indigenous Peoples in International Law.* Oxford: Oxford University Press.

Anderson, Benedict

In Press Nationalism and Cultural Survival in Our Time: A Sketch. In Bartholomew Dean and Jerome Levi, eds. *At the Risk of Being Heard: Identity, Indigenous Rights, and Postcolonial States.* Ann Arbor: University of Michigan Press.

1983   *Imagined Communities: Reflections on the Origin and Spread of Nationalism.* London: Verso.

Angeles, Mariscal

2000   "Buscan Confrontar Habitantes de Chalchihuitán y Polhó." *La Jornada*, 13 May.

Bonfil Batalla, Guillermo

1987   *México Profundo: Una Civilización Negada.* Mexico City: CIESA/SEP.

Burguete Cal y Mayor, Araceli

n.d.   Usos, Costumbres, Partidos, y Elecciones en Chalchihuitán, Altos de Chiapas, Centro de Investigaciones y Estudios Superiores en Antropología Social—Sureste, manuscript in author's possession.

Cancian, Frank

1992   *The Decline of Community in Zinacantán: Economy, Public Life and Social Stratification, 1960–1987.* Stanford, CA: Stanford University Press.

Cancian, Frank, and Peter Brown

1994   "Who is Rebelling in Chiapas?" *Cultural Survival Quarterly* 18(1):22–25.

Carrigan, Ana

2001   "Afterward: Chiapas, the First Postmodern Revolution." In Juana Ponce de León, ed. *Our Word is Our Weapon: Selected Writings, Subcomandante Insurgente Marcos*, pp. 417–443. New York: Seven Stories Press.

Collier, George

1997   "Reaction and Retrenchment in the Highlands of Chiapas." *Journal of Latin American Anthropology* 3(1):14–31.

Collier, George, with Elizabeth Quaratiello

1994   *Basta! Land and the Zapatista Rebellion in Chiapas.* Oakland, CA: Food First Book.

Díaz Polanco, Héctor

1997   *Autonomía Regional: La Autodeterminación de los Pueblos Indios.* Mexico City: Siglo XXI Editores.

Díaz Polanco, Héctor, and Consuelo Sánchez

2000   Self-Determination and Autonomy: Achievments and Uncertainty. In Aracely Burgete Cal y Mayor, ed. *Indigenous Autonomy in Mexico*, pp. 83–96. Copenhagen: IWIGIA.

Estrada Martínez, Rosa Isabel, and Graciela Vega Carrillo

1993   *Informe sobre el Programa de Atención a Comunidades Indígenas de la Sierra Tarahumara Primera Visitaduría General Coordinación de Asuntos Indígenas.* Mexico City: Comisión Nacional de Derechos Humanos.

Fox, Jonathan

1999   "Mexico's Indigenous Population." *Cultural Survival Quarterly* 23(1):26.

Fried, Jacob

2000   "Two Orders of Power and Authority in Tarahumara Society." In Raymond Fogelson and Richard Adams, eds., *The Anthropology of Power: Ethnographic Studies from Asia, Oceania, and the New World.* Pp. 263–269. New York: Academic Press.

Gómez, Magdalena

1995   *Derechos Indígenas: Lectura Comentada del Convenio 169 de la Orga-nización Internacional del Trabajo.* Mexico City: Instituto Nacional Indigenista.

Gómez Nuñez, Marcelino

2000   Autonomous Pluriethnic Regions (RAP): The Many Paths to De Facto Autonomy. In *Indigenous Autonomy in Mexico*, Aracely Burgete Cal y Mayor, ed., pp. 178–193. Copenhagen: IWIGIA.

González Rodríguez, Luis

1985   *Tarahumara.* Mexico City: Edición Privada de Chysler de México, S.A.

Gossen, Gary

1999   *Telling Maya Tales: Tzotzil Identities in Modern Mexico.* New York: Routledge.

Gutiérrez, Natividad

1999   *Nationalist Myths and Ethnic Identities: Indigenous Intellectuals and the Mexican State.* Lincoln: University of Nebraska Press.

Hansen, Tom

2002   Zapatistas: A Brief Historical Timeline. In *The Zapatista Reader.* Tom Hayden, ed., pp. 1–15. New York: Nation Books.

2001   Zapatista Timeline. In *Our Word is Our Weapon: Selected Writings, Subcomandante Insurgente Marcos.* Juana Ponce de León, ed., pp. 445–451. New York: Seven Stories Press.

Harvey, Neil

1998   *The Chiapas Rebellion: The Struggle for Land and Democracy.* Durham: Duke University Press.

Hernández Navarro, Luis

1998a   The Escalation of the War in Chiapas. *NACLA Report on the Americas.* 33(5):7–10.

1998b   Ciudadanos iguales, ciudadanos diferentes: la nueva lucha india. In *Acuerdos de San Andrés*, Luis Hernández Navarro and Ramón Vera Herrera, eds., pp. 15–32. Mexico City: Ediciones Era.

Hernández Navarro, Luis, and Kennedy, John G.

1996   *Tarahumara of the Sierra Madre: Survivors on the Canyon's Edge.* Pacific Grove, CA: Asilomar Press.

Kummels, Ingrid

2001   "Reflecting Diversity: Variants of the Legendary Footraces of the Rarámuri in Northern Mexico." *Ethnos* 66(1):73–98

Levi, Jerome

In press Indigenous Rights and Representations in Northern Mexico: Cultural Constructions of Rarámuri Voice and Silence. In *At the Risk of Being Heard: Identity, Indigenous Rights, and Postcolonial States.* Bartholomew Dean and Jerome Levi, Eds. Ann Arbor: University of Michigan Press.

2001   "Tarahumara." In *The Oxford Encyclopedia of Mesoamerican Cultures.* Davíd Carrasco, editor in chief. Vol 3. New York: Oxford University Press. 185–187.

2000   "Review of N. Harvey, The Chiapas Rebellion: The Struggle for Land and Democracy." *Journal of Interamerican Studies and World Affairs*, 42(4):151–157.

1999   "Hidden Transcripts among the Rarámuri: Culture, Resistance, and Interethnic Relations in Northern Mexico." *American Ethnologist* 26(1):90–113.

1988   "Myth and History Reconsidered: Archaeological Implications of Tzotzil-Maya Mythology." *American Antiquity* 53(3): 605–619.

Mallon, Florencia

1992   "Indian Communities, Political Cultures, and the State in Latin America, 1780–1990." *Journal of Latin American Studies* 24: 35–40.

Maybury-Lewis, David

1997   *Indigenous Peoples, Ethnic Groups, and the State.* Cultural Survival Studies in Ethnicity and Change. Series editors David Maybury-Lewis and Theodore MacDonald, Jr. Boston: Allyn and Bacon.

Molinari, Claudia, and William Merrill

1995   "Chiapas y Chihuahua: Cuatro Siglos de Resistencia India." *Ojarasca* 44:14–19.

Nash, June

2001   *Mayan Visions: The Quest for Autonomy in an Age of Globalization.* New York: Routledge.

1997   "The Fiesta of the Word: The Zapatista Uprising and Radical Democracy in Mexico." *American Anthropologist* 99(2):261–274.

Nigh, Ronald

1994   "Zapata Rose in 1994: The Indian Rebellion in Chiapas." *Cultural Survival Quarterly* 18(1):9–11.

Ochiai, Kazuyasu

1989　"Meanings Performed, Symbols Read: Anthropological Studies on Latin America." *Performance in Culture* No. 5. Tokyo: Tokyo University of Foreign Studies.

Ovalle Fernández, Ignacio (Director General)

1978　*INI 30 Años Despues: Revision Crítica.* Mexico City: México Indígena.

Paulson, Joshua

2000　"Rural Rebellion in Southern Mexico: The Guerillas of Guerrero." *North American Congress on Latin America (NACLA) Report on the Americas* 33(5):26–29.

Plancarte, Francisco

1954　"El Problema Indígena Tarahumara." *Memorias del Instituto Nacional Indigenista*, Vol 5. Mexico City: INI

Petrich, Blanche

2000　"Autoridades Indígenas Buscan Fortalecer la Política Rarámuri." *La Jornada*, 13 June.

1999　"Mantienen Reservas Sobre Desmilitarización: Rarómaris de San José del Pinal Apoyan Tres Puntos de la Consulta." *La Jornada*, 21 March.

Raat, Dirk, and George Janacek

1996　*Mexico's Sierra Tarahumara: A Photohistory of the People of the Edge.* Norman: University of Oklahoma Press.

Ramírez, Bertha Teresa

2001　"Tarahumaras, Tzeltales, Huicholes, y Nahuas, en la Cola de la Caravana: A un Paso del Zócalo, la Fatiga Casi Vence a los Indios, pero el Coraje los Levanta." *La Jornada*, 10 March.

Robles, Martha

1996a　"Muerte en la Tarahumara: Crimen Oficial y Privado." *Excelsior,* 10 December.

Romero Ruíz, Alejandro, and Rubén Villalpando

1996b　"Protestas por la Presencia Militar en la Sierra Tarahumara." *La Jornada,* 13 August.

Rus, Jan

1995　"Local Adaptation to Global Change: The Reordering of Native Society in Highland Chiapas, Mexico, 1974–1994." *European Review of Latin American and Caribbean Studies* 58:71–89.

1994 'Comunidad Revolucionaria Institucional': The Subversion of Native Government In Highland Chiapas, 1936–1968. In Gilbert Joseph and Daniel Nugent, eds., *Everyday Form of State Formation: Revolution and the Negotiation of Rule in Modern Mexico*, pp. 265–300. Durham: Duke University Press.

Rus, Jan, Rosalva Aída Hernández Castillo, and Sharon Mattiace

2001 "Introduction. The Indigenous People of Chiapas and the State in the Time of Zapatismo: Remaking Culture, Renegotiating Power." *Latin American Perspectives* 28(2): 7–19.

Stavenhagen, Rodolfo

2001 Toward the Right to Autonomy in Mexico. In *Indigenous Autonomy in Mexico*, Aracely Burgete Cal y Mayor, ed., pp. 10–21. Copenhagen: IWIGIA.

Stefani, Paola, Agusto Urteaga, and Luis González

1994 Descripción de la Situación Actual de la Población Indígena de la Sierra Tarahumara. In Luis González, Susana Gutiérrez, Paola Stefani, Margarita Urias, and Agusto Urteaga, eds., *Derechos Culturales y Derechos Indígenas en la Sierra Tarahumara,* Estudios Regionales 8, pp. 17–20. Ciudad Juárez, Chihuahua: Universidad Autónoma de Ciudad Juárez.

Stephen, Lynn

In press Indigenous Autonomy in Mexico. In *At the Risk of Being Heard: Identity, Indigenous Rights, and Postcolonial States.* Bartholomew Dean and Jerome Levi, eds. Ann Arbor: University of Michigan Press.

2002 *Zapata Lives! Histories and Cultural Politics in Southern Mexico.* Berkeley: University of California Press.

1999 "Introduction. Indigenous Rights and Self-Determination in Mexico." *Cultural Survival Quarterly* 23(1):23–26.

1997 "The Zapatista Opening: The Movement for Indigenous Autonomy and State Discourses on Indigenous Rights in Mexico, 1970–1996." *Journal of Latin American Anthropology* 2(2):2–41.

Turati, Marcela

2001 "Invade Narcoterror Sierra Tarahumara." *Reforma*, 30 April, 2001.

Villa Rojas, Alfonso

1976 Introducción. In *El Indigenismo en Acción.* Aguirre Beltrán, Gonzalo, Alfonso

Villa Rojas, Romano D., et al., eds., pp. 11–19. Mexico City: INI.

Vogt, Evon, Z.

1994   *Fieldwork among the Maya: Reflections on the Harvard Chiapas Project.* Albuquerque: University of New Mexico Press.

Warren, Kay

1999   *Indigenous Movements and their Critics: Pan-Mayan Activism in Guatemala.* Princeton: Princeton University Press.

Weinberg, Bill

2000   *Homage to Chiapas: The New Indigenous Struggles in Mexico.* London: Verso.

Yanes Rizo, Pablo Enrique

1997   "Indigenous Rights and Democratic Reform of the State." *Cultural Survival Quarterly* 23(1):48–49.

Acronyms

ACNC	Peasant Alliance of Northwestern Chihuahua
CASMAC	Advisory Council of the Sierra Madre
CDP	Committee for Popular Defense (Chihuahua)
CIOAC	Independent Confederation of Agricultural Workers and Peasants
CNC	National Peasant Confederation
CNDH	National Commission on Human Rights for the State of Chihuahua
CNI	National Indigenous Congress
COCOPA	Concord and Pacification Commission
COSYDDHAC	Commission for Solidarity and Defense of Human Rights
EPRI	Revolutionary Army of the Insurgent People
EZLN	Zapatista Army of National Liberation
FPF	Federal Preventative Police
ILO	International Labor Organization
INI	National Indigenist Institute
MODECH	Democratic Movement of Chalchihuitán
NAFTA	North American Free Trade Agreement
NGO	Non-Governmental Organization
OCEZ	Emiliano Zapata Peasant Organization
ORIACH	Indigenous Organization of the Highlands of Chiapas
PAN	National Action Party
PRD	Party of the Democratic Revolution
PRI	Institutional Revolutionary Party
RAP	Autonomous Pluriethnic Regions
SEDESOL	Secretariat of Social Development
SEP	Secretariat of Public Education
UU	Union of Ejidal Unions and United Peasant Groups of Chiapas

2

Appropriating the Indigenous, Creating Complicity: The Guatemalan Military and the Sanctioned Maya

Jennifer Schirmer

The discussion of the Maya in Guatemala leads to a distressing conclusion—that they, like so many other indigenous peoples in Latin America, find themselves caught, through no fault of their own, between forces over which they have little control. As in Mexico and Colombia, the indigenous people of Guatemala find themselves the targets of significant violence, a violence that is part and parcel of the undermining of their traditional systems of authority and social organization. The discussion in this chapter differs from the other chapters in this volume to the extent that it focuses on the perceptions and demands of the military, who are largely responsible for that violence and constitute the central actors in the undermining of traditional ways of life.

> "We brought government to the village . . . The key word in this initial strategy was 'participation' because the *indígenas* participated in the war effort."   —General Gramajo, 1990 interview

> Those who became complicit in the violence found themselves learning to be murderous through their "own" experience and were purposefully taught by others to think in certain ways as a result of punishing, fragmenting and isolating . . . [It was] indoctrination built on a hierarchy of "good people" versus "savages who deserve indoctrination" . . . turning neighbor against neighbor.
>
> —Montejo 1987, 63 and 56

The examination of power should "include the techniques and modalities of both the physically coercive forms of domination and the more ideological and discursive forms, and relations between the two . . ." (Andrew Turton, quoted in Green 1999, 230). What follows reflects this interplay between two domains of power used by the Guatemalan military vis-à-vis the indigenous population. Nowhere else in Latin America has an army managed to mobilize and divide an indigenous population against itself to such an extent—to the point of forcing victims to become accomplices in killing—as in Guatemala. If we are to better understand the dynamics between the political and violent restructuring of communities by the state and the cultural logics of everyday life, a close examination of the reasoning and mindset of state actors who hold and exercise such power is required.

The systematic policy of massacre, from the army's perspective, was intended to penetrate guerrilla-led mobilization structures and force complicity with the army, thereby producing fissures within indigenous communities possibly for generations as "insurance" against another insurgency. Underlying these actions is a worldview and a set of practices that assume a sophistry: We the army destroy you to save you, we re-define you so that you may maintain your identity. The army defines the Indian through the image of the "correct Maya," or what I refer to as the "Sanctioned Maya," and then justifies Indian beliefs and practices by reference to that definition. It's a kind of political solipsism—a mindset that says without hesitation that their view of politics, and their view of the Mayans' place within it, is all that exists or can be known. In sum, what the military does is create a world in which all that exists is what they know and how they know it. This is similar to many groups in power, but what is unusual is the extent to which they have been able to institutionalize their reality even within electoral civilian governance. This mental universe is effectively based on the extraordinarily contradictory belief that Mayans are at once mythical national superheroes and enemies of the state, objects to be honored and killed, mythologized and "forged" as part of the military's national project. (This is similar to the army's view of the Indian in the early part of the century as needing to be "civilized" in order to become "good soldiers.") And in order for the army to earn the Mayans' loyalty and complicity in killing, the Maya identity had to be "forged," shaped and affirmed through their own optic of the Sanctioned Maya.

Rather than falling back on the traditional dualism of ballots or bullets, civil or military, more finely tuned, contextualized, and ethnographic approaches to the ideology and belief systems of those who hold and exercise state power, in this case the protagonists of state political violence, are needed. I would argue that the anthropological approach is especially well suited for this purpose because of its ability to listen and enter the world of its subjects. Nonetheless, despite important attempts to describe relations between Indians and the state from an ethno-historical perspective (e.g., Smith 1990) or from "post-violence" perspectives of the victim and the community (e.g., Stoll 1993; Zur 1998; Green 1999), anthropologists have typically worked and mostly stayed within small, relatively homogeneous community boundaries and local indigenous culture. They, for the most part, have left the issues of power, domination, and "the state" to other disciplines.

In a reversal of this traditional optic on the state and indigenous communities, this chapter will focus on indigenous identity and life practices from the perspective of the army—a major state actor in Guatemala. Their massacre campaign and restructuring of indigenous communities in the early 1980s linked nation building with a particular sanctioned indigenous identity based on collusion. My purpose is to begin to contextualize the extent to which the recent history of the Maya is indelibly sculpted by the military's solipsistic view. It is my belief that without such contextualization and understanding, the army cannot be prevented in the future from once again fundamentally redefining and reshaping the lives of the indigenous population in its own image and on its own terms, reasserting its domination through its violent practices and frozen images.

Building on interviews with military officers over the last decade that capture the habits of mind and systems of meaning of those who have played key roles in the construction of a military project (Schirmer 1998), I examine the appropriation of the *indígena* and the construction of a "correct, Sanctioned Maya" from the army's perspective. My research, together with other scholars', indicates that the "appropriation" of the indigenous by the army has occurred on multiple levels:

1. The violent destruction and looting of the Maya's physical and cultural space

2. The robbing of an indigenous person's identity, to be replaced by one sanctioned by the army

3. The "neighborizing" of violence and the creation of a culture of fear of both the army and neighbors, both indigenous and ladino (civil patrollers and other collaborators)

To answer the question (to what extent is the recent history of the Maya indelibly sculpted by the military's solipsistic view), I focus on five major aspects of this appropriation of the indigenous to provide an avenue into this worldview, and its implications for the political future in Guatemala:

1. The pacification campaign
2. The Indian companies and civil patrols
3. The model villages and poles of development
4. Civil affairs and the Sanctioned Maya
5. The future of social intelligence

The chapter concludes with brief remarks about the peace accords and asks whether the military's attitudes toward the Maya are changing.

I. The Pacification Campaign

In Guatemala, for the past 36 years, state-crafting through political violence came in the form of direct, naked military power. But with the coup of 1982, a hybrid project of "strategic democracy" was "born" out of the womb of a counterinsurgency campaign that had already killed, according to interviews with army officers, 35,000 on both sides of the conflict, just between the months of November 1980 and February 1981. Several months later, an intensified campaign of what is referred to by the architect of the campaign, General Gramajo, as *matazonas*, (killing zones) would kill another 50,000 to 75,000 over the next 18 months—most of the killing in the first 8 months between April and December 1982 and primarily in the indigenous highland departments of Chimaltenango, Quiché, Huehuetenango, and the Verapaces. Ninety percent of these victims were noncombatants and indigenous. At least 440 villages were razed, again according to army estimates, and more than 1 million refugees were displaced. It was primarily the indigenous population in the most highly active guerrilla zones that was targeted in order to sever the guerrillas from their civilian support network. This meant literally emptying the local population from its sociocultural and geographic habitat in order to create logistical and recruitment difficulties of every order. Mass killing was thus inexorably connected to this campaign. It was the most closely coordinated, intensive massacre campaign in Guatemalan history. As Gramajo states: "One of the first things we did was draw up a document for the campaign with annexes and appendices. It was a complete job with planning down to the last detail" (Schirmer interview).

Drawing out the pacification campaign strategy on a table, he further explains:

> The Army attacked, here were the villages, here is the population supporting *la guerrilla* from behind, and the army attacked everyone and we continued attacking, attacking until we cornered them and we got to the point where the *población* was separated from the subversive leaders . . . (Schirmer interview)

As in every counterinsurgency war, the primary objective of this scorched-earth campaign, initially referred to as Operation Ashes, was to "separate and isolate the insurgents from the civilian population" with full military force (or, in militarese, the reverse: "to rescue the noncombatant civilian population" from the guerrilla (Cifuentes 1982, 26). President-General Rios Montt, in his weekly television sermons, called for the need to surgically excise evil from Guatemala and "dry up the human sea in which the guerrilla fish swim" (Richards 1985, 95). The searing contradiction of scorched-earth warfare, though, is that in order to accomplish this "separation," certain areas are targeted for massive killings: that is, the military must treat the civilians they are to "rescue" *as though they are combatants*, killing and burning all living things within the "secured area." No distinction is made between combatant and noncombatant; separation is purely rhetorical, as one colonel explains,

> Everyone, everyone was a guerrilla; no difference was made in killing them. The big difference [in the shift in strategy after the 1982 coup] was that we couldn't eliminate them all. Some were captured and their lives spared so they could serve as informers (Schirmer interview).

Although the army assumed that all guerillas—indigenous and ladino—were ideological heretics and thus the enemy of the state, the new High Command in 1982 also recognized that there was a particular historical hatred of the army as representatives of the state among the indigenous community. Not only was the army fighting an insurgency but also the legacy of a ladino-centered state in which the Indian had been not only marginalized politically and economically, but also perceived as minimally human. As one colonel surmised,

> Subversion comes from social contradictions: there is a higher class and a lower class. And there is much discrimination. We

military people committed a mistake: that most of the fruits of the infrastructure, if we can use this word, came only to the capital [city]. We might say it was a huge mistake. A disproportional development badly planned, or better put, badly executed since it has been well planned since 1800 (Schirmer interview).

As a result, the 1982 National Plan of Security and Development recognized that the causes of subversion were "heterogeneous, based on social injustice, political rivalry, unequal development, and the dramas of hunger, unemployment, and poverty; but it can be controlled if we attempt to solve the most pressing human problems" (1982, 1). The ability of the army to create a development component of counterinsurgency combat operations reflects their institutional flexibility. But it was a development intimately tied to security; there were to be no "beans" without the "bullets." However, the fundamental paternalism and authoritarianism implicit in the army's threat mentality concerning the Indian's susceptibility to manipulation by "foreign ideologies" would remain intact (and would hinder the effectiveness of their physical and ideological reordering). A 1981 army document entitled "Operation Ixil" reveals the army's extraordinary fear of difference with and lack of control over the Indian. At the same time, this document was one of the first to recognize why the indígena feels "distrustful of all that has come from the ladinos whom they associate unconsciously with the Spaniards and their descendants who have caused them so much suffering . . . [The guerrilla] offers them a dignity" in contrast to the "governments that have treated them like a subgroup, retarded and brutalized, by ignorance and the consumption of alcohol" (1982, 37, 28).

Penetration of the militarized state directly into the heretofore isolated and "abandoned" indigenous villages was underway. It was the first time in Guatemalan history when both the guerrillas and the army sought to gain the hearts, minds, and stomachs of the indigenous population.

Hence, a central part of the campaign was to appropriate the guerrilla vocabulary and strategy. To counter the guerrillas' ideology of redistribution and change, for example, the army drew refugees down from the mountains with food (i.e., the beans). It presented itself as an egalitarian, nationalist force of change and development, with stories of officers distributing relief supplies equally in villages, and sent in school teachers to rebuild schools (Steppentat forthcoming, 13). The appropriation of the image of order, honesty, justice, and state authority as used by Rios Montt in his political speeches was also central to their strategy in opposition to the "portable," partly invisible, state of la guerrilla with its localness, its village-centeredness, and its minimum of physical infrastructures and traditions (ibid., 12). It was this localness to which Gramajo addressed himself when he said "We brought government to the village."

II. Civil Affairs, Indian Soldiers, and Civil Patrols

Civil Affairs

Civil Affairs, established in June 1982, built on the Operation Ixil plan written by Navy Captain Cifuentes. Operation Ixil speaks of the need to adopt "an intensive, profound, and carefully studied psychological campaign to rescue the Ixil mentality." Several proposals are set forth: 1) the 100 percent formula for the army "to put all its efforts into Civil Affairs Units to complete its assigned mission [of] intensifying the ladinization of the Ixil population until it disappears as a cultural subgroup foreign to the national way of being." (38) By ladinization,

> one must understand it to mean *castellanizar,* to pressure the population to use Spanish language and culture, to suppress the distinctive indigenous dress and other exterior displays of differentiating oneself from the group. . . . Without these differentiating characteristics, the Ixils would stop thinking as they do and accept all the abstractions that constitute nationality, patriotism, etc. (1982, 46).

However, there are several "disadvantages" to this approach, Cifuentes points out: For one thing, for the last 400 years, the Ixils, more than other ethnic groups, have resisted *la castellanización.* "Efforts would be useless in changing their thinking and cosmogonic concepts even when they don't have the externally differentiating characteristics." Put simply, they may seem to be one of us, but they aren't; ladinization will make it even more difficult to know how differently they think, and "will augment [already existing] resentment of the Ixil toward the imposition [of the ladino]—a resentment that will fall right into the hands of the enemy [i.e., la guerrilla]" (46–47).

> The second proposal was to have the Civil Affairs Units follow a policy based on respecting the Ixil identity, customs, and language, giving them the opportunity to contribute, together with

the army, to the defense of their communities . . . Knowing the history of the Ixiles, this would be the only way to convince them to form part of the great Guatemalan nation with a pluralist society, more or less as in Switzerland . . . Another [advantage] would be to neutralize the strategy of the enemy, utilizing their own procedures [for defense] but with many more resources."

The disadvantage here, Cifuentes says, is that "there exists the possibility that if they organize themselves into self-defense patrols and are given arms, they could go into the mountains [to fight] with the guerrilla." (47). Thus, one can go just so far in respecting the Ixil as an equal. In short, without combining military and political actions—repressive force and ladinization through Civil Affairs-centered counterinsurgency campaigns—development or security alone would be insufficient. Cifuentes recommended proposal two: Civil Affairs with the addition of an intense ideological campaign in the Ixil language developed through psychological operations (OPSIC).

Much of the task of implementing the army's new strategy in 1982 fell on the *Asuntos Civiles* (Section of Civil Affairs) and Community Development (labeled S-5 in 1983). Civil Affairs "functions as advisor to the military commander of each military zone in reference to the political, economic, social, and psychological aspects of military operations. . . ." (Ejército 1987, 9). As a consequence, Civil Affairs units were assigned to garrisons in the zones of most conflict. They were there to transform guerrilla irregulars (FIL) into army soldiers and Civil Patrollers, oversee all settlements of the displaced in the highland areas of conflict, "reeducate" the refugees and internally displaced, and direct the psychological warfare and propaganda programs (OPSIC) targeting the civilian population, all the while gathering intelligence in situ. By 1983, all activities in the model villages, poles of development, and Civil Patrols, to which I turn below, were under Civil Affairs control and surveillance. In effect, Civil Affairs companies were put in charge of all civil-military actions of the state at the local level. Cifuentes's final proposal was to focus all government efforts on improving living conditions for the indigenous population. The advantages here were "the physical incorporation of this territory within a Civil Affairs plan . . . offering work to the Ixil population" with these projects. It would not, however, "resolve the problem in a definitive form . . . Knowing the Ixil nature, all of the process would be difficult [to achieve] as they would not collaborate," he concluded.

Civil Patrols

It was during the 1982–83 campaign that the army implemented a policy that would seriously implicate and divide the indigenous population against itself. With "participation" and "recuperation" of the Indian watchwords of the pacification campaign, indígenas "recuperated" from the massacre sweeps were mobilized to swell the army ranks and to deny guerrilla forces their irregulars (FIL) for surveillance and defense against the army.

Civil Patrols were part of the army's centerpiece for a more permanent counterinsurgency strategy in the highlands. But these Indian soldiers and patrols were directly looted from the guerrilla. Looting the self-defense network of the guerrilla, *fuerzas irregulares locales* or FIL, the army created and utilized special companies of Indian soldiers and Civil Patrols of Self-Defense. According to General Gramajo,

> We didn't have enough soldiers [to fill the new military zones] . . . So, since they had already been organized by the FIL, we recruited these *nuevos soldados lugareños* (new soldiers of the locale) . . . We tolerated the FIL in order to take it away from the guerrilla, and when we gave the new soldiers their [own] guns, we also gave them money so they would have a wage . . . and we did the same to their fathers, brothers, and whomever else. We gave them work. We built roads . . . That is, communal development, civic work, something in common, ok? The result of this was that they had their guns. If [the village] was afraid of [the subversives], it didn't matter because they had their guns . . . These were regular soldiers (Schirmer interview).

Integrated into various army activities, Civil Patrollers were established in the heart of guerrilla controlled areas, especially among the repatriated at refugee camps. Some were located within military attachments and patrolled with the army on the frontline, imparting their knowledge of the terrain, dialect, and local customs. Ixil company soldiers, for example, were "useful" in "explaining" the war to indigenous refugees with psychological warfare statements.[1] Officers commented that many of these soldiers were "from the very same villages that were destroyed and restructured into the poles of development. They return to these villages as members of Civil Affairs companies integrated into each infantry battalion stationed at the poles of development" (Schirmer interview).

As General Gramajo argues,

> By recruiting from these places [in the Ixil] we figured we would better know the places we were fighting and we would cease ethnic confrontation. And besides, we were putting money into these poor places. So it was a completely integrated effort (Schirmer interview).

Indian soldiers and Civil Patrollers, in this peasant "corporate patriotship" with the army, conveniently produced internal surveillance and complicity by the Indian (Steppuntat 15). Indians were forced to stand at the intersection of local and national violence to face a double bind. They were drafted officially to protect and defend the town from outsiders but in fact were there to monitor the activities of the townspeople and families and report suspicious behavior to military authorities on the outskirts of town. This forced the population, which found itself "between two fires," to choose sides. Many aligned themselves with the army to save their lives. Indian former soldiers, too, served with Civil Affairs units as "human force multipliers," providing "excellent intelligence sources" (Sheehan 1989, 144).

Indian companies of former soldiers were formed by the army in the Ixil Triangle, an area particularly brutally hit by the scorched-earth campaign, to patrol their locale, control the local population, and destroy the guerrilla network of irregulars. During the height of the campaign, 5,000 Ixils (most of them former soldiers and thus reservists) were re-inducted into the army. In many instances, former guerrillas were tortured and interrogated for several months and amnestied on condition that they join the army; after several months to a year of soldiering, they would be selected as *jefes* of Civil Patrols. Between 1983 and 1984, 1,300,000 indigenous men between the ages of 15 and 60 (or approximately 16.87 percent of the total population, and 20 percent of all males) were members of the Civil Patrols.

In extending soldiering and civil patrolling throughout much of the adult male indigenous population, the military was remarkably adroit at not only penetrating daily village life but also at spreading around responsibility for the killing. As one officer told the first patrollers in Nebaj, Quiché (Ixil Triangle): "Now we are all going to get our hands dirty" (Stoll 1993, 115). Every Indian soldier and patroller became implicated in or at least acquiesced to the new order, with the subject of "loyalty" and "support" within the climate of concealment and intimidation useful in the army's psychological war campaign. Neutrality for the indigenous population was thus impossible.

III. Restructuring Indigenous Life: Model Villages and Poles of Development

The military's 1984 booklet *Polos de Desarrollo (Poles of Development)* leaves little doubt that the military recognized the urgency of prioritizing security-qua-development and the need to assert state presence in the highlands, too long "abandoned" for the guerrilla and Catholic church to exploit:

> It is important to emphasize that . . . operations of security, development, countersubversive and ideological warfare will be conducted. In other words, having once attained security, the Army penetrates the population with the incentive for development, to correct the vulnerability of abandonment in our society in which [this population] has lived and which the subversion has exploited very efficiently after 12 years of good political work in the region, and which is necessary to counter in the same way. And it is this very reason that we enter into an era of ideological and developmentalist military operations, which up to now have provided very good results (Ejército 1984a, 57–58).

Presenting itself as reasserting order in the midst of chaos, the military's forceful social, economic, and physical reordering of indigenous life in the "well-massacred" highlands was institutionalized through its poles of development, within which model villages were constructed. They are best understood as high-security areas built to serve as forms of population control—moving the displaced from camps into model programs and "integrating" the local indigenous population into both the anti-subversive fight and the army's "nationalist" project.

Starting from the premise that past governments had abandoned indigenous communities, the Army General Staff, working within its paradigm of being the final arbiter of local indigenous village life, analyzed the indigenous social system, spatial distribution, and traditional beliefs to determine "what could be preserved and what had to be changed" to suit the military's security imperatives (Guatemala: *Acción Cívica* 1985, 16). The result was four large areas in the western highlands from which the insurgents had been "cleansed": the Ixil Triangle in southern Quiché, Chisec in Alta Verapaz, Chacaj in Huehuetenango, and Playa Grande in northern Quiché. Much of this work was carried out in less than one year. Although the plan was to construct 49 villages for 100,000 indigenous people within these four poles of development, only half were built, housing an estimated 50,000. Different poles served different counterinsurgency objectives: the Ixil Triangle, the area of most destruction, was the most restructured and served an exclusively internal function as a "demonstrative effect" for what the military considers to be a population "in resistance." Chacaj, on the other hand, was conceived exclusively to "attract those who cross over into Mexico" (Guatemala: *Acción Cívica* 1985, 6).

With new houses built in a grid and streetlights glowing in the dark, these "new villages" were intended to be viewed as "urban" and thus "developed." The settlements followed the Spanish colonial town grid of the New World (as well as that of a military base) with its tight rectangular nucleus, in contrast to the organic asymmetry of peasant settlements that typically follow the contours of the topography. With two houses between streets, and a water faucet on the corners, it became easier to keep in sight those who entered and left the houses as well as those who congregated for water and cleaning tasks (traditionally sites for gossip and information exchange). The military garrison was usually in an area overlooking the village from which the army could observe the roadways, church, and school.

Model villages themselves were not constructed on the site of the old village. The old village of Acul, for example, was spread out along the village floor "which meant little organization," according to one advisor. "To concentrate the population means you can protect and control it better as well as provide clean water and electricity" (Schirmer interview).

At the reeducation centers of Acamal model village, moreover, indoctrination sessions were held throughout the 1980s, during which the population was forced to listen to military marches on a record player or watch films about the horrors of life in the Soviet Union (Wilson 1991, 47). "My job is to brainwash the people (*lavarle el cerebro a la gente*). My work consists of first erasing the cassette that the subversion had recorded onto the people," explained one Civil Affairs teacher, "and later record onto them a new cassette" (Arias 1989, 207). In keeping with the army's Operation Ixil strategy, "an intensive, profound, and carefully studied psychological campaign to rescue the Ixil mentality" and "ladinize" it, was established. Villagers were expected to listen for hours to *pláticas ideológicas* (ideological talks) by S-5 teachers, to sing the hymn of the Civil Patrols in Spanish, and to participate in organizing "Queen of the Civil Patrols" festivals during the more traditional days of celebration.

Such forceful restructuring of sociocultural, economic, and settlement patterns of indigenous life represents the most significant reorganization of the indigenous population since the Conquest, when *pueblos de índios* were established. This disintegration of the economic, social, and cultural bases of a community, especially when land is one's site of origin, is a tearing asunder of established social relations to impose a new system of authority. It is also a breaking of ethnic history and memory in order to rewrite it (Arias 1988, 171). This form of myth robbery has created the military's own Sanctioned Maya.

IV. The Army's Construction of the Sanctioned Maya

In destroying, reconstructing, and penetrating the geographic and cultural fabric of villages in the northwest highlands in the form of model villages within poles of development, the army needed propaganda that sought ways to best reincorporate "the Indian" into the mental world of the military project. This propaganda rested on two ideas: the army was fighting the war, however reluctantly, with the support of the people (e.g., Civil Patrols), and the guerrillas were the authors of the massacres (Aguilera Peralta 1983, 94). As General Gramajo pointed out:

> We used propaganda [on the indigenous population] saying, 'The Army can help us, so let's not fight. Why do you want to fight the government if the government wants to work *with* you? We are Guatemalans. Why are we fighting one another?' In other words, to insert ideas of peace, ideas about civic culture—the color of the flag, the national anthem—into the minds of the population (Schirmer interview).

Attempting to evoke an illusion of re-creating the universe, officers speak of a "natal" democracy and of their development plan in the highlands as "a policy of a new man, a new country, a new Guatemala" (Peckenham 1983, 21). This modest sense of creation is also found in the military literature on the new model villages. One photograph of a scorched-earth village is captioned, "It appears to be a Christmas nativity and in some ways it is. *Tzalbal* in the corner of el Quiché at the hour of dawn, awakens from a dream refreshed to repeat another quiet day with renewed energy for its new corn plot which, in time, will become its daily bread." A sign at its entrance read, "A Village Reborn."

It is a kind of "reorganized truth" that appears to simplify, purify, and make things innocent of intent or contradiction. But it is more than creation mythmaking: it is a birthing discourse with numerous references to the military as though a parent. "As the only institution giving birth to democracy," the army "is the only one that has been pushing this baby into the light. The other institutions are irresponsible or immature." (Gramajo, *Crónica* interview, 19 May 1988, 22). Gramajo refers to the pacification campaign as his "baby"; General Rios Montt, too, remarked, "The democratic baby was very rapidly taken out of its incubator and that is why we have [the problems] we have [today]" (*Crónica* 26 Jan 1989, 8). This transsexual birthing discourse reveals just how much the military sees itself as creator (mother to the Fatherland) and parent-guardian (father to the Motherland), and its deep identification with the nation-state.

Such re-creation and guardian discourses should also alert us to the military's view of the indígena as a child needing to be disciplined, "ladinized," "entrepreneurized" and "forged" to fit the "new" Guatemala. Gramajo:

> To forge, you understand, refers to what a blacksmith does to make horseshoes. So we must forge *el pueblo* to force it to study, forge it to excel . . . *El pueblo* must earn everything [it receives]. There is no paternalism [involved]. But when they forge themselves, they do so by themselves, they are going to be free, they are going to have an education, they are going to have economic resources, but they will not be given anything free (Schirmer interview).

Part of this forging is accomplished by appropriating Mayan symbols to "rescue the Indians' mentality until they feel part of the nation" (Cifuentes 1982, 27–28). Maya numbers are used in military documents, the k'ekchí term for warrior, *kaibil,* refers to Special Forces. Many Task Forces participating in the massacre campaign were given Mayan names.

In the Cultural Magazine of the Army, the army's National Committee for Reconstruction appropriated Quiché Indian hero *Tecún Uman* and the *Popul Vuh* (the major religious text of the Quichés when fighting the Spaniards in the sixteenth century) as its own philosophy. "That you raise up everyone, that you call to everyone; that there is not a group, nor two among us, everyone forward and no one stays behind" (*Ejército* 1985, 6).

In explaining the army's new thesis of national stability, General Gramajo drew upon the military's presumptions of Mayan religious practices to present it as a kind of:

> exorcism of its *males* (wrongdoing). It is taking the worm out, as the *brujos* (shamans) do to cure you. They take an egg, passing it over your entire body, chanting. Once they are finished, they break the egg and it is dried, meaning they have extracted the evil. This [holding a copy of the thesis of national stability] is the army's egg! We are stating our evils, we are now satisfied . . . (Schirmer interview)

Absolving the army of all its sins, the Mayanified thesis represents a catharsis of the army's wrongdoing, a distancing from the past as well as from responsibility for the future. During the inauguration week of President Cerezo in January 1986, a radio OPSIC propaganda spot ran every hour or so, fixing the blame for the violence:

> [Ladino voice] Two years ago, with the destruction of the indigenous villages by the subversives, the Indians encountered in the Army of Guatemala a brave and loyal ally in the return to their place of origin. [Mayan drums and flutes] For their security, the Civil Patrols of Self-Defense were organized. For the reconstruction of their villages, the Inter-Institutional Coordinators functioned, and for their interconnection, the Army Corps of Engineers carried out their work, constructing highways and bridges as paths of rural development. [Marimba music, ladina voice] Today, two years later, new horizons have been opened in the country. The Army of Guatemala has fulfilled its obligation to you.

The Army's Sanctioned Maya

Clearly, such appropriations of Mayan custom and language do not serve to promote Indian identity and culture; instead, they stand as a form of Sanctioned Maya prototype constructed and continually reconstituted through the military's optic, deprived of memory and mute to the recent subversive past. These symbols nourish the distant, mythic heroics of war the military draws upon to fight a counterinsurgency campaign that brutally ravages indigenous highland communities. They then provide the rituals by which this same military purges itself of the stain of massacre to regain its professional status. All the while, the military attempts to reshape the contents of the "appropriate memory" of the "subversive" Mayan past. This in itself is an admission that memory is a potential resource for political action. But the evoking of a new world with "new traditions" and the inclusion of Indians in the Council of State is of vital importance for the military if it is to establish acceptable boundaries of "politically correct" Mayanism and an imagined community-nation.

Although military intelligence appears to have been quite precise as to guerrilla activity on the map during the campaign, there are contradictions in its claims as well as indications that its cultural understandings are not only racist but surprisingly outdated. Its claim to want to reestablish the *ancianos* (elders) conflicts with reports by survivors of massacres who have related how troops and officers took special care to kill the *costumbristas* and other local transmitters of indigenous tradition with their strong ties to the local habitat. What is more likely the case is that these military actions represent an attempt to "normalize" culture by restructuring it along lines that emanate from the military's idealized vision of frozen Mayan traditions and their desire for a loyal indígena. Gramajo's and Cifuentes's appraisals sought to create a radically altered cultural and religious—i.e., apolitical—Sanctioned Maya, to create an indígena who is not so much tied to local tradition as he is loyal to national symbols, the state, and by extension, the army. This is a vision partially attained with the "army-peasant partnership" of the Civil Patrols playing their part in the counterinsurgency apparatus (Kobrak 1997, 17).

The tragic irony is that Mayans represent a nationhood and yet are most marginalized from it; the "evil" of the Mayan shaman "exorcised" from the army was exercised precisely on that population. The army's correct, Sanctioned Maya is emptied of agency and history and is best illustrated by the army's Indian "eponymous[2] mascot of the poles of development" found on the back covers of two issues of the Army's cultural magazine in 1984 and 1985. This light-skinned human mascot in indigenous dress and Honor Guard spats is given the diminutive name *Polín Polainas* (Little Pole Leggings) and presented as

> omnidimensional, omnipresent, it doesn't matter his origin or attire. Yesterday from Quiché, today from Solola, Polín Polainas, candid and courteous, coming to plow the Guatemalan fields, leaving in his wake his exemplary studied love, and inspiring the portent of peace, development and accord, like the supreme yearning for a national unity (Ejército 1985a, 1984b).

In this mythical world, sophistries abound: "areas of conflict" magically become "areas of harmony," a village is destroyed to be "reborn."

V. Civil Affairs and Social Intelligence

Social intelligence gives us some sense of how little the military's view of the Maya's usefulness for its security project has changed. Social intelligence, "directed towards the population," penetrates much more fully into daily social activities of the population than does military intelligence "directed towards the enemy" (Schirmer interview). Its intent is to understand the conditions under which dissent may arise, and to catch out any dissent that may arise "in its infancy" and keep it within acceptable, controllable boundaries.

In the early 1990s, one military zone commander, General Camargo, came up with the idea of recruiting university-educated Maya women from the indigenous city of Quezaltenango to serve as *promotores especialistas*—nurses, social workers, and *operadoras psicológicas* (psychological operatives) as well as military recruitment teams. He explains how these women enter a village alongside a Civil Affairs unit to "converse" with people, especially the village women, to gather social intelligence for the army:

> "Those who work in psychological operations [psyops or OP-SIC] determine the levels of penetration that *el mensaje contrario* [counterinformation] has [on the village]. For example, everyone says that the army only serves *los ricos* (the rich), that the army *es la fuerza de los ricos* (is the force of the rich). These *operadoras* see how much the locals believe this and think of ways to counter it by propaganda and by actions to change people's minds."

Q: So these units enter villages, asking questions and calculating the level of penetration?

"In some cases, perhaps, but it's not so much from asking, as it crops up in the conversation, and that has to do with the unit's ability to get people to talk. The thing is not so much to enter to ask questions as it is to establish communication. Once that gets going, we can talk about everything, and in doing so, we can ascertain attitudes. One chats. Perhaps the first visit doesn't succeed in totally penetrating [what is going on in the village]. Perhaps we aren't able to go beyond the pleasantries, if things don't go well. But we don't lose hope; we just go to another village. They will eventually come to see that we are doing the same thing everywhere in the area" (Schirmer interview).

One could argue that social intelligence is an attempt to be in control of what politics *is*.

How successful this has been is yet to be known.

The Peace Accords

With the inauguration of President Vinicio Cerezo in 1986 and the appointment of General Hector Gramajo as defense minister in 1987, a regime of "co-governance" was established which opened the political space necessary for initiating a dialogue with the guerrillas (URNG). Esquipulas I and II meetings of the Central American presidents in 1986 and 1987 established the need for dialogue in the region, and in Guatemala this need was to be met by the National Reconciliation Commission (CNR). Yet both the government/army and the guerrillas continued a strategy of "peace as a tactic of war" for another four years (Palencia 1996, 8). In October 1987, for example, at a low-level Madrid meeting that included military observers, the URNG distanced itself from Esquipulas II and demanded a prior purge of the army and demilitarized zones as a condition for negotiations. In turn, the government demanded disarmament of the guerrillas and amnesty for all parties in the conflict as a prior condition to signing an accord.

In February 1989, a Grand National Dialogue was held with 47 organizations and 84 delegates participating, including, for the first time, indigenous groups. This participation by elements of civil society created a political climate that obligated the URNG and government/army to account for their positions and pressured both to move beyond the strategy of continuing the war by political means.

During this period the internal debate within the army intensified. On one side, institutionalist officers under the leadership of General Gramajo favored negotiations as a way to neutralize the URNG. On the other side, hardline officers accused the Christian Democratic president of "negotiating with criminals." In 1988 and 1989, this rift led to two coup attempts by "Officers of the Mountain" faced down by President Cerezo and General Gramajo (see Schirmer 1998). Despite such internal dissent and the army's public refusal to "dialogue with a bunch of ruffians," General Gramajo encouraged President Cerezo to appoint Bishop Quezada Toruno to head the CNR and reinvigorate the talks (Schirmer 1998). By the end of Cerezo's term, disarmament had been dropped as a condition for dialogue.

Between 1990 and 1993, Esquipulas was abandoned, and a CNR-URNG meeting in March 1990 in Oslo led to the approval of the Basic Agreement for the Search for Peace: peace through negotiation to build a participatory and stable democracy. Meetings of the URNG, the CNR, and representative social sectors would be followed by high-level negotiations between the army, government and URNG. The Oslo process, through its openness to different sectors other than the army and guerrillas, generated and promoted political participation. Indeed, in response to the failed *auto-golpe* (self-coup) of President Serrano in May 1993 (referred to as the *serranazo*), a Civil Society Assembly (ASC) was established in May 1994 and all sectors of society were invited, including indigenous organizations. Different groups began to develop their political positions. Mayan organizations[3] "managed to legitimize arenas of political discourse, which previously had not existed in Guatemala, expressing opinions about their cultural identity and the multiethnic and plurilingual nature of the nation." (Palencia 1996, 31) Indigenous women's groups alongside ladina organizations of the ASC also broke new political ground in creating a climate of tolerance and respect for dissent.[4]

Despite the rifts within the army, the increasing involvement of civil society in the peace process helped to soften the army's line. It was during this period that informal dialogues were held between the ASC and military officers about the memories of the past and post-war reconstruction. One product of these discussions was the bill presented to Congress stopping the army's forced recruitment of indigenous youth.[5]

Thus, after 7 long years of on-again, off-again negotiations, the peace accords between the guerrilla and the government were signed in December 1996. The Accord on the Identity and Rights of Indigenous Peoples contains four substantive parts. Part One urged the Congress to recognize the identity of indigenous peoples through constitutional reform. Part Two called for the eradication of discrimination on the basis of ethnicity by ending discriminatory legislation and promoting indigenous rights. Part Three provided for initiatives to officially recognize indigenous languages and their use in education, social services, and the courts and a program that would assure indigenous access to religious sites and freedom to undertake their own spiritual practices. Finally, in Part Four the government agreed to reform the constitution and to define Guatemalan national unity as multiethnic, pluricultural, and multilingual.

The September 1996 Accord on the Strengthening of Civilian Power and the Role of the Army in a Democratic Society required that the army be limited to providing external defense, and as such, that counterinsurgency structures be dismantled: 1) the network of 33,000 military commissioners first established in the 1960s; 2) the 1.3 million Civil Self-Defense Patrollers, and 3) the Mobile Military Police (PMA) stationed throughout the country. Nonetheless, 1996 and 1997 army documents contradict these agreements. One March 1996 document, for example, calls for "maintaining relations with the personnel of the demobilized military commissioners with the objective of organizing some type of group to be allied with the army, in order to develop all kinds of activities that promote the integration of this personnel and its unrestricted support of the armed institution" (Ejército 1996a, Anexo B, 7–8). Also, as noted in numerous MINUGUA (United Nations Verification Mission in Guatemala) reports, civil patrols are being converted into "other kinds of groups" collaborating with the army, with the intelligence web apparently shifting from officially recognized groups to unofficial ones. This maintenance of military and social intelligence networks in the countryside is particularly worrisome in the rural areas where civil affairs units maintain "a close relationship with the rural [indigenous] population, as officers proudly point out, apparently oblivious to the way in which this presence contradicts the "strictly external defense" clause of the agreement. The longer the army remains in these areas, the greater the potential for repressive action. With reports of lynchings by former civil patrollers in collusion with the army (MINUGUA), the army's policy of the "neighborizing" of violence in the early 1980s thus continues to haunt the indigenous community nearly 20 years later.

In addition, army documents continue to reflect the military's threat mentality. The National Defense Staff's *National Strategic Analysis* for 1996 speaks of "eliminating and/or neutralizing adverse factors for the Guatemalan state," including "the repatriated" whose poor living conditions allow them to "maintain their connection to terrorist groups, providing human resources and materials for their survival, and from there the logic is to continue organizing groups to reestablish themselves in the areas of armed skirmishes" (Ejército de Guatemala 1996a, 79, 99). Other "adverse factors" from the army's perspective include the emergence of a Pan-Mayan movement that "for the next 5 to 6 years will be run only by Mayan intellectuals and academics." But if this movement were to "succeed in resolving the differences within the Mayan community and create the conditions for leadership, it could form the basis for a new political party in the twenty-first century," according to one officer. Others voiced concerns that the Pan-Maya movement could easily be taken over by former guerrilleros being incorporated into political life with the peace accords: "Now everyone's a Mayan or ethnic or whatever they call themselves." Apparently, this threat mentality has not changed since the early 1990s, when during the months of negotiations, heated opinions were often expressed about the "indigenous threat" (Palencia 1996). General Julio Otzoy, an army officer of Cakchiquel-Mayan origin, said the ethnic problem was such a serious threat to the country that "the guerrilla movement of the next century may well be an indigenous movement" (Bastos and Camus 1995, 67).

But if the military does not appear to have changed its attitudes toward the indigenous population, does this indicate that officers would return to the "killing zones" of the 1980s, were a new crisis, such as an indigenous insurgency, to arise? The question to a great extent revolves around the extent to which the military itself has changed its thinking.

President Portillo, La Cofradía, and the Institutionalists

President Alfonso Portillo was inaugurated in January 2000 on the basis of the center-right platform of the FRG—a party founded by the general who headed the military government during the period of the massacre campaign, General Rios Montt. With little consensus in the ship of state—the president makes some decisions, "the general" others—there is an erosion of trust and legitimacy within and without the armed forces. Institutionalist officers who negotiated the peace accords were pushed out in July 1997 and today are competing with the retired intelligence "*cofradía*" to gain ascendancy with younger officers as to how to regain professional pride within the institution. The former suggest confronting the past, admitting to the "excesses and abuses," saying "let's get on with building for the future." The latter denounce and dispute the very foundations of the right to hold peace talks, sign an agreement, and establish a truth commission. But do the institutionalists represent a hope for real reform of the institution responsible for the "killing zones," and potentially the prevention of future mass violence against the indigenous population?

The military project, established with the coup of March 1982, did not produce the ability to go beyond the military's limited thinking on democracy or ethnicity, nor did it break from its own internal contradictions of fashioning a democracy out of the womb of a counterinsurgency campaign (Schirmer 1998). The project did begin to produce officers with the ability to visualize the future. What appears not to have changed is their inability to understand that a transition from authoritarian to democratic rule demands a new paradigm for the army that is based on purging and not on "professionalizing" those responsible for the majority of human rights violations. In short, the institutionalist officers are still shackled by their own history. In arguing that they would recover control of the apparatuses of repression in 1982, the political violence intensified and escalated into a systematic campaign of matazonas. In correcting the ship of state's listing into dictatorship in 1983 by "relieving" General Rios Montt from his position as head of state, the army stopped short of breaking free from its own shackles and demanding structural changes in the "power blocks" of the economic and political elites. In 1993, the army took actions against yet another attempt at dictatorship by refusing to support President Serrano's self-coup. Yet, once again, the military did not seize the opportunity to cross the line and develop alliances with the civilian population that supported the democratic transition—"a social pact which expresses a pact of national multiethnic, plural-lingual and multicultural unity"—against the traditional authoritarian "block of power" (Rosada 1998, 254).[6]

Nonetheless, the political climate in Guatemala has in fact shifted enough that new spaces for political alliances are possible. At the same time, the hardline officers still use violence as part of their political repertoire against those they deem opponents—even the less hardline, institutionalist officers and their families.

The army is still bitterly divided and bound by a threat mentality. We can only hope that out of these rifts and divisions, a military leadership based on a more direct connection to civil society, and in particular more respect for the indigenous communities in the rural highlands, can be created.

While it is important for the military to construct a more positive view of the Maya, the practices that emanated from the massacre campaign and the forging in violence of the Sanctioned and muted Maya must still be addressed by the Maya themselves.

Conclusions

Indigenous communities still shoulder the highest levels of poverty (three-quarters of Guatemala's population live in poverty or extreme poverty, of whom 93 percent are indigenous [PLADES 1995]), and still experience racial discrimination. Thus the conditions that existed before the peace accords to a great extent still exist. Given the new political freedoms and the increasing demands for economic and cultural justice, the question remains how either the cofradía or institutionalist officers will interpret these demands. Will the military reassert its old policies toward the Maya, including that of neighborizing the violence once again? No one can know.

What we do know is that the political space opened by the Assembly of Civil Society and the peace accords has meant an extraordinary intellectual and political effervescence of activity on the part of the indigenous community (see Montejo; Warren). The questions remain as to the extent to which the recent history of the Maya is indelibly sculpted by the military's solipsistic view. To what extent has the Sanctioned Maya of the military penetrated the core of Mayan society and if so, what effects is this having on the indigenous population today and will it have in the future? The answer to these questions needs to come from those who work with the Maya and from the Maya themselves. We know that when speech is stolen, as through the Sanctioned Maya, it is not clear how the restored Maya will see themselves:

> Speech, which is restored, is no longer quite that which was stolen: when it was brought back, it was not put back exactly in its place. . . . Things lose the memory that they once were made (Barthes, 125).

As Kay Warren writes, because of the military incursions, "one had to rely on people one could not trust in order to survive the violence. Silence, strategic evasiveness, and ambiguity were used as verbal tactics for over a decade when townspeople did not know for certain with whom they were speaking" (1998, 129).

> The voices we hear will have been shaped not only by internal forces of culture but by the institutions and actors who have had profound effects on the events, practices, memories, and experiences that have shaped and forged the reality to which the Maya respond and about which they speak. To place this reality in context, it is imperative we understand the actions of those who played, and continue to play, a central part in the shaping of those events, practices, and experiences. Without such an understand-

ing of the reasoning and mindset of state actors who hold and exercise such power, we are left with a Maya speaking of a world that is only partially of their own making.

It is toward understanding the world of appropriation and complicity, of the 'other side' of the Maya reality, and the mental universe of the military, that this essay is a beginning.

Notes

1 Gramajo mimicked such a message in an interview: "I'm sending a message to my cousin Juan because guerrillero Solomon is saying that I have been killed, but Solomon is telling lies because I gave myself up to the army and not only did they not kill me but they gave me medicine and treated my sores. And now that I am free, I am asking my cousin Juan to join me" (Schirmer interview).

2 To make eponymous means to give one's "name to anything, said especially of the mythical personages from whose names the names of places or people are reputed to be derived," *Oxford English Dictionary*.

3 Hector Rosada-Granados *Soldados en el poder. Proyecto Militar en Guatemala (1944–1990)* Funpadem: Universidad de Utrecht, Holanda, 1999

4 For example, the Mayan Unity and Consensus Body, *Nukuj Ajpop,* the Academy of Mayan Languages, and the Coordination of Mayan Organizations of Guatemala (COPMAGUA)

5 I am indebted to Tania Palencia Pardo for her analysis of this historic period of political mobilization.

6 Author's interviews with military officers and CONAVIGUA members (1997 & 1998).

Works Cited

Aguilera Peralta, Gabriel

1983   "Informe sobre el ejército guatemalteco" *Tribunal Permanente de los Pueblos Sesión Guatemala,* Madrid 21–31, Madrid: Iepela Editorial, 95–98.

Arias, Arturo

1989   "Changing Indian Identity: Guatemala's Violent Transition to Modernity" in *Guatemalan Indians and the Sate, 1540 to 1988,* Carol Smith, Ed. Austin: University of Texas Press. 230–257.

1988   "La respuesta del poder 1982–1986" in *Guatemala: Polos de desarrollo.* Guatemala: CEIDAC. 169–220.

Barthes, Rolande

1972   *Mythologies.* New York: Hill & Wang

Bastos, Santiago, and Manuela Camus

1993   *Quebrando el Silencio: Organizaciones del Pueblo Maya y sus Demandas (1986–1992).* FLACSO: Guatemala.

Cifuentes, H. Capt. de Navío DEMN Juan Fernando

1982   "Operación Ixil" *Revista Militar* 27 (September–December), 25–72. Ejército

1982   *Plan nacional de seguridad y desarrollo* PNSD-01-82 Guatemala City CEM 01 ABR82 RLHGCC-82

1984a *Polos de desarrollo.* Guatemala, Editorial del Ejército

1984b "Pensamiento y cultural." *Revista Cultural del Ejército* Edición Especial.

1985   "Polos de desarrollo." *Revista Cultural del Ejército* (January–February).

1987   *Forjar y libertar: Asuntos Civiles* Guatemala, Editorial del Ejército Gramajo, *Crónica* interview, 19 May 1988.

1985   *Guatemala: Acción cívica militar en la guerra de contrainsurgencia,* March 2. *ACEN-SIAG* 34.

Green, Linda

1999   *Fear as a Way of Life: Mayan Widows in Rural Guatemala.* New York: Columbia University Press

Kobrak, Paul H.

1997   *Village Troubles: The Civil Patrols in Aguacatán, Guatemala.* Ph.D dissertation, University of Michigan.

Montejo, Victor

1987   *Testimony: Death of a Guatemalan Village.* New York: Curbstone Press

Palencia Prado, Tania

1996   "Peace in the making. Civil groups in Guatemala. Briefing Report." London: Catholic Institute for International Relations.

Peckenham, Nancy

1983   "Guatemala 1983: A Report to the American Friends Service Committee" Philadelphia: AFSC.

Plan de Acción de Desarrollo Social (PLADES) 1996–2000 Gobierno de Guatemala, Guatemala, September 1995

Richards, Michael

1985   "Cosmopolitan Worldview and Counterinsurgency in Guatemala." *Anthropological Quarterly* 58, 3 (July):90–107.

Rosada-Granados, Hector

1999   *Soldados en el poder.* Proyecto Militar en Guatemala (1944–1990) Funpadem, The Netherlands: Universidad de Utrecht.

Schirmer, Jennifer

1998   *The Guatemalan Military Project: A Violence Called Democracy.* Philadelphia: University of Pennsylvania Press.

Sheehan, Michael A.

1989   "Comparative Counterinsurgency Strategies: Guatemala and El Salvador." *Conflict* 9:127–154

Smith, Carol A., Ed.

1990   *Guatemalan Indians and the State 1540–1988.* Austin: University of Texas Press.

Stepputat, Finn

2002   "Urbanizing the Countryside: Armed Conflict, State Formation and the Politics of Place in Contemporary Guatemala." In *States of Imagination, Ethnographic Explorations of the Postcolonial State.* Thomas Blom Hansen and Finn Stepputat, eds. Durham: Duke University Press.

Warren, Kay

1998   *Indigenous Movements and Their Critics: Pan-Maya Activism in Guatemala.* Princeton: Princeton University Press.

Wilson, Richard

1991   "Machine Guns and Mountain Spirits: The Cultural Effects of State Repression Among the Q'eqchi.'" *Critique of Anthropology* 11 (1): 33–61.

Zur, Judith

1998   *Violent Memories: Mayan War Widows in Guatemala.* London: Westview Press.

Acronyms

ASC	*Asamblea de la Sociedad Civil*, Civil Society Assembly
CNR	*Comision Nacional de Reconciliacion*, National Reconciliation Commission
FRG	*Frente Republicano Guatemalteco*, Guatemalan Republican Front
MINUGUA	*Mision de Naciones Unidas de Verificacion en Guatemala*, U.N. Verification Mission in Guatemala
OPSIC	*Operaciones psicologicas*, psychological operations
PMA	*Policia Militar Ambulante*, Mobile Military Police
URNG	*Unidad Revolucionaria Nacional Guatemalteca*, Guatemalan National Revolutionary Unity, the umbrella organization of the major guerrilla groups

SECTION

II

The Colombian War Zone

3

The Kuna of Panama: Continuing Threats to Land and Autonomy

James Howe

The San Blas Kuna of Panama are among the best known and most successful indigenous peoples of Latin America. Prosperous, well fed, educated, and secure—at least in comparison with their counterparts elsewhere—they participate actively in national affairs while at the same time holding to a semi-autonomous territorial reserve, one they secured through a rebellion against the national government three-quarters of a century ago. So tenacious have the Kuna been in defending their land and self-management that in 1998 their governing body, the Kuna General Congress, was awarded the Premio Bartolomé de las Casas by the Spanish government.[1] These notable successes, however, mask both serious ongoing threats and the structural weaknesses of the institutions through which the Kuna struggle to meet them.

In the year 2000, indigenous peoples constituted just over eight percent of the Panamanian population. The primary indigenous groups are the Kuna, with a population of 58,000; the Ngöbe and Buglé, often called Guaymí, who together include 150,000 people, and the Emberá and Wounaan, traditionally referred to as the Chocó, with 20,000. Two tiny populations, the Naso (2,324) and Bri-Bri (1,162), live on the frontier with Costa Rica. The Kuna themselves are divided into several subgroups, three of them on river systems in eastern Panama in the large region known as the Darién. The fourth, which forms the subject of this paper, lives to the north of the Darién, along the northeast or San Blas coast of the Isthmus (Congresos n.d; Dirección de Estadistica 2001).

I have chosen in this chapter (apart from some brief concluding re-marks) to focus exclusively on the San Blas Kuna, first because I have been following their struggles much more closely than those of Ngöbe-Buglé and Emberá-Wounaan, and equally important, because each of these three peoples so far deals with the government and other outsider forces largely on its own. The three groups have begun to support one another in small ways, most notably during a cross-country march by the Ngöbe-Buglé in 1996, but no effective pan-Indian group has emerged in Panama such as those described by Theodore Macdonald Jr. in Ecuador or Bret Gustafson in Bolivia elsewhere in this volume.[2] As will become apparent in the concluding section of the paper, Panama has developed a template for dealing with the question of Indian lands and governance, but the organs of the state responsible for indigenous affairs have not developed a genuine national policy, and as happened elsewhere in Latin America, Indian groups are increasingly turning to NGOs and foreign governments for assistance. Thus I will be concerned with threats to Kuna lands and autonomy over the last thirty years and with the impressive but still quite imperfect forms of organization with which they have met those threats.

The coastal Kuna inhabit some fifty villages, most of them on tiny coral islets, scattered along approximately 150 miles of coast ending at the Colombian border. Their territory, which encompasses the islands, shore, and mainland up to the crest of the cordillera running parallel to the coast, was established as the Comarca de San Blas in 1938 and renamed the Comarca de Kuna Yala at the end of the 1970s. Taken together, the marine and terrestrial areas of the comarca are said to encompass more than 5,000 square kilometers. The year 2000 census recorded 32,000 Kuna in Kuna Yala, 24,000 living in and around the cities of Panama and Colón, and another 1,400 scattered through western Panama. By law, the Kuna control access by non-Indians to the comarca, and they enjoy a considerable measure of autonomy within it, though not the kind of legal independence characterizing many reservations in the United States. Since the mid-1940s, they have been governed by three elected *saila dummagan* (big chiefs) or caciques, and by a semi-annual council of delegates from the fifty villages, the Kuna General Congress.[3] Even today, when many of its inhabitants have moved to the city, Kuna Yala is the greatest treasure the Kuna possess, and the General Congress is the weapon with which they defend it.

Threats to Kuna Yala

Intruders

Kuna lands and waters, like those of other indigenous peoples in Latin America, have been repeatedly invaded by non-Indian populations and organizations. At the beginning of the twentieth century, when the

San Blas coast was vulnerable mostly from the sea, outsiders entered the forests and inshore waters in search of ivory nut, balata latex, and turtle shell, provoking numerous clashes (Howe 1995, 1998). Much more recently, in the 1960s and 1970s, the southern, terrestrial border of the comarca for the first time faced threats close at hand, as the Pan-American Highway advanced eastward into the Darién and a large hydroelectric project flooded much of the Bayano Valley (see Wali 1989, 1995). Land-starved mestizo peasants began migrating into the region, rapidly converting the forest into cattle pasture (see Heckadon 1981).

The Kuna inadvertently facilitated the peasant invasion by agreeing to the construction of a dirt road financed by USAID leading up from the Pan-American Highway over the cordillera to the western end of the San Blas coast at Carti. In the 1970s, shocked to find that a handful of colonists had already started clearing land inside the comarca, the Kuna organized a project called PEMASKY (see below), which succeeded in demarcating the reserve's borders and peacefully evicting the invaders (Chapin & Herrera 1998, Chapin n.d.).

During the same years, other threats emanated from the east. In addition to intrusive Afro-Colombian settlers and gold miners, some of them travelling in well-armed groups, drug traffickers sent shipments up the coast by air and water. Drug processing plants and a network of air strips sprang up in the forests just to the south of Kuna Yala, and some young Kuna were drawn into the trade as sellers and consumers of cocaine and marijuana.[4] Most ominously, the principal Colombian revolutionary group, the Fuerzas Armadas Revolucionarias de Colombia or FARC, set up rest and refuge camps in the Darién.

By the mid-1990s, the turbulence in Colombia had begun to spill over into Panama, as refugees fled across the border and paramilitaries of the ACCU (Autodefensas Campesinas de Colombia y Urabá) actively pursued the FARC into the Darién. Left- and right-wing fighters, as well as apolitical but well-armed *desconocidos* (unknowns), began to turn up all across the region, leading to tense encounters in the forest, shoot-outs, kidnappings, and intimidation of local populations. The Panamanian national police lack the firepower to effectively defend the region, and the national government for a long time refused to admit the seriousness of the crisis. Between the two alien forces, the FARC has carried out several audacious actions in Panama, including the hijacking of two helicopters from Kuna Yala,[5] but the paramilitaries have proved more aggressive and menacing, even going so far as to "declare war" against the Panamanian government.[6] In the Kuna comarca, the paramilitaries have repeatedly terrorized Indian and Afro-Colombian communities near the border to deter them from supporting or tolerating the FARC. The situation has continued to deteriorate in the new century: FARC fighters, reportedly with a list of potential kidnap victims, lurk outside the town of Yaviza, and paramilitaries have driven the Roman Catholic bishop out of the Darién.[7]

Intrusive Resorts

Tourism, though less dramatic than armed invaders, has repeatedly called into question the integrity of the Kuna reserve. Several thousand tourists visit Kuna Yala each year, drawn by the natural beauty of the San Blas coast, the exoticism of Kuna culture, and the reverse-appliqué *mola* blouses sewn by Kuna women. Cruise ships of various sorts account for by far the greatest number of visitors, but yachts also pass through frequently, and dozens of tourists fly over each day from Panama City for day trips or stays of a night or two. The available accommodations include three small inns and a number of very basic rooms for rent maintained by the Kuna themselves, as well as several small resorts owned by non-Indians: of the latter, three are currently in operation, four others now defunct. Of all the worrisome and problematic aspects of tourism, what most concerns the Kuna is the presence of these outside interests and their attempts to evade local control and alienate indigenous land (see Chapin 1990; Doggett 1999; Falla 1979; Howe 1982; Snow & Wheeler 2000; Swain 1977; Tice 1995; Zydler & Zydler 1996).

Tourist trouble first began to develop in the late 1960s, when two North Americans, W.D. Barton and Thomas Moody, obtained permissions from the three big chiefs or caciques to explore for possible building sites in the reserve. Both men proceeded to rent uninhabited islands from their owners and build small resorts, Barton near Ailigandi on the central coast, Moody off Río Sidra or Urgandi much further to the west. Neither one bothered to obtain the permission from the General Congress required by law in order to rent land or build anywhere in the reserve. Many Kuna vehemently criticized the caciques, especially for travelling abroad at Barton's expense, but the General Congress, though it revoked Moody's exploration permit in 1969, failed at first to mount an effective resistance or to enlist government support.

Barton's resort lasted only a few years. He fell into disputes with the closest village, Ailigandi, over rent and wage payments, and the behav-

ior of his guests offended Kuna sensibilities. On two occasions the resort was torched, and after the second burning in 1974 the government
refused Barton permission to return (for details, see Howe 1982, 2001;
Falla 1979). Moody, on the other hand, was able to ignore regular
protests from the General Congress because he successfully cultivated
the patronage of powerful figures in the government as well as the
goodwill of nearby Río Sidra.

During the early 1970s, the national government proposed building
a large hotel on an artificial island, also near Río Sidra. The acute crisis
that ensued is discussed in the following section of this paper, which is
devoted to government-sponsored projects. Opposition to Moody's
presence, meanwhile, continued to grow. In early 1981, a special commission from the General Congress presented an ultimatum giving
him three months to depart. After four months had passed, the *intendente* or governor of the reserve, a young educated Kuna, pleaded in
vain with Moody that his safety could not be guaranteed (Tice n.d.). In
the early hours of June 20th, a party of twenty-five or thirty young men
attacked the resort, shooting Moody in the foot and attempting,
mostly unsuccessfully, to burn the rain-soaked cabañas. Later that
morning men from Río Sidra, angry that Moody had been hurt, mis-
takenly shot three Kuna members of the National Guard who ap-
proached the island out of uniform, killing one and seriously wound-
ing the others. In the aftermath of the incident, the Panamanian
government finally acted, sending a high-level delegation to a General
Congress session and agreeing to exclude Moody from Kuna Yala. To
forestall a feud with the home village of the ambushed guardsmen, Río
Sidra reluctantly gave up one of the shooters.

Following the Moody affair and the subsequent propaganda campaign he waged against the Kuna and the government, potential investors undoubtedly held back, and except for visits by cruise ships,
tourism throughout Panama fell off sharply during the years of confrontation between the Noriega government and the United States. In
the 1990s, however, following the U.S. invasion and the development
of an international eco-tourism movement, four small resorts were
built on uninhabited islands in Kuna Yala.[8] All four supposedly con-
formed to regulations passed by the General Congress restricting ownership of tourist facilities in the comarca to the Kuna themselves (Congreso General 2001), but a lawyer who investigated on the Congress's
behalf found that the Indian managers actually acted as front men for
tour agencies and outside investors. As of early 2001, three of the re-

sorts continue to operate, while the fourth has remained closed by order of the Congress.[9]

In the mid-1990s another crisis developed when it was learned that Panamanian investors proposed building a hotel a few yards beyond the western border of Kuna Yala, thus exploiting indigenous tourism without, they hoped, submitting themselves to indigenous control (IDICA/GRET n.d.). The crisis revived more general worries that the western border, as originally drawn in 1938, does not encompass all traditional Kuna lands in the area or provide a buffer zone adequate to deal with intrusions from that direction (Panamá América 7/26/00, Congresos n.d.). To date the resort has not been built.

Intrusive Government Projects

Perhaps the greatest threats presented to the comarca have come from a series of large-scale commercial, military, and development projects, all of them backed or initiated by the national government. Official support greatly increases the difficulty and cost to indigenous peoples of resisting outside proposals, and in the case of mining concessions, subsurface rights belong by law not to the landowners, individual or collective, but to the state. The first such projects—a manganese mine and two banana plantations—were imposed between 1915 and 1925, during the period in which Panama initially asserted control over the San Blas Coast and attempted to "civilize" the Kuna (see Howe 1995, 1998). By the early 1930s all three ventures had succumbed to banana blight and changes in the world economy, and with a few exceptions,[10] Kuna Yala remained free of major government-sponsored projects all the way through the 1960s.

In 1969 or 1970 the military government of Omar Torrijos proposed building a pipeline across the Isthmus to trans-ship oil from Alaska. The line was to terminate at the western end of Kuna Yala in Mandinga Bay, a body of water capable of accommodating deep-water tankers. Ultimately, because of changes in the international market, the project was abandoned. In the same period, the United States government considered a proposal calling for the construction of a sea-level inter-oceanic canal, to be excavated by nuclear explosions. Panamanian anthropologists carried out surveys in Kuna villages as part of an environmental impact assessment, but to the best of my knowledge, at the moment at which reason prevailed and the plan for a nuclear canal was abandoned, it had not yet been proposed to the General Congress.

Another failed project, but one with much more far-reaching consequences for the Kuna, emerged as an issue in the early 1970s (see Falla
1979; Howe 1982; Chapin 1990). The Instituto Panameño de Turismo
or IPAT proposed a scheme to promote tourism in four regions of the
country, including a resort hotel of almost 700 rooms to be built on an
artificial island in western Kuna Yala, thus, it was hoped, avoiding
problems with land claims by Kuna individuals or communities. Beginning in 1973, IPAT representatives presented the project to the
Kuna in several congress sessions. As had happened with Moody and
Barton, the three caciques signed a document authorizing a feasibility
study, although in this instance a public promise was later made by
IPAT that it would not proceed to construction until the General Congress as a whole had signed off.

Doubts and opposition took some time to develop. The project was
energetically supported by the three Kuna members of a national
council of *Representantes de Corregimientos* (District/Sector Representatives) established in 1972, which led to rumors that the three had
been bought off. Worries increased when a document was produced
offering support for the project, endorsed by a number of leaders in
western Kuna Yala, only to have several of them repudiate their signatures as forgeries. Kuna leaders also began to take in the ambitious
scope of the project; Río Sidra in particular, the village closest to the
proposed site, took note of the probable impact on its agricultural
lands of the airport and the workers' village proposed for the project,
both of which were to be located on the mainland.

In early 1975, a party of officials and technicians whose plane
landed at the Río Sidra airstrip were met by an angry mob, which
forcibly prevented them from deplaning. A few weeks later the head of
IPAT personally attended a session of the General Congress and defended the proposed resort. Although the agency soon scaled back the
project and called for implementation in stages, in August of 1975 the
General Congress revoked permission for the feasibility study.

In the ensuing crisis with the government, the Congress met again
in March of the following year and called for the removal of the three
representantes now widely perceived as sell-outs, and while still in session, it sent a special commission to communicate the decision to the
government. The delegation included the caciques, all three of them
frail men of advanced age, but when their plane arrived in Panama
City, they were whisked away, reportedly by government officials and

the three representantes, and within a few weeks a decree partitioned Kuna Yala into three districts, each to be headed by a cacique and rep-resentante.[11] In May, one week after the decree was issued, the General Congress met again and elected a new slate of caciques, whom the gov-ernment refused to recognize. Worse, the Kuna were themselves di-vided, since eight communities in the immediate spheres of influence of the old caciques refused to send delegates to the General Congress or recognize the decision of the other villages.

The stalemate and the partitioning of Kuna Yala continued into 1978, when the Kuna were finally able to patch together a compromise by which the three old caciques continued in office for a short time, while the three new men were named as their *suplentes* and designated successors. In the end, the IPAT resort was never implemented, in part because other branches of the government had never signed off on the grandiose project, and in part because the Kuna made it clear they would use violence to prevent construction. The General Congress had won its point but only with considerable pain and effort.

Panama did not attempt to impose any further large-scale projects in Kuna Yala for several years, until the late 1980s, when the govern-ment of Manuel Noriega announced that national security required a full-fledged military base in the comarca. When opposition quickly de-veloped, government spokesmen insisted that the government had the right to build regardless of Kuna wishes; ultimately, however, another standoff ensued, and the base was never constructed. The issue reemerged in new form in 1995, when it was announced that a naval base was needed near the Colombian border in order to counter the drug trade and armed intruders from Colombia. Most Kuna leaders recognized the necessity of the installation, but a majority at a General Congress session demanded that it be built directly on the border de-spite government insistence on a site much further into the comarca. The ensuing controversy and stalemate is discussed later in the paper.

Also in the mid-1990s, it became known that the government had signed contracts for mining concessions to explore for gold and copper in a region encompassing approximately three-quarters of the surface area of Kuna Yala, along with large concessions in other parts of Panama. Kuna objections provoked a heated statement by President Pérez Balladares in June of 1996 to the effect that he would not permit two legal systems in Panama, and that Indians must submit to national law. On June 14, the General Congress delivered an equally heated re-sponse, and on the following day, to great surprise, President Bal-ladares accepted an invitation to attend the current session of the Congress and pledged to respect its decisions (A. López 1996). Since then, mining operations have led to persistent conflict in western Panama, but the Canadian company holding the concessions in Kuna Yala has turned its attention elsewhere.[12]

Government Meddling and Non-Recognition of Kuna Autonomy

Another set of crises has been caused not by threats of physical encroachment but by government insensitivity to indigenous autonomy and democracy. These blowups have occurred most frequently when the General Congress repudiates its own leaders and representatives, in the case of the IPAT crisis the representantes and caciques, more often the governor or intendente of Kuna Yala. Beginning with the creation of the office of intendente in 1915, it was for more than half a century always occupied by a Latin Panamanian. Among the many men who held the post, one helped the Kuna reorganize comarca governance during the 1940s (Holloman 1969, 344–345), and another proved a good friend to the Indians in the late '60s and early '70s. Others were corrupt, incompetent, antagonistic to the Indians, or all three.

In 1978 the government for the first time appointed a Kuna, a young Spanish-trained sociologist named Eligio Alvarado. In 1981, however, while Alvarado was attending a conference in England, his enemies managed to have him removed from office. The crisis that ensued led to negotiations in which it was agreed that henceforth the government would choose the intendente from a slate of three candidates nominated by the General Congress. The government wasted no time in disregarding the agreement, in 1984 naming a Kuna active in the official party, the Partido Revolucionario Democrático (PRD), without consulting the General Congress. When the latter, as might have been anticipated, objected vociferously, a compromise was negotiated by which the man already appointed was accepted in return for a renewed pledge to honor the agreement.

During the late 1980s and early 1990s, the intendenteship did not function well: turnover was rapid and funding grossly inadequate. Then in 1995 and 1996 another crisis blew up concerning the intendente of the moment, who was by chance the same party functionary who had figured in the crisis ten years before. In this instance, the man strongly supported the efforts, mentioned above, by Panamanian businessmen to build a hotel just outside the limits of Kuna Yala, and many suspected that his enthusiasm was being subsidized. When Congress delegates confronted him, a dramatic shouting match broke out, and in the extended stalemate that followed after his repudiation, the headquarters on the island of El Porvenir were shut down for months at a time.

The government, finally, has consistently failed to support Kuna efforts at reform and self-governance. Since at least the beginning of the 1980s, the General Congress and special commissions have labored to write a constitution and basic laws for Kuna Yala, to replace the *Carta Orgánica* of 1945 and its enabling legislation, Law 16 of 1953, both of which the Kuna see as flawed and out-of-date. The General Congress has recently used funding from Spanish sources to publish the laws (Congreso General 2001), and it attempts to enforce them within the comarca, but it has never convinced the National Assembly to vote on them. Even the name change from San Blas to Kuna Yala has only been enacted into law in the last couple of years (La Crítica 7/26/00).

The Organization of Resistance

The Kuna deal with the government and national society through a variety of channels and organizations, some of them official agencies, such as the ministry of education, which operate in the comarca with minimal oversight from either the intendente or the General Congress.[13] In terms of fundamental collective relations, however, the Kuna interact with the rest of Panama through three institutions: national political parties, voluntary organizations, and the caciques and General Congress.

Political Parties

Political parties have coveted Indian votes since the 1920s, and the Kuna have been participating regularly in national elections since the 1930s, often in village and regional blocks (see Holloman 1969, 351–353). Although political parties were banned throughout Panama in 1968 after a military coup, in 1972 a new constitution paved the way for the creation of a national council of representantes, and a few years later for the return of political parties and the national legislative assembly.

At a few moments in their history, Kuna involvement in party politics has furthered their cause, notably in 1930, when party and labor organizations helped broker a rapprochement ending a five-year standoff with the government that followed the Kuna rebellion of 1925 (Howe 1998, 295–296). Political alliances very likely furthered the con-

solidation of Kuna land claims during the 1930s and the reorganization of the comarca in the 1940s (Holloman 1969, 345–353). Much
more recently, in the first years of the current government of Mireya
Moscoso, a Kuna legislator, Enrique Garrido, was president of the National Assembly.

Otherwise, however, from their revival in the 1970s until today, political parties have created discord and division among the Kuna. Parties often favor supporters with awards of facilities and infrastructure,
creating inequalities among villages, and the government party
throughout most of the '70s, '80s, and early '90s, the PRD, used its apparatus to divide and weaken Kuna resistance during crises. However
one judges the parties overall (one Panamanian political scientist
called them "looting machines"), they cannot be counted on to defend
Kuna lands and autonomy.

Voluntary Societies

A number of Kuna-run nongovernmental organizations have flourished since the 1990s. Their antecedents, which go back several decades,
include local cooperative societies (Holloman 1969, 209–221), numerous small projects organized by the Peace Corps in the 1960s; and especially a women's *mola* cooperative, still going strong after more than
thirty years (see Tice 1995; Salvador 1997). Also significant are the
many Kuna who have studied at the University of Panama, a number of
whom also took advanced degrees abroad. Pan-Kuna organizations included the Movimiento de la Juventud Kuna (MJK), which was at one
time affiliated with the Panamanian communist party; an organization
of Canal Zone workers called the Asociación de Empleados Kunas
(AEK); and the Centro de Investigaciones Kuna (CIK), a research body
that functioned from the mid-1970s through the 1980s.

University-educated Kuna, a number of them veterans of the Juventud, took a giant step forward in the 1970s, in response to the peasant
colonists advancing on the comarca. With the help of a $70,000 dona-
tion from the AEK, a young man named Guillermo Archibold and a
few friends began establishing a presence at the spot where the dirt
road from the Pan-American Highway meets the border of Kuna Yala.
Unfortunately, their efforts showed that ordinary agriculture could not
succeed atop the mountain ridge. It also became clear that the Kuna
could expect little help from the government, given the bias of politicians in favor of their mestizo countrymen and the involvement of
wealthy ranchers in buying up pastures cleared by peasant colonists.

Fortunately, the young men proved more successful in establishing or reviving ties with helpful foreigners, notably Mac Chapin, at that time an employee of the Inter-American Foundation, who as a Peace Corps volunteer had served with Archibold at an agricultural school in Kuna Yala (Chapin & Herrera 1998, Chapin n.d.).

In 1982 the Centro Agronómico Tropical de Investigación y Enseñanza (CATIE) in Costa Rica received a grant from USAID to assist the Kuna in planning a forest reserve in the threatened area, leading, it was hoped, to environmental education, ecotourism, cooperative scientific studies, and ultimately a biosphere reserve. In 1983 PEMASKY (El Proyecto de Estudio para el Manejo de Areas Silvestres de Kuna Yala) was officially launched, and with grants from the Interamerican Foundation, World Wildlife Fund, the MacArthur Foundation, and other foreign organizations, total funding passed one million dollars. The project, held up as a model both of indigenous self-management and of cooperation with environmental organizations, received a great deal of positive publicity.

The praise and attention were in many respects warranted. Project technicians, supported by relays of volunteers from the coastal and island villages, surveyed and demarcated more than 150 kilometers of the threatened boundary, and with great tact they managed to evict and buy out the peasants already inside the comarca. Through reports and traveling shows taken to many individual villages as well as to sessions of the General Congress, they raised the environmental consciousness of the whole Kuna population (along with their own) and focused attention on the threats to indigenous territory. On a much reduced level, moreover, PEMASKY continues today.

The project's more ambitious goals, on the other hand, could not be achieved. The forest management plan did not take sufficient account of the distribution of ecological knowledge in Kuna society, in which older, traditional men knew a great deal more than young *técnicos*. Neither the project staff nor their outside advisors had sufficiently anticipated the financial and managerial demands of the plan's implementation, and the document itself was not completed until 1987 (González & Solís 1/24/01). The fault lay not so much with the individuals involved as with the rapid growth of the project and—despite the relative sophistication of the Kuna—the inexperience of its technical staff, who were simply asked to do too much too fast. At the moment of its greatest fame abroad, PEMASKY had already begun to implode (Chapin & Herrera 1998, Chapin n.d.).

The wreckage, however, has been effectively retrieved and recycled. Staff alumni, as well as other Kuna who observed and learned from PE-MASKY, have gone on to establish a number of new organizations (see Chapin & Herrera 1998; Congresos n.d.; Ventocilla et al. 1995, 123–124). They include the Fundación Dobbo Yala, headed by the former intendente, Eligio Alvarado; Fundación Osiskun, dedicated to the marine environment and directed by Guillermo Archibold, past head of PEMASKY; a project called DESOSKY (Desarrollo Sostenible de Kuna Yala), concerned with sustainable development; an umbrella organization called IDIKY (Instituto para el Desarrollo Sostenible de Kuna Yala); a militant cultural group called Twiren; Koskun Kalu, the research arm of the Kuna Cultural Congress (on which, see below); Asociación Nabguana, a cultural and environmental organization;[14] and the now-defunct Consultoria de los Pueblos Indígenas de Panamá. Both PEMASKY and the Movimiento de la Juventud Kuna also persist. The Catholic Church has periodically provided substantial funds to some organizations, and in recent years the European Union, the Spanish government, and other bodies have donated several million dollars.[15] The Kuna NGOs have achieved a great deal, especially in the areas of indigenous publication and consciousness-raising. Despite many problems typical of young grassroots organizations (lack of expertise, misguided plans, factionalism, under- and over-funding, embezzlement, and general entropy), they will undoubtedly accomplish more in the future. But it is unlikely that any one of them will play the crucial role that PEMASKY once did or emerge as the primary guardian of Kuna Yala.

The General Congress

The Kuna have enjoyed remarkable successes in meeting outside threats through the General Congress. These victories, however, have not come easily,[16] and as often as not, they have been achieved only by overcoming basic structural weaknesses (see Holloman 1969, 336–371; Moore 1984, 1985). The first of these is a lack of administrative continuity. Until recently the Congress was represented between sessions only by a general secretary, by the caciques (about whom see below), and by ad hoc commissions created to study or negotiate pressing issues. The situation has improved somewhat: the Congress now rents office space in the city and collects a modest tax from the villages; the organization IDIKY oversees (at least in theory) projects proposed for

Kuna Yala; and a second body, the Congreso General Kuna de la Cultura, attends to cultural and religious issues.[17] IDIKY has recently begun acting as an administrative and financial office for the Congress. The administrative evolution of the Congress still has a long way to go, however. It still lacks a reliable enforcement power, moreover, and as often as not acts in a fitful and episodic fashion.[18]

The congress system also suffers from weak leadership. Quite a few capable and strong-willed men have served as cacique, but they find their powers tightly circumscribed. Caciques must account at each Congress session for their actions since the last one; any decisions or negotiations they make are subject to review and rebuke; and they may not travel or deal with outside powers without the company of at least a secretary. Rumors often circulate that people are fed up with the current caciques and about to boot them out. It would be wrong to say that Kuna fears are entirely misplaced, given the frequency with which indigenous leaders around the hemisphere have exploited or sold out their followers, but the result is a less than forceful executive power.

The General Congress must also contend with divisions within the Kuna population based on differences in age, education, ambition, or party politics, or on past regional and factional oppositions. Before the establishment in 1945 of the present system, with its regular congresses and three ranked caciques, the coast was divided between two major indigenous confederacies and one small cluster of acculturated villages. Although the confederacies disappeared in that year, and today each of the three ranked caciques theoretically represents Kuna Yala as a whole, old loyalties do resurface, and the islands in three sectors within the comarca often meet separately to hash out positions. Regional loyalties are by no means automatic, however: some issues pit villages against each other *within* the same sector (see the case immediately below).

The Panamanian government has shown few scruples about exploiting or even creating divisions,[19] as happened during the IPAT controversy in the mid-1970s. In the more recent affair concerning a proposed naval base, the government wished to site the base at Punta Escocés, twenty-odd miles in from the border, thus giving its patrols lead time to intercept suspicious vessels coming out of Colombia. Although at least some of the caciques and other leaders were sympathetic to this point of view, opponents insisted that the base be located next to the non-Indian border town of Puerto Obaldía. Of the nine

Kuna communities in the region, the one closest to Punta Escocés, called Koetupu, initially opposed that site but then reversed itself. Sasardi/Mulatupu, an island community encompassing two villages whose members actually own Punta Escocés,[20] went from acceptance to rejection. As the issue heated up at the end of 1996, a government delegation pressured the leaders of the two villages, Mulatupu and Sasardi, into signing an agreement accepting the base; their acquiescence so angered the rank and file of Mulatupu that they threw their first chief out of office. Afterward, it was alleged that activists in the government party, the PRD, had instructed merchant vessels not to land at Sasardi/Mulatupu, and conversely, that local authorities had denied the services of the island health clinic and high school to people from other islands. Despite this turmoil, delegates at the next General Congress voted almost unanimously to "paralyze" the construction of a base at Punta Escocés, and although President Balladares threatened to proceed regardless, the project has not been revived since the inauguration of President Mireya Moscoso in 1999.[21]

At several periods in their history the Kuna have also been divided by age and education, especially during the ten years leading up to their rebellion against Panama in 1925 (Howe 1998). In the early 1970s, teachers and other young educated Kuna often showed great interest in economic development and national culture, as well as an impatience with *tradición*. During the 1970 Congress at which the government presented its proposal for an oil pipeline, a group of Kuna youth delivered a letter welcoming the project, and the educated speakers who managed discussion of the issue, headed by a prominent trilingual Kuna missionary, deflected negative commentary and questions about the project's environmental impact.[22] Although the Congress authorized only a study of the pipeline's feasibility, one government representative told me privately that they now had sufficient authorization to proceed with construction.

Just a few years later, however, young educated Kuna were swept up in a nativistic revival, and although plenty of room remains for different viewpoints (not to mention pursuit of individual and village self-interest), a broad consensus has taken hold concerning the worth of traditional culture and the necessity of preserving Kuna land and autonomy (see Chapin 1991).[23] The Kuna have also shown on numerous occasions an ability to patch up their differences, in several cases following severe and prolonged schism.

The cost, however, has been high, in terms of distraction from other pressing tasks as well as the effort needed to repair the torn social fabric. Both the Kuna themselves and sympathetic outsiders have repeatedly expressed concern about a wide range of issues beyond territorial defense, including degradation of the natural environment, rapid social and economic change, wholesale migration to the city, endemic health problems, malnutrition in some sectors, the erosion of the economic base in the coconut trade, loss of self-sufficiency in food production, increasing monetarization of the local economy, breakdown of the traditional marriage system, and limited job opportunities in the city (see Bonilla 2000; Chapin 1991; Congresos y Organizaciones Indígenas de Panamá n.d.; Instituto de Estudios Nacionales; Leis 1992; Turpana 1995; Ventocilla, Herrera & Núñez 1993; Ventocilla et al. 1995). Most of these issues involve a combination of outside influences—economic, social, political, and ecological—as well as the practices of the Kuna themselves; almost all of them have been considered in the General Congress, but the need to respond to territorial threats has reduced the already limited time available for discussion in meetings of the Congress, which except for extraordinary sessions take place only twice a year. It may be hoped that Kuna NGOs, already active in environmental issues, may also be able to take the lead in addressing some social and economic problems, but to date their impact has been limited.

It is also notable that after decades of countering threats, the General Congress finds it easier to say "No" than "Yes," even in cases, such as the recent ejection of the Smithsonian's marine laboratory, where "Yes" might have been wiser (Chapin and Howe n.d.). Perhaps most of all, the Congress has little idea of how to counter the threat it has never seen before, that of well armed, aggressive, and mutually hostile military forces.[24] It has met to discuss the crisis on the Colombian border and issued a statement, which had no noticeable effect on the FARC or the paramilitaries. It is hard to see what else the Congress *can* do: certainly, if the Kuna were to arm themselves and forcibly resist incursions, they would run a great risk of being drawn into the conflict. Under such conditions, even indigenous peoples depend on the power of the state, and so far Panama has shown little inclination or ability to come to the defense either of the Kuna or of other citizens on its eastern borders. For the moment at least, the worst threats come from the east, and it is the weakness of the national government rather than its power that presents the greatest danger.

Threatened Comarcas in the Rest of Panama

Although I have been concerned here only with the San Blas or coastal Kuna, several key features of their situation apply, at least in general terms, to other Panamanian indigenous peoples. In the western half of the country, these consist primarily of the very numerous Ngöbe and Buglé (or Guaymí), who together represent 65 percent of the country's indigenous population. In the east are the Emberá and Wounaan (collectively called the Chocó), who constitute 9 percent of the indigenous population, and three small Kuna populations of Madungandi, Wargandi, and Tagargunyala, found in the watersheds of the Bayano, Chucunaque, and Tuira Rivers respectively.

The territorial and governmental institutions of almost all these groups—comarca, general congress, and caciques—are borrowed from the coastal Kuna.[25] In Madungandi and Wargandi, these institutions rest on the same social base as in Kuna Yala and seem to function about as well as they do there (see Moeller 1997), though the small forest populations enjoy much less influence with the government than their coastal cousins. In the case of the Ngöbe-Buglé and the Emberá-Wounaan, on the other hand, Kuna forms were imposed on groups without the political culture, leadership traditions, or nucleated settlement patterns that underly the Kuna political system.[26] The general congresses and regional leadership of the two groups have been plagued by faction and schism, and they do not, at least as yet, function very effectively.

The cacique/comarca/congress system was generalized to include groups other than the San Blas Kuna between 1969 and 1978: the process, which involved a number of Panamanian anthropologists, a new national constitution, and a Kuna cacique named Estanislao López, has been described in detail by Peter Herlihy (1995, 82–86). After a special commission composed of social scientists, bureaucrats, and native activists studied indigenous problems in 1977, General Torrijos announced a plan the following year to demarcate Indian territories.

The actual creation of comarcas has proceeded more slowly, in most cases after years of agitation by indigenous groups and their supporters on one side, and delays and opposition by non-Indian interests on the other. One strong positive impetus has come from the International Development Bank (IDB) which in recent years has demanded the titling of indigenous lands as a condition for the millions of dollars it is putting into the development of the Darién region (Mac Chapin, personal communication).[27] The Comarca Emberá-Drua, consisting of two large blocks in the Darién, was established in 1983, the Comarca Kuna de Madungandi in 1996. A comarca for the Ngöbe-Buglé was enacted into law in early 1997 following a dramatic national campaign that included a hunger strike and crosscountry march, and the Comarca Kuna de Wargandi was created only very recently, in July of 2000. The Naso, Bri-Bri, and Tagargunyala Kuna are all reportedly campaigning for comarcas.

The geographer Peter Herlihy (1995) has characterized the comarca system in glowing terms, as "something revolutionary." I find the comarca less unusual as an organizational form than does Herlihy, and (as he would undoubtedly agree) the strength of legal protections for indigenous lands can only be established in practice, in the give and take of interactions with the government and outside interests, a point made forcefully in a number of articles in this volume. All of the new comarcas have been compromised by the presence within their boundaries, at the time of their legal enactment, of non-Indian populations and claimants to land. In western Panama, Ngöbe-Buglé lands are most threatened by ranching, coffee, and mining interests (the latter have been attempting to revive the notorious Cerro Colorado copper mine), and by land disputes that have erupted within the native population itself.

In the Darién, indigenous comarcas and congresos have been subject to endless problems and complications. The Comarca Emberá-Drua overlaps the largest forest reserve on the Isthmus, the Parque Nacional de Darién (created in 1980), a source of friction and legal ambiguity. Half of the approximately eighty Emberá and Wounaan communities lie outside the comarca, which led them to form an alternative congress, the Congreso de Tierras Colectivas Emberá-Wounaan, which was not officially recognized by the government until 1997. In 1999 the Wounaan, feeling dominated by the more numerous Emberá, seceded to form a congress of their own (Julie Velásquez Strunk, personal communication). Both groups, meanwhile, live thoroughly interspersed among mestizo colonists, and the Afro-Panamanians known as Darienitas—the Darienitas preceded both Emberá and Wounaan historically in the Darién, but as non-Indians they lack a comarca or territorial guarantees. All of the indigenous lands in the region, finally, have suffered from uncontrolled logging (with which the Madungandi and Wargandi Kuna have sometimes cooperated); from the huge wave of mestizo peasants that has poured into the region since the 1960s; and most recently from the armed incursions out of Colombia.

What will happen with indigenous lands in Panama is hard to predict. On the one hand, it might not have been anticipated that all major native groups would secure comarcas, now equaling about twenty percent of the surface area of Panama, or that they would prove as determined as they so far have. The recent "Arnulfista" government headed by Mireya Moscoso, in power since 1999, has been tied less closely to extractive interests than was the PRD, which, except for the brief period following the U.S. invasion, held power for the better part of thirty years. But extractive interests and Colombian intruders have proved unrelenting, and the PRD looks very likely to retake the presidency in the next elections.

Moreover, as Indians have organized, so have their peasant and landlord antagonists: in a revealing incident from recent years, when the Kuna of Madungandi, who were demanding the expulsion of 125 colonist families, briefly blocked the Pan-American highway and threatened to destroy hydrographic measurement stations, the head of the local union of (non-Indian) agricultural workers countered that the colonists were there by legal right, and besides, it was the Indians who were selling off timber. The provincial governor responded by threatening the Kuna leaders of the demonstrations with prosecution for rebellion and sedition (*La Prensa* 12/11/96 and 8/02/96). As this case illustrates, in conflicts over indigenous land, the alignments, actors, and practices may change with time, but not the intensity of the struggle.

Notes

1 *La Prensa* 10/14/98.

2 An ineffective and factionalized inter-tribal council called PAPICA suffered from indifference and hostility, at least from the Kuna.

3 Each village sends two or three delegates. Each village has one vote, on those infrequent issues that come to a formal vote. Each congress session is hosted by a particular community, usually by pre-arrangement at the previous session.

4 *La Prensa* 2/19/00.

5 *La Prensa* 11/15/99.

6 *La Prensa* 9/13/99.

7   *La Prensa* 1996 (10/24, 11/10, 11/12, 11/15, 11/16, 11/20, 11/22, 11/22, 11/24, 12/03, 12/05); 1997 (1/26, 2/27, 3/03, 3/27, 4/02, 4/05, 4/07, 4/09, 4/25, 5/22, 6/23, 6/26, 7/02, 7/07, 7/08, 7/09, 7/10, 7/11, 7/12, 7/15, 7/19, 8/02, 8/15, 8/16, 9/23, 10/07, 12/08, 12/31); 1999 (9/15, 9/20, 10/19, 10/2511/02, 11/10, 11/18, 11/19, 11/24, 12/01, 12/17, 12/22); 2000 (1/20, 5/03, 5/19, 10/05, 10/16, 10/17, 10/20, 11/12). *La Crítica* 1999 (8/04, 9/27, 10/26, 10/28), 2000 (7/26). *Panamá América* 7/30/99, 11/10/99. *Washington Post* 7/11/97. FOR Panamá Update No. 20, Summer 1997 (http://www.forusa.org/panama/0797-6.html). FOR Panama Update No. 27, July 1999 (http://www.forusa.org/panama/35.html). "Colombian Paramilitary Violence Spreads Into Panama" (http://burn.ucsd.ed/archives/ats-1/1997.Apr/0066.html). Mendel (2000). World News Interpress Service 6/01/99 (http://www.oneworld.org/ips2/june_99/16-45-073.html). (Websites defunct.) foreign wire.com 4/23/97 (http://www.foreignwire.com/Darien.html). Benjamin Howe, Jesús Alemancia: personal communications.

8   Kuanidup, near Río Sidra; Kwadule Eco-Lodge, near Akkwanusadub or Corazón de Jesús; Iskardup, near Playón Chico; Dolphin Island Lodge or Uaguitupo, near Achutupu.

9   *La Prensa* 4/10/95, 4/16/95, 1/28/97, 3/10/97, 8/12/99.

10 During World War II the United States operated several plane-spotting stations. A plantation venture and narrow-gauge railroad was briefly revived at one point, and in the late 1960s and early 1970s, a small exploratory copper mine sponsored by the United Nations operated at the eastern end of the coast.

11 The partitioning requires further study: the three districts corresponded to units in the populist structure of regional and national councils instituted by the Torrijos government, which in Kuna Yala were incongruent with the indigenous system of local gatherings and regional General Congress.

12 News release 6/11/97, "Western Keltic Purchases Minority Interest in Panamanian Subsidiary" (http://www.keltic.com/news/news97.06.11. html). John Parnell, 9/06/96, "Western Keltic Mines land grab of Native land in Panama" (http://www.hartford-hwp.com/archives/47/082.html). FOR Panamá Update Spring/Summer 1996 (http://www.forusa.org/panam/696urgen.html). FOR Panamá Update No.21, 12/97 (http://www.forusa.org/panama/1297-10.html). (Websites defunct.) News Release 2/11/97, "M.I.M. withdraws from Panama option" (http://keltic.com/news/news97.02.11.html).

13 However, the local representatives of these agencies (teachers, health aides, development workers, etc.), who more often than not are Kuna, are closely scrutinized by the communities in which they work. Some government programs, however flawed and anemically funded, have significantly improved Kuna well-being.

14 http://geocities.com/TheTropics/Shores/4852/home.html.

15 The Kuna General Congress is set to receive approximately $800,000 from the Asociación Española de Cooperación Internacional (AECI) (Mac Chapin: personal communication).

16 It is evident that Kuna pride and forthrightness have themselves often provoked hostility on the part of office-holders and other Panamanian nationals.

17 The spheres of influence of the two congresses and their two slates of caciques are not entirely clear, resulting in moderate friction and rivalry.

18 Regular sessions occur twice a year, but extraordinary sessions can be called as needed.

19 The government also exploited Kuna divisions in the first quarter of the century (Howe 1998).

20 Punta Escocés is a peninsula, the site of a famous and short-lived Scots colony in 1700. Although there is no officially recognized village on the point, Sasardi/Mulatupu maintains a work camp of about a dozen houses there.

21 *La Prensa* 1995 (4/17), 1996 (10/16), 1997 (1/16, 2/14, 2/26, 2/28, 3/10, 4/28, 8/05); 1999 (11/29). Panamá América 7/26/00.

22 Ironically, many of those doubtful about the project had apparently been fed information about its possible negative impact by Moody and/or Barton.

23 It should be added that this general consensus goes along with an accelerating loss of traditional learning, a rapid adoption of national cultural forms, and an observance of Kuna culture in self-conscious and compartmentalized forms.

24 It might be argued that the situation immediately after Panamanian independence was in some respects similar, in that both Panama and Colombia pressured the Kuna for their allegiance and assistance. The crucial difference was that in 1903, both nations were in military terms extremely weak, which is not true of either the FARC or the paramilitaries.

25 Strictly speaking, the three riverine Kuna groups traditionally had political systems similar to that of the San Blas Kuna, but the formal system of caciques and congresses was created by national law, as it was for the Ngöbe-Buglé and Emberá-Wounaan.

26 The Emberá-Wounaan were brought together into nucleated villages in the 1960s and 1970s; the Ngöbe-Buglé still live in dispersed hamlets.

27 The term *reserva* has also been used, in early periods as a semi-synonym or synonym for comarca, more recently to indicate a territorial unit earmarked for an indigenous group but not yet endowed with the legal permanence of a comarca.

Works Cited

Bonilla, Arcadio

2000   "El matrimonio kuna." *La Prensa* 3/18/2000, Panamá: Trasfondo, pp. 64.

Chapin, Mac

1990   "The Silent Jungle: Ecotourism among the Kuna Indians of Panama." *Cultural Survival Quarterly* 14(1):42–45.

1991   "Losing the Way of Great Father." *New Scientist,* 10 August 1991.

n.d.   "Defending Kuna Yala: the Study project for the Management of Wildland Areas of Kuna Yala (PEMASKY)." Unpublished manuscript.

Chapin, Mac, and Heraclio Herrera

1998   "Defending Kuna Yala: the Study project for the Management of Wildland Areas of Kuna Yala (PEMASKY)." In Ronald Trosper, ed., *Bridging Traditional Ecological Knowledge and Ecosystem Science.* Flagstaff, Arizona: Northern Arizona University School of Forestry, pp. 81–96.

Chapin, Mac, and James Howe

n.d.   "S.T.R.I. Gets the Boot: the Breakdown in Communication between the Kuna and the Smithsonian." Unpublished manuscript.

Congreso General Kuna

2001   *Anmar Igar: Normas Kunas.* Panama: Congreso General Kuna & Manos Unidas de España.

Congresos y Organizaciones Indígenas de Panamá

n.d.   "Informe de la situación de los derechos humanos de los pueblos indígenas de Panamá." Report presented to *La Comisión Interamericana de Derechos Humanos,* June 6, 2001.

Dirección de Estadística y Censo, Contraloría General de la República, República de Panamá.

2001   *Censos nacionales, X de población, VI de vivenda,* Vol. II.

Doggett, Scott

1999   *Panama.* Hawthorne, Australia: Lonely Planet.

Falla, Ricardo

1979   *El Tesoro de San Blas: Turismo en San Blas.* El indio panameño serie 4. Panamá: Centro de Capacitación Social.

González, Otoniel, and Vivienne Solís

2001 "Kuna-Yala, Panama, Sustainability for Comprehensive Development." (http://www.iucn.org/themes/ssp/panama.html) (Website defunct.)

Heckadon Moreno, Stanley

1981 "Dinámica social de la cultura del potrero en Panamá." *Actas del IV Simposium Internacional de Ecología Tropical*, tomo III.

Herlihy, Peter

1995 "La revolución silenciosa en Panamá: las tierras de comarca y los derechos indígenas." *Mesoamérica* 29:77–93.

Holloman, Regina

1969 *Developmental Change in San Blas.* PhD dissertation, Northwestern University.

Howe, James

1982 "Kindling Self-Determination among the Kuna." *Cultural Survival Quarterly* 6:15–17.

1995 "La lucha por la tierra en la costa de San Blas (Panamá), 1900–1930." *Mesoamérica* 29:57–76.

1998 *A People Who Would Not Kneel: Panama, the United States, and the San Blas Kuna.* Washington, D.C.: Smithsonian Institution Press.

IDICA/GRET (Instituto para le Desarrollo Integral de la Comarca de Kuna Yala/Group de Recherche e d'Echanges Technologiques)

n.d. [August 1995] "Invasión de terrenos comarcales: la percepción de la comunidades kunas del sector Cartí (Kuna Yala, Panamá)"

Instituto de Estudios Nacionales (Universidad de Panamá) and Diócesis Misionera de Colón

1991 *Colón y Kuna Yala: Desafío para la iglesia y el gobierno.* Panamá: Diócesis Misionera de Colón, Talleres de Materiales de Evangelización.

Leis, Raúl

1992 *Machi: Un kuna en la ciudad.* Panamá: CEASPA.

López, Atencio

1999 "Mining Concessions and Indigenous peoples in Panama." (http://www.ecouncil.ac.cr/indig/conventi/panama2-eng.html) (Website defunct.)

Mendel, William

2000   "Under New Ownership—It's *Panama's* Canal." *Military Review* July–August 2000. (http://call.army.mil/call/fmso/fmsopubs/issues/newowner/newowner.html) (Website defunct.)

Moeller, Eric John

1997   *Identity and Millenarian Discourse: Kuna Indian Villagers in an Ethnic Borderland.* PhD dissertation, University of Chicago.

Moore, Alexander

1983   "From Council to Legislature: Democracy, Parliamentarianism, and the San Blas Cuna." *American Anthropologist* 86:28–42.

1985   "The Form and Context of the Kuna General Congress" In William D'Arcy and Mireya Correra, eds. *The Botany and Natural History of Panama.* St. Louis: Missouri Botanical Garden, pp. 333–343.

Salvador, Mari Lyn

1996   "Looking Back: Contemporary Kuna Women's Arts." In Mari Lyn Salvador ed., *The Art of Being Kuna.* Los Angeles: Fowler Museum of Cultural History, pp.150–211.

Snow, Steven, and Cheryl Wheeler

2001   "Pathways in the Periphery: Tourism to Indigenous Communities in Panama." *Social Science Quarterly* 81(3):732–749.

Swain, Margaret

1977   "Cuna Women and Ethnic Tourism." In Valene Smith (ed.), *Hosts and Guests: The Anthropology of Tourism.* Philadelphia: University of Pennsylvania Press.

Tice, Karin

1995   *Kuna Crafts, Gender, and the Global Economy.* Austin: University of Texas Press.

n.d.   (1982) "Conflict and Resolution: Events Leading up to the Expropriation of a Foreign–Operated Hotel in Kuna Yala (San Blas, Panama)." Unpublished manuscript.

Turpana, Arysteides

1995   "To be or not to be." In Ventocilla, Jorge, Heraclio Herrera, and Valerio Núñez eds., *Plants and Animals in the Life of the Kuna.* Austin: University of Texas, pp. 111–114.

Ventocilla, Jorge, Heraclio Herrera, and Valerio Núñez

1993   *Plantas y animales en la vida del pueblo kuna*. First Spanish-language edition, Panamá, [Instituto Nacional de Cultura] & Smithsonian Tropical Research Institute; first English-language edition, 1995, Austin: University of Texas Press; second Spanish-language edition, 1997, Barcelona: Icaria Editorial; third Spanish language edition, 1999, Smithsonian Tropical Research Institute & Abya Yala (Ecuador).

Ventocilla, Jorge, Valerio Núñez, Francisco Herrera, Heraclio Herrera, and Mac Chapin

1995   "Los indígenas kunas y la conservación ambiental" *Mesoamérica* 29:95–124.

Wali, Alaka

1989   *Kilowatts and Crisis: Hydroelectric Power and Social Dislocation in Eastern Panama*. Boulder, Colorado: Westview Press.

1995   "La política de desarrollo y las relaciones entre región y estado: el caso del oriente de Panamá, 1972–1990." *Mesoamerica* 29:125–158.

Zydler, Nancy Schwalbe, and Tom Zydler

1996   *The Panama Guide: A Cruising Guide to the Isthmus of Panama*. Brookfield WI: Seaworthy Publications.

Acronyms

ACCU	*Autodefensas Campesinas de Colombia y Urabá*
AEK	*Asociación de Empleados Kunas*
CATIE	*Centro Agronómico Tropical de Investigación y Enseñanza*
CIK	*Centro de Investigaciones Kuna*
DESOSKY	*Desarrollo Sostenible de Kuna Yala*
FARC	*Fuerzas Armadas Revolucionarias de Colombia*
IDIKY	*Instituto para el Desarrollo Sostenible de Kuna Yala*
IDB	International Development Bank
IPAT	*Instituto Panameño de Turismo*
MJK	*Movimiento de la Juventud Kuna*
PEMASKY	*El Proyecto de Estudio para el Manejo de Areas Silvestres de Kuna Yala*
PRD	*Partido Revolucionario Democrático*
USAID	United States Agency for International Development

4

Caught in the Crossfire: Colombia's Indigenous Peoples during the 1990s[1]

Jean Jackson

This paper examines the emergence of Colombia's indigenous people as a political force, and identifies the effects of the crisis on the nation's indigenous *pueblos*.[2] It focuses on the period following the signing of the new Constitution in 1991. I begin with some general information about Colombia's pueblos, then summarize the discussions during the National Constituent Assembly (*Asamblea Nacional Constituyente*, henceforth ANC); next I provide a short overview of the Constitution's successes and failures with respect to indigenous concerns, then briefly discuss the implications of the indigenous movement, and, finally, describe a specific case that illustrates the kinds of problems that the nation's indigenous people are facing.

Overview of Colombia's Indigenous Communities

Colombia's indigenous people form at least 81 distinct *pueblos*[3] and speak 64 different languages. The 1996 national census gives a figure of 638,606 Indians,[4] 2 percent of the total population of 36,762,000.[5]

From the comparatively densely populated Andean communities to the smaller and more dispersed communities in the plains and tropical forests regions, the nation's indigenous people have always been extremely socially, politically, and economically marginalized. During the colonial era the Crown created a system of *resguardos*, collectively owned indigenous reservations,[6] in part to protect the communities from such rapacious exploitation that they were in danger of disappearing entirely (and, with them, a valuable labor source). Independence from Spain and Portugal ushered in an ideology of nation-building, which required forging a single national identity, a process seen to eventually result in a homogeneous Spanish- or Portuguese-speaking, Catholic, and patriotic citizenry. State policies of *indigenismo* (a policy directed at helping to incorporate Indians into the general population, through racial mixing and cultural assimilation [see Ramos 1998, 5–6]) appeared throughout almost all Latin American countries with indigenous populations. In Colombia, indigenous communal landholding came to be seen as especially inimical to the nation-building project, and legislation intended to dismantle the resguardos was promulgated. However, Law 89 of 1890, passed by the conservatives then in power, slowed down the "progressivist" legislative trend that had arisen during the 19th century, which aimed at eliminating tribute-paying and privatizing collective lands. The new legislation recognized the official status of the resguardo and legalized the indigenous councils, known as *cabildos*, which governed the communities.[7] It strengthened Indian claims to lands with colonial titles (all in highland areas), and became the foundation for repossessions during the 1970s and 1980s. In 1988, Decree 2001 defined the resguardo as a special kind of legal and socio-political institution formed by an indigenous community or entire indigenous ethnic group (see Ramírez, this volume).

During most of this century the Colombian state left much of the job of governing and civilizing its indigenous population to the Church; for example, a January 1953 Treaty put it in charge of all indigenous education. In 1962 the Summer Institute of Linguistics/Wycliffe Bible Translators was permitted to begin placing linguist-missionaries in indigenous communities (see Stoll 1982, 165–197). The *División de Asuntos Indígenas* (DAI: Division of Indigenous Affairs), the official government agency representing the state to the country's pueblos, was founded in 1960. Presumably an advocate for indigenous interests, it has consistently been criticized by some for implicitly supporting an indigenist approach and only gesturing to the need to respect cultural difference (Jimeno and Triana 1985; also see Jackson 2002). Needless to say, traditional vested interests continue their attempts to colonize indigenous lands, to promote their version of development, and to find ways to exploit indigenous labor.

History of Indigenous Organizing

Colombian Andean indigenous communities began to organize to fight for land rights during the first half of the twentieth century. In the 1920s, Marxist Indians involved in the effort partially rejected the assimilationist positions held by both the Left and Right, and spoke of indigenousness and the "indigenous proletariat." The most famous leader of that time, Manuel Quintín Lame, a Páez (a pueblo now known as Nasa) eventually came to support indigenous separatism (see Pineda 1984; Gros 1991; Rappaport 1990). During the 1930s and 1940s, the struggle for land by indigenous communities and non-indigenous peasants was taken up by the *Movimiento Agrarista* (Agrarian Movement) in the southern part of the department of Tolima; Marxist and Liberal guerrillas continued this struggle against the Conservative government of the 1950s, forming "independent republics" which evolved into the insurgent groups of the 1980s and 1990s.

In 1970, the *Asociación Nacional de Usuarios Campesinos* (ANUC: National Association of Peasants) was formed to ensure enactment of the land reform laws passed in the early 1960s. ANUC soon divided, and indigenous people from Cauca, Nariño, Putumayo, San Andrés de Sotavento and Antioquia formed a *Secretaría Indígena Nacional* within one faction. Upon realizing that ANUC was only interested in "peasantizing" (*campesinar*) its indigenous members, they left and formed the *Consejo Regional Indígena del Cauca* (CRIC: Regional Indigenous Council of Cauca) in early 1971 to continue the fight for land rights and as a defense against severe repression from guerrilla armies and the national armed forces. Demanding implementation of agrarian reform laws passed in the early 1960s that mandated expansion of indigenous resguardos, and reclaiming resguardos titled by the Crown, CRIC (and, subsequently, other organizations representing highland pueblos) fought many bloody battles. When the state realized that the repossessions were going to continue, despite imprisonment and other forms of repression, legal and illegal, it reversed its position and sought to institute a way to make land recovery occur within a legal framework. The Instituto Colombiano de Reforma Agraria, INCORA, the Land Reform Institute was established, but it would take further struggle before its notion of communally held land would dovetail with that of the indigenous communities (see Findji 1992, 119–121; Jimeno and Triana 1985).

These politicized Indians' activism was opposed not only by local landowners and the government, but also by the Church, which owned extensive landholdings in some areas. For example, earlier in the century the Church had mounted a campaign to convince Indians that they had no claim to the land because it was actually unused public land (*baldío*), and therefore available to "whoever would work it and make it worth something" (Jimeno 1985, 184), an attitude many continue to hold today about sparsely populated indigenous territories in the plains and tropical forests.

Although CRIC declared itself to be an indigenous organization, it has never identified itself with a particular pueblo, although most of its members are Nasa.[8] Findji states that CRIC lacked an "ethnic" vision (she also calls it anti-indigenist[9]), its organizing principle social class (1992, 118). While CRIC certainly maintained links with other sectors of the rural society, helping amplify its potential for mass mobilization, in the fall of 1971 it modified its charter to include the defense of "indigenous history, language and customs" (*Consejo Regional Indígena del Cauca* 1981, 12). CRIC's own version of its history acknowledges that at the very beginning "we ourselves believed that being *indio* wasn't good, and that in order to progress we had to copy what came from the exterior" (*Consejo Regional Indígena del Cauca* 1981, 11). In 1974 CRIC began *Unidad Indígena*, a newspaper currently published several times a year.

During 1976–1981 the government attempted to pass a repressive "Indigenous Law" that effectively gave the state extensive power over the pueblos, including specifying who was and was not indigenous (Triana 1978). But the organizing efforts were kept alive, in part due to the national and international attention several scandals generated,[10] and by alliance-building with peasant groups and other left organizations, leading eventually to government recognition of the indigenous organizations. A nation-wide group, the National Organization of Colombian Indians (Organización Nacional Indígena de Colombia, ONIC) was founded in 1982, and by 1986 sixteen indigenous organizations had appeared (Avirama and Márquez 1995, 84). ONIC was recognized by the government in 1983 and became an official participant in several governmental programs concerned with indigenous affairs.

Ever since the stepped-up land repossessions in the Andean regions in the 1960s, and the 1970s activism demanding implementation of land reform legislation begun in 1961, Colombia has been handing over land, at times very large tracts, to its indigenous pueblos. Today the pueblos collectively and inalienably own approximately 28 million fully demarcated hectares, 85 percent in the plains and tropical forest, constituting one fourth of the national territory.[11]

One result of the organizing has been a substantial portion of the country's indigenous pueblos coming to see the collectivity of the nation's pueblos as an "imagined community" (Anderson 1983), a major change from the more limited pueblo-specific identity that dominated in the past. Indeed, in earlier periods, when given the chance, Indians who militantly affirmed their pueblo membership would explicitly disavow membership in the highly stigmatized category "indio." Findji, discussing several Guambiano communities' decision to leave CRIC over disagreements about (among other things) how to conceptualize territory, provides an example of people who wanted to be seen as neither campesino nor indigenous in a generic sense, but strictly as Guambiano.[12] Beginning in the 1970s, a process of change and restructuring has provided both incentives and opportunities for the development (and politicization) of a generic indigenous identity. As was happening elsewhere, political liberalization reduced repressive responses to indigenous demands, creating space for broader organization and more inclusive claims. Colombian indigenous people also learned of indigenous organizing elsewhere in the Western Hemisphere, and of the environmentalist movement. A resignification of "indigenous" occurred, its meaning increasingly relying on the interplay between negotiated otherness and cultural continuity. What had been a stigmatizing identity for those Guambiano, among others, turned into symbolic and political capital, becoming what political scientists call a political opportunity structure. Consequently, indigenous demands began to be couched less in a discourse of minority rights, and more in terms of their rights as a "people." As elsewhere in Latin America, the Colombian movement continued its efforts to gain access to the political institutions of the state, but also focused more than before on strengthening the pueblos' own institutions. Cultural recovery projects increased in number and visibility, and their significance heightened, both for the pueblos themselves and in their interactions with the outside.

These evolving notions and new strategizing possibilities had far-reaching effects. The meaning of indigenous territory, for example, and, hence, of land claims, changed, as did the way such claims were legitimized. Territory came to be seen in more comprehensive ways: as land, yes, but also as the underpinnings of self-determination, a "fundamental and multidimensional space for the creation and re-creation of the social, economic, and cultural values and practices of the communities" (Grueso et al., 1998, 20). Claims to a core, intrinsic, positively valenced indigenous identity, and to demands for autonomous jurisdiction were increasingly validated by a performance of cultural distinctiveness as represented by customary practices and traditions. The way collective land rights were secured or denied increasingly depended on notions about just what indigenous identity consisted of. Of course, the state had denied land claims before by denying that the applicants were indigenous; what was new was the latitude increasingly given to the pueblos themselves to define their otherness, formulating the criteria on which to make the decisions.

In sum, new parameters emerged for indigenous involvement in state affairs. The country was moving toward a pluralist conception of itself, a notion that, once enshrined in the 1991 Constitution,[13] required a respect for the autonomy of indigenous institutions never before imagined.

Indigenous identity had itself become a strategy in many important venues. What it meant, never predetermined, became much more unstable as all actors repeatedly modified their discourses in response to multiculturalism's new role and the shifting terms of engagement. And indigenous identity not only became a political resource, it turned into a moral reproach to status quo hegemonic institutions like the state and the Church, and, indeed, a critique of Western society as a whole.

The 1991 Constitution

Advocates for rewriting the country's constitution felt that the old 1886 constitution was extremely rigid, inefficient, and overly centralized (de la Calle 1994). Democratic foundational charter in name only, it favored the Conservatives and, more generally, the privileged and powerful. Colombia is a "façade" democracy: as Alvarez et al. (1998, 9) note, in such countries the majority of citizens have come to regard politics as the private business of the elites, and civil society is embryonic.

The drive for constitutional reform arose from awareness that the current social order, in which access to the government was gained exclusively through political parties (all other attempts being ignored or treated as subversion), was incapable of adapting to changing social conditions (Van Cott 2000, 63–89). The political and moral crisis resulting from the insurgency, the increase in violence as landowners and security forces attempted to stamp it out, and a pervasive distrust of a state controlled by the oligarchy and deeply corrupt,[14] also strengthened arguments promoting constitutional reform (see Assies 2000, 3). Especially during the 1980s, the unending states of siege and the depredations of the drug cartels at times seemed to paralyze the state, making its inadequacies glaringly apparent.

Constitutional reform was intended to decentralize power and create a more open and legitimate political system. The original agenda had not included benefiting the country's minorities, but during the ANC deliberations, several political interests, not just indigenous and Afro-Colombian, realized that advocating pluralism brought them closer to their own goals. The debates opened up new spaces for democratic participation, and civil society hesitantly began to give voice to its concerns (Van Cott 2000). These democratic reforms began a process of reconfiguring the relationship between state, market and civil society. Notions of participation and empowerment, previously limited to oppositional social movements and NGOs, began to appear in governmental discourse, notably in the Constitution itself (see Assies 2000, 2, 3).

Indigenous Pueblos and the Constitution

With respect to indigenous rights Colombia's new constitution is the most far-reaching in Latin America. The remarkable media focus during the ANC on the three indigenous representatives, Francisco Rojas Birry, Lorenzo Muelas, and Alfonso Peña Chepe,[15] did not signal any real political clout on their part, but rather the extent to which the nation's indigenous pueblos had come to symbolize tolerance and pluralism, a rediscovered national identity, historic reconciliation, justice, political effectiveness, and participatory legitimacy (see Cepeda 1995, as cited in Van Cott 2000, 72). The participation of the three men in the ANC conveyed the promise of a new ways of solving conflicts, based on respect and dialogue rather than violence. Murillo suggests that the indigenous representatives gave legitimacy to the government and the entire ANC, an opinion shared by others (1996, 22). The Gaviria administration (1990–1994) "offered the protection of ethnic minority rights as a highly visible emblem of the new regime of rights protection" (Van Cott 2000, 74). A government that had been closely associated with assimilationist policies doing an about-face and guaranteeing the rights of its most marginalized population would show how the most peripheral sectors were being incorporated into the democratic process, both as citizens in good standing *and* as citizens belonging to unique communities whose distinctiveness the state recognized, valued, and promised to protect (Van Cott 2000, 74). The reconstitution of state-indigenous relations, by moving from a paternalistic, assimilationist stance to one recognizing the pueblos' rights—to autonomy, dignity, and self-determination—became an emblem of the overall goal of reconstituting relations between the state and society as a whole.

Achievements in Constitutional Reform Related to the Pueblos

The new Constitution most significantly benefits Colombia's indigenous pueblos in its mandate that the new territorial ordination would include "indigenous territorial entities" (*Entidades Territoriales Indígenas*—ETIs) (see Dover and Rappaport 1996; Jackson 1996; Padilla 1996; Roldán 2000, 33–59). It also confirms collective ownership of resguardos and the pueblos' right to use their territories as they see fit, including any decision-making about development. Unfortunately, these territorial guarantees, coupled with assignment of subsoil rights throughout the country to the government, reveals one of several serious contradictions contained in the charter. The ETI legislation has yet to be written, and territorial units following this model are very unlikely to materialize, given the worsening of the crisis.

Another benefit is the recognition of customary law (*usos y costumbres*), which allows indigenous communities to settle their internal affairs as they see fit, even in criminal cases, so long as the basic law of the land is not violated (see Sánchez 1998, 71–120).

Among the legal mechanisms set up by the Constitution, the writ of protection—*acción de tutela*—has definitely benefited the nation's indigenous pueblos, for it "empowers citizens to appeal for immediate court action when their fundamental constitutional rights are violated and no other judicial means are available" (Van Cott 2000, 87). Another reform, the Constitutional Court, has defended the rights of many citizens, including Indians (see Ministerio de Justicia y del Derecho/Ministerio del Interior, Dirección General de Asuntos Indígenas 1997).[16] Van Cott notes that the Court has issued an accumulated jurisprudence on indigenous rights and jurisdiction far more extensive than anywhere else in Latin America (2000, 112).

In addition, the Constitution strengthened ethno-education and other programs tailored to permit cultural distinctiveness (for example, in health) which had been legislated during the 1980s. The Constitution mandated more direct transfers of state resources to the resguardos, and legislation to implement this change began under Gaviria (Dirección General de Asuntos Indígenas 1998).[17]

The Post-Constitution Situation

Continuing Problems

As might be imagined, several long-standing problems not sufficiently addressed, or not addressed at all, by the Constitution virtually guaranteed that it would not accomplish many of its creators' goals. First, the traditional parties, legislature, and post-Constitution administrations have successfully limited effective participation by citizens in many domains. Second, despite the changes targeted at rural areas, the state still does not control a significant amount of the national territory; its presence in many rural areas is limited to military and police, and its total absence in others leaves the local population under the rule of guerrilla forces or local elites, in many cases backed up by illegal paramilitaries.

The violence now gripping the country has deep roots. The decade known as "La Violencia" (1948–1957), characterized by horrendous inter-party warfare in which an estimated 150,000 to 200,000 people died (Van Cott 2000, 39), was ended by a military coup which created a Popular Front and mandated that power-holding between the parties alternate, and important posts be distributed equally. It lasted until 1974. The governments of Betancur (1982–1986) and Barco (1986–1990) began reaching out with peace initiatives and discussion about how to establish a more open political system. The decision was made to reform the 1886 constitution, which would spearhead the peace process and thereby successfully defuse the situation and decrease the left's appeal.

Throughout the twentieth century the Colombian state has responded to even legal protest with vicious repression of the country's leftists. Of the rural guerrilla groups that arose during the Violencia, two are still in arms today: the Revolutionary Armed Forces of Colombia (FARC), and the pro-Cuban National Liberation Army (ELN). Other armed groups demobilized in 1990 in order to be able to participate in the ANC debates.[18] The nation's pueblos were guaranteed two seats in the senate, and in fact, three indigenous senators were elected.

During the last decade the violence has escalated. Readers of the Colombian press are treated to a hellish vision of civilian massacres, "disappeared" individuals, approximately 3,000 kidnappings a year (Forero 2000), assassinations, extortion, and sabotage. Assassinations of human-rights activists, politicians, journalists, and judges continue, maintaining a climate of intimidation and, in many rural areas, sheer terror. Thirty-five hundred trade unionist leaders were murdered by state and paramilitary forces between 1986 and February 2002. Other acts of violence, death threats, and nearly innumerable actions terrorizing the populace for the most part receive little attention, so frequently do they occur. Evidence of human rights abuses linked to the army and police, who operate with near-total impunity, abounds. According to Amnesty International, fourteen politically motivated homicides occur each day (website posting, December 21, 2000). The judicial system continues to be paralyzed with respect to prosecuting criminals and enforcing sentencing. Nearly 2 million Colombians, almost 4 percent of the population, are internally displaced, fleeing the numerous areas of intense conflict, and living in the *zonas de miseria* that surround every urban center. According to a UNICEF report, this total exceeds the number of internally displaced refugees in Rwanda, Burundi, and Congo combined (as cited in Van Cott 2000, 251, 252).

Other remaining problems include the glaringly obvious failure of the neoliberal economic model to democratize the distribution of the nation's wealth. Van Cott notes that if one were to use conventional economic measures (i.e., no balance of payments debt, yearly growth), the Colombia of the early 1990s could boast of a robust and stable economy. Soon, however, the economic dislocations caused by *la apertura*, the neoliberal opening legislated during the decade, increased the sense of crisis, for it aggravated already serious income disparities. Even at the beginning of the 1990s, approximately 50 percent of the population was already living in absolute poverty (Van Cott 2000, 49, 248). The Constitution is totally mute regarding these ever-increasing inequalities of wealth, and subsequent court decisions have not taken such reforms as their mandate.

Colombia's drug problem remains extremely serious. The U.S.-dominated international market guarantees that vast sums of narcodollars will continue to flow into the country, and so it is no surprise that both guerrillas and paramilitaries quickly filled the spaces left by the dismantling of the cartels during the Samper administration.

Nor did the constitutional reform touch the military, either in its structure or in its abysmal performance with respect to human rights abuses, which puts the reform's main goal, ending the cycle of violence, completely out of reach. The role of the United States in the violence is substantial. The United States cannot claim publicly to be fighting communism as in its Cold War interventions in Latin America, but it is amply clear that supporting the Colombian government means supporting the security forces regardless of their glaring human rights abuses and links to paramilitaries. The U.S. Congress and the Executive branch have stressed the links between guerrillas and drugs to justify their programs (currently Plan Colombia and the Andean Regional Initiative), paying much less attention to the paramilitaries' involvement with narcotrafficking or their appalling record of human rights abuses. The U.S. mass media for the most part reflect this distortion.

Post-Constitution Problems Specifically Affecting the Pueblos

During the ANC, indigenous activism was weakened by divisions within the movement, some of them resulting from organizations with a national presence like ONIC sponsoring their own candidates for election. Although the movement comes together during times of crisis, such as the two-year negotiation with various government agencies that culminated in the final 1995 proposal over legislating the Indigenous Territorial Entities, and during the series of strikes that occurred over the summer of 1996 (see Jackson 2002), divisions were forming even as the movement was gathering strength during the 1980s. The same events—participating in the ANC and in the 1994 elections—that led to the movement's achieving a new degree of maturity also, perhaps inevitably, led to factionalization within ONIC. By 1994 electoral politics had proven so disruptive that the only recourse for ONIC was to stop.[19] ONIC has always struggled to define its role in the national political scene, both with respect to its mandate to represent all of the country's pueblos, and with respect to the kind of political activism it should adopt. It felt shut out during the Gaviria administration, which dealt mainly with the indigenous senators and congressional deputies.

As noted, counter-reform efforts by the executive and legislative branches emerged soon after the adoption of the new Constitution. The reforms could not resolve the various crises the country was experiencing. The fault lines within the national indigenous movement that had always weakened its political power were also apparent in their negotiations during this time, even though the movement presented a single front in public.

A tight connection exists between democratic reforms throughout Latin America and neoliberal policies being adopted. As Alvarez et al. point out, implementation of structural adjustment policies requires a concomitant "social adjustment" (1998), which includes movement toward a more participatory civil society. The state goal of "minimalist" government, one depending much more on the private sector (including NGOs, which often function as para-state institutions), carries enormous consequences for Colombia's pueblos. Decentralization as such does not empower or enhance their participation in civil society. Furthermore, although Colombia has established a "safety net" (*Red de*

Solidaridad, Solidarity Network) to ease the burden of structural adjustment on the poorest sectors, public services have been drastically cut. The elimination of price supports and subsidies for the agrarian sector further disadvantages both highland and lowland pueblos.

The adverse consequences of the neoliberal policies of the 1990s did less harm, however, than the violence virtually all pueblos are currently experiencing. Indigenous communities are targeted by all the armed groups: military, paramilitaries and guerrillas. More than 400 indigenous leaders have been killed since the early 1970s, and not one of their killers has been brought to justice (Murillo 1996, 21). Although the government as such has dropped its repression of indigenous organizing and no longer assumes that political opposition equals subversion, many authorities in the rural areas continue to assume that Indians are either actual or potential supporters of the guerrillas—due to their geographical location and their poverty—and hence appropriate targets for counterinsurgency measures (see Van Cott 1994, 10).

Large sections of indigenous territory are occupied by guerrillas, paramilitaries and military detachments, and Indians are compelled to serve as guides or informers, often by threatening their families (Roldán 2000). A meeting in 1998 between Francisco Rojas Birry, the indigenous senator, Abadio Green, then president of ONIC, and Carlos Castaño, the head of *Autodefensas de Colombia* (AUC, Colombian Self-Defense Army), the main paramilitary organization, illustrates the extent of indigenous vulnerability, for the agenda was negotiation of a ceasefire of sixty days in the highly conflictive zones of Córdoba and Urabá (*El Espectador* Sept. 25, 1998). Some Indians do voluntarily join the guerrillas and, occasionally, even the paramilitaries—to protect their families in areas under paramilitary control, or for the promise of a uniform and pay.

Indians have also been involved in other kinds of conflict; in the Chocó region on the Pacific coast, for example, Indians and blacks have clashed over land demarcation (Achito 1997; Wade 1993, 353; Pizarro 1997). In this instance, however, attempts have been made to ease the situation: the local indigenous organization has attempted to build alliances in the fight against environmental degradation, and black peasant associations often invite Indians to their meetings to build trust (Wade 1993, 353, 357).

Narcotrafficking seriously imperils indigenous communities in many regions and in many ways. Both highland and lowland Indians grow illegal crops (coca and opium poppies), sometimes by choice, sometimes under duress, with severe impact on the traditional subsistence economy and social order. In addition to intrafamilial disputes, health problems and possible legal penalties, Indians face potential loss of livelihood and health risks from fumigation of fields, as well as a scarcity of essential commodities like gasoline, due to government efforts to decrease production of coca paste.

Discussion

The shift by the Colombian state to a stance that promotes inclusion of the nation's indigenous pueblos while also encouraging them to remain apart has meant that the nature of such pluralism must be worked out in a highly politicized context. ANC debates over internal self-determination were fierce, and while victory was achieved in several key areas, as noted, the resulting document at several crucial points is vague and ambiguous.[20] The actual legislation to put the reforms in motion has slowed to a standstill in some areas, including laws concerned with collective territorial ownership.

Although a pueblo's claim to self-determination does not in principle require it to freeze-dry its traditions, both pueblos and the state have moved in dangerous ways toward closure, reifying identity and customary law and traditions. Ideally, Colombia's indigenous peoples will have the space to transform their cultures (and hence their identities) selectively, according to their own customs, rules, and de facto *realpolitik*. Because such processes always involve power relations, internal and external, questions of authenticity often arise. A related worry concerns the potential for inter-ethnic polarization, for example, between blacks and Indians on the Pacific coast, and between Indians and colonos in the Amazon and plains regions (see Ramírez, this volume).

We have seen that the Constitutional Court seeks to maximize the autonomy of indigenous jurisdiction, but a number of cases have already been heard involving clashes between a pueblo's judgment and the basic law of the land guaranteeing the right to life and protection from slavery and torture. The liberal construction that automatically links indigenous rights with human rights starts to unravel when an individual is sentenced to be whipped or put into stocks (see, for example, Gow and Rappaport 2002), or when traditional authorities require execution of witches or the abandonment of orphans or twins (see Sánchez 2000). Another controversial domain is gender rights. That indigenous women might organize to both change their traditional *usos y costumbres* and defend them illustrates my point above about selective transformation and the highly politicized arenas in which it must occur.

Which leads us to a basic and often neglected point: any indigenous community will be riddled with conflicts, some ongoing, others resolved but not forgotten, as well as factions, hierarchies, and decision-making mechanisms that exclude and marginalize some members. It will, in short, display values and actions that are anything but fair, democratic, or egalitarian, as these concepts are defined and valorized in the West. (Western institutions and values are no less conflict-ridden and exclusionary.) The romantic view of pueblos as cohesive and consensus-based totalities can be sustained only from a distance. Just how indigenous customary law interfaces with codified positive law, and what compromises are necessary, points again to the danger of imposing Western legal premises and procedures on systems that are anything but codified, and that depend on kinship relations, shamanic consultations, and so forth, and thus differ fundamentally from Western notions of justice, due process, and conflict resolution.

Alliances between the indigenous movement and environmentalists, in Colombia and elsewhere, raise their own potential problems, many of them functions of the authenticity question and the tendency to "freeze-dry" custom. When indigenous peoples are stereotyped as the preservers of biodiversity, changes in traditional patterns may jeopardize the legitimacy of territorial claims. Indigenous people can pursue distinctive visions of development (sometimes referred to as "ethnodevelopment"), but the directions such development takes are unduly restricted when they must conform to Western images of born ecologists. If the World Bank is any indication, international lending agencies often simply equate indigenous issues with environmental issues. Exactly what projects developed by "ethnodevelopment" might look like is highly ambiguous in these agencies' literature (see Brysk 1995). Such programmatic statements about ethnodevelopment do not invite a true reexamination of the dominant notion of development, and all too often the goal of these agencies is either to encourage pueblos to participate in business-as-usual capitalist development, or else to increase their ability to withstand its depredations.

This particular representation of Indians as Nature itself also tends to disenfranchise the large majority of indigenous peoples (70 percent) who are poor highland peasants (Brysk 2000, 6), and the many more who are uncounted urban dwellers. If, as Albert (1997) argues, the market value of "indigenous identity" results in the marginalization of groups seen to be less traditional, then indigenous citizenship will become indexed to an "identity rent," and new forms of dependency and clientelism will result. That the patrons would be international lending agencies and NGOs rather than traditional party politicians is no guarantee a pueblo would ultimately benefit.

An Example: The Tukanoans [21]

The Amazonian region of the Vaupés illustrates many of the effects of the Colombian crisis on its pueblos. Goldman writes that during his period of fieldwork in 1939, the Cubeo (now spelled Kubeo), told him they believed they were living in a "golden age," far better than the previous hunting and gathering period when, according to their traditions, they were always on the verge of starvation and reduced to eating tree sap and bark (1979, 51). And in 1973, French sociologist Christian Gros commented that, when compared to other Amazon regions, the Vaupés seemed a relatively tranquil island (1991, 16). The rubber boom was in its death throes, and neither guerrillas nor the narcotraffickers, who arrived later during the coca boom of the early 1980s, had yet appeared.

The Vaupés of 1939 or the early 1970s was not, of course, a tranquil island, nor did every settlement boast of cornucopias of foodstuffs. Goldman and Gros, however, are correct in their statements that Tukanoans did indeed enjoy *relative* safety and economic self-sufficiency. Sadly, this is no longer the case. The coca boom brought the euphoria and disappointments that booms always bring, and a FARC raid in 1988 on Mitú, the departmental capital, in which nine people and at least twelve guerrillas died (*El Espectador* April 21, 1988) resulted in the establishment of a military base on the outskirts of the town.[22] Up to then the Vaupés had been the only department depending entirely on police to maintain public order. A subsequent gold rush in a region to the south brought more disruption. While the 1988 military base was later dismantled, in part due to pressure applied by the local indigenous organization, security steadily declined in the region, and plummeted when FARC launched an all-out assault on Mitú at dawn on Sunday, November 1, 1998. An estimated force of 700 to 1,000 guerrillas killed 16 policemen and 13 auxiliaries, all of the latter Tukanoan, and took 51 police and 24 auxiliaries prisoner[23] (28 guerrillas were reported dead—*El Tiempo* Nov. 4, 1998). Because they were out of uniform, without arms, and in their houses, the young Tukanoan police auxiliaries who were killed and taken prisoner should have been considered civilians. Using homemade missiles fashioned from modified propane gas cylinders, the guerrillas leveled the police garrison and the nearby *Caja Agraria* (farmer's bank), mined the airstrip, and blew up the microwave communications tower. Mitú, with a population of 14,000, has always been accessible only by air and water, making it an excellent choice for demonstrating FARC power, because planes could not land at the mined airstrip, and the rapids-filled Vaupés river did not permit a water-based attack. The besieged town was retaken only on November 4, after an earlier unsuccessful attempt. Even though permission had been refused, the Air Force launched the attack from an airstrip in Brazil (Mitú is 30 km. from the border). Issuing a "vehement protest," Brazil recalled its ambassador (Esnal 1998).

While taking Mitú brought no strategic military gain (apart from prisoners to be used in exchanges), FARC clearly strengthened its position right before peace talks were to begin with the government, which lost face, nationally and internationally. The attack's only benefit, in my opinion, was that it flushed out about 200 Colombian troops from the Brazilian side who reentered Colombia to help break the stranglehold, their presence a long-standing rumor. Of course this disclosure further embarrassed the government.[24]

Mitú was virtually defenseless; the police were there to maintain public order (and, ostensibly, to control narcotrafficking), not to protect the town from guerrilla attack.[25] Although those killed and taken prisoner were mostly police, the bombs destroyed the homes of 3,000 people and a school, seriously damaged the hospital, and destroyed the pharmacy. Following the attack, many people with vital roles to play in the region, including five physicians, left on the earliest possible flight (only three remained).

The majority of the population in Mitú is indigenous, and, with a few exceptions, the surrounding area (the Vaupés *resguardo*, consisting of more than three million hectares) is entirely Tukanoan. The attack on Mitú presents in an extremely stark and ugly manner many of the ways the nation's Indians have been caught up in the war.

First is FARC's presence in the region. FARC detachments, whose numbers vary, are able to move through the resguardo at will. The number of indigenous guerrillas in the region is unknown. Tukanoans have complained for some time about the forced recruitment of indigenous children, and, when their sons and daughters disappear, they have registered formal complaints with the authorities. The degree to which these youths are coerced is, of course, anyone's guess, but it is very clear that FARC has many soldiers under 18, some as young as 12.

Second is the fact of coca. Coca is grown and partially processed into paste in the Vaupés, and many Tukanoans are involved. I do not know whether FARC runs plantations within the Vaupés resguardo as it does in Guaviare to the northwest, but undoubtedly FARC is involved in the coca industry in the region to some degree.

Third is the overall effect of the attacks on the indigenous population. Following the attack, dozens of Tukanoans came to Mitú from other settlements, seeking refuge in the church of the Prefecture, the various Protestant halls, in the schools, in a communal longhouse, or with relatives. A nighttime curfew was ordered, and a permanent army base was established at the airport. This tight security regime has severely disrupted commerce and communication, as virtually everything but the most basic foodstuffs must be flown into the region.

Fourth is the threat of paramilitary activity. Apparently some of the houses near the garrison were empty prior to the attack, which explains the relatively light civilian deaths (eight, including one Tukanoan). If true, obviously some people were warned ahead of time, and, equally obvious is the fact that they did not warn the police.[26] A greatly ratcheted up repression, consisting of paramilitary death threats, torture, disappearances and executions[27] similar to what is happening to many indigenous communities elsewhere in the country, is a real possibility, though hard evidence on this point has not yet been received.[28]

Conclusions

The remarkable emergence of Colombia's indigenous peoples—their success at finding a political voice and gaining recognition as valued citizens, some of that value deriving from their "otherness"—constitutes an impressive achievement. Mobilizing and alliance-building, both national and international, accompanied by democratic reforms and the new pluralist vision produced changes no one could foresee. We can envision a future in which Colombia's pueblos selectively revise cultural practices under conditions that provide them the space to accomplish this, autonomously and with some degree of participatory democracy (although perhaps not along Western majority-rule lines). Such conditions require, first, open dialogue within a given community, as well as between the community and outside institutions and interests; second, respect for one another as people with different visions of the cosmos and ways of doing things; and, third, mutual accountability.

However, all these achievements and promising future scenarios appear extremely vulnerable in the current context of the political and moral crisis the country is undergoing, and the increased poverty caused by structural adjustment and shrinking state services. Worst is the civil war. Despite the possibilities of developing a more participatory citizenry and of a civil society finally being born, we have seen that in the last decade the position of many pueblos has actually worsened. Uncontrolled colonization of indigenous territories in the plains and Amazon regions, accompanied by the armed conflict, coca-crop spraying, and land-clearing in virgin forest make a mockery of indigenous ownership and control of the nation's resguardos. Drug traffic and daily battles and repression of civilians so characteristic of guerrilla warfare make life a horror for many pueblos, as assassinations and forced migration increase. Massive development projects also produce forced migration and promote disease and death rather than the benefits touted by multinational corporations in their slick project statements (See Brysk 2000, 10). In addition to the communities internally displaced by the violence, economic conditions have forced many indigenous people to move to urban centers and try to cope with the horrendous conditions there.

We need to hope, difficult though it may be, that a solution to the extremely complex and wide-ranging crises the country is experiencing will be found and that it won't involve a massive bloodbath.

Notes

1   In Colombia, thanks to all who have helped my research on indigenous organizing, in particular Raúl Arango, Jaime Arocha, Ana Cecelia Betancourt, Guillermo Carmona, Francois Correa, Martín Franco, Segisfredo Franco, Abadio Green, Leonor Herrera, Victor Jacanamejoy, Myriam Jimeno, Gladys Jimeno, Hernando Muñoz, Guillermo Padilla, Roberto Pineda, María Clemencia Ramírez, Elizabeth Reichel, Esther Sánchez, María Lucía Sotomayor, Adolfo Triana, Enrique Sánchez, Roque Roldán, Carlos Uribe, Martín von Hildebrand, Simón Valencia, Miguel Vázquez, the Instituto Colombiano de Antropología, the Department of Anthropology at the Universidad de los Andes, various members of the Consejo Regional Indígena del Vaupés—the Regional Indigenous Council of the Vaupés (CRIVA), and various officials of the Organización Nacional de Indígenas de Colombia (ONIC). Trips to Colombia (1985, 1987, 1989, 1991, 1992, 1993, 1996, 2000) have been funded in part by the Dean's

Office, School of Humanities, Arts and Social Sciences, M.I.T. For help thinking through the ideas presented here, thanks to David Maybury-Lewis, James Howe and Donna Van Cott. The responsibility for the ideas set forth here is entirely my own.

2   *Pueblo* ("people," "community") is the official term for a distinct indigenous group.

3   The actual number of indigenous pueblos in Colombia is somewhat uncertain, some authors, like Roldán, listing 81, others 82 or 84. For example, the Kankuamos are a recently resurrected indigenous community living in the Sierra Nevada de Santa Marta (1994, 2), which presumably increases the total number of indigenous communities to 85 (Gros 1994; *Unidad Indígena* 1993, 14; Jackson 1996, endnote #10).

4   Where stylistically possible I use "indigenous" rather than "Indian," but retain the latter term when a noun referring to one or more individuals must be used, despite the term's controversial status. "Indigene" is not really English, and I find "native" or "aborigine" equally problematic. See Gow and Rappaport, forthcoming.

5   Roldán (2000, 128). That these are estimates is illustrated by Padilla's (1996, 93) total of 972,000 people who consider themselves indigenous.

6   The first resguardo legislation, in 1549, stipulated that the Indians would collectively be managed and also would work and pay tribute to the Crown (see Rappaport 1990, 45–46; Triana 1993, 101–106). Efforts in later centuries to expropriate resguardos led to many of them falling into decline.

7   *Cabildos,* the indigenous councils governing resguardos, were part of the Crown's attempt to centralize and urbanize the scattered "uncivilized" indigenous populations. They continue to be the legal institution governing each pueblo's internal affairs, in accordance with its traditions.

8   Van Cott (personal communication, 2001) has suggested that CRIC is not identified more tightly with the Nasa because many of the organization's leaders have been from the Coconuco pueblo. The Coconuco are less able to perform indigenousness successfully because they lost their language years ago; nor do they wear pueblo-specific costume. Drawing on the political purchase of pueblo identity, therefore, might empower the Nasa section of CRIC.

9   Note that "indigenist" has two well-established, often confusing meanings. The first, most often used in reference to state policy toward indigenous peoples, indicates an integrationist position; this is particularly the case with the word's Spanish and Portuguese cognates. The second meaning refers to any individuals (indigenous or non-indigenous) or institutions in favor of indigenous rights. The first meaning usually carries a negative connotation, the second a positive one.

10   One scandal, following a 1967 massacre of fifteen Guahibo Indians in the eastern plains region of the country, was widely cited because one of the assailants, a settler, said in his defense at the trial that he hadn't seen anything wrong with the killings, because they were Indians. He was acquitted (see Bodley 1990, 29). Discussing another massacre occurring in 1969, one of the killers said that as Indians have no soul they cannot be considered human beings (*El Tiempo* 1988).

11   Colombia has 469 areas reserved for indigenous occupation (460 resguardos and 9 indigenous reserves). Eighty-three percent of these are new resguardos and 81 percent of Colombian Indians live in territory collectively owned by them (see Roldán [2000 xxiii, xxiv, 49, 50]). Also see Jimeno and Triana 1985 on the history of resguardo creation following agrarian reform in the 1960s.

12   "We don't want to be 'humiliated' indígenas—we want to defend, for our children's sake, our right to be Guambianos" (Findji 1992, 122). Note also that the Wayúu, who live in both Venezuela and Colombia on the Guajira peninsula, are well-known for a lack of enthusiasm for the national movement.

13   Article 7 of the Constitution states, "The State recognizes and protects the ethnic and cultural diversity of the Colombian Nation."

14   In 1990 *The Economist* named Colombia one of the world's five most corrupt countries (Buenahora 1991; as cited in Van Cott 2000, 49).

15   Birry was ONIC's representative, Muelas represented the Southwest Indigneous Authorities, and Peña Chepe represented demobilized Quintín Lame guerrillas from Cauca.

16   The number of cases the Court heard is truly remarkable: by mid 1996 more than one hundred thousand citizens had exercised the writ of protection (Van Cott 2000, 112).

17   In order to educate the indigenous communities about the reforms, the DAI commissioned translations of the constitution into seven major indigenous languages (Rojas 1997), and established, in collaboration with ONIC, educational programs to allow Indians to achieve a basic understanding of their constitutional rights (Van Cott 2000, 90).

18   The Democratic Alliance M-19 party, previously a guerrilla organization famous for occupying the Palace of Justice in Bogotá in 1985, along with the Army of Popular Liberation (EPL), the Revolutionary Workers Party (PRT), and Quintín Lame (Movimiento Armado Quintín Lame, MAQL), a mostly Nasa (Páez) armed group in Cauca. An extremely important piece of the puzzle of why violence is so endemic is the fate of many of these demobilized insurgents. For example, the *Unión Patriótica* party, formed by FARC members to participate in electoral politics, is nearly extinct; for a while they saw one of their compatriots assassinated

every two days. The demobilized EPL saw 274 of its members assassinated between 1991 and 1994 (Van Cott 2000, 252, 254). Eduardo Pizarro (1989) has pointed out that the near-impossibility of establishing a democratic left within the political process helped guarantee that any resistance to the status quo would be armed.

19 ASI (Alianza Social Indígena), the party formed by the indigenous guerrilla group Quintín Lame when it demobilized, continued as a party, later on successfully sponsoring Jesús Piñacué for senate. MIC (Movimiento Indígena de Colombia) was founded as the electoral vehicle for senator Gabriel Muyuy, an Inga from the Putumayo, previously ONIC's candidate. In 1997 Rojas Birry was elected by an open (non-indigenous) district. AICO (Indigenous Authorities of Colombia) continued its support of Lorenzo Muelas, a Guambiano.

20 As Assies notes about all the new constitutions, such confusion is sometimes deliberate (2000, p. 297).

21 "Tukanoan" includes Makú and Arawak-speaking communities.

22 The raid was a hit-and-run operation; four policemen were killed and two medical personnel kidnapped and taken upriver to treat wounded FARC members. The base was rather pathetic as bases go (one could tell from the river that the tanks were dummies), but nonetheless had a significant negative impact, in the form of much tighter control, diseases, including venereal disease, and unwed indigenous mothers whose children would have no fathers at all in the social sense, a new development in the region.

23 *El Tiempo* Nov. 6, 1998, León Restrepo, 1998; *El Espectador,* Dec. 1, 1998.

24 *Agence France Presse* Nov. 4, 1998; *Boston Globe,* Nov. 3, 1998.

25 Interestingly, the 1998 press reports made no mention of the 1988 FARC attack on Mitú, despite a number of similarities (although on a much smaller scale), nor the subsequent gradual buildup of FARC presence in the region. The mayor was quoted in the press as saying "we had been enjoying peace and tranquility for a long time" (León Restrepo 1998).

26 There had been so many rumors of imminent attack that the recently arrived colonel in charge of the police seems to have adopted a "boy who cried wolf" attitude.

27 "Disappearances" and vigilante executions have occurred, although not in any systematic way. In 1993 I was shown a photograph of a man killed by a self-appointed "justice" committee by the proud photographer (and committee member).

28 According to María Clemencia Ramírez, when the news of the Mitú attack arrived in the town of Puerto Asís in the Putumayo (see this volume), people commented about how accustomed inhabitants of much of the Western Amazon had become to everyday violence and threats of

violence, in contrast to the shock and surprise expressed by Mitú residents (personal communication, 2000). It should also be noted that many Tukanoans live at the headwaters of the Vaupés and in Guaviare, some of them recent migrants, others having been transported there from downriver communities by rubber gatherers earlier in the century. Margarita Chaves, a Colombian anthropologist working in the region, told me that these Tukanoans continue to claim Tukanoan identity and try to live as their cousins downriver do, for example, continuing to practice language exogamy (personal communication 2000). These communities are far more involved in the coca trade and far more repressed by the military, the FARC, and, periodically, by paramilitary "cleansings," which can be extremely grisly.

Works Cited

Achito, Alberto

1997   "Autonomía territorial, jurisdicción especial indígena y conflictos interétnicos en el Pacífico." In *Ministerio de Justicia y del Derecho*. Ministerio del Interior/Drección General de Asuntos Indígenas.

Albert, Bruce

1997   "Territorialité, ethnopolitique et développement: À propos du mouvement indien en Amazonie Brésilienne." *Cahiers des Amériques Latines*: 177–210.

Alvarez, Sonia E., Evelina Dagnino, and Arturo Escobar, eds.

1998   Introduction: "The cultural and the political in Latin American social movements." In *Cultures of Politics and Politics of Cultures: Re-visioning Latin American Social Movements*. Boulder: Westview Press: 1–32.

Assies, Willem

2000   "Indigenous peoples and reform of the state in Latin America." In Willem Assies, Gemma van der Haar, and André Hoekema, eds, *The Challenge of Diversity: Indigenous Peoples and Reform of the State in Latin America*. Amsterdam: Thela Thesis: 3–22.

Avirama, Jesús, and Rayda Márquez

1995   "The indigenous movement in Colombia." In Donna Van Cott, ed., *Indigenous Peoples and Democracy in Latin America*. New York: St. Martin's Press.

Bodley, John

1990   *Victims of Progress.* 3rd edition. Mountain View, California: Mayfield Publishing Company.

Brysk, Alison

2000   *From tribal village to global village: Indian rights and international relations in Latin America.* Stanford: Stanford University Press.

1995   "Acting globally: Indian rights and international politics in Latin America." In Donna Lee Van Cott, ed., *Indigenous Peoples and Democracy in Latin America.* New York: St. Martin's: 29–51.

Consejo Regional del Cauca (CRIC)

1978   *Diez años de lucha: historia y documentos.* Bogota: CINEP (Centro de Investigación y Educación Popular) Serie Controversia.

De la Calle, Humberto

1994   "La carta del 91: Instrumento contemporáneo." *Lecturas Dominicales,* Nov. 13:8, 9.

Dirección General de Asuntos Indígenas

1998   *Los pueblos indígenas en el País y en América: Elementos de política colombiana e internacional.* Bogotá, Serie Retos de la Nación Diversa.

Dover, Robert V.H., and Joanne Rappaport

1996   Introduction. In Rappaport, J., ed., "Ethnicity reconfigured: Indigenous legislators and the Colombian Constitution of 1991." *Journal of Latin American Anthropology* 1, 2:2–18.

El Spectador

1988   "Asalto en Mitú y choques en la frontera." *El Espectador,* April 21.

1998   "Tregua indígena con 'paras': 60 días para evaluar papel de los indígenas en el conflicto." *El Espectador,* Sept. 25.

1998   "En Mitú quieren olvidar la tragedia." *El Espectador,* Dec. 1.

El Tiempo

1988   "La historia sí se repite: Violencia y comunidades indígenas." *El Tiempo,* Sept. 18

1998   "No habrá cese del fuego, dice 'Tirofijo'." *El Tiempo,* Nov. 4.

1998   "Selva perdió el rastro de su amor: Tenente indígena busca a su esposo." *El Tiempo,* Nov. 6.

Esnal, Luis

1998   "'Colombia violó nuestra soberanía': Brasil." *El Tiempo*, Nov. 4.

Findji, María Teresa

1992   "From resistance to social movement: The Indigenous Authorities Movement in Colombia." In Arturo Escobar and Sonia E. Alvarez, eds., *The Making of Social Movements in Latin America: Identity, Strategy, and Democracy.* Boulder: Westview Press, pp. 112–133.

Forero, Juan

2000   "Rightist squads in Colombia beating the rebels." *New York Times*, Dec. 5.

Goldman, Irving

1979   *The Cubeo: Indians of the Northwest Amazon*, 2nd ed. Urbana: University of Illinios Press.

Gow, David, and Joanne Rappaport

2002   "The indigenous public voice: The multiple idioms of modernity in native Cauca." In Kay B. Warren and Jean E, Jackson, eds., *Indigenous Movements, Self-Representation and the State in Latin America.* Austin: University of Texas Press.

Gros, Christian

2000   *Políticas de la etnicidad: Identidad, estado y modernidad.* Bogotá: Instituto Colombiano de Antropología e Historia.

1996   "Un ajustement à visage indien." In Jean-Michel Blanquer and Christian Gros, Coord., *La Colombie: à l'aube du troisième millénaire.* Paris: Éditions de L'IHEAL: 249–275.

1995   "Identitiés Indiennes, identités nouvelles": Quelques réflexions à partir du cas colombien. *Caravelle* 68.

1993   "Derechos indígenas y nueva Constitución en Colombia." *Análisis Político* 19, Mayo-Agosto: 8–24.

1991   *Colombia Indígena: Identidad Cultural y Cambio Social.* Bogotá: Fondo Editorial CEREC.

Grueso, Libia, Carlos Rosero, and Arturo Escobar

1998   "The process of black community organizing in the southern Pacific coast region of Colombia." In Sonia E. Alvarez, Evelina Dagnino, and Arturo Escobar, eds., *Cultures of Politics and Politics of Cultures: Re-visioning Latin American Social Movements.* Boulder: Westview: 196–219.

Jackson, Jean

2002 "Contested discourses of authority in Colombian national indigenous politics: The 1996 summer takeovers." In Kay Warren and Jean Jackson, eds, *Indigenous Movements, Self-Representation and the State in Latin America*. Austin: University of Texas Press.

1996 "The impact of recent national legislation in the Vaupés region of Colombia." *Journal of Latin American Anthropology*, 1, 2:120–151.

Jimeno, Myriam

1985 "Cauca: Las armas de lo sagrado." In *Estado y Minorías Étnicas en Colombia*, Myriam Jimeno and Adolfo Triana Antorveza, eds., Bogotá: Editorial Gente Nueva: 149–212.

Jimeno, Myriam, and Adolfo Triana

1985 "El estado y la política indigenista." In *Estado y Minorías Étnicas en Colombia*, Myriam Jimeno and Adolfo Triana Antorveza, eds., Bogotá: Editorial Gente Nueva: 65–143.

León Restrepo, Orlando

1998 "Para Mitú la guerra era muy lejana." *El Tiempo* Nov. 8.

Ministerio de Justicia y del Derecho, Ministerio del Interior/Drección General de Asuntos Indígenas

1997 *"Del olvido surgimos para traer nuevas esperanzas": La jurisdicción especial indígena*. Bogotá.

Murillo, Mario

1996 "Confronting the dilemmas of political participation." *NACLA* 29, 5:21–22.

Padilla, Guillermo

1996 "La ley y los pueblos indígenas en Colombia." *Journal of Latin American Anthropology* 1, 2:78–97.

Pineda, Roberto

1984 "La reivindicación del Indio en el pensamiento social Colombiano (1850–1950)." In J. Arocha and N.S. de Friedemann, eds., *Un siglo de investigación social: Antropología en Colombia*. Bogotá: ETNO: 197–252.

Pizarro, Eduardo

1997 "Hacia un sistema multipartidista? Las terceras fuerzas en Colombia Hoy." *Análisis político*, 31, May–Aug: 82–104.

1989   "Los orígenes del movimiento armado comunista en Colombia." *Análisis Político* 7, May–Aug.

Ramírez, María Clemencia

2001   *Entre el estado y la guerrilla: Identidad y ciudadanía en el movimiento de los campesinos cocaleros del Putumayo.* Bogotá: Instituto Colombiano de Antropología e Historia.

Ramos, Alcida Rita

1998   *Indigenism: Ethnic politics in Brazil.* Madison: The University of Wisconsin Press.

Rappaport, Joanne

1990   *The politics of memory: Native historical interpretation in the Colombian Andes.* Cambridge: Cambridge University Press.

Rojas Curieux, Tulio

1997   "La traducción de la Constitución de la República de Colombia a lenguas indígenas." In Ministerio de Justicia y del Derecho/Dirección General de Asuntos Indígenas, *"Del olvido surgimos para traer nuevas esperanzas": La jurisdicción especial indígena.* Bogotá: 229–244.

Roldán Ortega, Roque

2000   *Pueblos indígenas y leyes en Colombia: Aproximación crítica al estudio de su pasado y su presente.* Bogotá: Tercer Mundo.

Salcedo, Mauro

1998   "Indígenas sionas denuncian su extinción en el Putumayo." *El Espectador*, March 2.

Sánchez, Esther

2000   "The tutela-system as a means of transforming the relations between the state and the indigenous peoples of Colombia." In Willem Assies, Gemma van der Haar, and André Hoekema, eds., *The challenge of diversity: Indigenous peoples and reform of the state in Latin America.* Amsterdam: Thela Thesis: 223–245.

1998   *Justicia y pueblos indígenas de Colombia.* Bogotá: Universidad Nacional de Colombia.

1997   "Conflicto entre la jurisdicción especial indígena y la jurisdicción ordinaria (enfoque antropológico)." In Ministerio de Justicia y del Derecho/Dirección General de Asuntos Indígenas, *"Del olvido surgimos para traer nuevas esperanzas": La jurisdicción especial indígena.* Bogotá: 287–292.

Stoll, David

1982   *Fishers of men or founders of empire? The Wycliffe Bible Translators in Latin America.* London: Zed Press.

Triana Antorveza, Adolfo

1978   "El estatuto indígena o la nueva encomienda bonapartista." *Controversia* 79. Bogotá, CINEP: 29–41.

Unidad Indígena

1993   "Los Kankuamo: Reencuentro con sus raíces." No. 105, Aug 10.

Van Cott, Donna Lee

2000   *The friendly liquidation of the past: The politics of diversity in Latin America.* Pittsburgh: University of Pittsburgh Press.

Wade, Peter

1993   *Blackness and race mixture: The dynamics of racial identity in Colombia.* Baltimore: The Johns Hopkins University Press.

Acronyms

ANC	*Asamblea Nacional Constituyente,* National Constituent Assembly
CRIC	*Consejo Regional Indígena del Cauca,* Regional Indigenous Council of Cauca
CRIVA	*Consejo Regional Indígena del Vaupés,* Vaupés Regional Indigenous Council
DAI	*División de Asuntos Indígenas,* Division of Indigenous Affairs
ELN	*Ejército Nacional de Liberación,* National Liberation Army
ETIS	*Entidad Territorial Indígena,* Indigenous Territorial Entity
FARC	*Fuerzas Armadas Revolucionarias Colombianas,* Revolutionary Armed Forces of Colombia
INCORA	*Instituto Nacional Colombiana de Reforma Agraria,* National Colombian Institute for Agrarian Reform
MAQL	*Movimiento Armado Quintín Lame,* Quintí Lame Armed Movement
NGO	Non-governmental organization
ONIC	*Organización Nacional de Indígenas de Colombia,* National Organization of Colombian Indians
UNICEF	United Nations International Children's Emergency Fund

5

The Politics of Identity and Cultural Difference in the Colombian Amazon: Claiming Indigenous Rights in the Putumayo Region[1]

María Clemencia Ramírez

Ethnicity in Colombia's Amazon region has become a central concept in the formation of a cultural politics of difference, shaped by and in contestation to state policies. The state's differential legislative treatment of the indigenous population, in relation to other social groups, has resulted in distinct constructions and negotiations of identities. This differential legislation has produced conflicts not only between *colonos*[2] and indigenous groups, but among indigenous groups around the issue of authenticity—"real" Indianness and the degree to which leaders truly represent their constituency. To illustrate these processes, I will consider two cases taking place in the department of Putumayo, located in the eastern part of the Colombian Amazon region, a frontier colonization area.

The first case concerns the emergence of a new indigenous group called the Quillacinga-Pasto, which is located in the Valley of Sibundoy (upper Putumayo region), an area traditionally inhabited by the Inga and Kamsá indigenous groups (see map 1). The second case involves the Cofanes, whose communities are located in the main coca cultivation area in the lower Putumayo region, also the location of major oil reserves (see map 2).

Upper Putumayo is constructed in relationship and contraposition to Lower Putumayo according to historical variables and to their respective indices of violence. Upper Putumayo (in the northwestern end of the Putumayo department) comprises the municipalities of Santiago, Colón, San Francisco, and Sibundoy, all located in the Sibundoy

Valley (see map 5-1). Since the end of the nineteenth century the valley has been the center of activities for Capuchin missionaries, who built and maintained primary and secondary schools that still exist today. People in the valley do not identify with the violence that characterizes Lower Putumayo since coca is not grown in Upper Putumayo; dairy farming and milk processing are the principal economic activities in Upper Putumayo, and guerrillas pass through but are not based there. The same holds true for Mocoa, the department's seat of government.

Valle del Guamués (La Hormiga), Puerto Asis, Orito, Puerto Caicedo, San Miguel (La Dorada), and Puerto Guzmán, located in Lower Putumayo (see map 2), are the municipalities defined by the growing of coca and are home to Fronts 48 and 32 of the FARC. Among them, Valle del Guamués (La Hormiga) and San Miguel (La Dorada), places where the Cofanes are located, are most stigmatized as violent and most associated with the coca economy. The Cofanes who cultivated coca as a traditional crop have also been cultivating it for commercial purposes since the 1980s; as a result, they have been affected by the state actions against coca cultivation.[3] However, the concentration of homicides in the Lower Putumayo towns coincides not only with the existence of a coca economy, but also with an ongoing armed conflict. Since 1997, paramilitarism has become a more prominent political actor in Putumayo, sharpening political violence. As a result, the civilian and indigenous populations are caught within a web of confrontations among the guerrillas, the paramilitaries, and the army, and are continually harassed. Death threats are the most common human rights violations in the department, coming from all three armed groups.[4] As a result, the Cofanes have requested the human rights defenders, governments institutions, and national and international NGOs to take actions in "respect of our indigenous territories and protections of our lives" (*Declaración del Pueblo Cofán y los Cabildos Indígenas del Valle del Guamués y San Miguel*, January 2001).

In this context, the Cofán Foundation of Traditional Authorities ZIO-AI, created by the initiative of the elders in 1998, has been directed to search for alternative ways to achieve peace, to find solutions to the conflict that lives in the region, and to guarantee the physical, economic, and cultural survival of the eighteen indigenous communities situated in the rural area of the municipalities of Valle del Guamués (La Hormiga) and San Miguel (La Dorada).

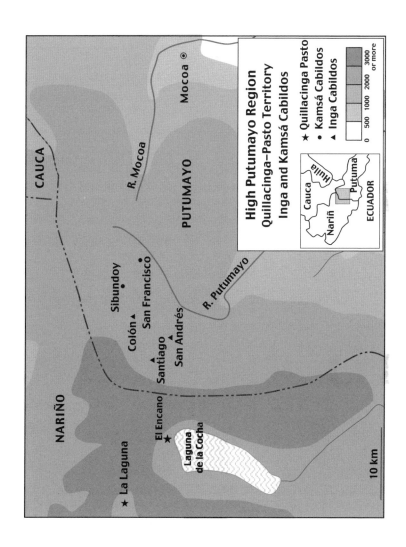

Map 5-1

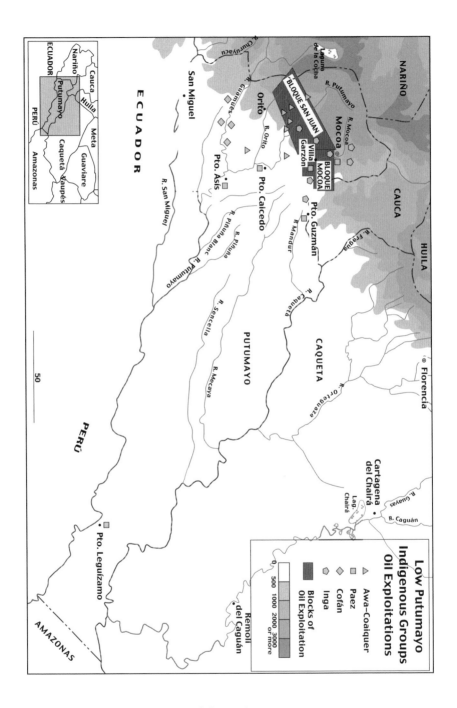

Map 5-2

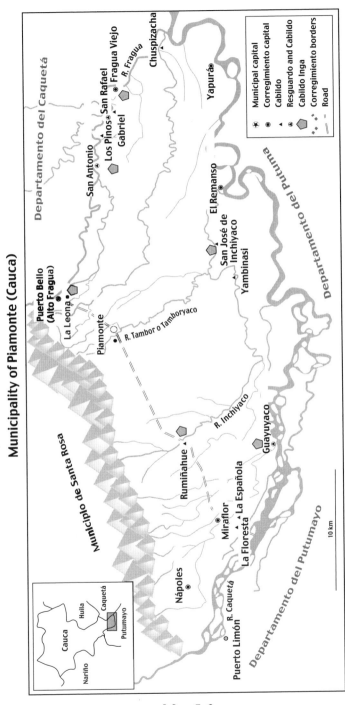

Map 5-3

Colombian Legislation and Indigenous Rights

The new 1991 constitution recognizes the ethnic and cultural diversity of the nation and the right of Indian groups and ethnic minorities to maintain, perpetuate, use, and defend their patrimony as distinct populations. This recognition is the result of the nation's indigenous communities' long-standing struggle to maintain their rights as minorities. The constitution also assigns special rights to the indigenous people, such as bilingual education, university scholarships, free health service, exclusion from military service, and two seats in the Congress, one in the Senate and one in the House of Representatives. Protection of communal lands and of associative and solidarity forms of ownership are also part of the package. Titles to communally owned lands and *resguardos*[5] are inalienable and nontransferable (Arts. 63 and 329). These norms not only assure the stability of indigenous landholdings, but also limit the accessibility of resguardos for public works, state-sponsored mineral exploitation, etc. (DNP 1993, 15).

The new constitution specifies that exploitation of natural resources in indigenous territories be carried out "without affecting the cultural, social and economic integrity of the indigenous communities" (Art. 330). To achieve this aim, "the Government will promote participation of the representatives of each of the indigenous communities involved in the decisions concerning exploitation of natural resources" (Art. 330). In addition, Law 21 of 1991, which ratifies the 1989 agreements contained in Convention 169 of the International Labor Organization regarding rights of indigenous peoples, states that indigenous peoples have the right to participate in the use, administration, and conservation of their natural resources. Although the subsoil is property of the state, before authorizing or initiating a plan for exploration or production, the government must consult the indigenous peoples inhabiting the territory in order to ascertain whether their interests are affected and, if so, to what extent (Art. 15). This general principle has been implemented into general Law 99 of December 1993, in what has been called the *Proceso de consulta previa* (Previous Consultation Process), established for both indigenous and black communities so that any decisions taken regarding the exploitation of natural resources have to occur after consultation with representatives of those communities (Art. 76). This article has been made operational by various decrees from the Ministry of the Environment (Decree 1397 of August 1996 and 833 of March 1997), which define diverse types of impacts depending on which kind of project is being considered, as well as the requirements of the Previous Consultation Process, whose main purposes are:

1) To instruct the state on the way it must meet its legal and constitutional obligations to respect the ethnic and cultural integrity of the indigenous peoples.

2) To inform traditional indigenous authorities and organizations about the characteristics of the national and regional projects that can affect their communities, and to elicit their point of view concerning such projects, including their expectations about participating, and to reach an agreement about the terms under which the project will be carried out.

Indigenous participation is guaranteed by means of consultation with *cabildos mayores y menores*,[6] indigenous traditional authorities, their legal representatives,[7] and any legally constituted local, regional, or national indigenous organization.[8] To be legally constituted, an organization has to obtain its *personería jurídica,* indicating that a number has been assigned by the Ministry of the Interior granting the organization legal status.

Finally, following the Previous Consultation Process and approval, the projects have to be adapted to the requirements imposed by this intercultural context, incorporating the conditions negotiated with the indigenous peoples (Dirección General de Asuntos Indígenas 1998).

The Previous Consultation Process does not need to take place in peasant communities, known as "civil communities," located inside these indigenous territories. Moreover, when exploitation of natural resources or any work on a region's infrastructure (like roads, electricity, etc.) is going to be carried out in peasant areas, the law states that community members only have to be informed. Peasant organizations such as the *Juntas de Acción Comunal* (Community Councils) are merely convoked and notified of the project; they are not taken into account when possible negative impacts are being evaluated or damages settled. Negotiations are done individually, by talking with each affected family and arranging their relocation if necessary.

The above is an example of how the new constitution and its accompanying legislation ignore important segments of the population, such as peasant communities living within Indian territories. These peasant groups, characterized by a low socio-economic status and a lack of land, educational opportunities, and health care, are suddenly faced with the necessity of defining their identity and fighting for equal rights—or, more accurately, "the right to have rights" (Dagnino 1997). Such is the case of the local-born non-indigenous population of the Putumayo, children of the older generations of colonos who came during the first wave at the beginning of the 20th century and who, for almost a century, have shared with various native indigenous groups the region that extends from the eastern Andean slopes to the Amazon lowlands of the Putumayo and Caquetá departments.

The new constitution has radically shifted the balance of power between the indigenous groups and the colonos and challenges the colonos' perception of their cultural identity and relationships with their neighbors, which at times results in conflict. The colonos face challenges not only from the Colombian state and extractive industries but from the Indian population that has been granted a special place in the national political arena. In all the Constitutional Amendment articles, the emphasis is on the ethnic groups or Indian communities, culturally differentiated by language, customs, and collectively owned property.

Thus, the assertion of distinct traditions, not only by indigenous but also by non-indigenous groups, as a political strategy to gain a national political space has in effect been promoted by the Colombian state. Several authors have analyzed the effects of this ten-year-old process in different regions and among various ethnic groups.[9]

Case 1: The Emergence of the "Quillacinga-Pasto" Indigenous Group

In the Valley of Sibundoy, two traditional Andean indigenous groups have been recognized since colonial times. From this period on, the Inga and the Kamsá have shared this territory, and they are politically organized into four Inga *cabildos* (San Andrés, Santiago, Colón, and San Pedro), and two Kamsá *cabildos* (Sibundoy and San Francisco). (See map 5-1.) Taita[10] Domingo, former governor of the Inga cabildo of Santiago, emphasizes that these six cabildos "are legally constituted, filling all the requirements that the law demands" (from the meeting held in the Santiago Cabildo, March 22, 1998). The assumption that cabildos and Indians exist by virtue of the state's legal system mediates all the discussion that has occurred among members of the Inga and Kamsá groups regarding the 1998 appearance of a new cabildo, the

Quillacinga-Pasto of the municipality of El Encano, located in the highlands of the valley near the Nariño department.

This new cabildo made its appearance during a Previous Consultation Process that dealt with paving a road between El Encano and Santiago. When the company in charge of the work asked the Indigenous Affairs Office of the Ministry of the Interior about which indigenous groups resided in the area, the Inga and Kamsá groups were named. However, on arriving at the Valley of Sibundoy, the company was informed of a new ethnic group, the Quillacinga-Pasto, whose governor had taken office authorized and recognized as such by the mayor of Santiago, the act that legitimizes the existence of an ethnic group.[11] Following this, the national Office of Indigenous Affairs had recognized the Quillacinga-Pasto as an indigenous group residing in the area and with whom the company should also conduct a Previous Consultation Process. When the company initiated the Consultation Process with this new group, the Kamsá and Inga of the Valley of Sibundoy protested, and open conflict began. Taita Domingo stated the problem as follows:

> ... as Inganos here [in Santiago] or the six cabildos here in the Valley, we have jurisdiction as far as Quilinsayaco (Páramo de Bordoncillo). I don't see why Olimpo [the governor of the Quillacinga-Pasto cabildo] has to go starting new cabildos. Don Olimpo is usurping our autonomy. We have to see that our autonomy is respected. As the real owners of this land, we have our own culture, our way of life, our rules, and for legislation we have our laws that are based on the Constitution, so the government respects our zone where we exist, our language, everything of ours is officially recognized because the government respects our jurisdiction where we exist. So now why isn't the law going to help us when another intruder comes in and just declares an imaginary cabildo? We have to decide this here, in the Association of Cabildos of the Valley. The Director of Indigenous Affairs of the Ministry of the Interior should come here to explain why her representative accepted the Quillacinga cabildo without knowing what's going on in the Valley. The six cabildos of the Valley are like a big family, the Kamsás and the Ingas. We as a people are the ones who can accept [or reject] it (Meeting held in the Santiago Cabildo, March 22, 1998).

The creation of the Quillacinga-Pasto cabildo is seen as a territorial threat because it does not appear to be linked to a specific bounded territory. And it is true that the Quillacinga-Pasto define themselves as inhabitants dispersed over the Valley of Sibundoy. To the question of how many settlements there were, the Quillacinga-Pasto governor answered:

> We are all united; for example we Quillacingas-Pastos living in the Sibundoy Valley, the Quillacingas-Pastos in the Carrizal zone, and the Quillacingas-Pastos in El Encano, La Laguna, Santa Clara, San Bernardo, Santa Isabel (Meeting in Santa Clara, March 15, 1998).

Taita Domingo's statement reveals how indigenous people have incorporated the national law framework as part of the definition of their ethnic identity. Rappaport (1990b), in her analysis of the indigenous groups of the Nariño department in the Andean region (Pastos), argued that for the national and local governments in Colombia, the Indian was perceived as a "legal category" instead of a "cultural being." Thus, recognition of Indian identities by the state was grounded in the existence or not of legal entities, such as the resguardos. This assumption was manipulated by state representatives in order to undermine and even deny the recognition of indigenous communities during the 1950s, 1960s, and 1970s. Paradoxically, today, this same argument is made by Taita Domingo to dispute the Quillacinga-Pasto ethnic identity.

A statement by another member of the Inga cabildo of Santiago, Taita Jesús, referring to the letter sent by the six cabildos to the Director of Indigenous Affairs rejecting the creation of the Quillacinga-Pasto cabildo, argues that their ancestral territory cannot be invaded by another ethnic group, and added that he was sure official authorities would defend his position. In addition, he finds it "curious" why the persons creating this cabildo could possibly be allowed to claim indigenous status today, given that in earlier times they persecuted indigenous people; "those people will be respected as persons, but not as cabildos or Indians, only as owners of property at the side of the road, property they have possessed for a long period of time." (Meeting in the Inga cabildo of Santiago, March 22, 1998.)

In sum, traditional cabildos justify their claims to rights as ethnic groups by relying on collective memory seen as materially inscribed in the territory. Rappaport (1990a, 9) has pointed out, for the case of another Indian group of the Andean region (Paez, or Nasa of Tierradento in the Cauca department), how these people "have encoded their history of struggle in their sacred geography, so that past meets present in the very terrain on which they live, farm, and walk. Memory has built upon memory, connecting events of the distant past, the more recent past, and the present in the topography of Tierradentro." Consequently, the Inga stipulate that the new cabildo Quillacinga-Pasto can be created only by circumscribing its territory between El Encano and Quilinsayaco, a completely different territory from the one inhabited and recognized by the Ingas and Kamsá. The words of Taita Domingo refer to the testament of the cacique Carlos Tamoabioy written in the eighteenth century, which states that the Inga and Kamsá territory in the Valley of Sibundoy was bought by the cacique Tamoabioy "for his Indians, Ingas and Kamsá and goes from the *páramo* to the Río Blanco in the Putumayo." Taita Domingo emphasizes that the cacique Tamoabioy never spoke of the Quillacinga. This argument spells out why the Ingas and Kamsá can recognize the new ethnic group only if it is located in a different territory. To define this other territory they refer to oral tradition:

> My grandfather always said that they had a cabildo in El Encano [name of a lake in the Andean area of Nariño]. There was a governor, a mayor, everything. They treated the people here as *compadres*. Before, the Inganos worked as guards and they had their post at El Encano, because from El Tábano to here belonged [to the cabildo]. Some ambitious leaders let friends in and they lost cattle and money, and the people from La Laguna, called *Laguneros*, came back. Otherwise it would belong to us, the Inga. So what we have is we control the valley from Quilinsayaco to here; that's why. So we and the six cabildos all agree that we would open up the dialog, as it should be, that the *campesinos'* [peasants] interests would be defended according to our laws, even though they don't belong to the cabildo. You know you can get along here as a campesino, because the law provides compensation for their losses, too. They can be taken care of; there's no need to shake things up by forming a new cabildo (Meeting at the Inga cabildo of Santiago, March 22, 1998).

Oral tradition does trace the genealogy of a people referred to as the Laguneros (from the lake called the Encano in Nariño department).

Even though the Inga's ancestors considered the Encano to be Inga territory, this territory is said to have been occupied a long time ago by foreigners, the Laguneros, and from then on the Inga territory was redefined. If the new cabildo jurisdiction is defined as the area of the Encano, the traditional cabildos say they can accept this new ethnic group. This example demonstrates how migration by groups leads to redrawing the boundaries of their territories, producing in turn a renegotiation of identities. Thus, spatiality is at the core of the Inga's resistance to recognizing the new Quillacinga-Pasto group, and it is through the delimitation of a specific territory for the new ethnic group that the Inga's authorities propose the conflict be solved.[12] Taita Domingo is implicitly stressing that indigenous people have succeeded in being recognized as citizens with special rights only after many struggles. For Taita Domingo it is not fair that colonos benefit from Indians' protracted struggles, which is the case of the leader of the new Quillacinga-Pasto group who wanted to run for governor of the Inga cabildo of Santiago. Despite being married to an Inga woman, he was not accepted as a candidate because he was not an Indian. Having been rejected in this way, and in order to gain access to power and certain privileges, he decided to promote the idea of creating the Quillacinga-Pasto cabildo among the colonos of the Valley of Sibundoy.

The Quillacinga-Pasto, grandchildren of colonos who came to the Putumayo from the Andean department of Nariño during the first wave of colonization between 1900 and 1946, are constructing the specifics of their claim to be an indigenous group by stating that they are descendants of the Pasto ethnic group of the central area of Nariño, and the pre-hispanic Quillacinga group that inhabited the northeastern area of Nariño and the Valley of Sibundoy. "Authentic" indigenous last names, such as Botina and Chanaque, have been listed by the governor of the Quillacinga-Pasto cabildo, Olimpo, and are a prerequisite to become a member of the Quillacinga-Pasto cabildo. This is the way Olimpo assures the linkage with the Nariño ancestors, creating an "authentic" indigenous identity in consequence. Moreover, in one of the meetings held with the official representatives of the Office of Indigenous Affairs of the Ministry of the Environment, the governor of the Quillacinga-Pasto cabildo explained that the socio-cultural study that had to be carried out by an anthropologist during the Previous Consultation Process would help them reconstruct and establish their traditions. The anthropologist was asked to help define their characteristics and traditions as an ethnic group, drawing on an investigation by an archaeologist and ethnohistorian documenting the Quillacinga and Pasto pre-hispanic territories, on which the new community was basing their claim. The governor of the Quillacinga-Pasto said that from that time on, indigenous rights would be fully exercised because they were no longer "ignorant Indians,"[13] meaning that an identity suppressed and hidden for centuries had re-emerged.[14] This case is an example of how ethnicity[15] can, in certain circumstances, turn into a political stance.

Case 2: The Cofanes' Appropriation of the Previous Consultation Process

As it has been pointed out, the Cofanes' location in the Putumayo department coincides not only with an area containing coca plantations but also with major oil reserves. In this case, negotiations with the oil companies over exploration and exploitation of oil reserves located in indigenous territories become a central debate not only between the region's inhabitants and the oil companies and government representatives, but among the local, regional, and national leaders of the indigenous movement as well. The interests of the movements' national leaders often diverge significantly from those of the regional and local indigenous organizations, a situation clearly revealed during negotiations with the oil companies, and during interactions between the regional and local organizations. Conflict takes place within the communities over the following issues: Which is the most representative organization? With whom should the state or the private companies negotiate? How are the indigenous communities' representatives elected and on what basis is authority determined? All of these issues are mediated and shaped by recent Colombian legislation.

As a result of the preferential treatment given to the region's indigenous population following the Previous Consultation Process legislation discussed above, the government has taken the Cofanes' claims into account. Pile's (1997) concept of a politics of location[16] helps us understand how these indigenous groups are empowered, in particular the oil companies having to permanently negotiate with the Cofanes' representatives to be able to continue with their work. Oil exploration and exploitation have depended on the establishment of new resguardos or the amplification of existing ones, because the indigenous groups demand land before signing any agreement.[17] Thus, the Cofanes, known as one of the indigenous groups of the Amazon region most affected—numerically and culturally—by the waves of colonization, have been able to redefine their political struggles in response to their location in an oil exploitation area. This location and the Previous Consultation Processes that has to take place for the petroleum companies to be able to work, have meant that the Cofanes had to be taken into account by the state. Thus, instead of disappearing as an ethnic group, as had been expected, the Cofanes emerge as an empowered and revitalized community, stressing their indigenous identity as a political stance.

I will discuss two Previous Consultation Processes that involved the Cofanes during 1997 and 1998: the first, in Orito, was with the Canadian Oil Company, and the second, in La Hormiga, concerned the construction of the International Bridge over the San Miguel river on the frontier with Ecuador. These consultation processes illustrate the problem of representativeness within indigenous organizations. I will also draw upon an earlier Consultation Process between the National Petroleum Company (Ecopetrol), and the indigenous groups (mainly Ingas) that inhabit the area of Bloque San Juan (Villagarzón), to illustrate the oil company's position and that of the regional and national indigenous organizations regarding oil exploitation in the Putumayo.

In contrast to the Valley of Sibundoy, the indigenous communities of the Putumayo lowlands never had the Andean political and territorial institutions such as the cabildos and colonial resguardos.[18] Among the Cofanes, the traditional governance structure was made up of shamans known as "Curacas" and "Taitas" and councils of elder men. And rather than resguardos, in 1966 the government designated indigenous territories in the lowlands as *reservas indígenas*, as provisional collective territories. Triana (1992, 112) states:

> The main idea was that the indigenous groups who didn't have resguardo lands but had possession of their ancestral lands, were located on *terrenos baldíos* (no-man's land) belonging to the nation (the usual case in the Orinoco and Amazonian areas and in Chocó on the Pacific coast), lands that could be allocated to them as long as it didn't affect the economic activities of the colonos and they weren't designated for a national park or forest reserve.

Between 1966 and 1972, 74 reservas indígenas were created in the Amazon, Orinoquia, and Pacific regions of Colombia, and by 1977, these reservas began to be designated as resguardos (Arango y Sánchez 1989). By 1996, 121 resguardos had been established in the Amazon region (Ariza, Ramírez y Vega 1998, 109). In 1988, the cabildo became the form of governance for all indigenous territories nationwide (Decree 2001), definitively formalized in the new constitution of 1991, following the trend toward centralizing political offices. And beginning in 1988, along with the establishment of cabildos in the Amazon region, the office of *capitán*[19] was transformed into *gobernador*, in order for the state to have visible indigenous representatives to negotiate with.

In February 1997, when the Canadian Oil Company began a Previous Consultation Process to permit explorations in the area of La Hormiga, Orito, and Puerto Caicedo, 21 cabildos were on the books, but by the end of the month, 25 cabildos were listed. Indigenous communities can organize cabildos without having a resguardo,[20] and through the cabildo institution indigenous groups gain a negotiation stance with the state. Indeed, while in the Valley of Sibundoy there are two resguardos and six cabildos, in the Cofán area, there are twenty-five cabildos and only five resguardos.

In addition, Canadian Oil encountered members of other ethnic groups such as Awas, Paeces, and Emberas, who since the 1970s had been migrating from the departments of Nariño and Cauca in the Andean region and Chocó in the Pacific, who had had to flee from their communities because of violence, development programs, loss of lands, or even in response to traditional settlement patterns (e.g., Paeces considered the piedmont area of the Andes as part of their traditional territory, so they considered themselves entitled to migrate and occupy the lowlands) (Ariza, Ramírez y Vega 1998, 100–102). These communities saw the Amazon region as offering the possibility of reconstituting themselves as ethnic groups, and they are also organized into cabildos. As such, they legally must be included in the Consultation Process, although the companies' representatives always pose questions regarding their recent appearance in the region. These ethnic groups are fighting to establish resguardos of their own.[21]

The first step of a Consultation Process is to carry out a socio-economic study of the indigenous communities in the area where the work is going to take place. This document is called a Document of Valuation and Environmental Management (DEMA), and it has to present the possible negative as well positive impacts of the proposed project. Once completed, it is presented to the communities' representatives for their approval. An Act of Agreement is signed stating clearly the obligations of the company to the communities. In the case of the negotiations with the Canadian Oil Company, the following local and regional representatives were present at the first meeting to discuss the DEMA document: Zonal Indigenous Organization of the Putumayo

(OZIP) and the local associations of cabildos, such as Association of Cabildos from Puerto Caicedo (ASOCIPCA), Association of Cabildos from Valle del Guamués (ASCINVAGUA), as well as some independent cabildo governors from other municipalities. Creating these regional and local associations during the 1990s was intended to strengthen the communities' negotiating power with official and private institutions. However, these centralized organizations tend to silence the voice of the communities. In this meeting, the discussions focused on previous experiences with other oil companies, in particular the damage they caused, and emphasis was placed on the need to create an indigenous committee to ensure that the agreements were carried out. However, local leaders stressed the need to expeditiously arrive at an agreement and not hold up the company's project.

A discussion about the rights of those indigenous people not organized into cabildos followed, and leaders suggested that they should form cabildos because an indigenous community lacking a cabildo was invisible to the state. Paradoxically, although national legislation supports indigenous autonomy and indigenous forms of government, it in fact favors the centralized cabildo as the only form of political organization authorized to establish dialogue and negotiations with indigenous communities. Members of the Cofán community pointed out the division and disorganization resulting from the continuous emergence of small cabildos, composed of 60 to 80 members, as compared to up to 3,000 members previously. One participant commented that although they had been more isolated before, there had been more solidarity.

An ONIC (National Indigenous Organization) representative attended the second meeting alongside the regional and local representatives. The purpose of the meeting was to sign the Agreement Act and elect the members of the supervising committee. As the meeting started and the record of the previous meeting was read, the ONIC representative questioned the way it was written and asked the oil company representatives to leave so the representative could to talk with the local leaders. After the oil people left, he told the local leaders that they were signing agreements about local issues, such as guaranteed employment, construction of schools, and financing training workshops, that were not in accordance with the agenda of the national indigenous movement. Although these agreements might be important locally, at the national level the indigenous organizations' main demand concerned land; he reminded them of how Cofanes had lost almost 80 percent of their ancestral land;[22] hence, if they signed the agreement they would be wasting a political opportunity to demand the establishment and enlargement of resguardos.

> We must make general proposals because we indigenous people are also operating within a democracy. We're meeting here today in what should be the beginning of the process. We should keep in mind what happened with the 33,000 hectares of the Cofanes in the Guamués Valley. Environmental management is the study of our lives, of our land. It is we indigenous people who love and defend the land; we are born of the land and live off it. We can't sign any document that could affect us adversely. We should set a date to meet again (Meeting in Orito, February 1998).

This national leader not only questioned local leaders' decisions but also insisted on delaying the Consultation Process. Although he gestured to the ideal of democratic participation, he was in fact not letting the local leaders participate. Implicitly the ONIC representative was asking the local leaders not to betray the national indigenous movement. One of the representatives of the local associations of cabildos confronted him, telling him that national leaders always appear at the last minute to decide for the local communities, without having participated in the entire process. However, this man was not supported by the others; instead, one of the governors at the meeting; stood up to argue that indigenous peoples had rights "not because the government wanted us to have them but because we have struggled, we have organized strikes, and some have even given their lives." He concluded by stating that he supported following the "indigenous leader's guidance" in learning their rights (Meeting in Orito, February 10, 1998).

This example illustrates the reason the oil companies had been complaining about the way that the meetings were managed. A regional newspaper, writing about an earlier Consultation Process with Ecopetrol, in the area of Villagarzón, stated that although there had been several meetings between Ecopetrol and the regional authorities and indigenous people, "they haven't come to an agreement, since on each occasion indigenous people came forward with new leaders and new petitions." The paper also quotes an official of Ecopetrol saying that "he didn't understand the attitude of the indigenous people, since in previous meetings they have accepted some agreements and then they come back with new things and completely different petitions and new representatives" (*La Nación*, December 1996, 12). The article continues,

> the authorities have proved that many of the indigenous groups that express disagreement with the Ecopetrol project aren't from communities in the department and have been brought from other departments. The same holds true for the communications received by Ecopetrol, which come from people not identified with the indigenous groups of Putumayo. All this represents incalculable economic losses for Ecopetrol. A few indigenous people have been able to create an obstacle that has impeded progress on regional projects (*La Nación*, December 1996, 12).

Clearly, inconsistencies among the different levels of indigenous organization result in the obstruction of the oil companies' projects, threatening their financial solvency. Although indigenous representatives and decisions do change through the different stages of the Consultation Process, what has to be underscored is that the national indigenous movement has interpreted the recognition of cultural diversity in the national legislation as a political opportunity to demand and recover what has been taken from indigenous people ever since the conquest, and from this perspective, nothing the companies offer is ever enough. In response, in order to proceed with their projects, the companies are trying to delegitimize the indigenous representatives; in this case, as in the other, one of their arguments is the fact that indigenous people have come from other parts of the country and are not natives to the Putumayo.

As it was pointed out, even though the indigenous groups have designated their territories as neutral zones in the paramilitary-guerrilla conflict, this decision has not been respected by the armed groups in conflict. Not only have violent actions against indigenous leaders taken place, but also opposition to indigenous groups' interests. For example, Ecopetrol asked the FARC to pressure the OZIP Executive Committee to sign the agreement to begin work in Villagarzón (Bloque San Juan). In February of 1997, the Organization of the Indigenous People of the Colombian Amazon region (OPIAC, representing Vaupés, Putumayo, Caquetá, Amazonas, Guaviare and Guainia) protested and demanded that Ecopetrol cease employing such tactics. This is an example of how Ecopetrol, like other actors in the area (i.e., colonos, indigenous people, political parties), use the FARC to their own advantage. FARC's intrusion can be explained in two ways. First, FARC intervened because they stood to benefit financially if an oil deal was signed. Such an outcome actually happened in Piamonte (The southern "boot" of Cauca department) during the beginning of oil explorations in 1990. The Inga groups,[23] trying to oppose the projects, were stopped by FARC. The head of the colono Community Council told me that he thought FARC was looking for money from the oil company instead of services for the communities and that he presumed that the oil company must be giving the FARC a monthly amount of money to authorize oil exploration. A second possible explanation is FARC's wanting to support the colonos, who, as we will see, counter to the indigenous organizations' stance, wanted the oil company to begin oil exploration and give them jobs.

OPIAC also refused to recognize an agreement signed between the oil company and the cabildos of the Bloque San Juan, a consequence of the Second Congress of the OZIP in February 1997, when it was decided that oil exploration should be stopped for a period of five years, during which the government had to enlarge the resguardos as well as protect the economically important natural resources. The OZIP Congress also specified that a program to train and strengthen the indigenous organizations must be established in order to understand and deal with the impact of the oil projects (*Pronunciamiento* of OZIP and OPIAC 1997).

The colonos of the region used their *Juntas de Acción Comunal* (Community Action Committees) to undercut the indigenous position:

> The whites and the Juntas de Acción Comunal from the districts of La Castellana and Hualchayaco, among other places, sent a document to Ecopetrol in which they officially lent their support to the petroleum project in the Bloque San Juan. There is also the expectation of employment in the municipality of Villagarzón and more than fifty surrounding districts that will benefit from petroleum operations (*La Nación*, December 23, 1996, 12).

Clearly, the colonos and local officials perceived the indigenous people as obstacles to developing the Putumayo, and the authorities in the area—mayors, council members and even the governor—reminded the indigenous representatives that "their rights end where the rights of others begin" and that the indigenous organizations "are opposing projects that will benefit a large number of Putumayans" (*La Nación*, December 23, 1996, 12).

That the indigenous organizations were aware that both colonos and local officials held this perspective is clear in the following quote by Taita Querubin Queta in a meeting between the Cofán and various state representatives of the central level:

> Don't think that we're the obstacles to developing this place. We also want to be given what belongs to us, our rights, the land. In reality this region was ours, the Cofanes, which is why we insist on respect as the Cofán people. We were here first and we haven't disappeared. We still have our traditional clothing and our language. Look at us. You can see with your own eyes that we haven't completely lost our culture (Meeting in La Hormiga, May 1998).

At the beginning of the meeting, Taita Querubín spoke in Cofán; the leaders sitting in the main table were wearing Indian clothes, and a Cofán group performed their music. By representing themselves as "authentic Indians," the Cofán were establishing their ancestral rights to their Putumayo lands.

At this meeting, Aureliano, the representative of OZIP, supported the Cofán demand for recovery of their ancestral land[24] and emphasized the obligation of the state to bring this about:

> I think that a viable proposal would be to create a resguardo throughout the territory of the reserve, and to later establish plans for annual or biannual review of the territory, to buy back plots held by non-indigenous landholders. What the state must do, through INCORA [Colombian Institute of Agrarian Reform], is safeguard the ancestral land rights of the indigenous communities in the zone. . . . It would also be necessary to set up information sessions for the colonos, because some of them have the wrong idea, thinking that if the resguardo is created they're going to lose their rights. Really their situation is the same for them, whether in a reserve or a resguardo, neither better nor worse. Their land titles would maintain a similar legal status (Comments of OZIP leader in a meeting on May 13, 1998).

In the case of the Bloque San Juan in Villagarzón, the confrontation between colonos and indigenous people made it necessary for

Ecopetrol to finance three workshops to reconcile both sides: one for Indians, one for colonos, and one for both. The goal of these workshops was to "sensitize the colonos about indigenous rights and teach them to tolerate each other and live together in harmony" *(Acta de la reunión de concertación Bloque de perforación exploratoria* San Juan, Agosto de 1997, 3).

This kind of threat generated interethnic conflict not only in the Putumayo but in other places, such as Piamonte, where FARC had had to intervene to stop a confrontation between colonos and indigenous groups. In this case, the colonos, who had been living in the region for 30 years, were talking about arming themselves in order to defend their lands from the indigenous people. FARC made the colonos aware that this confrontation and factionalization would only benefit the petroleum company and, moreover, paramilitaries would be able to gain access to the region. Fighting each other meant loosing the combined strength they needed to confront outside intervention. FARC emphasized that this confrontation had to be resolved in order to prevent open conflict (interview with a *colono* in Piamonte, 1997).

Another issue discussed by Aureliano, the OZIP leader, had to do with interculturality:

The [Cofán] indigenous community has been organized and has its identity, even if there are a lot of cultural influences from other social groups, because they're valid too. We can't stay buried in our own culture. Interculturality is important, but taking your own identity into account (Comments by OZIP leader in the meeting of May 13, 1998).

What we learn from the above quote is that OZIP wants to reaffirm the Indianness of the Cofán, but not at the expense of their relationship with the government and the colonos in the region. The intercultural relationship to which Aureliano refers is made concrete for the national indigenous leaders in the *planes de vida* (life plans). These development plans are elaborated by each ethnic group under the guidance provided by the Office of Indigenous Affairs of the Ministry of the Interior. These planes de vida are instituted as "an instrument for culture and identity strengthening" (ONIC-IICA—Instituto Interamericano de Cooperación para la Agricultura 1998, 15), and as such, each ethnic group is expected to propose its particular customized plan. Subsequently the plans must be coordinated with the municipality's and the department's development plans. The indigenous leaders conceive of the planes de vida as "proposals for the future that respond to the new needs that the relationship with the non-Indians has imposed on indigenous people, in order to maintain the equilibrium that provides sense to our continuation in the world" (ONIC–IICA 1998, 13). ONIC gives four reasons supporting the elaboration of a plan de vida: 1) strengthening ethnic identity; 2) participation in official decision making; 3) open discussion of indigenous needs and the possibility of proposing alternative solutions; 4) coming up with strategies to construct a new type of relationship with social actors at different levels: first, internally, among members of the community; second, locally, with other ethnic groups, social groups and public and private entities working in each indigenous territory; and third, with public and private institutions. Finally, ONIC states that it is the sole national representative of the region's indigenous groups (ONIC-IICA 1998, 14).

In other words, ONIC wants to have the final say in any negotiation with the state or oil companies. This position has been established as a political practice at all the different levels (national, regional and local) of indigenous organizations. It is in this context that we can understand why OZIP negotiated a major Integral Development Plan for Indigenous People supported financially by Ecopetrol (U.S.$25,000). Because it is a regional plan and thus needs to be approved by the national organizations' plan for the national indigenous movement, this departmental plan constrains the local planes de vida proposed by different ethnic groups.

In order to gain regional and national representation without the mediation of the established regional and national indigenous organizations, the local Cofán communities held the first Congress of the Cofán People in March of 1998, creating *La Mesa Permanente de Trabajo por el Pueblo Cofán* (Permanent Council Working for the Cofán People). This Council consists of the traditional authorities, the cabildo governors, and two members representing the community, totaling 22 members; its purpose is to centralize the decision making regarding the Previous Consultation Processes and state intervention in their area.[25] The first action taken by this Mesa was to convoke a meeting with all the state representatives working in the area to announce the creation of this new entity and to find out about each official institution's projects. It was made clear that any future government action needed the Mesa's prior approval; as the Mesa was the sole legitimate representative entity, no other organizations need be consulted. The Cofanes were indirectly legitimizing an assumption held by the oil companies and the state that they need to negotiate only with the "real" natives, and not with other immigrant ethnic groups. In sum, empowerment is gained through assertions of "nativeness"; when successful, inter-ethnic confrontation results.

The government is clearly promoting centralization of power within the various indigenous communities, as well as the bureaucratization of their organizations. Although the need to support the autonomy and the indigenous forms of government is explicitly stated in the new constitution and accompanying decrees, in practice, the legally recognized leaders are not only designated by the government as the "real" representatives, but within the communities these leaders play the role of mediator between the national government and the traditional leaders of the indigenous communities. Clearly, as Dover and Rappaport have pointed out,

> the danger in Colombia is that governmental and developmental agencies, as well as the indigenous elite, begin, increasingly, to 'adjudicate the traditional,' leading to a diminishing of traditional authority and the redefinition of the politics of indigenous resistance in terms of electoral politics (Dover and Rappaport 1996a, 13).

The central point I want to make is that, as legislation is enacted recognizing and reifying *usos y costumbres* (indigenous traditional practices and customs), an elite of indigenous leaders legally recognized by the state is fortifying and reproducing national political practices, such as the centralization of decision making. Moreover this elite is defining, in dialogue with the national government rather than local leaders, what is an ethnic group and what are its members' needs. As we saw in the second case, because different instances of representation mentioned above do not always agree, a discourse around the definition of representation occurs when a Previous Consultation Process takes place, resulting in internal division and factionalization. The perception of the indigenous communities as collectivities with no interior conflicts, where common interest is assumed, derives from an idealized image of indigenous peoples and a reification of ethnicity. The result is that community members often feel their voice is not heard, because the indigenous elite monopolizes the discussion, imposing an "ethnic" discourse as well as certain indigenous fight for rights—a central one being the fight for land. As a result, this hegemonic "ethnic" discourse is homogenizing and shaping the negotiations being conducted with the state institutions' or private companies' representatives.

To conclude, it is clear that state policies aimed at centralizing local political office and the creation of indigenous organizations on the national, regional, and local level had two unintended consequences in this region: first, since the most important negotiations are taking place among the leaders at the regional and national levels, community voices are seldom heard. This is paradoxical because these leaders' discourse was framed in terms of democratic participation. Second, the process in which local leaders are creating different types of local associations such as the cabildos associations and the Mesas Permanentes de Trabajo, which seek to reunite the cabildos that have emerged in search of political recognition by the state, has resulted in conflict between ethnic groups in the area and in confrontations between the indigenous organizations at the regional (OZIP) and national (ONIC) levels. This poses the question: are these centralized indigenous organizations strengthening the indigenous movement and local representation? Or are they closing the spaces within which the indigenous communities can express other political stances? Dover and Rappaport (1996a and 1996b) document how similar "indigenous elites"—state-sponsored leaders—have diminished traditional authority in the Andes. The two cases discussed above reveal that these elites have reproduced the political culture that has characterized the Colombian political elites for decades. Padilla (1996, 88–89) has pointed out, too, that the model of political participation that the Colombian state has implemented in the Constitution of 1991 requires from the indigenous people a "modern" representation (indigenous leaders are expected to speak correct Spanish and to be able to discuss all type of topics). As a result, "better educated" young leaders are taking the place of traditional authorities, who now only deal with internal community affairs. Furthermore, Padilla poses an important question: is cultural diversity really exercised as it is recognized in the Constitution of 1991, or is this modernization of the traditional indigenous power a way to integrate indigenous people into the hegemonic nation?

Finally, it has to be emphasized that the conflicts that have been emerging in response to the new legislation that recognizes multiculturalism, traditional usos y costumbres, and indigenous participation in decision-making are nurturing the conflict between the guerrilla and paramilitary. Thus, additional research to examine the relationship between the indigenous groups and the armed actors in the area clearly needs to be undertaken.

Notes

1   My fieldwork was carried out in Putumayo and the southern "boot" of Cauca department during 1998, funded by dissertation grants from the United States Institute of Peace and the Wenner-Gren Foundation for Anthropological Research.

2   White settlers and the local-born non-indigenous people who have moved to the Amazon as a result of different waves of migration since the beginning of the 20th century. Colonos migrated to the Amazon region in response to the social, political, and economic upheavals in Colombia's heartland. For information on the different periods of migration to the department of Putumayo, see Ariza, Ramírez and Vega (1998).

3   Thirty-seven hundred hectares of coca cultivated by the indigenous communities inhabiting the Putumayo have been estimated (Plante functionary, personal communication, 2000). Even though the indigenous territories have been formally excluded from the areas targeted for fumigation of illicit crops, and the National Alternative Substitution Plan (PLANTE) has been financing medicinal gardens as an alternative to coca cultivation, since December 22, 2000, the indigenous groups located in Valle del Guamués and San Miguel experienced the spraying not only of their coca crops but of their licit ones. To prevent the continuation of aerial spraying, on January 12, 2001, the Cofán, among other indigenous groups of the Putumayo, signed an agreement with the government to eradicate manually their coca plantations within a year (*Pacto Social de desarrollo alternativo y erradicación voluntaria*, January 12th, 2001).

4   On January 3, 2001, Emilio Díaz Queta, a Cofán leader, vice president of the Cofán Foundation of Traditional Authorities ZIO-AI, was killed by armed groups, presumably paramilitaries in the municipality of San Miguel. On December 26, 2000, the ex-governor of a Cofán cabildo and member of the Permanent Working Assembly of the Cofán people, and his spouse, Lidia Queta, who was four months pregnant, were also assassinated by paramilitaries in the community of Yarinal.

5   Decree 2001 of 1988 defines the resguardo as a special kind of legal and socio-political institution, formed by an indigenous community or an entire indigenous ethnic group, that collectively owns its territory. The resguardo is internally governed by a legal organization called cabildo

and defined, by the same decree of 1988, as a political administrative entity, whose members are elected and recognized by a specific indigenous group living in a specific territory, and are to represent the group and execute functions according to their traditional values and customs (DNP 1993, 81). The institution of resguardo was created in the second half of the fifteenth century. In the Amazon region, resguardos were created only in 1977.

6   During the colonial period, in response to the Spaniards need to control indigenous communities, cabildos emerged as a syncretistic local political authority promoted by the Spaniards through the appropriation and reshaping of the *cacicazgos* (from cacique or chief). Cabildos consisted of a governor (the cacique), a mayor and other officials known as *alguaciles* and *mayordomos,* and played an important mediating role between the Indian communities and the Spaniards, regulating tribute both in kind and in labor or personal services to the conquerors (corvée). This mediation by the caciques constituted a means of resistance to assimilation promoted by the Spanish. Indigenous authorities learned and used Spanish laws in order to defend their lands and their cultural distinctiveness.

7   The importance given to these legal representatives is a response to the new constitution's support of indigenous autonomy and forms of government. The Constitution states that indigenous authorities have jurisdiction over their territories in compliance with their own norms and procedures to the extent that they do not go against the Constitution and national laws. It is expected that subsequent legislation will establish the coordination between this special jurisdiction and the national judicial system (Art. 246).

8   Such as OZIP-Zonal Indigenous Organization of the Putumayo, created in 1986, the ONIC-National Indigenous Organization of Colombia, founded in 1982, and OPIAC-Organization of the Indigenous People of the Colombian Amazon created in 1995.

9   The Tukanoans of the Vaupés (Jackson 1989, 1995 and 1996), black communities of the Pacific Coast (Wade 1993, Escobar 1992), Cumbales of Nariño in the Andean region (Rappaport 1994 and 1996), Yanaconas of Cauca (Zambrano 1993) and Ingas of the Sibundoy Valley in the Putumayo (Dover 1995 and 1996). Chaves (1998 and 2001) has pointed out the emergence of competitive subaltern discourses of identity among indigenous groups and colonos in the Putumayo department.

10   Taita is the name given to senior members of the community, generally ex-governors and respected shamans, those who have the traditional knowledge and wisdom to guide the community.

11   The Office of Indigenous Affairs of the Ministry of the Interior has spec-

ified that the only requirement for a cabildo to be constituted is the act of taking office as a governor recognized by the local state authorities. This act represents the certification of the inhabitants of the area that is the representative of an indigenous group.

12 This is an example of what Pile (1997, 27) calls the "politics of lived spaces," when he points out that "at the heart of questions of resistance lie questions of spatiality."

13 Meeting in the town of Santa Clara with official representatives, March 10, 1998.

14 This case can be contrasted with Findji's (1992) analysis of the emergence of an indigenous movement in the Andean region of Colombia, which although it was fighting for a "territory" and to be recognized as a *pueblo* (or people), possessed a political identity and was fighting for its right to exist as such.

15 Self-differentiation is at the core of the definition of ethnicity: Barth (1969) defines ethnic groups as "categories of ascription and identification by the actors themselves," an aspect that has become of paramount importance in the constitution of new identities. Nash (1989, 10) discusses the issue of self-ascription, noting that although ethnicity is a historical product and as such is subject to redefinition, "cultural categories with social and group referents are the focus of ethnic inquiry. Where there is a group, there is some sort of boundary, and where there are boundaries, there are mechanisms to maintain them." Sollors (1989) sees ethnicity in the modern world as identities being continually reinvented and reinterpreted.

16 Pile's definition:

The politics of location involves not only a sense of where one is in the world—a sense gained from the experiences of history, geography, culture, self and imagination—mapped through the simultaneously spatial and temporal interconnections between people, but also the political definition of the grounds on which struggles are to be fought. In this sense, location has more to do with the active constitution of the grounds on which political struggles are to be fought and the identities through which people come to adopt political stances than with the latitude and longitude of experiences of circumscription, marginalization and exclusion (Pile 1997, 28).

17 The successive waves of colonization hit the Cofán population especially hard, mainly due to the entry of petroleum companies since the 1960s, and the coca boom during the 70s and 80s. As a consequence, the Cofanes have lost a great part of their ancestral territory, and their main struggle has been to recover it.

18 See notes 5 and 6.

19   The first Westerners entering the Amazon region called the settlement headman *capitán* and saw him as the community representative, often attributing more power to the office than headmen traditionally held.

20   This means that cabildos can be created in places where their members do not necessarily own their territory collectively or where resguardos have been established.

21   In the jurisdiction of Mocoa, a Paez resguardo of 98 hectares has been constituted, as well as 74 hectares in Puerto Guzmán, and an Embera resguardo of 131 hectares in the jurisdiction of Orito. Paez communities which total 3,500 or more members can be found all over the Putumayo, in the municipalities of Mocoa, Villa Garzón, Puerto Guzmán, Puerto Caicedo, Puerto Asís and in Puerto Leguízamo (Ariza, Ramírez y Vega 1998, 101–102). See map 5-2.

22   Today Cofán leaders are fighting for the recuperation and legalization of 28,000 hectares as a resguardo, arguing this was the ancestral reserva once recognized by the state as such. However, as the colonization advanced, members of the community sold their land and today only 5,671 hectares have been legalized as resguardos, coinciding with the area occupied today by the Cofán communities (Mesa Permanente de Trabajo por el Pueblo Cofán 1998). The rest of the land is occupied by colonos.

23   These Inga groups have been organized into the Zonal Indigenous Council of the southern "boot" of Cauca as a sector of the CRIC-Regional Indigenous Council of the Cauca department. Fourteen cabildos make up this organization and are also fighting for resguardos. Until 1997, six resguardos had been constituted: San Antonio and San José del Fragua (Fragua Viejo), La Leona (Puerto Bello) Rumiñahue and Guayuyaco (Miraflor), San José del Inchiyaco (Remanso). See map 5-3.

24   This goal coincides with that of the National Indigenous Organization of Colombia (ONIC): to recover all ancestral indigenous territories that have been invaded by colonos. The tension between the Cofanes and the colonos has risen as the struggle has escalated. Unfortunately, this specific conflict is nourishing the broader conflict between the paramilitaries and the guerrilla.

25   The Permanent Council Working for the Cofán People has the following functions:

1) That the 22 members of the Permanent Council prepare themselves to defend the life of the Cofán people. They should be aware of the history and the present situation of the Cofán and should be conscious of their most important needs and expectations.

2) The Permanent Workgroup should represent the Cofán People in decision making, after consulting the Cofán community in general and the traditional authorities.

3) It should be the entity that follows up on the implementation of projects in Cofán territory.

4) It should contribute to the defense of the territory, the culture, the traditions, and the wisdom of the Cofán people.

5) It should begin to prepare for meetings with the institutions of the Colombian state (*Mesa Permanente de Trabajo por el Pueblo Cofán,* 1988).

Works Cited

Acta de la reunión de concertación dentro del perfeccionamiento del Proceso de Consulta Previa y participación a los pueblos indígenas Inga y Awa de las comunidades indígenas Bella Vista, Siloé, Playa Larga, Chulaiaco, San Andrés Islas, el Espingo, Damasco Vides, Villa Unión, Las Vegas y San Miguel de la Castellana, ubicadas en el área de influencia indirecta del Bloque de Perforación Exploratoria San Juan, Pozos Unicornio 1, Pegaso 1 y Troyano 1, en Jurisdicción del Municipio de Villagarzón (Putumayo) Agosto 20 de 1997.

Arango, Raul y Enrique Sánchez

1989   *Los Pueblos Indígenas de Colombia.* Bogotá: División Nacional de Planeación.

Ariza, Eduardo, María Clemencia Ramírez and Leonardo Vega

1998   *Atlas Cultural de la Amazonia Colombiana: la construcción del territorio en el siglo XX.* Bogotá: Ministerio de Cultura-Instituto Colombiano de Antropología, Corpes Orinoquia, Corpes Amazonia.

Barth, Fredrik

1969   *Ethnic Groups and Boundaries. The Social Organization of Cultural Difference.* London: George Allen and Unwin.

Chaves, Margarita

2001   "Discursos subalternos de identidad y movimiento indígena en el Putumayo." *Movimientos sociales, Estado y democracia en Colombia.* Mauricio Archila y Mauricio Pardo, eds., pp. 234–259. Bogotá: CES Universidad Nacional, Instituto Colombiano de Antropología e Historia.

1998   "Identidad y representación entre indígenas y colonos de la Amazonía Colombiana." *Modernidad, Identidad y Desarrollo.* María Lucía Sotomayor, ed., pp. 273–386. Bogotá: Instituto Colombiano de Antropología y Colciencias.

Constitucion Política de Colombia

1991   Bogotá: Ediciones Emfasar.

Departamento Nacional de Planeación (DNP)

1993   *Bases para la conformación de entidades territoriales indígenas.* Bogotá: Departamento Nacional de Planeación.

Dagnino, Evelina.

1998   "The Cultural Politics of Citizenship, Democracy and the State." In *Cultures of Politics and Politics of Cultures. Re-visioning Latin American Social Movements.* Alvarez Sonia, Arturo Escobar and Evelina Dagnino, eds., pp. 33–63. Boulder: Westview Press.

Declaración del Pueblo Cofán y los Cabildos Indígenas del Valle del Guamués y San Miguel, Putumayo: January 2001.

Dirección General de Asuntos Indígenas

1998   *Los Pueblos Indígenas en el País y en América.* Bogotá: Ministerio del Interior.

Dover, Robert

1995   Nucanchi gente pura: *the ideology of* recuperación *in the Inga communities of Colombia's Sibundoy Valley.* Dissertation submitted to the faculty of the University Graduate School of Indiana University in partial fulfillment of the requirements for the degree Doctor of Philosophy in the Department of Folklore. Indiana University.

Dover, Robert, and Joanne Rappaport

1996a   "Introduction." *Journal of Latin American Anthropology* 1(2):2–17.

1996b   "The construction of difference by native legislators." *Journal of Latin American Anthropology.* 1(2):22–45.

Findji, María Teresa

1992   "From resistance to social movement." In *The Making of Social Movements in Latin America.* Arturo Escobar and Sonia Alvarez, eds. pp. 112–133, Boulder: Westview Press.

Jackson, Jean

1989   "Is there a way to talk about making culture without making enemies?" *Dialectical Anthropology* 14:127–143.

1995   "Culture genuine and spurious: the politics of Indianness in the Vaupés, Colombia." *American Ethnologist* 22(1):3–27.

1996   "The impact of recent national legislation in the Vaupes region of Colombia." *Journal of Latin American Anthropology* 1(2):120–151.

La Nación.

1996   "Indígenas se oponen al desarrollo que brinda Ecopetrol." Mocoa: December 23.

Ley 99 del 22 de Diciembre de 1993. Bogotá: Ministerio del Medio Ambiente.

Nash, Manning

1989   *The Cauldron of Ethnicity in the Modern World.* Chicago: University of Chicago Press.

ONIC-IICA

1998   *Planes de Vida de los Pueblos Indígenas. Guías de Reflexión.* Bogotá: Organización Nacional Indígena de Colombia, Instituto Interamericano de Cooperación para Agricultura, Ministerio de Agricultura.

Mesa Permanente de Trabajo por el Pueblo Cofán

1998   *Plan de Vida del Pueblo Cofán.* Bogotá: Fondo DRI, Gobernación del Putumayo, Alcaldías Municipales de Orito, La Hormiga y San Miguel.

Pacto Social de Desarrollo Alternativo y Erradicación Voluntaria, suscrito por las comunidades indígenas Cofán, Awa, Embera, Páez, Quechua y Pastos. Putumayo: Enero 12 de 2001.

Padilla, Guillermo

1996   "La ley y los pueblos indígenas en Colombia." *Journal of Latin American Anthropology* 1(2): 78–95.

Pile, Steve

1997   "Introduction. Opposition, political identities and spaces of resistance." In *Geographies of Resistance.* Steve Pile and Michael Keith, eds., pp. 1–32. New York: Routledge.

Prounuciamiento de la Junta Directiva de la Organización Zonal Indígena del Putumayo-OZIP y de la Organización de Pueblos Indígenas de la Amazonia Colombiana-OPIAC (Vaupés, Putumayo, Caquetá, Amazonas Guaviare, Guainia). Mocoa: 27 de Febrero de 1997.

Rappaport, Joanne

1990a   *The Politics of Memory: Native Historical Interpretation in the Colombian Andes.* Cambridge: Cambridge University Press.

1990b   "History, Law and Ethnicity in Andean Colombia." *The Latin American Anthropological Review* Vol. 2(1):13–19.

1994   *Cumbe Reborn: an Andean Ethnography of History.* Chicago: University of Chicago Press.

Sollors, Werner, Ed.

1989   *The Invention of Ethnicity.* New York: Oxford University Press.

Triana, Adolfo

1992   "Grupos étnicos, Nueva Constitución en Colombia." In *Antropología Jurídica.* Esther Sanchez, ed., Bogotá: Sociedad Antropológica de Colombia, Comité Internacional para el Desarrollo de los Pueblos y VI Congreso Nacional de Antropología.

Wade, Peter

1995   "The Cultural Politics of Blackness in Colombia." *American Ethnologist* 22(2):341–357.

Zambrano, Carlos Vladimir

1993   *Hombres de Paramo y Montaña: los Yanacona del Macizo Colombiano.* Bogotá: Instituto Colombiano de Antropología-PNR, Bogotá.

Acronyms

ASCINVAGUA	Association of Cabildos from Valle del Guamues
ASOCIPCA	Association of Cabildos from Puerto Caicedo
CRIC	Regional Indigenous Council of the Cauca Department
DEMA	Document of Valuation and Environmental Management
FARC	*Fuerzas Armadas Revolucionarias de Colombia,* Revolutionary Armed Forces of Colombia
INCORA	Colombian Institute of Agrarian Reform
ONIC	National Indigenous Organization
OPIAC	Organization of the Indigenous People of the Colombian Amazon
OZIP	Zonal Indigenous Organization of the Putumayo
PLANTE	National Alternative Substitution Plan
ZIO-AI	Cofán Foundation of Traditional Authorities

SECTION

III

The Andean Countries

Ecuador: Indigenous Peoples and Nationalities

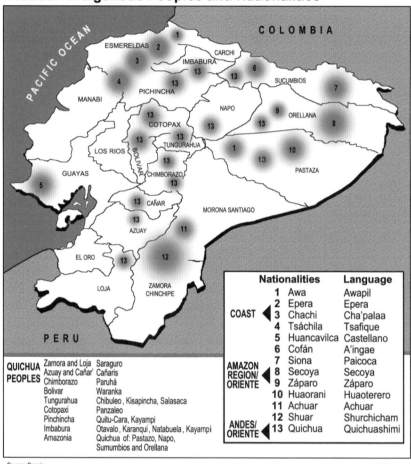

		Nationalities	Language
COAST	1	Awa	Awapil
	2	Epera	Epera
	3	Chachi	Cha'palaa
	4	Tsáchila	Tsafique
	5	Huancavilca	Castellano
AMAZON REGION/ ORIENTE	6	Cofán	A'ingae
	7	Siona	Paicoca
	8	Secoya	Secoya
	9	Záparo	Záparo
	10	Huaorani	Huaoterero
	11	Achuar	Achuar
ANDES/ ORIENTE	12	Shuar	Shurchicham
	13	Quichua	Quichuashimi

QUICHUA PEOPLES		
Zamora and Loja	Saraguro	
Azuay and Cañar'	Cañaris	
Chimborazo	Paruhá	
Bolivar	Waranka	
Tungurahua	Chibuleo , Kisapincha, Salasaca	
Cotopaxi	Panzaleo	
Pinchincha	Quitu-Cara, Kayampi	
Imbabura	Otavalo, Karanqui , Natabuela , Kayampi	
Amazonia	Quichua of: Pastazo, Napo, Sumumbios and Orellana	

Source: Conaie

El Universo

Map 6-1

6

Ecuador's Indian Movement: Pawn in a Short Game or Agent in State Reconfiguration?

Theodore Macdonald, Jr.

Introduction: The "Shortest Coup" [1]

For approximately three hours, beginning shortly before midnight on January 21, 2000, Antonio Vargas Huatatuca rose higher on the political ladder than any Indian since *Abya Yala* [2] became Latin America. As president of the Confederation of Indian Nationalities of Ecuador (CONAIE), Vargas represented the country's Indians in a governing triumvirate and a *Junta de Salvación Nacional*, which, during the course of the day, coordinated a *Levantamiento* (uprising) that, much to its own surprise, took over the National Congress and the Supreme Court, forced President Jamil Mahuad to flee his offices, declared an end to government by "oligarchy," and placed itself in charge of the country.

An unlikely ally—the Ecuadorian army—propped up the Indians' ladder. For several months prior to the coup, Colonel Lucio Gutiérrez and other young colonels had evaluated, with considerable frustration and anger, the deteriorating national economy. They also talked with CONAIE's leaders, who, for over a decade, had been formulating and advancing plans for an expanded "plurinational" democracy. There was mutual agreement on the need for political change and economic adjustment.

Shortly before the coup, more than 10,000 Indians set up camp in Quito, where they were visited regularly by army officers. Thousands of other Indians blocked roads throughout much of the country, where the army and police simply watched. On January 21, with the National Congress besieged by Indians, Colonel Gutiérrez and his troops arrived. The guards then opened the barricades and allowed Indians and troops to enter. That night General Carlos Mendoza, head of the Joint Military Command, hoisted hands with Vargas and Carlos Solózano (a former President of the Ecuadorian Supreme Court and the leader of the Social Movements Coordinating Group) to proclaim a triumvirate government.

The following day the triumvirate was dissolved. Escorted into office by the Joint Military Command, Vice President Gustavo Noboa was installed into the presidency and constitutional order was reestablished. Public attention then shifted largely to the policies of the new government and to an analysis of the coup. Meanwhile, thousands of tired and disgruntled Indians vacated their campsite and headed home. It appeared that the Indians' high profile in the "shortest coup" had simply fizzled out like a sparkler during the long night. Some observers lamented the Indians' actions as an unfortunate, perhaps naïve, but nonetheless understandable response to their increasingly bleak economic situation (Lucas 2000). Others considered that CONAIE's leaders had not only violated constitutional rule but, in doing so, had shifted the Indian movement's tactics away from a steady nonviolent inclusion into the broader Ecuadorian society and politics to a shortsighted scramble for power (*El Comercio* 20 February 2000, *El Comercio* 22 February 2000).

This chapter, by contrast, suggests that the events surrounding January 21 were not an anomaly and the outcome was not a tragedy. Rather, analysis unfolds a graphic metaphor for an Ecuadorian indigenous movement that, in little more than twenty years, has progressively elevated Ecuador's Indians to unparalleled national and international visibility. In doing so, the organizations have awarded indigenous peoples a new political status and role in a country where they served and were seen, for the most part, and for the previous 500 years, as little more than a faceless, laboring, and impoverished mass. The January 21 events served as a fulcrum to open more political space, as a stimulus for internal reflection and self-criticism, and, subsequently, as a motive for a more structured and rational political plan.[3]

Almost exactly a year later, and stripped this time of any short-term military alliance, the January 2000 actions provided the Indian leaders with the moral authority and hindsight to confront the Noboa government and negotiate means to decrease the Indians' general economic hardships and expand their organizations' political presence. Placing the short-lived phenomena of the January 2000 coup against the larger landscape of the movement demonstrates, in time and space, that the apparent "losers" in the January 2000 coup may, in the long run, have "won" more for themselves than any other sector involved.[4]

Background: The Events of January 2000

The January 2000 Levantamiento was, in many ways, a reaction to the actions and inaction of President Mahuad and his government. Between November 1998 and February 1999 five large Ecuadorian banks suddenly collapsed. The government's immediate responses—freeze all personal bank accounts, provide funds to shore up the banks, and increase the sales tax—were widely interpreted as imposing personal hardship on the populace while bailing out banking cronies. The Indians and the army further resented the Mahuad administration for pouring money into the foundering banks while abandoning promises of funds for Indian social services and for military salary increases and equipment purchases.

Most Ecuadorians were fully aware that a large part of the economic crisis had been inherited from the earlier, highly corrupt administration of President Abdala Bucaram. Economic problems were exacerbated by a coastal agricultural crisis that resulted from weather patterns provoked by the 1998 "El Niño" and the 1999 "La Niña," and were compounded by a precipitous decline in the world price of oil, which makes up about 40 percent of Ecuador's state income.[5] Nevertheless, the populace directed its frustration and anger toward President Mahuad's perceived inaction in the face of the economic crisis, exacerbated later when the president and/or his political party was reported to have received, but not reported, a major campaign contribution from a bank owner deeply involved in the banking scandal. The negative image of the government was easily translated into strong sympathy for the highly symbolic indigenous economic plight. Indigenous leaders, meanwhile, demonstrated their frustration by establishing strongly-participatory shadow governments, or *gobiernos comunitarios* (popular parliaments) in local *alcaldías* (mayoralties). Then, while thousands of Indians marched into Quito in January 2000, they scaffolded an analogous "National Parliament of the Peoples of Ecuador." In doing so the Indian leadership illustrated that its expressed goals for the January 2000 Levantamiento went far beyond palliative measures to meet the immediate economic crisis. Invoking threats made for over a decade (CONAIE 1993), they drew on their models for local mayoralties to demand a similar democratization through the destitution of all three branches of the national government.

On Friday, January 21, following the arrival of soldiers and mid-rank officers led by Colonel Gutiérrez, troops opened the barricades surrounding the National Congress and accompanied over 2,000 Indians as they stormed inside to install the new Peoples' Parliament. By afternoon they had taken over the Supreme Court offices and, late that night, the Indians and the soldiers occupied the Presidential Palace, where they proclaimed the new Junta of National Salvation that, after General Mendoza replaced Colonel Gutierrez as the military member of the group, was renamed the triumvirate.

Shortly after midnight, General Mendoza announced that he was leaving the junta for personal reasons. At about 3 a.m. on January 22, another member of the military high command informed the Indians that the triumvirate government was dissolved and that Vice President Gustavo Noboa would assume the presidency.[6] Vargas decried the military's reversal as "treason" by the old guard, added that the Indians would be back, and said that he could no longer assure they would be nonviolent.

For many observers the conjunction of a complex, perhaps inevitable, national economic crisis and President Mahuad's actions and inactions produced a coup in which Indians played a highly visible, but short-lived and largely symbolic, role. However, to focus only on the events and alliances that surrounded January 21 and then to suggest that indigenous actions can be understood solely, or even largely, in terms of immediate national political events and responses to a brief political opening provided by the military diminishes the significance and intent of indigenous agency, masks their deep-seated sentiments, neglects their long-term goals, and ignores their recent steps toward increased political participation. Conversely, to counter argue, as this chapter does, that the Indians' actions illustrated yet another step, albeit bolder and more dramatic than most of their earlier ones, in their progressive entry into Ecuador's national political and economic arena raises two obvious questions regarding the Indians' short-term behavior, and a third related to their broader agenda.

1. Why would the Indians link themselves in an alliance with the military, generally seen as a repressor of indigenous groups and rights in Latin America?

2. Why would Ecuadorian Indian leaders participate in unconstitutional and apparently undemocratic actions, and thus jeopardize their perceived, and highly applauded, status as peaceful

agents of essential change, an image that they had been building successfully for almost twenty years?

3. How was the Indians' short-term engagement with state actors linked to their broad goals for future inter-ethnic relations in an expanded democracy?

I. The Indian-Military Alliance: Why?

Shared Socio-economic Status

The Indians' January 2000 alliance was with the army. The navy and the air force did not support the dramatic coup attempt. The Ecuadorian army, unlike the navy and air force, has an officer corps that draws much of its ranks from the middle to lower socio-economic sectors. Many of the troops are Indians, particularly those serving in elite combat units. Consequently, the Ecuadorian army does not see itself as part of a *social* elite but rather as an *organizational* elite, one that can rise above petty political infighting and "get the job done efficiently." The Ecuadorian army, at least since late 1960s, when it modeled itself after Peru's progressive Velasco military dictatorship, has rarely acted against popular opinion and has never turned systematically against indigenous peoples.

Shared Complaints

The Indians' and the army's complaints extended beyond the economic downslide that affected the entire country. CONAIE had also been told that the organization would be part of a permanent dialogue with the government (*El Comercio* 8 Jan 2000). But with the government absorbed by the banking crisis, no effective talks took place. This left the Indians feeling once again marginalized. The military, in turn, resented the marginalization that followed President Mahuad's successful negotiation in 1998 of the long-standing border dispute with Peru. He subsequently reduced the military budget, in proud response to the International Monetary Fund's recommendations for trimming the public sector budget. The army, however, saw his actions as a diminution of their previously high national status and role, and as obeisance to foreign financial agents.

Five years earlier, the army had been lauded as national heroes after the 1995 border war that the Ecuadorians proudly proclaimed that they had "won" in combat. Consequently, many soldiers and officers felt that the government had neglected them economically and "forgotten" them historically. In brief, for the Indians and the army, the Mahuad government's economic policies and priorities were perceived as personal and sectional slights as much as economic depravation.

Perspectives of Contrast

Some Indian leaders have argued that, in general, it is not naïve to assume military support for indigenous needs.[7] They state that Ecuador's indigenous peoples had obtained their most significant advances during times of military dictatorships. Between 1994 and 1998, Indians say that the democratically elected government claimed that it recognized Ecuador as a multiethnic and pluricultural state, with collective rights. However, the Indians argue that the government never respected these rights in practice. By contrast, under military dictatorships Ecuador had passed agrarian reform legislation, established a development plan for the country, approved and supported bilingual education projects, and advanced the acceptance of bilingualism.

In 1980, they add, the Ministry of Defense acknowledged the "national" nature of Amazonian populations and encouraged Ecuador to recognize indigenous peoples' basic differences and historical roots. The minister, a military officer, suggested that Ecuador allow indigenous peoples a degree of self-determination, allocate a percentage of oil revenues to development projects, recognize indigenous languages, establish primary bilingual education, provide secure land tenure and sufficient land for three generations, and create an institute to train indigenous anthropologists, linguists, economists, and other specialists. By contrast, Indians note that in July 1991, the democratic government of President Rodrigo Borja caused deaths and injuries during the Levantamiento General.

The Military as Refraction

Indigenous comments on military rule and the contrasts drawn with civilian regimes speak more toward the shortcomings of Ecuadorian democracy than any support of military rule. Otherwise, how do Indians explain CONAIE's previous confrontations with the armed forces (CONAIE, October 1991) and the armed forces' interpretation of the concept of "plurinationalism" as divisive to the state (CONAIE, May 1991)? At the time of the January 2000 events, CONAIE charged that the army's "old guard" clearly "tricked" and "betrayed" the Indians when the high command ended the triumvirate and installed a conservative vice president. Also, military rule, almost by definition, would have precluded the expanded democracy currently promoted by CONAIE.

In summary, indigenous support for the military was, in fact, linked only to a small group of individual officers who expressed complaints common to indigenous peoples as well. This small group, with or without the full knowledge and support of the military high command,[8] created a strategic alliance with CONAIE at a particular time and undertook a loosely planned action to replace the existing political authorities.

II. The Ecuadorian Indian Movement's Unconstitutional and Apparently Undemocratic Actions: Why?

While the events of January 2000 were undeniably dramatic, they were nonviolent. CONAIE's president proudly emphasized, at each stage of the Indian's move to power, that there had been no bloodshed. The Ecuadorian press remained consistently non-alarmist and generally sympathetic to the Indians' overall position. Despite Vargas's departing comment that nonviolence could not be assured in the future, the Indians have remained nonviolent. They are fully aware of the stigma and subsequent loss of national and international support if they resort to violence.

A Threat to Constitutional Order?

The actions of January 2000 were also, for several hours, an undeniable breach of constitutional procedures. Few of the actors, however, commented directly on constitutional issues (e.g., see statements by Vargas, Pacari, Macas, in Lucas 2000). Indians spoke only of the immediate political nature of their actions, stating repeatedly that they sought to expand participation in an Ecuadorian democracy that they had helped to redefine and institutionalize through the 1998 constitution. This was to be done by removing from office a small political and power elite whom they considered to have "kidnapped" Ecuadorian democracy. There was no indication that any form of Jacobin revolution would replace them. Quite the contrary, the Indians' goals and motives expressed a simple desire for inclusion. The 1998 constitution, and the numerous antecedent and subsequent actions toward increased indigenous political participation, briefly reviewed below, illustrate the pragmatic nature of indigenous agency.

III. How Do Current Actions Relate to Earlier Expectations?

The Ecuadorian Indigenous Movement: A Summary

The indigenous movement in Ecuador is, at present, the most organized and institutionalized of any in Latin America. CONAIE is one of the few truly national organizations, linking Indians—about 35 percent of Ecuador's population—from all three geographic regions. Through a combination of coordinated and centralized organizations and consistently nonviolent actions, CONAIE maintains an extraordinary capacity to mobilize the indigenous population. Mobilizations paralyzed much of the country in 1990 (*Levantamiento General*), 1992 (*Gran Marcha para la Vida*), 1994 (opposition to breakup of communal lands), 1999 (opposition to economic policies, freezing of bank assets, and decreased social services), January 2000 (reviewed here) and, again and most successfully, in February 2001.

Ecuadorian indigenous peoples' most visible actions have almost all taken place at the national level and have centered in the Andean capital of Quito.[9] Also, Andean Indians are about 95 percent (1.5 million) of the total Indian population, far more than the diverse linguistic nationalities of the Amazonian region, whose 75,000 members make up less than 5 percent of the total. However, Amazonian Indians have provided more than half of CONAIE's leaders. More important, it was the Amazonian Indians who provided the initial stimulus and structure for ethnically based organizations in the 1960s, and these lowland groups consistently spoke to broad issues and concerns. By contrast, the Andean communities, though organized, were more class-oriented than ethnically focused. Though Andean Indians developed many of the movement's current tactics—strikes, road blockages, and similar patterns of resistance—Andean actions were, until recently, isolated *reactions* to local concerns. By contrast, the Amazonian organizations focused more on broad regional patterns and policies such as colonization and land rights.

It was not until the 1990s that movements, Andean or Amazonian, melded and focused many of their demands on broad national economic concerns (e.g., price increases for basic commodities or gasoline) and national political issues (e.g., land rights, education, health, and indigenous political status).[10] The two periods and groups are reviewed separately. While any temporal and geographic separation is arbitrary, and neglects many of the period's regional actions and cross-regional ties, the distinctions nonetheless illustrate general patterns within the indigenous movement.

Amazonian Organizations: Bellwether of the 1980s

The first Amazonian ethnic federation arose in 1961 among the Shuar (Jivaro) Indians in Ecuador's Southern Oriente. Beginning in 1961 and in reaction to an influx of Andean colonists and to government agrarian politics that encouraged and supported colonization, the Shuar joined disparate settlements to form the *Federación de Centros Shuar*, or Shuar Federation (Federación de Centros Shuar 1976; CONAIE 1988).

The Shuar situation and response spurred similar organization among several Amazonian Quichua[11] groups. In 1981 the Lowland Quichua joined with the Shuar to form the Confederation of Indigenous Nationalities of the Ecuadorian Amazon (CONFENIAE), which in 1982 began actively recruiting the region's smaller groups—Cofan, Siona-Secoya, and Huaorani—and supporting their land claims.

CONFENIAE leaders also met with leaders of Ecuarunari, one of the largest and oldest (1972) Andean Indian organizations to form the *Consejo de Coordinación de las Nacionalidades Indígenas del Ecuador*, or CONACNIE. In November 1986, they moved beyond simple coordination to organize, at the national level, the *Confederación de Nacionalidades Indígenas del Ecuador,* or CONAIE. They thus linked the Amazon region with groups from the highlands and coast with similar concerns—land rights, respect for culture, and representation within a pluricultural nation. However, it was the Amazonian Indians' responses during the 1980s to external threats to their land, resources, and identity, that led to the mobilization of a national political sector with a shared "ethnic" identity—*indio* (Macdonald 1999).

1980s Goals and Actions: Organizing Space

Ecuador's Indians, as happens with most social movements, responded to a political opening and extended their own agency. However, in Ecuador, indigenous agency has been a more powerful and consistent stimulus for action than has any political opening. While the movement has used a wide range of short-term strategies, the goal—inclusion—has remained steady across a range of government regimes.

Strategic actions in the Amazon region, and the resulting sense of strong indigenous agency, are illustrated during the three quite distinct governments of that period. The actions and resultant visibility set the stage and helped to define the indigenous agenda for the more widely known and highly publicized direct actions of the 1990s.

1980–1984: "Open Doors"

During the presidencies of Jaime Roldos and Oswaldo Hurtado,[12] relations between Indian organizations and the government were generally direct and cordial. The government established the first *Oficina de Asuntos Indígenas* (Office of Indian Affairs) to provide assistance (including land claims) to Indian communities, and also created a Central Bank-funded small-loan program, the Fund for Development of the Urban and Rural Marginal Populations, or FODERUMA. The Indian organizations regarded both agencies as services and thus began to work closely with those government institutions and representatives, which provided the federations with increased national and local visibility.

At the same time, the Indians worked to expand their own control by directly challenging other government agencies such as IERAC, the national agrarian reform agency. IERAC, the Indian organizations claimed, should simply recognize and title land based on traditional community boundaries, not establish its own criteria for land tenure, as if the land were state property. To press their point, some Amazonian organizations began to *auto-linderar*, or "self-demarcate" their territorial boundaries.

Also, in 1983 the government granted approximately 67,000 hectares to 900 Huaorani Indians, as their communal territory, and included an additional 250,000 hectares as their exclusive "reserve." Up until that time (i.e., since the beginning of the agrarian reform policies in the 1960s) only about 40 percent of the land titles adjudicated in the Amazonian region had been awarded to the original indigenous occupants, and none had been on such a scale. Equally important, the president's address emphasized that the government was not *giving* land to the Huaorani, but was formally *recognizing* claims that the land had been theirs for centuries (Uquillas 1984, 94).

Rather than applaud the president's actions, the Indian federations argued that the combination of land grant and adjacent reserve of the Huaorani was neither an accurate reflection of that group's rights nor an appropriate guarantee of tenure. The "reserve" still remained in government hands and provided no means for local control over extractive industries. They thus challenged IERAC's and, by extension, the government's authority to determine what was or was not "traditional" land.

Similar responses had occurred in 1981, when the Ecuadorian Congress passed forestry laws that put community forestry and conservation programs on a par with more environmentally questionable activities such as cattle raising, which some indigenous groups, most noticeably the Shuar and Quichua, had adopted largely to demonstrate possession and land rights (Macdonald 1999). The laws sparked no interest. The Indian organizations were more concerned with how laws were drafted and promulgated than with their specific content. To them it was another government effort to exercise control over land and resources without consulting with the organizations. They thus shifted course away from requests for government favors, limited participation, and individual land titles toward a more expanded playing field in which entire groups engaged the state on basic policies and practices.

1984–1988: "Closed Doors"

Beginning in 1984, the government of President León Febres Cordero entered with significantly different priorities—unrestrained economic activities for the private sector, colonization of the Amazonian region, and opposition to the ethnic federations, particularly their efforts at *auto-linderación*. The previously helpful *Oficina de Asuntos Indígenas* was suddenly elevated to the status of a directorate (*Dirección Nacional de Poblaciones Indígenas del Ecuador*), and assumed many of the roles that the ethnic federations had been working to establish for themselves.

The León government also encouraged "alternative" Indian organizations, often made up of only a handful of self-appointed and government-approved Indian "leaders" (Amanecer Indio 1985a). Foderuma, in turn, began to provide or promise funds to the newly formed organizations or directly to Indian communities, thus circumventing and weakening the lines of authority recently established by the federations to coordinate development actions.

In 1985, IERAC's support for the expansion of African Palm plantations provoked widespread outcries from the regional and national Indian organizations (Amanecer Indio 1985b; CONFENIAE 1985a, 1985b). The established Indian organizations decried IERAC's actions as government efforts to weaken their power. The protests drew wide support from national and international solidarity organizations and donors (*Latin American Weekly Report* 1985).

By 1986, the conservative León government was reacting to any popular actions or protest as if it were a direct and subversive threat to the country. Public political actions were quickly and often violently halted by heavily equipped, masked police. Consequently, accusations and accounts of human rights violations drew in international organizations such as Americas Watch to a country that had, till then, been one of the few havens from government repression in a troubled hemisphere.

The Indian organizations, throughout this period, continued to hold public meetings and maintained a relatively high public profile. Through congressional contacts, Indian leaders held two general assemblies in the main salon of the National Congress, where outspoken leaders criticized government policies.

Consequently, the national and international visibility and status of Ecuador's Indian organizations soared. They stood out as the only popular organization that maintained its agenda in open and direct opposition to the León government.

1988–1992: "Open Doors"

Shortly after President Rodrigo Borja took office in 1988, he publicly proclaimed Ecuador's strong commitment to the preservation of the Amazonian rain forest and described his country as "pluricultural." The indigenous leadership seized on his progressive words, hoping to hold the administration to its proclamations and, by extension, to open political doors even further. The regional Amazonian organization, CONFENIAE, began to demarcate their members' entire *territorios*, or areas of traditional occupation. The federations thus moved away from a concern with specific community borders to larger ethnically defined units over which the entire group claimed a set of rights.

Territorial claims were a sudden, quantum leap in indigenous relations to the state. The organizations, by shifting to broader territorial demands, were working to change the basic rules regarding land in general, not simply its boundaries.

In summary, throughout the 1980s the movement worked to define land rights, and with it, a means to enter the political arena, without a loss of indigenous self-identity that determined those rights. To a large extent the actions can be understood as a response to state corporatist policies. The indigenous organizations worked to keep the assimilationist tendencies of corporatism in check by reacting to government policies in ways that retained and even strengthened their distinct indigenous identity and claims.

Andean and Amazonian Organizations: Entering the State in the 1990s

Levantamientos and Marches

As if somehow keyed to the calendar, Ecuador's indigenous peoples began and ended the decade of the 1990s with major uprisings. The 1990 Levantamiento General (National Uprising) thrust Indian concerns onto center stage and established CONAIE as a prominent actor. Throughout the 1990s Indian leaders, working inside the state through Congress and outside it through CONAIE, moved progressively, and with even more clearly articulated political steps, toward permanent inclusion.

The 1990 Levantamiento General, however, was one of the most dramatic actions, if not the most, ever undertaken by Ecuador's Indians, and it set the pattern for future mobilizations. In a loosely organized but highly effective series of actions, CONAIE's member groups paralyzed the entire country by peacefully blocking all roads. Then approximately 10,000 Indians marched into Quito and occupied the plaza in front of Quito's oldest cathedral, San Francisco, where they placed a broad set of demands before the government of President Borja.

This short chapter permits only a brief review of the 1990 Levantamiento and the other direct actions of the decade. Moreover, to focus solely on dramatic strikes, marches, and demonstrations, overlooks other, more subtle actions—e.g., internal debates, papers, emerging political parties and their practices, and redefined ethnic boundaries. The indigenous actors used each method to think about and act upon their position as citizens and as groups.

From Multiculturalism to Plurinationalism

Among the main demands of the 1990 "uprising" were formal recognition of Ecuador as a "multiethnic and multicultural state," and respect for communal indigenous land tenure. Though President Borja had spoken in support of these issues shortly after his election, there was little formal implementation. The 1990 strike, in fact, provoked a backlash. By 1991 landowners and some government officials were accusing the Indians of attempting to create a state within a state and under-mining the unity of the state through demands for recognition of in-dependent communal lands that, by extension, denied others the right to private property. Army officers, in turn, wrote a public letter stating that "extremist" elements were taking advantage of indigenous naivete by encouraging an indigenous state (CONAIE 1992).

Sharply contested, such statements hardened the movement's stand. In mid-March 1992, the Organization of Indigenous Peoples of Pas-taza (OPIP) staged a 2,000-person six-day march from a small Ama-zonian city, Puyo, to Quito. This *Marcha Indígena por la Vida* was a de-mand for government recognition of broad pan-ethnic territories in the province of Pastaza. However, the event quickly captured popular good will, drew in CONAIE, and added a broader theme—respect—that galvanized national support for indigenous rights, as Ecuadorian citizens. As the marchers moved into the highlands they picked up thousands of Andean Indian supporters before they arrived, colorfully and ceremoniously, in Quito's Plaza San Francisco. The subsequent agreement with the Borja government provided land only for ex-panded community land holdings, not the broad ethnic territorial claim. The visibility and negotiations nonetheless placed the indige-nous movement on even higher ground with regard to the national so-ciety. Likewise, with the exception of the military, which interpreted the demands as "separatist," the indigenous march accumulated even more political goodwill and power for the movement in general. Their needs were acknowledged as legitimate and the nonviolence was applauded.

Beyond, between, and throughout these spectacular events of the 1990s, the Indians themselves began to define and create a new na-tional fabric. They progressively drew themselves away from a focus on single issues, short-term actions, and exclusively "indigenous" prob-lems. Such positions, they argued, had distinguished Indians *too* much from the rest of the national society and thus promoted a false di-chotomy between "Indians" and the "national society." As the Indian leaders moved to redefine national society, ethnic distinctions were to *be* the national fabric, not simply a fragment of it. Moreover, by defin-ing the new national structure, indigenous peoples also placed them-selves in a position to reconstruct related economic and political prac-tices in ways that reflected and supported a "plurinational" identity, rather than simply highlighting Indians as a distinct, and generally marginalized, population.

Following the OPIP march and the 1992 hemispheric fanfare that accompanied the five hundredth anniversary of Cristóbal Columbus' arrival in the Americas, CONAIE in 1993 issued a very clear and lengthy paper, "The Political Declaration of Ecuador's Indigenous Peoples," their proposal for a "New Multinational Nation" (CONAIE 1993). CONAIE emphasized that its organizational work of the previous decade made the organization into a recognized, alternative political force, which now sought to create a "multinational, democratic government attentive to the interests of all of the nationalities that make up Ecuador and guaranteeing the material and spiritual well-being of the family, the community, and society in general" (CONAIE 1993). "Multinationalism," the document states, is simply the recognition of and subsequent exercise of power by all sectors of the ethnically diverse country.

CONAIE thus moved to alter non-indigenous perceptions of indigenous peoples as being somehow "separate" from the national society. This was seen as an essential step toward a government that could respond to broad national problems—e.g., land, unemployment, health, education, and discrimination—as self-help rather than paternalism.

The new structure was to include, as equals, all of the "nationalities" that Ecuador comprised. Each indigenous group was to be understood as a "nationality" with a separate origin, history, tradition, and territory. Previously, the Indian organizations had lumped themselves into the general category of "*indio*." Though the term had served as an essential, unifying ethnic category during the 1980s, leaders began to suggest that the term "pluriculturalism" was too vague and served only to lump together all those who are marginal to the "national society." By redefining themselves as "nationalities," Ecuador's indigenous peoples sought to institutionalize diversity through recognition of the differences that exist *within* the broad categorization of "Indians."

By mid-decade the lexicon of ethnicity had shifted from "multinational" to "plurinational," and the terms and ideas became more sharply defined in the CONAIE congresses of 1996 and 1997. The organization has consistently recognized nine indigenous nationalities: Quichua, Shuar-Achuar, Chachi, Tsachi, Siona-Secoya, Huaorani, Cofán, Awá, Epera. As such, "plurinationalism" existed in the traditionally ethnic (and linguistic) distinctions in the Amazon region and Pacific lowlands. In the 1990s, however, those included in the largest and previously singular Andean/Amazonian "nationality"—

Quichua—began to subdivide, identify, and seek ascription formally through a more diverse set of ethnic terms designating *pueblos* (peoples). Some of these Andean groups have long been recognized as somehow distinct and named—e.g., those of Otavalo, Saraguro, Cañar, and Salasaca. But in the 1990s existing distinctions were institutionalized and new "ethnic identities" and related territories emerged for groups previously seen simply as Quichua-speaking campesinos. These "new" Andean groups distinguished themselves as smaller, distinct pueblos—the Puruhuá, Waranka, Panzaleo, Chibuleo, Quitu, Cayambi, Caranqui, and Natabuela.[13]

While some, perhaps most, social scientists would question the sort of "lumping" and sharply defined ethnic boundaries between and within "nationalities" that now appear in indigenous public discourse, indigenous emphasis rests on the outcomes of a dynamic, internally debated process, not some rigid definition of nationalities. Boundaries are defined not so much by geography and ancestry, but rather by the manner in which the various nationalities relate to and work with each other. Whether or not some Quichua populations later redefine their pueblos as a *nacionalidades* remains an open question. In the meantime, there is absolute clarity as to the desired end result—*inclusion as equals in a plurinational state.*

To emphasize the point, CONAIE also classifies Afro-Ecuadorians and Hispanic-Ecuadorians as nationalities. The combination of nationalities thus constitutes the plurinational Ecuadorian fabric. Within that society, indigenous peoples now argue that the state—its legislative, judicial and executive branches—must reflect all national differences if it is to be truly democratic. Otherwise, the indigenous peoples suggest, the country is little more than a democratic façade, defined and controlled by elites and closed to social sectors such as indigenous peoples. The state, for CONAIE, is one in which all of the different nationalities have agreed on the same constitution and the same governing procedures. Democracy, in turn, is understood as permanent participation in political and administrative decision making by all peoples and nationalities. Such ideas are radical redefinitions only because they have not been practiced before.

Advancing Plurinationalism

Indian leaders were able to advance significantly their plurinational agenda when the *Ley de Elecciones* (Election Law) was modified in 1996. The law permitted the creation and inclusion of new parties into the political process. This prompted the creation of the Movimiento de Unidad Plurinacional Pachacutik (MUUP, or Pachacutik as it is most commonly known). Pachacutik, based on a Quichua term meaning a remaking or recreation of the earth, was far from any millenarian quest. The movement simply sought the democratic order that the traditional and poorly institutionalized political parties had failed to provide. The emergence of Pachacutik thus allowed the Indians to end alliances with traditional patronage-based and poorly institutionalized parties, and to create an independent political status that would reflect their interests more accurately and consistently.

In the subsequent 1996 elections, Pachacutik won eight congressional seats, even though the majority of Indians continued to vote along traditional, often paternalistic, party lines. Pachacutik, with its assemblage of progressive, nontraditional members, also distanced itself from the winning candidate, Abdala Bucaram.

Perhaps as a consequence of not allying itself with Bucaram, the potential unity of the Pachacutik candidates was quickly weakened as the new president temporarily derailed the program. First, he created a new ministry, the Ministry of Indian Affairs, which drew its two co-ministers from among indigenous leaders. President Bucaram's populism quickly deteriorated into a corrupt tragicomedy in which two Pachacutik deputies were jailed for receiving public monies in exchange for their support to the flailing president. President Bucaram's actions temporarily ruptured government ties with CONAIE, estranged some Indian leaders from the movement, and disrupted the effective entry of Pachacutik into the national political arena.

The removal of Bucaram (on charges of mental incompetence) was followed by a rapid, chaotic, often humorous series of successions and claims to succession.[14] By contrast, Pachacutik deputies such as Luis Macas, an earlier president of CONAIE, remained above the feeding frenzy that surrounded President Bucaram's patronage, while those who had entered it were later welcomed back into the movement's fold.

The Indians' greatest long-term advance occurred in the months before the 1998 election, as a constitutional assembly, with a significant number of indigenous delegates, drafted a new constitution. The 1998 constitution included broad recognition of indigenous rights and a promise to consolidate Ecuador through recognition of regional diversity of peoples, ethnic groups, and cultures. Such statements drew heavily on the International Labor Organization's Convention Number 169, a landmark international legal instrument ratified by Ecuador in 1998, which established Indians as legal subjects with broad collective as well as individual rights, medical practices, law, identity.[15]

Equally important, although formal recognition of Ecuador as a "plurinational" state was not part of the new constitution, the term was included indirectly, and in such a way that it opened the possibility for subsequent change. Pachacutik, and with it the indigenous movement in general, thus perceived itself not simply as a new and legitimate political party, but as a, if not *the*, vanguard for advancing broad popular participation and democratization. Indians were filling the void between elections and democracy created and perpetuated by traditional parties.

In the August 1998 elections Pachacutik gained additional seats, and initial relations with the government of President Jamil Mahuad were quite good. President Mahuad's Minister of Government, Ana Lucia Armijos, worked closely and amicably with CONAIE to create the highly participatory *Consejo de Desarrollo de las Nacionalidades y Pueblos del Ecuador* (Development Council for the Nations and Peoples of Ecuador, or PRODENPE), and to create an "indigenous fund" for local development projects. Equally important for CONAIE, the organization negotiated the time and space for a regular dialogue with the government. Consequently, through early 1999 the government was receiving strong praise from CONAIE's president (*El Comercio* 18 January 1999).

The positive working relationship, however, was short-lived. In February 1999—when the banking crisis, frozen assets, and subsequent scandals emerged—the funds promised for PRODENPE were unavailable, and dialogue was stalled.[16] By March 1999, CONAIE was calling for another levantamiento and a general strike. Since the Indian organization was expressing broad public frustration with unpopular issues, there was strong popular support. Again, CONAIE dramatically but peacefully brought the country to a halt. The subsequent March 19, 1999 agreement between CONAIE and the government included a progressive and flexible "thawing" of "frozen" bank accounts and general lowering of prices for basic food commodities and fuel, as well as more specific "indigenous issues" such as the re-creation of the PRODENPE development fund for indigenous peoples and support for bilingual education.

Equally important, and again illustrative of indigenous efforts to go beyond integrating their organizations and parties into state decision-making and to serve as the vanguard for broad national political participation, the agreement with CONAIE established a regular dialogue with indigenous peoples and another one for a broader national dialogue. The second *mesa de dialogo* (dialogue table) would include CONAIE and numerous other members of the public sector in discussions of ways to resolve national political and economic issues.

Unfortunately, as the economic situation deteriorated and the political crisis worsened, agreements were not met. Equally unsettling to CONAIE and others, the Pachacutik/CONAIE plans for participatory decision making were neglected. Any actions or planning undertaken by the government were done through closed decision making. This was understood as a direct rejection of the dialogue agreements, which CONAIE had proudly brokered, for broad-based and open mesas de diálogo. The idea, let alone implementation, of broader "plurinationalism" virtually disappeared from the government's viewing screen. The government was thus perceived as unwilling or unable to accept and implement the advances in broad participatory governance and state management that the indigenous movement advocated and worked to achieve, theoretically and practically, throughout the decade. The resulting sense of marginalization from the decision-making process provoked, in large part, the unlikely alliance with the army officers and the levantamiento/coup of January 2000.

Revisiting January 2000 in February 2001: Continuity Amid Transitions

Neither the indigenous movement nor its public presence died when the Indians walked away from their Quito encampment, El Arbolito, in January 2000. On the contrary, CONAIE's presence increased notably. In the immediate post-coup period, official visits to Ecuador by Cesar Gaviria (OAS Secretary General) and Thomas Pickering (President Clinton's "drug czar") each included meetings with CONAIE. Vargas also met with Noboa. Likewise, CONAIE's plans to restructure the Congress and Supreme Court did not dissipate. During the first half of 2000, CONAIE worked to compile a list of signatures, which it would present to the Supreme Electoral Tribunal (TSE) which, in turn, would determine whether or not a national plebiscite would be called. However, when the signatures were reviewed in September 2000, the TSE charged that many had been falsified. The charges proved true. Corruption, compounded by an existing conflict between CONAIE and Pachacutik (along with another Indian organization, Feine) over the political utility of another CONAIE-called levantamiento, provoked national interest and led to a special CONAIE congress to evaluate the leadership. Many non-Indians assumed, and critics hoped, that the accusations and disagreements would weaken CONAIE's political power. They did not. At the special congress Vargas publicly acknowledged the CONAIE leadership errors, and the assembly debated the matter. The Indians decided that organizational solidarity and continuity were essential. So the CONAIE congress participants simply slapped Vargas's wrists, and then the organization continued to press forward with its demands.

During the late months of 2000, it became increasingly clear to CONAIE that President Noboa's economic policies, glossed in indigenous discourse as broad criticism of "neo-liberalism," left little space to attend to CONAIE's needs and requests. Likewise, and consistent with CONAIE's self-ascribed role as vanguard leader, the organization began to speak out strongly on such national issues as the impact of Plan Colombia on Ecuador and similar "non-Indian" issues. So, as the anniversary of the January 2000 coup arrived, CONAIE called for another levantamiento.

This time, however, there would be no military alliance or support. During the year President Noboa had deftly retired army generals Carlos Mendoza and Telmo Sandoval, and placed a loyal naval admiral in charge of the Ministry of Defense. The Noboa government then confidently warned that it would put down any form of "civil disruption," and his military supported the need to do so.

Nevertheless, in late January 2001 CONAIE began to mobilize Indians throughout the country for another general strike in the first week of February. They were successful in bringing out the Indians. But unlike previous "uprisings," and as warned by President Noboa, the February 2001 demonstration was met with considerable military and police opposition, force, and occasional violence. Indians en route to Quito were escorted off of buses by the police and army. Efforts to block roads were thwarted. Indians were also denied access to their highly symbolic campsite, El Arbolito. Consequently, many sought the refuge offered by the Salesian University. Later, police cordoned off this complex and the Indians were temporarily unable to receive food and other basic supplies. Nevertheless, the Indians' actions during the levantamiento were once again nonviolent,[17] and the actions in general won wide popular support. By contrast, the government's repressive and violent acts were highly publicized, circulated internationally, and generally condemned. Consequently, on February 6, 2001, President

Noboa and cabinet members, after several days of intransigence and demands that the strike actions be lifted before any talks could get underway, agreed to meet with CONAIE leaders. In one day they drafted and signed a twenty-point agreement, the main points of which, for most Indians, were a freezing, or lowering, of gasoline and natural gas prices and credit programs to small businesses. These were small but significant gains. For CONAIE, perhaps the more important point was the administration's commitment, with established dates, to an open dialogue with CONAIE on the solution of Ecuador's financial, social, commercial, and monetary policies. With this, CONAIE once again assumed a leadership status in the development of national policy and, by including other sectors of civil society into the dialogues, was indirectly advancing its broader agenda toward "plurinational" governance.

At the same time, partly in response to the previous year's aborted efforts to assume the apex of national power and partly to retain the broader goals of participatory government, CONAIE shifted its focus toward popular assemblies at the mayoral level. They thus shifted away from efforts to obtain power at the executive level and toward expanded popular participation at the local level. During the CONAIE-Noboa government negotiations, CONAIE's new focus was highlighted by the visibility and popularity of one of the main negotiators, Auki Tituaña, the Indian mayor of Cotacachi and one of those who had been most successful in establishing CONAIE's *gobiernos comunitarios* or Popular Parliaments.

Equally important, and to a certain extent a landmark achievement, was the social capital obtained by CONAIE from non-Indian sectors of society. That new status was perhaps most accurately revealed in an editorial in the widely read but relatively conservative daily newspaper, *El Comercio* (7 February 2001).

> . . . what happened this week was a great leap onto the train leading to an inevitable utopia: the search for an economically and socially equitable society, one that is not oppressive at home, and much more democratic in its policies. . . . Ecuador is changing its skin. If someone now shouts, "shoot" because "Indians are in revolt" yet the Presidential Palace "attends to the legitimate demands of the indigenous people," that's good. It's because something is moving beneath our feet.

Such statements demonstrate that the indigenous presence in the January 2000 coup cannot be simply dismissed as a *golpe detrás de los ponchos* (military coup hidden behind Indian ponchos) as some have suggested (Alvarez 2001). While that dramatic gesture failed to place an Indian into a presidential seat, subsequent actions and attitudes suggest that Ecuador's indigenous nationalities need not forget their ideas of pluriculturalism, and their perceived role within the state. Likewise, even if the Indians' current, outspoken leadership role in the democratization of national political life and similar interventions into such broad national issues as the impact of "neo-liberal" economics and regional geopolitics (e.g., "Plan Colombia") diminish as the organizations shift toward local politics and local needs, the support derived from their constituency will only strengthen the leadership's legitimacy and representation. Local input will also foster the sort of democratic, broadly participatory reviews that are essential for politically mature responses to inevitable questions, disagreements, and accusations, which like the crisis that surrounded the plebiscite issue of 2000, have and will punctuate the indigenous politic participation.[18] In the meantime, there is no doubt that Ecuador's Indians have creatively advanced their ideas, their practices of inclusion, and their political presence beyond the point of any paralysis or reversal.

Amid Transition

Ecuador is, currently and almost "as usual," in political transition. Ecuador's Indians, by contrast, continue to open space toward a more inclusive society through their representatives in Congress and their local level politics. This has been a consistent pattern. While the country's indigenous people have pushed some "doors" more easily and frequently during "open" political regimes, the impetus for that pressure has been regular. Patterns developed in the early 1970s have remained consistent, regardless of whether a particular administration provided them with "political openings" or opened "revolving doors."[19]

While specific actions obviously change, there has been a persistent pattern of proactive politics, *all focused on inclusion and participation.*

The ideas and aspirations of "plurinationalism," and the related engagement with the state, clearly demonstrate CONAIE's successful rejection and reconfiguration of state-managed corporatism. Alternatively, their most recent negotiations with the government also suggest that any political and economic analysis must separate and distinguish the wide range of national economic and political policies and practices rather than presume a tidal wave of inevitable impacts glossed as "neoliberal" reforms. There is no doubt that the "neo-liberal package"—decentralization, privatization of common lands, increased oil concessions, cuts in social service programs, and a general emphasis on individual rights and responsibilities—clashes with and thus challenges many of the political and economic changes that CONAIE had sought since it was founded. Most likely, neither trend will disappear. But, considering recent indigenous actions and government responses, many economic "reforms" will, again most likely, have to be negotiated rather than accepted as inevitable "globalization." Likewise, the indigenous movement's current oscillation between local, national, and international political and economic concerns and actions defies any definitive prediction of future directions and goals. All such questions and predictions are premature as Ecuador's Indians continue to establish, de facto, their place in the plurinational state that they have imagined.

Conclusion: Ecuador's Plurinationalism in a Regional Context

Since the February 2001 *Levantamiento,* Ecuador's Indians have, by and large, been replaced in the national and international press by national economic issues and regional concerns with the impact of Plan Colombia. Nevertheless, the indigenous movement led by CONAIE has increased its political trajectory and enhanced the always-precarious links between organizations, representatives, and communities. As always, Ecuadorian Indian actions illustrate their unique approach to the state and to each other, yet also show strong similarities—shared patterns with and images of indigenous communities and movements—with their counterparts in many of the other countries detailed in this book.

As occurred most notably in Brazil in the 1970s and, at present, most strongly in Mexico, Colombia, Bolivia, Peru, as well as Ecuador, for those non-Indians who see themselves and/or their society as marginalized from power and wealth, Indian actions and claims serve as highly concise metaphors for the demands of broad democratic participation and consultation in each country. Likewise, as illustrated by the essays on Mexico, Colombia, Bolivia, and Peru, indigenous interests and demands highlight norms and similar expressions of participatory democracy included in recent national and international laws and national constitutions but rarely practiced satisfactorily and much negotiated or debated locally (see Maybury-Lewis, Levi, Jackson, Ramírez, Gustafson, Gelles, and Dean in this volume).

At the same time, much like those of Colombia and Peru, and using tactics quite different from Mexico's Zapatistas yet similar to those of

Bolivia (but eliciting a far more sympathetic non-Indian response than that described for Bolivia by Gustafson in this volume), Ecuadorian Indian organizations have created considerable and regular political space for CONAIE and Pachacutik through direct and active participation in the political process. What distinguishes the new Ecuadorian congressional presence from that in other countries is the *form* through which they seek to reconfigure society and the state—i.e., plurinationalism. This ideal state formation—a set of constituent "nations"— would create as a federated political mosaic that moves beyond simpler respect for and recognition of cultural difference by the state, as expressed in terms of "multiculturalism" or "pluriculturalism" in many other countries. While plurinationalism is equally an "idea," the term has been converted into active politics for those of Ecuador's Indians not waiting for or demanding that change filter down from the top.

To illustrate, unlike in 2000, CONAIE no longer seeks to leap to the "top." CONAIE's new leadership, with Leonidas Iza as president and Tito Puanchir as vice-president, has displayed indigenous political aspirations less dramatically and they project less charismatic public personae than Antonio Vargas. But there is no less inclination toward radical change or any suggestion of a major shift in direction. In fact, the same opportunism in creating political alliances with other sectors demonstrated in "the shortest coup" is currently playing itself out again as the national Pachacutik movement and its provincial chapters maneuver between different blocks of political parties in the 2002 electoral process. The practical challenge at hand is to balance the at times competing and at times converging interests of supporting an indigenous candidate for the presidency and of creating a coalition broad enough to ensure a reversal of the "neo-liberal" policies that, CONAIE insists, have been so devastating for indigenous populations.

Ecuador, at present, contrasts with the Colombian situation detailed by Ramírez in this volume, by Jackson in related publications, in Ecuador during the León government, and latent in any country at any time. That is, in many areas and times, political positions, activities, and priorities sometimes divide the interests and priorities of organizations or representatives from those of the communities. That could, of course, change. However, the Ecuadorians have worked recently in ways that increase checks and balances between communities and representatives, and they now use the same democratizing mechanism— "People's Parliaments"—to create a national role for themselves as vanguard for political and economic initiatives that incorporate a wide range of sectors and interests.

To illustrate, CONAIE convoked all social sectors for a 16 February 2002 (and first) session of the Parliament of the Peoples (Pueblos) of Ecuador by stating that:

> According to the government, the Ecuadorian national economy has grown by 5 percent, but only favors the rich, the business-men, and the industrialists. WE ASK: How much has it grown for the poor of Ecuador? Nothing. On the contrary, there is now more poverty, more unemployment, and more misery.
>
> Consequently, the social path to overcome these problems is through the Parliaments of the Peoples of Ecuador, space consti-tuted by means of the unity of the distinct organizations of a Community, Parroquia (township), Canton (county), and Province. It is a space to enlarge the *minga* (Quichua term for good-spirited, communal reciprocal labor) between Indians and non-Indians—young people and women, artisans and mer-chants, students and workers, farmers and intellectuals, educa-tors, retired people, and transport workers—to jointly seek the solutions for our country.
>
> The parliamentarians are leaders of representative organiza-tions with a legitimate social base from which to help. Their strong work ethic, permanent militant stand, and transparency permit them to serve as spokespersons of the local Parliament and to the provincial and national parliaments.

This CONAIE memo clearly illustrates the Indians' current efforts to blend a continued push towards Ecuador's unique goal—plurina-tionalism—through democratic representations built on strong ties with the grass roots, and with effort to create links and stimulate proactive policies within the broader national society. As such, Indians continue to speak for and to the national society through voices that—it would appear—emanate from and reflect local interests.

Notes

1 The coup and *Levantamiento* events reviewed here are drawn from a va-riety of sources, primarily national and international news services and newspapers (*El Comercio, El Hoy,* CRE radio, *New York Times,* and CNN, as well as Lucas [2000], *El Comercio* [2000] and Alvarez [2001]). The in-

formation from each source is similar. Consequently, lengthy and cumbersome citations are not included, except where there are differences or where citations are otherwise deemed essential. I would like to thank Carlos Espinoza and Bret Gustafson for their comments on an earlier draft. I would also like to thank David Edeli, currently a Fulbright Scholar in Ecuador, for his comments on and additions to the "Postscript."

2   The term comes from Panama's Kuna Indians but is now used widely in Central and South America to indicate all "Indian Lands."

3   For the most recent events (1999–2001), this paper draws mainly on primary sources—newspaper articles and public documents—as well as personal interviews with indigenous leaders, who will remain anonymous here.

4   This paper was initially drafted prior to the February 2001 Levantamiento, or "uprising." As of this writing (March 2001), Indians have won some clear economic and political gains, and landed on high moral ground. However, insufficient time has passed to permit any detailed evaluation of the most recent events.

5   The price of oil dropped from U.S.$14 per barrel in December 1997 to U.S.$6 in December 1998, as inflation rose from 31 percent to 45 percent. The price of natural gas, imported and widely used for domestic cooking, rose over 450 percent.

6   On the night of February 12, Cesar Gaviria, Secretary General of the Organization of American States (OAS), and Peter Romero, U.S. State Department's Undersecretary of State for Latin American Affairs (and former U.S. Ambassador to Ecuador), spoke several times, and in the clearest possible manner, by telephone to Mendoza and others. The apparent coup, they said, was unconstitutional and unacceptable, and the actions would lead to sanctions. Some observers suggest that these interventions persuaded the army to end the coup (*New York Times* 22 February 2001). Others argue that the replacement of Mahuad by Noboa had been considered and planned for months (*El Comercio* 2000, Alvarez 2001). While it now appears that the change in leadership was, indeed, considered and suggested for some time before February 2000, such analysis is beyond the scope of this paper.

7   Most of these statements are drawn from a paper prepared for a May 2000 conference "Indigenous Sovereignty and Multicultural States" hosted by the Weatherhead Center for International Affairs, Harvard University, by Ampam Karakras, a Shuar Indian who works closely with CONAIE.

8   See Alvarez 2001 for alternative interpretations.

9   OPIP's *Marcha Indígena por la Vida*, reviewed here, was one of the few exceptions.

10 Each direct action—levantamiento, march, or strike—also produced a long list of local demands. However, the organizational thread that linked each was a focus on national or otherwise broad regional issues that required a national response.

11 In Ecuador the Quechua language (widely spoken from Bolivia to southern Colombia, with approximately 1.5 million in Ecuador) is consistently and widely referred to as Quichua. Though dialects vary throughout the region, Quichua and Quechua are the same language.

12 President Jaime Roldos died in a plane crash (1981) and was succeeded by his Vice President, Oswaldo Hurtado.

13 These "new" terms are often drawn from historical names or archeological styles.

14 At one time there were three claimants to the presidency—Bucaram, Fabian Alarcon, and Vice President Rosalia Arteaga.

15 These included establishment and administration of indigenous territories, political representation, control over natural resource and natural resource exploitation, consultation, intellectual property rights, and respect for traditional authorities and languages.

16 Alvarez (2001, 117) writes that CONAIE and Ecuarunari refused to meet, so as not appear too supportive of the government prior to the elections of CONAIE officers, and, when they met later, requests for funds increased exponentially and unacceptably.

17 There was one deadly violent action, perhaps an accident, that occurred in the Tena-Archidona area of the Amazonian region. Several people, police and citizens, were shot and killed.

18 Rumors have already begun to circulate that Vargas had met secretly with Noboa prior to the formal meeting, and the same rumors talked of bribes. CONIAE will meet on this, but has already added that such rumors are to be expected from those who resent the Indians' power and progress.

19 These openings, and closings, are significantly different from the broader, post-military dictatorship "political openings" that Yashar (1999) identifies as markers for the rise of many of Latin America's indigenous movements.

Works Cited

Alvarez Grau, Vladimiro

2001   *El golpe detrás de los ponchos.* Quito: Endino.

Amanecer Indio (Bulletin, Confeniae, Quito, Ecuador)

CDDH (Comisión de Derechos Humanos)

1993   *El levantamiento indígena en el Ecuador.*

CONAIE

1989   *Las nacionalidades indígenas en el Ecuador.* Quito: Ediciones Tinkui.

1991   Ecuador: Indians want "a State within a State," say landowners.

1992   Indian Uprising in Ecuador Protester Killed by Army: Many Wounded and Detained.

1992   *Indigenous Plurinational Mandate.* CONAIE.

1993   *Political Declaration of Ecuador's Indigenous Peoples.* The Fourth Congress of the Confederation of Indigenous Nationalities of Ecuador (CONAIE) was held December 15–18, 1993.

1998   *Derechos de nacionalidades y pueblos indígenas del Ecuador.* Fundacion Hanns Seidel-Conaie.

CONFENIAE

1985a   *Palma Africana y etnocidio.* Quito: Cedis-Confeniae.

1985b   *Defendemos nuestra tierra! Defendemos nuestra tierra!* Quito: Cedap-Confeniae.

CRE (Radio/Internet: Guayaquil, Ecuador)

El Comercio (Newspaper, Quito, Ecuador)

Hoy (Newspaper, Quito, Ecuador)

Karakras, Ampam

2000   Indigenous Sovereignty in Ecuador. Paper presented at the conference "Indigenous Sovereignty and Multicultural States" hosted by the Weatherhead Center for International Affairs, Harvard University. May 2000.

Latin American Weekly Report

1985   African Palm and ethnocide. 8 November (WR-85–44).

Lucas, Kintto

2000   *La rebelión de los indios.* Quito: Ediciones Abya Yala.

Macas, Luis

1992   *El levantamiento indígena visto por sus protagonistas.* Quito: Instituto Científica de Culturas Indígenas.

Macdonald, Theodore

1999   *Ethnicity and Culture amidst New "Neighbors": The Runa of Ecuador's Amazon Region.* Boston: Allyn and Bacon.

New York Times (Newspaper, New York, USA)

Uquillas, Jorge

1984   Colonization and spontaneous settlement in the Ecuadorian Amazon. In: *Frontier Expansion in Amazonia.* Marianne Schmink and Charles Wood, eds. Gainesville, FL: University of Florida Press.

Yashar, Deborah

1999   Contesting Citizenship: Indigenous Movements and Democracy in Latin America. *Comparative Politics*, October 1998.

Acronyms

CONACNIE   *Consejo de Coordinación de las Nacionalidades Indígenas del Ecuador,* Coordinating Council of Indigenous Organizations of Ecuador

CONAIE   *Confederación de Nacionalidades Indígenas del Ecuador,* Confederation of Indigenous Nationalities of Ecuador

CONFENIAE   *Confederación de Nacionalidades Indígenas de la Amazonia Ecuatoriana,* Confederation of Indigenous Nationalities of the Ecuadorian Amazon

FODERUMA   *Fondo para el Desarrollo de Poblaciones Rurales y Urbanos Marginales,* Fund for Development of Urban and Rural Marginal Populations

IERAC   *Instituto Ecuatoriano de Reforma Agraria y Colonización,* Ecuadorian Institute for Agrarian Reform and Colonization

MUUP (Pachacutik)   *Movimiento de Unidad Plurinacional Pachacutik,* Movement for Plurinational Unity Pachakutik

OAS   Organization of American States

OPIP   *Organización de Pueblos Indígenas del Pastaza,* Organization of Indigenous Peoples of Pastaza

PRODENPE   *Programa para el Desarrollo de las Nacionalidades y Pueblos del Ecuador,* Development Program for the Nations and Peoples of Ecuador

TSE   *Tribunal Supremo Electoral,* Supreme Electoral Tribunal

7

State Power and Indigenous Peoples in Peruvian Amazonia: A Lost Decade, 1990–2000[1]

Bartholomew Dean

Cultural citizenship—or what Renato Rosaldo has called "the right to be different and to belong, in a democratic, participatory sense" (1996, 243)—is not yet very well developed in Peru.[2] This is perhaps nowhere more apparent than in the country's Amazonian regions, where indigenous societies continue to struggle against state-sponsored economic abuses, cultural discrimination, and pervasive violence. Throughout the Peruvian Amazon, indigenous peoples have long faced centuries of evangelizing missionary work and unregulated streams of colonists. They have endured land-grabbing, decades of formal schooling in an alien tongue, pressures to conform to a foreign *national* culture, and more recently, explosive expressions of violent social conflict fueled by a booming underground coca economy. The disruptions accompanying the establishment of extractive economies, coupled with the Peruvian state-sanctioned *civilizing* project, have led to a devastating impoverishment of Amazonia's richly variegated social and ecological communities. Anyone who has spent even a short time among putatively "uncivilized" peoples of the Peruvian rainforest is well aware of the high operating costs accrued by those who are made to suffer such dehumanizing distinctions.

Implicit in the Peruvian state's neoliberal, and at times populist, project is a political philosophy with the imperative of creating a national citizenry—a "national community" (Rosaldo 1996)—out of a heterogeneous mix of culturally, linguistically, and historically diverse peoples. By promoting the cultural homogeneity of a *unified* Peruvian citizenry, schoolteachers, military officers, bureaucrats, and local elites have long reinforced the naturalizing impulse of the state's relentless attempt to forge the singular nation. An indispensable part of policy formulation in the present, a historicized account of Amazonia's past (Cleary 2001, 71) facilitates understanding the shifting nature of the Peruvian state's relations with indigenous peoples in its midst. The relatively small and politically vulnerable indigenous societies of Amazonia have long been susceptible to the social and demographic distortions associated with the Peruvian state's coercive assimilationist policies. Poverty tends to disproportionately affect indigenous peoples, especially in rural zones of Amazonia where malnutrition and illiteracy, as well as increased health and environmental risks, accompany the limited availability of basic social services.[3]

Representing 12 major linguistic families, and at least 63 "distinct" societies, the native peoples of the tropical Andes and lowlands of Peru represent the largest indigenous groups in the Amazon Basin (La Torre 1999, 32; Nájar 1998, 7).[4] The precise population of Peruvian Amazonia is difficult to specify. Population estimates range from between two and three million inhabitants, of whom at least a half a million are considered indigenous peoples (Gray 1997, 75; Chirif 1998). The numerically largest indigenous societies of the region are the Asháninka (approx. 60,000); Awajun [Aguaruna] (approx. 45,000); Kichwa (Lamas, Napo, Pastaza, and Tigre [Alamas]—approx. 35,000); Shipibo (approx. 25,000); Shawi [Chayahuita] (approx. 14,000); Kukama-Kukamiria [Cocama-Cocamilla] (approx. 11,000); and the Machiguenga (approx. 10,000). The society that I am most familiar with, the Urarina, number at least 5,000. In Peruvian Amazonia there are numerous indigenous societies whose numbers have dwindled to the hundreds—such as the once mighty Omágua; the Shiwilu [Jebero]; and the Bóóraá [Bora]—or those societies that are literally on the verge of cultural extinction—such as the Maijuna [Orejón], Dukaiya and the Ibo'tsa [Ocaina], and the Taushiro [Pinchi]—of whom only a handful remain.

Comprising nearly sixty percent of national territory (775,650 square km), Amazonia has long been presented in Peru's official and elite discourse as a vast and empty frontier simply awaiting penetration, civilization and finally, full national incorporation (Smith 1982). Tracing its intellectual genealogy to the myth of the teeming fecundity of the forests of *El Dorado* (M. Wood 2000, 187–229), the ideological construct—"Amazonia awaiting conquest"—persists in the Peruvian state's modernist fantasies of "development" predicated on productive extraction.[5] Yet state presence in the region has been historically partial and usually contingent on interests emanating beyond Amazonia. Since its inception in the nineteenth century, the Peruvian state has been motivated by nationalist sentiments aimed at guaranteeing territorial dominion. A painful reminder of this is Peru's long-standing border dispute with its Andean neighbor to the north—Ecuador (Martínez Riaza 1998; Rivera 1994). After much saber rattling and periodic outbreaks of armed conflict, Peru and Ecuador finally agreed to a formal truce in October of 1998. The peace treaty in effect confirms Peru's territorial claims, while granting to Ecuador (as private property) a square kilometer of Peruvian territory at Tiwintza, the place where fallen Ecuadorian troops lie interred following a fierce 1995 battle.[6] In addition to facing external threats to national sovereignty in Amazonia, the Peruvian state has had to deal with regionalist ire,[7] not to mention those forces that have threatened to topple it—namely armed rebel groups, such as the *Movimiento Revolucionario Túpac Amaru*, or MRTA (the Tupac Amaru Revolutionary Movement), and *Sendero Luminoso* (Shining Path).

From the perspective of indigenous peoples, the actions of the state have been arbitrary and profoundly unpredictable (Gray 1997, 71). State intervention in Amazonia has often followed on the heels of particularly brutal entrepreneurs, many of whom have operated above the law that they themselves imposed. The infamous Putumayo rubber boom scandal is a good case in point. The surfacing in 1907 of wild allegations of brutality, slaving, and genocidal murder of Bóóraá [Bora] and Uitoto peoples by the rubber baron's henchmen set into motion an international scandal that focused world attention on Amazonia.[8] Nearly a century later, large-scale exploitation of natural resources and raw materials in indigenous territories remains commonplace. In addition to the ecological impact of the boom in coca cultivation and processing, some of the most egregious cases of environmental degradation have been committed by multinational lumber, mining, and oil companies operating in the Peruvian Amazonia (De Sakar 1996; Sala 1998; Knight 2000).

In spite of the disruptions accompanying the expansion of extractive economies, social relationships in regions of intensive intercultural contact involve a dialectic that is always much more complicated than subaltern versus dominant (García Canclini 2001, 126; Dean 2001).[9] Notwithstanding this caveat, my chapter explores indigenous peoples' supra-local relationships from the vantage point of the Fujimori dictatorship (1990–2000), a perspective that admittedly obscures the complex history of zones of cultural encounter. Indeed, colonial, national, and indigenous modes of production and circulation have long interacted, even in the far reaches of the Upper Amazon (Myers 1990; Dean 1994; 1995b; Myers and Dean 1999). More recently, encroachments on indigenous territories have come from a variety of sources: Andean colonists; peasant and indigenous communities displaced during the civil war; *cocaleros* (coca growers); rebels in search of new bases of operation; business interests; and adventure seeking eco-tourists (El Comercio 1998, 2000a; Portillo 1999; El Matutino 2000a, 2000b; Balaguer 2001).

Violence and the Authoritarian State: Fujimori's Civil-Military Regime, 1990–2000

Following the tumultuous events of the 1980s, and the failed economic policies of Alan García Pérez's presidency (1985–1990), many Peruvians turned to a political "outsider" to solve the country's record rates of joblessness, inflation, monumental fiscal deficit, and grinding poverty. Soundly defeating the novelist Mario Vargas Llosa, Alberto Fujimori first came to power in 1990. His independent political party emerged from total obscurity to defeat Vargas Llosa, a political favorite backed by the patrician old guard and Lima-based conservative business elites. Many political observers interpreted Fujimori's decisive electoral victory as a vote of protest against the status quo. In an effort to create the "market conditions" that would attract international monetary loans, Fujimori's government moved quickly to implement drastic economic reforms. This included privatization of state-run industries, liberalization of imports, and the reduction of tariffs and trade barriers. The government's stringent 1990 macroeconomic program—dubbed *Fujishock* by some—had a tremendously high human cost (Crabtree 2000, 172). While taming hyperinflation, the sudden economic changes accompanying the structural adjustment program sent millions into deeper impoverishment. The real economic "benefits" from the *Fujishock* were, needless to say, selectively distributed in a manner that, "made the wealthiest groups in society even wealthier" (Reyna 1997, 34).

The populist political system that emerged under Fujimori depended on the time-honored ploy of doling out state resources on the basis of political patronage. Fujimori established a special ministry—the Ministry of the Presidency, representing up to forty percent of the annual budget—responsible for managing the allocation of targeted social spending aimed at enhancing political support (Crabtree 2000, 174). New patronage networks accompanying Fujimori's corrupt pork barrel policies took their place in Amazonia alongside older and more localized forms of clientelism. Some indigenous representatives supported the Fujimori regime in return for direct material assistance. Along the Corrientes River, for instance, Achuar community leadership's public expression of support for Fujimori's 2000 re-election campaign was directly tied to old-style political patronage (*El Matutino* 2000a).

At the national political level, Congress approved a proposal for the creation of a new governmental commission exclusively designated to work on indigenous issues. Pursuant to Peru's international commitments and domestic legislation, Ministerio de Promoción de la Mujer y del Desarrollo Humano, or PROMUDEH (the Ministry for Promotion of Women and Human Development), was charged with overseeing official programs aimed at improving indigenous peoples' welfare. These efforts were co-coordinated through PROMUDEH's *Secretaría Técnica de Asuntos Indígenas* (SETAI: Secretariat for Indigenous Affairs) which received financing from the World Bank. Created by Fujimori's government in 1998, the Secretariat for Indigenous Affairs is heir to the *Instituto Indigenista* (Indigenous Institute) of the 1940s, which eventually became part of the Ministry of Labor, and finally the Ministry of Agriculture (Olivera and Paredes 2001, 69–70).

Fujimori's government instituted several programs that purportedly benefited indigenous peoples, such as the *Proyecto Especial de Titulación de Tierras* (PETT: Special Project for Land Titling).[10] Meanwhile, the *Defensoría del Pueblo* (National Ombudsmen) became active in publicizing human rights abuse cases in indigenous communities (Santistevan 1997; Yañez 1997). The Defensoría del Pueblo was created by constitutional decree and given the mandate of defending the constitutional rights of individuals and communities. Since its inception in 1993, the Defensoría del Pueblo established a series of special human rights programs, such as a special initiative dedicated to defending the collective rights of indigenous peoples (*Programa Especial de Comunidades Nativas*). Through its non-partisan, intermediary role, the National Ombudsman's office promotes compliance of state obligations. It has, for instance, mediated problems communities have had with the Ministry of Agriculture over land titling, and provided important assistance in electoral disputes involving indigenous communities in Manseriche (Loreto), Yarinacocha and Tahuanía (Ucayali), and the Río Tambo (Junín). In collaboration with pro-indigenous advocacy groups, the Defensoría del Pueblo implemented a civil rights media training project in the run-up to the 2000 general electoral campaign. This included public service announcements and voter education via radio broadcasts in three indigenous languages: Asháninka, Shipibo, and Awajun.

In spite of these tangible achievements, the limited fiscal resources at the Defensoría del Pueblo's disposal have stymied the effectiveness of this respected public institution. Even though the Fujimori's government offices of the Defensoría del Pueblo and PROMUDEH's Secretariat for Indigenous Affairs did not signal any substantive deviation from the *civilizing* project of erstwhile governments, the mere existence of these pro-indigenous advocacy agencies within the bureaucratic structures of state governance represents an important precedent for the future negotiation of indigenous peoples' rights claims. In the absence of political will, such negotiations during the Fujimori regime amounted to little more than paper promises.

Instead of the give and take characteristic of democratic, participatory governance, intimidation, complicity, and censorship were common leitmotivs of Fujimori's authoritarian regime (D. Wood 2000), which actively promoted a culture of fear and suspicion. Fujimori resorted to the removal of checks and balances of democratic accountability and encouraged the systematic harassment of the opposition in order to consolidate his grip on state power. Restless with Congressional opposition, Fujimori closed the legislature in 1992, and suspended the 1979 National Constitution during the notorious *autogolpe*. With the political opposition in disarray, Fujimori handily won a second presidential term in 1995, defeating former U.N. Secretary General Javier Pérez de Cuellar. Fujimori's reelection was facilitated by the forging of an alliance with a Limeño based business-military caste that appropriated the state apparatus for its own material and ideological ends.

Fujimori's regime had by 1996 implemented neoliberal structural adjustment plans and won key military victories against the MRTA and *Sendero Luminoso* (see Obando 1996, 1998; Oliart 1998; Cotler and Grompone 2000). The key role of the military in Fujimori's government was evident from the considerable power wielded by the Rasputin-like figure of Vladimiro Montesinos, the former chief of the political police (the National Intelligence Service, SIN). Under Montesino's direction, the SIN developed into a formidable espionage and extortion network with close ties to paramilitary death squads (Tamariz Lucar 2001).

Countless human rights violations were the result of Fujimori's efforts to maintain an authoritarian political regime (Amnesty International 2000; Defensoría del Pueblo 2000; Youngers and Burt 2000).[11] In the wake of the purported defeat of the subversive forces waging war against a besieged state, Fujimori's civil-military regime skillfully manipulated widespread social polarization, mistrust, and economic distress. As in Guatemala (Schirmer 1998; Taylor 1998), the erasure of governmental culpability during the decade and a half (1980–1995) of Peru's civil war, combined with the pervasive militarization of society, enabled Fujimori and his cronies to consolidate his neoliberal authoritarianism (Burt 1998). Nevertheless, insurgent groups, most notably *Sendero Luminoso* and the MRTA, maintained an unyielding grip on large swaths of Peru's tropical Andes and Amazonian regions, which by the 1990s had come to supply nearly half of the globe's cocaine from its lucrative coca harvest.[12]

Beginning in the early 1980s, the Peruvian state had initiated a fitful yet savage counterinsurgency campaign that resulted in the death of more than 35,000 people. Initially concentrating its scorched-earth counterinsurgency efforts on the region of Ayachucho, the Peruvian military impelled members and sympathizers of *Sendero Luminoso* to seek refuge and new bases of operation in the sparsely populated tropical rainforests that lie east of the Andes. Similarly, MRTA defeats in the Andean department of Junín obliged this rebel group to move its base of operations into Peru's *selva central* (or central jungle, especially the provinces of Satipo and Oxapampa). By the end of the 1980s and the beginning of the 1990s, the armed insurgent groups had gained significant popular bases of operation in the selva central and some regions of the northern jungle, such Jaén (Regan 2001, 51). Both indigenous and *colonos* (mestizo colonists) either were coerced or volunteered to support the subversives. The killing of Asháninka, Yánesha, and Nomatsiguenga leaders, as well as a series of massacres committed by rebel groups and the Peruvian military gave rise to the formation of local self-defense patrols—or *rondas campesinas*—which in turn further militarized the region and intensified the violence that the state was often simply incapable of controlling (Rojas Zolezzi 1994; Espinosa de Rivero 1995, 1996; Gray 1997; see also Rodríguez 1993; Brown 1996; Degregori 1996; Starn 1999).

The impact on indigenous communities, particularly Asháninka and Nomatsiguenga, has been profound and lasting. This is reflected in terms of the actual number of war casualties, as well as by the psychological trauma accompanying the conflict (*El Comercio* 1998, A32) and by the forced displacement of families and, in some cases, entire communities (Villapolo and Vásquez 1999; Roldán and Tamayo 1999, 241–265). The magnitude of coercive violence in Peru's selva central has diminished significantly over the last few years, but human rights violations continue throughout this region where chronic, low-intensity conflict has now become endemic. In spite of its triumphant rhetoric, and a slew of decisive military victories, the Peruvian state has failed to address the armed conflict at the level of a negotiated political settlement. Both the MRTA and Sendero continue to operate in the Peruvian Amazon, albeit with diminished capacitates (Burt 1998, 37; *El Comercio* 1998, *El Comercio* 2000a, 9).[13]

Border skirmishes, counterinsurgency efforts, and the demands of drug interdiction have promoted *leva* (forcible recruitment) and *servicio militar obligatorio* (compulsory military service) in Peru. Military recruiters regularly implement the leva, particularly when recruitment goals are not met due to draft evasion and absenteeism (González-Cueva 2000, 89). The contrast between the universal nature of conscription and its unfair application demonstrates the state's active support of coercive social distinctions. Reinforcing the notion that the Peruvian state is the legitimate monopolizer of violence, the leva disciplines citizen subjects by defining certain groups—like indigenous peoples—as hazardous to the social order. Those young men unable to produce their military cards (*libretas militares*) are forced to serve in the military (Dean 1999b). Conscription is a publicly acknowledged sign of inequity: everyone knows that those lacking contacts or financial means must serve. Most indigenous peoples in rural Amazonia lack basic identity documents, such as birth certificates, military service cards, and voter registration papers that normally would certify them as full-fledged citizens—albeit notwithstanding all the ambiguities of citizenship such *national* documents imply (Anderson 2000; Gray 1997, 68).

White Gold and Social Dread

The pervasive corruption, endemic violence, and militarization that have recently characterized the Peruvian Amazon are intimately associated with a massive shadow economy in coca—the raw product for cocaine hydrochloride, PBC (*pasta básica de cocaína*), which is the unrefined form of cocaine. At its peak in the 1990s, trade in PBC was estimated to be worth a billion dollars annually from an industry involving more than a half a million people (Soberón 1999). Over the past two decades, the cultivation and processing of coca for the illicit PBC trade represents arguably the most significant socio-economic transformation in Peruvian Amazonia since the collapse of the rubber economy around the time of the First World War (Fujimori 1992; Chaumeil 1984, 13). This was particularly apparent in the early 1990s in frontier towns like Iquitos, which had a thriving informal economy of money exchangers and business fronts for laundering cash, or in the Alto Huallaga Valley, a region intimately involved in the cultivation and processing of coca (Portillo 1996). The proliferation of the illicit coca trade was also visible in Amazonia from the wide circulation of elite consumer goods (from speedboats to designer perfumes) in an endless sea of poverty.

As is demonstrated by a number of cases outlined in this volume (e.g., Colombia, Bolivia, Mexico, and Panama), the reconfiguration of indigenous peoples' relation to the Peruvian state has been complicated by violent social conflicts accompanying the illicit drug trade. Economic dislocation, coercion, and political violence have followed in the wake of the expansion of the shadow coca economy in Amazonia (AAA 2001; Cultural Survival 2001). So too has the involvement of the United States, which is driven to act by the anxious logic of a "War on Drugs" that has now spun out of control. Following the twilight of the Cold War fight against real or imagined "communist insurgency," drug interdiction efforts have become a primary rationale for U.S. military involvement in Latin America (Call 1991; Zirnite 1997; Youngers 2000). Evidence for this shift in U.S. policy was reflected in 1989 by the then Secretary of Defense Dick Cheney, who stated that the new U.S. role of "detecting and countering" drug production and trafficking was a "high priority national security mission" (Quoted in Youngers 2000, 18). Working closely with Peru's rogue National Intelligence Service, the United States vigorously expanded its security-assistance programs. Assisted by a well endowed "narcoenforcement complex" made up of more than 50 federal agencies and bureaus (Youngers 2000, 18), the U.S.-backed counterinsurgency efforts in Peru have conveniently overlapped with drug interdiction efforts.[14] The United States has spent nearly $80 million to establish a secret drug interdiction base in the Peruvian Amazonia. Under a joint Peruvian–U.S. program, 30 suspected narco-trafficker's planes have been either shot from the skies or forced down since 1995. Ostensibly established to aid the training of the Peruvian military in its war against the *narcotráficos* (drug-runners), this joint U.S.–Peruvian military operation has been responsible for the seizure of approximately one ton of coca paste since its establishment two years ago (Marshall 2001). According to official figures, Peru's coca production dropped to fewer than 100,000 acres by 2000, having peaked in 1992 with more than 300,000 acres under cultivation.[15]

In concert with U.S. support, Peruvian military pressure on the Alto Huallaga Valley's coca operations drove the narcotráficos to seek new regions of coca cultivation and safe zones for the processing of PBC. As a result, the drug runners diversified the geographical orbit of their activities to include areas away from the Alto Huallaga, such as the Alto Marañón Basin (homeland to the Awajun and Wampis [Huambisa]); the Pichis-Palcazu and Ene-Tambo regions (inhabited by the Asháninka and Yanesha peoples); the Ucayali Basin (home to the Uni [Cashibo-Cacataibo] and Shipibo-Conibo); the Urubamaba Valley (the traditional territory of the Machiguenga); and the Tambopata and Madre de Dios watersheds where the Ese'Ejja and Harakmbut reside (Mora and Bernex 1994, cited in Brack 1997, 17). Disruptions from the expansion of coca and poppy cultivation for heroin production have been noted in the Alto Chambira Basin, homeland to the Urarina, and the Tigre-Corrientes River watershed, inhabited by a number of indigenous peoples, including the Alamas Kichwa. The counterinsurgency campaign against Sendero Luminoso—especially in the Alto Huallaga, Junín and Puno regions—resulted in the actual transformation of key segments of both the armed forces and the guerilla groups into drug traffickers themselves (Gray 1997, 73).[16] Proceeds from the illicit production and commerce in PBC enriched some members of the military and government, while enabling Sendero Luminoso and the MRTA to partly reconstitute themselves (Lazare 1997; Kay 1999; Pezo 2001). However, by effectively supplanting Sendero Luminoso as the primary intermediary between the narcos and local coca growers, the Peruvian military managed to gain the "upper hand" in its war on drugs (Youngers 2000, 18, 19).

Concern over the purported growth in "narco-terrorism" has been a major factor in shaping recent U.S. foreign policy toward the entire Andean region (see Gillert 1998; Marquis 2002). In 2000, the United States approved Plan Colombia, a $1.3 billion foreign aid package designed to reduce Colombia's coca production and to stabilize the continent's oldest ongoing civil war. The U.S. State Department has proposed approving an additional $880 million program for Colombia's Andean neighbors, including Peru, where coca prices are now on the rise and the air war on the narcotráficos is temporarily on hold following the killing of an American Baptist missionary and her infant daughter in a botched drug interception air raid mission in April 2001.

The failed war on drugs has demonstrated that imposing a military solution to a problem that is at root socio-economic is myopic. The illicit drug economy, and the vigorous efforts to eradicate it, have left indigenous communities to face the disruptive consequences of involvement in clandestine activities, not to mention weather the violent conflict and bear the social dread of the boom in white gold (among others, see Macdonald 1991). Fear of drug-financed insurgency has shaped recent state interventions in the Peruvian Amazon. Similarly, a generation ago state policy toward Amazonia and its inhabitants was also shaped by reaction to insurgency—but at that time, the perceived threat came not from narco-terrorism, but from growing agrarian discontent in the Andes.

Secure Homelands: From Reform to Reaction

Coinciding with the rise to power of the so-called "Military Radicals," the Peruvian state's most proactive involvement in advancing the rights of Amazonia's indigenous peoples has been in the arena of securing their traditional homelands. General Juan Velasco Alvarado's assumption of power following the 1968 *golpe de estado* that overthrew the civilian led Belaunde government heralded a number of significant, albeit temporary changes in the state's historical posture toward indigenous peoples (Seligmann 1995). In addressing the nation's grossly inequitable "feudalistic" social order, Velasco's military government instituted a series of structural reforms formulated to diffuse the growing rural agrarian revolt in the Andean highlands. The reformist military regime nationalized key sectors of the economy and initiated one of Latin America's most extensive land redistribution programs. In Amazonia, the Peruvian state embraced a development strategy tempered by strong *indigenista* (pro-indigenous) sentiment (Montoya et al. 2001). This found expression in the promulgation of the *Ley de Comunidades Nativas y Promoción Agropecuaria de las Regiones de Selva y Ceja de Selva* (Law of Native Communities). Supplanting legislation passed in 1909 (*Ley de tierras de Montaña N. 1220*) that had rendered the tropical rainforests the exclusive property of the state, the 1974 Native Communities Law was the first instance in modern Peruvian history in which the state recognized the explicit right of its Amazonian indigenous peoples to hold communal title to their ancestral home-lands (Uriarte 1985, 40; CAAAP 1999, 20–1).

Under the combined direction of the Ministry of Agriculture and the corporatist popular mobilization agency, SINAMOS (*Sistema Nacional de Apoyo a la Movilización Social*), a process of indigenous land entitlement began in the Peruvian lowlands. Marred by many contra-dictions, the implementation of the Native Communities Law in Ama-zonia mirrored the state's model of agrarian reform in Andean peasant communities (Hvalok 1998, 100). While the Native Communities Law recognized mobile residential patterns and conceded communal rights to territories used for foraging, fishing, hunting, and slash and burn agriculture, a primary issue not stipulated in the 1974 legislation was exactly how much "migratory" territory the state was obliged to deed to legally recognized *comunidades nativas* (indigenous communities). Implementation of the 1974 legislation resulted, in some instances, in the fragmentation of common property and in the segregation of local indigenous groups. The phenomenon of territorial fragmentation of ethnic groups was by no means universal. Among the Urarina of the Chambira Basin, for example, SINAMOS presence was quite limited. During its brief existence, this state agency only titled three Urarina communities (for a total extension of 23,143 hectares).

Though at the time significant, the long-term impact of SINAMOS in Amazonia is unclear. While a group of well-meaning anthropolo-gists staffed the upper reaches of SINAMOS, those who worked di-rectly in implementing the state reforms often lacked appropriate training, and many harbored romantic, if not negative, stereotypes re-garding indigenous peoples. Moreover, rural extension workers were often just as patronizing as the most overbearing of proselytizing mis-sionaries or as abusive as the local labor bosses. The extension workers' message tended to be not that different: labor not for the *patrón* or for the Church, but rather for the State (Corry 1984, 53; Dean 1990). In spite of real shortcomings, the Velasquista reforms were in fact a wa-tershed in state relations with Peru's substantial indigenous populace. The legislative reforms implemented during Velasco's government marked a historic recognition of the basic human right of indigenous peoples to be *culturally different* (Montoya, Burgos and Paredes 2001, 102).

The transformation in the Peruvian state's assimilationist posture toward indigenous peoples was only short-lived. Under the presiden-tial leadership of General Francisco Morales Bermudez Cerruti

(1975–1980), the military government disbanded SINAMOS in 1977 and replaced the Native Community Law with legislation liberalizing the terms under which large-scale extractive industries (mining, petroleum, and lumber) could operate in Amazonia. Laws subsequently enacted further relaxed constraints on land ownership. This in turn allowed the Peruvian state to begin allocating generous land concessions to private investors. Even though the 1974 Native Community Law was left intact, the process of granting land titles to indigenous communities came to a virtual standstill. In the name of modernity, national progress, and economic prosperity, big business was yet again given a free reign in its quest to develop the Amazon (Dean 1990, 70; Corry 1984, 55–5; Burger 1987, 97).

The stampede for nonrenewable natural resources, namely petroleum, natural gas, and gold, has wreaked havoc on ecosystems and local communities in Peruvian Amazonia. During the second government of Fernando Belaunde Terry (1980–1985), colonization of Amazonia was reemphasized, and the state-directed indigenous land-titling program came to a grinding halt. Financed by international lending agencies, ambitious Amazonian highway construction projects were launched, and so too were top-down mega-development schemes, such as the Pichis-Palcazu Special Project. The government of Alan García Pérez (1985–1990) publicly expressed greater understanding for the need to recognize the plight of indigenous communities, but political crisis, economic chaos, and the growing threat of Shining Path's armed struggle prevented a besieged state from doing much in the way of concrete programs for the welfare of indigenous peoples, let alone the vast majority of the impoverished citizenry (Gray 1998).

During Fujimori's decade in power, rural Amazonian communities witnessed a dramatic upswing in the rate of privatization and parceling of communal areas. By the end of Fujimori's grip on state power in 2000, there were literally dozens of oil exploration fields, gold mining outfits, and timber companies operating in indigenous homelands throughout Peruvian Amazonia. Fujimori's brand of neoliberalism—with its lucrative tax abatements, lax environmental standards, and generous territorial concessions—clearly advanced the interests of the primary-product exporters, particularly the foreign-dominated mining sector (such as the U.S.-based Peruvian Copper Corporation) and numerous petroleum companies (Reyna 1997, 35–36), not to mention the profitable market in tropical hardwoods.[17] Assessing the Peruvian state's promotion of hydrocarbon exploration in Amazonia illustrates the Fujimori government's priorities, which tended to emphasize economic "development," regardless of the consequences this had for the livelihood and communal well-being of the region's politically vulnerable indigenous peoples.

Black Gold: Oil, the State and Indigenous Communities

Fujimori reactivated the national petroleum company's search for Amazonian oil soon after coming to power (Juárez Carmona 1991). The Fujimori-controlled legislature subsequently passed laws that paved the way for the return of foreign oil investors and the eventual privatization of the national petroleum industry, Petro-Perú. To this end, Fujimori signed the Law of Organic Hydrocarbons (Ley 26221) that encouraged the growth of the petroleum industry on the basis of free market competition and unlimited access to profits. According to this 1993 law, lots are awarded in concessions spanning from 40 years for natural gas exploration to 30 years for the extraction of oil. Moreover, the concessionaire is the legal owner of the natural resources extracted (La Torre 1999, 16). Fujiomori's neoliberal land titling program in Amazonia appears to have been designed with the aim of dividing the region into "concessionary blocks" to attract tenders for oil exploitation rights.[18]

The threat from oil is apparent throughout the Peruvian rainforest, where many indigenous communities find themselves locked in bitter disputes with unresponsive petroleum companies (AIDESEP 1999). This is evident in Peru's northern jungle, particularly in the territory of the Jivaroan and Urarina speaking peoples of the upper Amazonian region along the border with Ecuador; in the homelands of the Asháninka, Nomatsiguenga, and Yánesha peoples of the central jungle; as well as in the southern jungle department of Madre de Dios, home to the Harakmbut and neighboring groups such as the Machiguenga and Yine (Piro) peoples.

To promote and manage the exploration and production contracts, Fujimori's government created a state agency (confusingly called Perú-Petro). Many transnational petroleum companies—including among others, Chevron, Mobil, Shell, Exxon, and Occidental—vied for concession rights during what some observers have deemed a new Amazonian economic "boom" in hydrocarbons. This included Shell's controversial exploitation of the Camisea natural gas field in the Urubamba Valley. In 1995, the government awarded ARCO an exploration and production contract for a northern block (Katsouris 1995), and a conglomerate led by the French oil giant Elf Aquitaine was awarded an exploration and production contract for the central Peruvian Amazon (Reuters 1995; Espinosa de Rivero 1996, 125). The following year, Pluspetrol, an Argentine oil firm, was awarded exploration and development rights for the country's northern oilfields (Bowen 1996, 31). By 1998, 21 million hectares of Amazonian rain forest had been granted in 34 exploration and production lots (La Torre 1999, 16).

For their part, indigenous communities in Peruvian Amazonia do not enjoy any special rights over the use of natural resources, such as the water in their territories (navigable and nonnavigable), nor do they enjoy the right to extract subsoil resources in their own traditional homelands. Indeed, the Peruvian state has complete discretionary control over natural resource management.[19] Neoliberal legislation implemented during Fujimori's ten-year regime countermanded constitutional and statutory protection of indigenous peoples' land rights established under previous governments. While the 1993 Constitution guarantees communal property and reaffirms the legal recognition of Native Communities, the inalienability of communally held land was revoked. As a result, the outright sale of communal lands is no longer prohibited under current law.[20] The Peruvian Constitution recognizes the state's inalienable and absolute ownership of all mineral resources, which are exploited under a concession system. Given that the promotion of mining investments is considered to be in the national interest, and the fact that communal title to land does not encompass mineral or other subsoil rights, disputes between petroleum companies and indigenous communities are quite common. Moreover, private and commercial interests with sufficient resources and political influence have been very successful at subverting the spirit of those laws designed to defend the rights of indigenous communities.

Titling indigenous people's homelands in Peru is a long and Byzantinely complex procedure (Parellada and Hvalkof 1998). Numerous indigenous communities have endured years of bureaucratic red tape and have borne (often futilely) the cost of pursuing land title. As a result, there are presently thousands of indigenous and peasant communities that lack official governmental recognition of their ancestral lands (Inter-American Commission on Human Rights 2000). In spite of obstacles, loopholes, and governmental heel-dragging, indigenous rights organizations were by the close of the 1990s able to secure the legal recognition of more than seven million hectares of territory—or roughly ten percent of the Peruvian rainforest (Brack 1997, 21, 213). While a sizeable chunk of national territory, the amount granted to indigenous communities is less than a third of the total of rainforest territory conceded to the oil companies during Fujimori's decade in power (La Torre 1998, 20–21).

Amazonian Indigenous Federations

Throughout Fujimori's tenure, land privatization schemes persisted, as did the threat from petroleum companies, loggers, gold miners, and even cocaleros who were granted concessions, auctioned territorial "blocks," or allowed to operate with little or no oversight. In response, indigenous peoples and their allies mobilized around the issues of land titling, intellectual property rights, and rights claims in relation to exploitation of oil, minerals, lumber, and community defense. Influenced by their travels to urban and peri-urban Amazonia, the presence of pro-indigenous and development NGOs in their midst, and the general appeal of indigenismo, a new generation of indigenous leaders has come to realize that multiethnic confederations may be one of the most appropriate mechanisms for indigenous societies to articulate and defend their human rights (Dean 2002a; Verber 1998; Gray 1997; Brown 1993).

In light of the limited successes achieved at the national level, struggles for local and regional autonomy have been redirected to the international arena, where transnational indigenous organizations are now asserting their claims for self-determination and sovereignty. An unprecedented rise in political organization and activism by indigenous federations and their advocates in Amazonia has marked the past quarter of a century (Dean 2000). National indigenous organizations—such as CIDOB of Bolivia and CONAIE of Ecuador—and the transnational pan-ethnic confederation COICA (*Coordinadora de Organizaciones Indígenas de la Cuenca Amazónica*) have emerged as a vibrant political force in Latin America (among others, see Montoya 1998; Maybury-Lewis 1997; Varese 1996a, 1996b; Brysk 1996; Levi and Dean 2002). In Peru, indigenous advocacy organizations increasingly pressed their legal grievances by citing ILO Convention 169, which the state officially ratified in 1993. Nevertheless, when compared with its Andean neighbors—Bolivia and Ecuador—Peru's indigenous movement is considerably less well articulated at the national political level (Burga 2001, 68). Alliances between highland and lowland indigenous political organizations have remained virtually nonexistent in Peru, a country marked by its profound regionalism, and mutual antipathy dividing the Andean and Amazonian imagined communities.

The recognition and consolidation of indigenous peoples' rights to their distinctive ways of life and "traditional" homelands is still very much an unresolved matter in Peru.[21] Peruvian legislation is often contradictory when it comes to the rights of indigenous peoples. In some instances, laws recognize indigenous communities' rights, while in other cases laws recognize the absolute authority of the state. More generally, national legislation tends not to favor indigenous peoples' demands, and the political power of the indigenous movement remains relatively weak at the national level (cf. *El Comercio* 2000). In Peruvian Amazonia problems associated with territorial management, including controlling the access of miners, oil companies, and lumber concerns, continue to plague indigenous communities. This is evident from a series of ongoing conflicts over resource use and management. In the southern jungle department of Madre de Dios, unregulated gold mining is wreaking havoc; in the central jungle (*selva central*) the violent aftermath of the civil war has been exacerbated by continued conflicts over coca, and in Loreto, a massive oil spill by the Argentine oil company Pluspetrol has recently threatened the livelihood of thousands of indigenous peoples and imperiled the mighty Marañón river and its countless micro-environments, including the Chambira watershed (Rijke 2000).

Political mobilization has occurred in the face of the challenges to the cultural survival of Amazonia's indigenous societies. The two primary national ethnic federations representing the interests of indigenous peoples of Peruvian Amazonia are AIDESEP (*Asociación Interétnica de Desarrollo de la Selva Peruana*—Inter-Ethnic Association for the Development of the Peruvian Amazon) and CONAP (*Confederación de Nacionalidades Amazónicas del Perú*—Confederation of Amazonian Nationalities of Peru). Established in 1980, AIDESEP is the senior pan-ethnic organization in Peruvian Amazonia. In contrast to the numerically less powerful ethnic federation CONAP, AIDESEP is resolutely opposed to territorial encroachments by government, commercial, and other interests. For its part, CONAP believes that extractive activities and other development operations are inevitable. Established in 1987, CONAP advocates a more pragmatic strategy that encourages indigenous communities to actively share in the planning and benefits of development initiatives, particularly those activities initiated on their territories.

AIDESEP and CONAP share similar concerns, even though both claim to be the sole legitimate and authoritative voice of all indigenous peoples. Both, for instance, vociferously criticized the 1995 legislation allowing for the sale of putatively uninhabited territories or "unproductive" lands in Amazonia. Throughout the 1990s, both AIDESEP and CONAP requested the creation of communal reserves for hunting and subsistence activities (*El Comercio* 1998, L1). Moreover, both organizations have actively promoted cultural survival through their ongoing support of inter-cultural, bilingual educational reform.

Intercultural Education

A fundamental obstacle inherent in minority education in Peruvian state-run schools is that the educational environment does not accommodate cultural and linguistic plurality. Configured by an urban, monolingual-based model of pedagogy, formal schooling in Peru tends to be deeply authoritarian in practice and hierarchical in its organization. Following independence, Spanish was transformed from an imperial to a national language: formal instruction in the Spanish language became an important part of making the singular vernacular part of the Peruvian nation-state. The creation of a national language in Peru, as elsewhere in the postcolonial world, was "the result of the symbolic and literal violence required to forge and govern a standard language out of the vernaculars and dialects that marked the modern state" (Willinsky 1998, 199). The forced imposition of Spanish—castilianization through literacy—separates indigenous peoples from their traditional means of socialization and their customary modes of expression that emphasize oral and culturally specific local knowledge. Not only do indigenous students learn skills that are not appropriate for their particular socioeconomic and historical situation, they are also indoctrinated into becoming ashamed of their own cultural and linguistic heritage.

In many respects the educational situation in rural Peru is emblematic of the long history of culturally inappropriate modes of schooling found throughout much of Latin America, and in particular, native lowland South America. It is estimated that for every 100 indigenous students in Peru only three receive formal education designed to meet the cultural and historical needs of the community (Montoya 1998, 48). The academic school calendar in Peru is oriented to a coastal, urban existence—not to the practicalities of pastoral life in the Andes or in the Amazonian rainforest. Put quite simply, the national school calendar does not reflect the seasonal nature of agrarian life and is partly responsible for the state's dismal failure in providing appropriate educational opportunities in Peru's countryside.

School-based, formal education by itself will not be able to resolve all of the dire predicaments facing Peru's indigenous societies. Nevertheless, a community-based educational program that features language preservation (in terms of stressing not only formal methods of reasoning and literacy but oral and verbal genres from many diverse male and female points of view) and cultural awareness can in fact help counter the deleterious effects of Peru's ethnocidal social policies and rampant economic exploitation. Bilingualism and multiculturalism in situations of linguistic dominance require concerted political mobilization and support. In Peruvian Amazonia, indigenous peoples' ethnic federations, human rights organizations, and NGOs have politicized language and culture. Since the emergence of the transnational indigenous rights movement in the early 1970s, language has increasingly been celebrated as a validation of authentically performed native culture. The revalorization of language through educational programs is a means of ensuring cultural survival. Peru's national indigenous federation, AIDESEP has a bilingual intercultural education program (*Programa de Formación de Maestros Bilingües de la Amazonía Peruana*, PFMB) that is particularly noteworthy in this respect.

AIDESEP's Bilingual Teachers' Training Program (PFMB) was established over a decade ago in an effort to counter folkloric characterizations of indigenous peoples and their cultural traditions in mass-produced school primers, which are informed by a singular national curriculum and largely non-indigenous epistemologies. Involving long-standing collaborative relationships among native speakers, linguists, educators, and anthropologists, the PFMB represents one of the most significant efforts at stemming language shift and promoting cultural survival in Peruvian Amazonia. Indeed, the PFMB has been responsible for producing a new generation of appropriately trained intercultural teachers who are now helping to revitalize the moribund community school so that they can assume a role as the vibrant force behind cultural and political innovation in indigenous communities.[22] What is perhaps most noteworthy from the vantage point of this essay is the extent to which indigenous peoples, rather than the Peruvian state, have taken the lead in promoting cultural survival and community well-being through intercultural, bilingual education.

Uncertain Prospects: State and Indigenous Agendas for the Future

When it comes to evaluating the Peruvian state's promotion of the full political, economic, and social participation of Amazonia's indigenous peoples in national society there has been little to celebrate during the past decade. In what some have claimed is an empty gesture aimed at resolving the perennial tensions between self-determination and sovereignty, Fujimori's government promoted the Indigenous Affairs Office, which as previously noted, was chaired by the Ministry of Women's Advancement and Human Development (PROMUDEH). Similarly, the Peruvian Congress created its own Indigenous Affairs Committee in 1999. However, under the tutelage of Fujimori's state machine, both commissisons were largely ineffectual (*El Matutino* 2000a). The Peruvian state officially embraced the principles of ethnic and cultural pluralism in 1993 when it modified the National Constitution (Avalos Cisneros 1999, 5).[23] But just as the movement toward acknowledgment of the right to be *different* has gained official acceptance, so too has disregard for the rights of indigenous peoples continued largely unchecked.

The establishment of supra-local organizations that allow indigenous peoples to defend their human rights through political and legal means has been a slow process in the making. Many factors have impeded the ability of indigenous people to participate in, and facilitate their deliberate exclusion from, decision-making directly affecting their lands, cultural traditions, and the allocation of natural resources. The centralization of state power in Lima limits the access and participation of indigenous peoples in Peruvian national society. In addition to their cultural exclusion from the "mainstream" national mestizo society, the political unification of Amazonia's indigenous peoples has been hindered by their geographical isolation, by the nature of their dispersed settlement patterns, by their long history of intra- and inter-ethnic rivalry, and political factionalism. Attempts at countermanding, or at least subverting, the authority of rival groups is a common stratagem marking relations between rival factions. Moreover, the "egalitarian" character of many indigenous societies mitigates against hierarchical models of political organization (Clastres 1987; Dean 2002b). This has been a perennial challenge to indigenous political organizations, "which seek to permit maximum participation with a minimum of concentration of power" (Smith 1982, 29). Indeed, there are many reasons to be uneasy with contemporary versions of *indigenismo*,[24] particularly in the Peruvian Amazon where it continues to conceal the endurance of systematic social distinctions through its appeals to a putatively universal indigenous subjectivity (Dean 2002a). The illusion of an atemporal past and internal social cohesion intimated by the pan-ethnic confederations' reliance on a discourse of ethnic primordialism[25] allows its leaders to conceal both accommodation and resistance to hierarchical organizational structures that often exacerbate gendered disempowerment (cf. Dean 1995a, 1998; cf. Hobson Herlihy 1996). As is true elsewhere in lowland South America, such as in the central Brazilian Amazon, "political relationships between local people and political actors representing wider scales of action (NGOs, etc.) remain distinctly top-down" (Hoefle 2000, 497). Not withstanding these limitations, indigenismo continues to be identified—at least in the industrialized West—with a discourse of equality, and as such carries with it an enormous moral weight capable of generating much needed support (material and otherwise) for collective social action.

A review of the major events of the last decade—conveniently framed by the rise and fall of the Fujimori dictatorship—highlights indigenous peoples' political mobilization, which has occurred in the context of the ongoing crisis of political legitimacy in Peru. However, under Fujimori's leadership the state pursued policies that undermined the cultural integrity of the region's indigenous societies and embraced short-sited developmentalist strategies that led to ethnocide and widespread violence, particularly in Peru's central jungle.

One of the primary causes for the democratic crisis gripping Peru at the end of the 1990s was Fujimori's autocratic effort to retain power for an unconstitutional third term (Andean Report 2000). Fujimori's attempt to remake the Peruvian body politic through what Degregori (2000) aptly calls an "anti-politics" was in the end blocked by chronic political violence and rampant corruption. The abrupt departure of Alberto Fujimori and his reviled and feared head of espionage—Vladimiro Montesinos—from the reins of state power has opened up a Pandora's box, bringing to light a sordid host of abuses, such as graft, censorship, torture, and politically motivated extrajudicial killings.

Peruvian political culture is renowned for its weak democratic intuitions and its embrace of populism. In this regard, Peru contrasts with its two Andean neighbors, Ecuador and Bolivia, where indigenous peoples' involvement in national political life has generally been more pronounced. From the *Oncenio* of President Augusto Leguía (1919–1930) to Fujimori's authoritarian regime (1990–2000), Peruvian political history illustrates the consequences of the failure to address popular demands at the national level and of neglecting to effectively institutionalize mass political participation (Crabtree and Thomas 1999; Crabtree 2000; Degregori 2000). In Amazonia, the challenges to democratic participation, and hence *national belonging*, have been legion. Touted as a means of incorporating the absent indigenous voice, roundtable dialogues, such as the 1998 consultation involving AIDESEP, CONAP, development agencies, and the World Bank, were encouraged by the state (Promudeh and Banco Mundial 1998). Critics rightfully claimed such events amounted to nothing more than window dressing, since actual participation of indigenous communities in the planning and implementation of large-scale development initiatives has, to date, been all but absent in the Peruvian Amazon.

From the vantage point of the cultural survival of indigenous peoples, the Fujimori regime represented a lost decade. Indeed, the previous decade of the 1990s provides very little in the way of a model for directing future state relations with indigenous peoples and their homelands. On the contrary, if state-driven development initiatives continue to go unchecked in Peruvian Amazonia as they did under the Fujimori dictatorship, fragile environments will continue to be degraded, and the region's indigenous peoples will invariably lose their traditional homelands, their communities will be shattered, and their distinctive ways of life irrevocably lost. As a result, the human remnants of once vibrant indigenous cultures will be obliged to inhabit the precarious spaces at "the margins of the 'civilized' world with assimilation into the mainstream their sole viable option for the future" (McIntosh and Maybury-Lewis 2001, 4). In contrast to the state's assimilationist project of forging the Bolivaran liberal citizen, the challenge now is to imagine a national community where "indigenous Peruvian" is not oxymoronic.

Notes

1 I would like to thank David Maybury-Lewis for organizing the conference "Indigenous Peoples and the State in Latin America," which was convened by the Weatherhead Center for International Affairs, Harvard University (March, 2000). My gratitude goes to the conference participants for sharing their expertise, and for their generous and constructive feedback on my paper. I have also benefited from the collective energy and intellectual vitality of my students and colleagues at the University

of Kansas and the Universidad Nacional Mayor de San Marcos. My soul partner and colleague, Michelle McKinley, has been a boundless source of wisdom and critical reflection—I gratefully acknowledge her endless contributions. The research on which this chapter is based was conducted over forty months (1988–2000). Grants from the following institutions and organizations have supported my research in Peruvian Amazonia: The Department of Anthropology, Harvard University; Sheldon Traveling Fellowship, Harvard University; Peabody Museum of Archaeology and Ethnology, Harvard University; Mellon dissertation award, Harvard University; IIE-Fulbright Fellowship; Fulbright-Hays Fellowship; Wenner-Gren Foundation; Emslie Hornimam Scholarship, Royal Anthropological Institute; 1998–99 Fellowship in Urgent Anthropology, Royal Anthropological Institute and Goldsmiths College, University of London; Tinker Foundation; the Sigma Xi Research Society; the MAPFRE America Fundación; New Faculty Research Grant, University of Kansas; Faculty Travel Grant, Hall Center for the Humanities, University of Kansas; Tinker Field Research Grant, Latin American Studies Center, University of Kansas; and the General Research Fund, University of Kansas. This essay is dedicated to the many nations of Peru.

2 The term *cultural* emphasizes vernacular conceptions of communal belonging and mutual entitlement that provides the basis for human dignity (Rosaldo 1997, 243). In Peru, Rosaldo's notion of cultural citizenship raises the question of whether indigenous peoples can in fact be culturally distinctive, as well as being citizens in the full sense of the term.

3 UNICEF estimates that infant mortality rates in the region are double the national average, while one third of Amazonian children under age five are chronically malnourished (FENAMAD 2000). On the complex issue of indigenous rights and reproductive health in Peruvian Amazonia, see Dean, Elías, McKinley and Saul (2000); McKinley, Dean, and Arévalo-Arévalo (n.d.).

4 This includes: Arawak; Cahuapana; Harakmbet; Huitoto; Jíbaro; Pano; Peba-Yagua; Quechua; Tanacana; Tucano; Tupí-Guaraní and Záparo. In addition, three languages—Cholón (Seeptsa); Ticuna (Duéxégu); and Urarina—still remain linguistically unclassified (Dean 1999a; cf. Pozzi-Escot 1998).

5 Henry Pearson captures this perspective in his 1911 account of the Amazonian rubber industry. In Pearson's estimation, "[t]he province of Loreto [Peru], of which Iquitos is the capital, is so rich in forest products that Humboldt spoke of it as the 'dining hall of the world'"(1911, 152). Many observers have imagined Amazonia in terms of a cornucopia of productive potentials, much in the way Antonio Raimondi characterized Loreto during the mid-nineteenth century. In Raimondi's learned esti-

mation, "[n]o hay palabras para dar una idea de la inmensa variedad de producciones naturales y de la actividad de la naturaleza en el continuo desarrollo de sus seres" (1942, 97).

6   While failing to achieve the autonomous access it desired, Ecuador was ceded navigation rights on the Amazon River and its tributaries within Peruvian national territory (Manrique 1999).

7   In Loreto, Peru's largest Amazonian Department, regional demonstrations for increased autonomy were mixed with violent protests against the 1998 peace agreement with Ecuador. This latest expression of Loreto's desire for autonomy follows a long line of regionalist movements, such as the 1921 uprising led by Captain Guillermo Cervantes, which was eventually crushed by the central government based in Lima.

8   On the coercive relations of labor and the social dislocations accompanying the Amazonian rubber boom, among others, see Casement 1912; Arana 1913; Valcárcel 1915; Flores Marin 1987; Taussig 1987; Barham and Coomes 1996; Rumrrill 1998; Ochoa Siguas 1999 and Stanfield 1998. Stanfield's path breaking ethno-history of northwestern Amazonia's rubber boom (1850 to 1933) assesses the transformation this frontier region between roughly 1850 and the 1930s, just as this backwater region experienced rapid and violent incorporation into the political and economic systems of rival nation-states of Peru, Ecuador, Colombia, Brazil, the United States, and Western European powers. By paying close attention to previously unstudied archival materials, Stanfield examines how the rubber boom and international trade radically altered local indigenous communities and the environment. Stanfield's research demonstrates how indigenous peoples were not merely victims. Indigenous peoples both aided and resisted economic and environmental change in subtle and profoundly contradictory ways.

9   As David Palumbo-Liu has recently argued, cultural fields, "accommodate both dominant and emergent social groups who differently and significantly inflect the consumption and production of an increasingly global and hybrid culture" (1997, 8). In the same collection of essays exploring the multiplex nature of *streams of cultural capital,* Appadurai makes a related point by arguing that, "the world has for a very long time been constituted by overlapping congeries of cultural ecumenes" (1997, 29).

10 By the end of 1999, the PETT project had finished the physical demarcation of some 1.7 million lots, of which 700,000 were inscribed in the government's official property registers (Inter-American Commission on Human Rights 2000).

11 On the authoritarian political history of Peru, among others, see Flores Galindo 1999.

12 It was estimated that approximately 500,000 Peruvian peasants were involved during this time in the illicit cultivation of coca (Pezo 2001, 93).

13 Media accounts suggest *Senderista* activity in "la selva ayacuchana" where the Maoist insurgents are said to have a base of operation in the rainforest east of Ayacucho at Viscatan in Huanta. *Ronderos* from the community of Llochegua—located on the Río Apurimac—captured 2 suspected members of Sendero Luminoso in March, 2001 (March 6, *El Comercio*).

14 Among other institutions and agencies, this includes the U.S. Defense Department, the Customs Service, the Drug Enforcement Administration, the State Department's international narcotics bureau, and the Central Intelligence Agency.

15 Recent official figures estimate that Peru had approximately 86,500 acres of coca cultivation in 2001. However, many believe that these state estimates are too low and may be as high as 173,000 acres in 2001 (Reuters 2002).

16 Gen. Nicolás Hermoza, the former chief of the Peruvian armed forces from 1992 to 2000, currently stands accused of aiding drug smugglers in return for millions of dollars in kickbacks, which are now frozen in Swiss bank accounts. Numerous other senior Peruvian officers have been formally charged with assisting the drug smugglers for financial gain. This has included the sale to *narcos* of sensitive intelligence information about the air war and bilateral policy of "shoot-down/ask later." In their critical review of the joint U.S.–Peruvian "anti-drug patrols" (which the United States orchestrated with Montesinos) Faiola and Wilson of the *Washington Post* noted, "U.S. officials repeatedly have uncovered evidence of Peruvian pilots and military officers conspiring with drug traffickers, forcing the United States to continually take steps to protect the operation's integrity"(2001, A01).

17 La Torre estimates that since commercial logging began in Peru, almost seven million hectares of territory have been deforested. Over-harvesting has resulted in the virtual extinction of some species, particularly in their natural high jungle habitat (La Torre 1999, 26–27).

18 The Peruvian state's encouragement of Amazonian oil prospecting differs little from its enthusiastic support for other extractive economies, such as the rubber industry. This point is supported by Pearson's observation during the height of the rubber bonanza that the Peruvian state, "has been exceedingly generous with those taking up lands and has voted many valuable concessions to the companies that have constructed roads" (1911, 160).

19 For a nuanced study of the complex interaction of local and state directed models of natural resource management, see Gelles' (2000) path breaking study of the politics of Andean irrigation. As Gelles has demonstrated, "the ongoing clash between state and local models of [natural resource management] is conditioned by a racist colonial legacy (Gelles

2000, 156). As in the Andes, local peoples in Amazonia often reject state models because they are seen as constituting "a form of cultural hegemony by a nation-state that neither shares nor respects highland cultural values" (Gelles 2000, 156).

20   The only right to communal land tenure still remaining intact is that of "unassignability," which in essence prevents land titles from being reassigned to nonindigenous tenants simply on the basis of the length they have resided on the lands in dispute.

21   This is not to suggest that the official recognition of territory is the final objective of the indigenous movement. Stefano Varese's comment in a recent interview is apropos in this regard. "Qué es lo que el Estado neocolonial peruano reconoce a la comunidad nativa? Unos cuantos centímetros de suelos? El ashaninka Juaneco de Tsisontire, en su sabiduría ambiental de siglos, decía hace años en una reunion en Iquitos: 'Es que solamente la gente necesita tierras? Acaso los monos, los pájaros, las huanganas y los venados no necesitan también de la tierra para vivir?"(Montoya, Burgos and Paredes 2001, 102).

22   Based in Iquitos—the provincial capital of Peruvian Amazonia—the Bilingual Teachers' Training Program is co-managed by AIDESEP and the Teachers College of Loreto (*Instituto Superior Pedagogico "Loreto"*). This novel intercultural teacher training program presently works with students selected by their communities and ethnic federation from fourteen participating indigenous groups (Achuar, Awajun, Wampis, Kandozi, Asháninka, Nomatishigenga, Shipibo, Shawi, Shiwilu, Kukama-Kukamiria, Uitoto, Tikuna, Kichwa del Pastaza and Bóóraá). Community-based research projects (which involve participation from students, teachers and community members) are combined with postgraduate teacher training in a conventional classroom setting at the Teacher College in Iquitos. Trainee teachers are nominated by their local communities and supported through scholarships throughout their six-year study program at the PFMB (Dean 1999a; AIDESEP/PFMB/Fundación Telefonica 2000; Pizango 2001).

23   Peru's 1993 constitution explicitly prohibits discrimination based on ethnicity and provides for the right of all citizens to speak their natal languages.

24   Peruvian *indigenismo* should be understood in terms of a broader Latin American intellectual movement whose stated objectives were, as Deborah Poole notes, "to defend the Indian masses and to construct regionalist and nationalist political cultures on the basis of what mestizo, and largely urban, intellectuals understood to be autochthonous or indigenous cultural forms" (1997, 182). The complex nature of *indigenismo* is highlighted by Raúl Romero's excellent review (2001) of José Maria Arguedas' contributions to Peruvian debates over cultural *mestizaje*. This

includes Arguedas' characterization of *hispanists* as those intellectuals who were ardent champions of Hispanic and *mestizo* cultural forms (Romero 2001, 126; Arguedas 1977).

25   Typical of such rhetoric is a recent published statement by FENAMAD (Federación Nativa Madre de Dios) regarding "foreign" economic practices which they contend disregard indigenous peoples' "ancient knowledge of nature, and attack our people's self-esteem, have undermined the strong ties built on unity, solidarity and reciprocity that have characterized our communities for thousands of years"(2000, 21).

Works Cited

AIDESEP

1999   "Actividades Hidrocarburíferas en Territorios Indígenas." Memorial Indígena. XVIII Congreso Nacional de la Asociación Interétnica de Desarrollo de la Selva Peruana (AIDESEP), 16 October, Lima, Peru.

AIDESEP/PFMB/Fundación Telefónica

2000   *El Ojo Verde: Cosmovisiones Amazónicas.* Lima: AIDESEP/PFMB/Fundación Telefónica.

American Anthropological Association (AAA)

2001   "Preliminary Draft Action Plan: Fostering Partnerships with South American Indigenous Communities." AAA Task Force on the Status of Indigenous Peoples, June 8–9.

Amnesty International

2000   *Perú: Continúan las torturas.* London: Amnesty International, International Secretariat.

Andean Report

2000   "Fujimori Starts third term with Fresh Cabinet and Tear Gas." 27(29). July 24–31.

Appadurai, Arjun

1997   Consumption, Duration, and History. In *Streams of Cultural Capital: Transnational Cultural Studies.* D. Palumbo-Liu and H. U. Gumbrecht, eds., pp. 23–45 Palo Alto: Stanford University Press.

Arana, Julio C.

1913   *Las cuestiones del Putumayo: Declaraciones prestadas ante el Comité de investigación de la Cámara de los Comunes, y debidamente anotadas.* Foleto N. 3 Barcelona: Imprenta Viuda de Luis Tasso.

Arguedas, José María

1977   *Nuestra Música Popular y sus Intérpretes.* Lima: Mosca Azul.

Avalos Cisneros, María

1999   "Compendio a favor de pueblos nativos." *El Peruano.* 18 October, 5.

Balaguer, Alejandro

2001   "Los Kandozi: Guardianes del lago más rico de la Amazonia Loretana." *Rumbos* 5(27):6–17.

Barham, Bradford, and Oliver T. Coomes

1996   *Prosperity's Promise: The Amazon Boom and Distorted Economic Development.* Dellplain Latin American Studies, No. 34 Boulder: Westview Press.

Bowen, Sally

1996   "The Americas: Repsol group wins auction for refinery" *Financial Times.* June 12, p. 31.

Brack Egg, Antonio (ed.)

1997   *Amazonia Peruana: Comunidades indígenas, conocimientos y tierras tituladas. Atlas y Base de Datos.* Lima: GRF, PNUD and UNOPS.

Brown, Michael

1996   "On Resisting Resistance." *American Anthropologist* 98(4):729–749

1993   "Facing the State, Facing the World: Amazonia's Native Leaders and the New Politics of Identity." *L'Homme* 33(126–128):307–326.

Brysk, Alison

1996   "Turning weakness into strength: the internationalization of Indian rights." *Latin American Perspectives* 23(2):38–58.

Burga, Manuel

2001   "Lo andino hoy en el Perú." *Que Hacer.* Enero-febrero pp. 64–68.

Burt, Jo-Marie

1998   "Unsettled Accounts: Militarization and Memory in Postwar Peru." *NACLA: Report on the Americas* 32(2):35–41.

Call, Charles

1991   *Clear and Present Dangers: The U.S. Military and the War on Drugs in the Andes.* Washington, D.C.: The Washington Office on Latin America.

Casement, Roger

1912   "The Putumayo Indians." *The Contemporary Review* (102):317–28.

Centro Amazónico de Antropología y Aplicación Práctica (CAAAP)

1999   *Amigos desde hace 25 años.* Lima: CAAAP.

Chaumeil, Jean Pierre

1984   *Between Zoo and Slavery: The Yagua of Eastern Peru in their present situation.* IMGIA Document No. 49. Copenhagen: International Work Group for Indigenous Affairs.

Chirif, Alberto

1997   "Población indígena subestimada." *Kanatari.*(Iquitos) June 14, 7.

Cleary, David

2001   "Towards an Environmental History of the Amazon." *Latin American Research Review* 36(2):64–96.

Cotler, Julio, and Romeo Grompone

2000   *El Fujimorismo: ascenso y caída de un régimen autoritario.* Lima: IEP Ediciones.

Crabtree, John

2000   "Populisms old and new: the Peruvian case." *Bulletin of Latin American Research* (19):163–176.

Crabtree, John, and Jim Thomas (eds.)

1999   *El Perú de Fujimori, 1990–1998.* Lima: IEP and Universidad del Pacífico.

Cultural Survival

2001   "Action Update: Plan Colombia." *Cultural Survival Voices* 1(1):5.

Dean, Bartholomew

2002a   "At the margins of power: gender hierarchy & the politics of ethnic mobilization among the Urarina." In *At the Risk of Being Heard: Identity, Indigenous Rights & Postcolonial States.* B. Dean and J. Levi., eds. University of Michigan Press.

2002b   "Critical Re-vision: Clastres' Chronicle & the optic of primitivism." In *The Best of Anthropology Today.* Jonathan Benthall, ed. London: Routledge Press.

2001   "Digitizing indigenous sounds: cultural activists and local music in the age of Memorex®." *Cultural Survival Quarterly* 24(4):41–46.

1999a "Language, Culture & Power: Intercultural Bilingual Education among the Urarina of Peruvian Amazonia." *Practicing Anthropology* 20(2):39–43.

1999b "Intercambios ambivalentes en la amazonia: formación discursiva y la violencia del patronazgo." *Anthropologica* XVII(17):85–115.

1998   "Brideprice in Amazonia?" *The Journal of the Royal Anthropological Institute* 4(2):347–345.

1995a "Forbidden fruit: infidelity, affinity and brideservice among the Urarina of Peruvian Amazonia." *The Journal of the Royal Anthropological Institute* 1(1):87–110.

1995b "Towards a Political Ecology of Amazonia." *Cultural Survival Quarterly* 19(3):9.

1994   "Multiple Regimes of Value: Unequal Exchange and the Circulation of Urarina Palm-Fiber Wealth." *Museum Anthropology* 18(1):3–20.

1990   The State and the Aguaruna: Frontier Expansion in the Upper Amazon, 1541–1990. M.A. thesis in the Anthropology of Social Change and Development, Harvard University.

Dean, Bartholomew, Eliana Elías, Michelle McKinley and Rebecca Saul

2000   "The Amazonian Peoples' Resources Initiative: Promoting Reproductive Rights and Community Development in the Peruvian Amazon." *Health and Human Rights: An International Journal* 4(2):3–10.

Defensoría del Pueblo

2000   *Informe Anual de la Representación Defensorial con sede en la ciudad de Iquitos* (26 de mayo 1999–25 de mayo 2000). Iquitos: Defensoría del Pueblo.

1998   *Análisis de la normatividad sobre la existencia legal y personalidad jurídica de las comunidades nativas.* (August) Lima: Defensoría del Pueblo.

Degregori, Carlos Iván

1999   *La Década de la antipolítica.* Lima: IEP.

1996   *Las rondas campesinas y la derrota de Sendero Luminoso.* Lima: Instituto de Estudios Peruanos.

De Sakar, Dipankar

1996   "Peru Indigenous: Worried About Shell." *Inter Press Service.* London, Oct. 24.

El Comercio

2000a "Terroristas mantuvieron cautivos a nativos." *El Comercio.* July 6, A9.

2000b "Tres nativos de la selva postulan al Parlamento por Somos Perú." *El Comercio.* July 6, A9.

1998 "Nativos asháninka desalojan invasores utilizando plantas de ortiga silvestre." *El Comercio.* September 6, A32.

El Matutino

2000a "Comunidades indígenas respaldan reelección del Presidente Fujimori." *El Maututino* (Iquitos) Feb. 22, 8.

2000b "INRENA y Policía Ecológica decomisan lote de madera de la especie caoba." *El Maututino* (Iquitos) March 14, 5.

2000c "Posición sistemática contra intereses indígenas." *El Maututino* (Iquitos) May 28, 2.

2000d "Varias ONGs desarrollarán proyectos de ecoturismo y manejo agroforestal del Pacaya-Samiria." *El Maututino* (Iquitos) July 9, 7.

Espinosa de Rivero, Oscar

1996 "El pueblo Asháninka y su lucha por la ciudadanía en un país pluricultural." In *Derechos humanos y pueblos indígenas de la Amazonia Peruana.* Lima: APEP & CAAAP pp. 77–132.

1995 *Rondas Campesinas y Nativas en la Amazonia Peruana.* Lima: Centro Amazónico y Aplicación Práctica.

FENAMAD

2000 "Life and Death in the Peruvian Amazon." *NACLA: Report on the Americas* 34(1):20–22.

Fabián, Beatriz

1995 "Cambios culturales en los Asháninka desplazados." *Amazonia Peruana.* 13(25):159–176.

Faiola, Anthony, and Scott Wilson

2001 "U.S. Took Risks In Aiding Peru's Anti-Drug Patrols: Control, Standards Conceded." *Washington Post.* April 29, A01.

Flores Galindo, Alberto

1999 *La Tradición Autoritaria: Violencia y democracia en el Perú.* Lima: APRODEH & SUR.

Flores Marín, José Antonio

1987 *La explotación del caucho en el Perú.* Lima: CONCYTEC.

Fujimori, Alberto

1992 "Excerpt from relay of speech at the UN Conference on Environment and Development, UNCED, Rio de Janeiro." *British Broadcasting Corporation,* BBC Summary of World Broadcasts, June 16.

García Canclini, Néstor

2001   *Consumers and Citizens: Globalization and Multicultural Conflicts.* Minneapolis: University of Minnesota Press.

Gelles, Paul H.

2000   *Water and Power in Highland Peru: The Cultural Politics of Irrigation and Development.* New Brunswick, N.J.: Rutgers University Press.

Gillert, Douglas J.

1998   "Southern Command Aids Search for Narcotraffickers." *American Forces Press Service.* January.

González-Cueva, Eduardo

2000   "Conscription and Violence in Peru." *Latin American Perspectives* 27(3):88–102.

Gray, Andrew

1998   "Demarcating Development: titling indigenous territories in Peru." In *Liberation Through Land Rights in the Peruvian Amazon.* Alejandro Parellada and Søren Hvalkof, eds. Document No. 90. Copenhagen: IGWIA pp. 163–216.

1997   *Indigenous Rights and Development: Self-Determination in an Amazonian Community.* Oxford: Berghahan Books.

Hvalkof, Søren

1998   "From Slavery To Democracy: the indigenous process of upper Ucayali and Gran Pajonal." In *Liberation Through Land Rights in the Peruvian Amazon.* Alejandro Parellada and Søren Hvalkof, eds. Document No. 90. Copenhagen: IGWIA pp. 81–162.

Hobson Herlihy, Laura

1996   "Empowering Native Women in Central America." *Aba Yala News* 10(1):14–15.

Hoefle, William

2000   "Patronage and empowerment in the central Amazon." *Bulletin of Latin American Research.* (19):479–499.

Inter-American Commission on Human Rights

2000   *Second Report on the Situation of Human Rights in Peru.* Organization of American States.

Juárez Carmona, Víctor

1991   "Petro-Perú reinicia trabajos de exploración petrolera en la selva." *El Comercio.* April 17, A1, 3.

Katsouris, Christina

1995   "ARCO signs E &P contract with Perupetro as firm recovers from tender offer flop." *The Oil Daily.* 45(December 11) p. 1.

Kay, Bruce

1999   "Violent Opportunities: The Rise and Fall of 'King Coca' and Shining Path." *Journal of Interamerican Studies and World Affairs* 41(3):97.

Knight, Danielle

2000   "Isolated Amazon Tribes Threatened by Logging." *Inter Press Service,* Washington Jan. 28.

La Torre López, Lily

1999   *All We Want Is To Live In Peace: Lessons learned from oil operations in indigenous territories of the Peruvian Amazon.* Lima: International Union for the Conservation of Nature and Racimos Ungurahui Working Group.

Lazare, Daniel

1997   "Drugs and Money." NACLA: *Report on the Americas.* 30(6):37–43.

Levi, Jerome, and Bartholomew Dean

2002   "Introduction" In *At the Risk of Being Heard: Identity, Indigenous Rights & Postcolonial States.* B. Dean and J. Levi, eds. University of Michigan Press.

Macdonald, Theodore

1991   "From Coca to Cocaine: The political and economic implications for tribal Amazonian Indians." In *Coca and Cocaine: effects on People and Policy in Latin America.* D. Pacini and C. Franquemont, eds. Cultural Survival Report 23. Cambridge, MA. and Latin American Studies Program, Cornell University. Pp. 145–160.

Manrique, Nelson

1999   "Perils of Nationalism: The Peru-Ecuador Conflict." *NACLA: Report on the Americas.* 32(4):6–10.

Marquis, Christopher

2002   "U.S. to Explore Aid to Colombia, Citing Threat of Terrorism." *New York Times* March 3.

Martínez Riaza, Ascensión

1998   "Estrategias de ocupación de la Amazonia: la posición Española en el conflicto Perú-Ecuador (1887–1910)." In *Fronteras, colonización y mano de obra indígena en la Amazonia Andina (Siglos XIX–XX)*. Pilar García Jordán, ed. Lima: Pontificia Universidad Católica del Peru y Universitat de Barcelona. Pp. 241–335.

Marshall, Claire

2001   "Peru Set to be Drug Leader." *BBC World Service*, February 17th, 21:28 GMT.

Maybury-Lewis, David

1997   *Indigenous Peoples, Ethnic Groups, and the State*. The Cultural Survival Studies in Ethnicity and Change. Boston: Allyn & Bacon.

McIntosh, Ian, and David Maybury-Lewis

2001   "Cultural Survival on 'cultural survival' " *Cultural Survival Quarterly*. 25(1):4–5.

McKinley, Michelle, Bartholomew Dean, and Blanca Arévalo-Arévalo

(n.d.)   "Women's Perceptions of Quality of Care in Reproductive Health Services in the Peruvian Amazon." Ms. under review for publication in *Human Organization*.

Montoya, Rodrigo

1998   *Multiculturalidad y Política: Derechos Indígenas, Ciudadanos y Humanos*. Lima: Sur Casa de Estudios de Socialismo.

Montoya, Rodrigo, Hernando Burgos and Martín Paredes

2001   "En la selva sí hay estrellas: Una entrevista con Stéfano Varese." *Que Hacer*. 128:98–105 enero-febrero.

Myers, Thomas P.

1990   *Sarayacu: Ethnohistorical and Archaeological Investigations of a Nineteenth-century Franciscan Mission in the Peruvian Montaña*. University of Nebraska Studies, New Series No. 68. Lincoln: University of Nebraska.

Myers, Thomas, and Bartholomew Dean

1999   "Cerámica prehispánica del río Chambira, Loreto." *Amazonia Peruana*. 13(26):255–288.

Nájar, Fernando

1998   "Pluriculturalidad y multilingüismo peruano." *Kanatari* (Iquitos) May 24, 7–10.

Ochoa Siguas, Nancy

1999 *Nimúhe: tradición oral de los Bora de la Amazonia Peruana.* Lima: CAAAP & Banco Central de Reserva del Perú.

Olivera, Luis, and Martín Paredes

2001 "Indios o ciudadanos: una entrevista con Jaime Urrutia." *Que Hacer* (128):69–78.

Palumbo-Liu, David

1997 "Introduction: Unhabituated Habituses." In *Streams of Cultural Capital: Transnational Cultural Studies.* D. Palumbo-Liu and H. U. Gumbrecht, eds. Palo Alto: Stanford University Press Pp. 1–21.

Parellada, Alejandro, and Søren Hvalkof (eds.)

1998 *Liberation Through Land Rights in the Peruvian Amazon.* Document No. 90. Copenhagen: IGWIA.

Pearson, Henry

1911 *The Rubber Country of the Amazon.* New York: The India Rubber World.

Pezo, Aldinger

2001 *La Danza de la Coca: Crónicas del negocio ilícito, el problema de la drogadicción y posibles alternativas de solución al cultivo de la coca.* Tarapoto, Peru: Syndisgraf.

Pizango, Hermógenes Patty

2001 "Reflexiones sobre la experiencia en el PFMB durante seis años de formación magisterial." *Kuúmu* (Iquitos)(3):19–22.

Poole, Deborah

1997 *Vision, Race, and Modernity: A Visual Economy of the Andean Image World.* Princeton: Princeton University Press.

Portillo, Zoraida

1999 "Colonization Threatens the Indigenous Ashaninka." *Inter Press Service.* Jan. 22.

1996 "Former Coca Growers in Vanguard of War on Drugs." *Inter Press Service.* August 5.

Pozzi-Escot, Inés

1998 *El Multilingüismo en el Perú.* Cuzco: CBC & PROEIB.

Promudeh and Banco Mundial

1998   *Consulta Amazónica: Para el plan de desarrollo indígena.* (Memoria) Iquitos, June 1–5.

Raimondi, Antonio

1942   [1862] *Apuntes sobre la provincia litoral de Loreto.* Iquitos: El Oriente.

Regan, Jaime

2001   *A la Sombra de los Cerros: las raíces religiosas de los pueblos de Jaén, San Ignacio y Bagua.* Lima & Jaén: CAAAP & Vicariato Apostólico de Jaén.

Reuters

2002   "Peru Burns Seized Drugs Worth Millions." *Reuters,* January 23.

Reyna, Carlos

1997   "Peru: Oligarchs with New Faces." NACLA: *Report on the Americas.* 30(6):32–36.

Rijke, Els

2000   "Ya No Es Como Antes . . . Een antropologisch onderzoek naar de gevolgen van oliewinning in Chambira, Peru." Doctoraalscriptie Culturele Antropologie, Universiteit Utrecht.

Rivera, Fernando

1994   "A Nineteenth-Century War in the Amazon: Indigenous Communities Caught in the Ecuador/Peru Dispute." *Abya Yala News.* 8(4):6–7,38.

Rojas Zolezzi, Enrique

1994   *Los Ashaninka: un pueblo tras el bosque.* Lima: Pontificia Universidad Católica.

Roldán, Roque, and Ana María Tamayo

1999   *Legislación y derechos indígenas en el Perú.* Lima: CAAAP & COAMA.

Romero, Raúl

2001   *Debating the Past: Music, Memory, and Identity in the Andes.* Oxford: Oxford University Press.

Rosaldo, Renato

1996   "Social justice and the crisis of national communities." In *Colonial discourse/postcolonial theory.* F. Barker, P. Hulme and M. Iversen eds. Manchester: Manchester University Press. Pp. 239–252.

Rumrrill, Róger

1998   "Las masacres del hombre y de la naturaleza: el Putumayo, el río de la violencia sin fin." *Kanatari* (Iquitos) Sept. 13, 13.

Sala, Mariella

1998   "Shell o no Shell: medio ambiente y poblaciones nativas." *Quehacer* (Mayo–Junio) pp. 57–65.

Santistevan de Noriega, Jorge

1997   "La Defensoría del Pueblo y las Comunidades Nativas." In *Desarrollo y Participación de las Comunidades Nativas: Retos y Posibilidades.* Lima: CAAAP and La Defensoría del Pueblo. Pp. 31–35.

Schirmer, Jennifer

1998   *The Guatemalan Military Project: A Violence Called Democracy.* Philadelphia: University of Pennsylvania Press.

Seligmann, Linda

1995   *Between Reform & Revolution: Political Struggles in the Peruvian Andes,* 1969–1991. Stanford: Stanford University Press.

Smith, Richard Chase

1982   *The Dialectics of Domination in Peru: Native Communities and the Myth of the Vast Amazonian Emptiness.* Cultural Survival Occasional Paper No. 8. Cambridge, MA: Cultural Survival.

Soberón, Ricardo

1999   "Impacto del narcotráfico en la economía local y nacional." *Kanatari.* (Iquitos) Jan. 31, 23–24.

Stanfield, Michael

1998   *Red Rubber, Bleeding Trees: Violence, Slavery, and Empire in Northwest Amazonia,* 1850–1933. Albuquerque: University of New Mexico.

Starn, Orin

1999   *Nightwatch: The Politics of Protest in the Andes.* Durham: Duke University Press.

Tamariz Lucar, Domingo (ed.)

2001   *Montesinos: Toda la Historia.* Lima: Caretas Dossier.

Taussig, Michael

1987   *Shamanism, Colonialism and the Wild Man.* Chicago: University of Chicago.

Taylor, Clark

1998 *Return of Guatemala's Refugees: Reweaving the Torn.* Philadelphia: Temple University Press.

Varese, Stefano

1996a "The ethnopolitics of Indian resistance in Latin America." *Latin American Perspectives.* 23(2)58–72.

1996b "The New Environmentalist Movement of Latin American Indigenous People." In *Valuing Local Knowledge Indigenous People and Intellectual Property Rights.* S. Brush and D. Stabinsky, eds. Washington, D.C. Island Press.

Veber, Hanne

1998 "The salt of the Montaña: interpreting indigenous activism in the rainforest." *Cultural Anthropology.* 13(3):382–413.

Valcárcel, Carlos A.

1915 *El proceso del Putumayo y sus secretos inauditos.* Lima: Horacio La Rosa & Co.

Villapolo, Leslie, and Norma Vásquez

1999 *Entre el juego y la guerra: recursos psicológicos y socio-culturales de los niños asháninka ante la violencia política.* Lima: Centro Amazónico y Aplicación Práctica.

Willinsky, John

1997 *Learning to Divide the World: Education at Empire's End.* Minneapolis: University of Minnesota Press.

Wood, David

2000 "The Peruvian Press under recent authoritarian regimes, with special reference to the *autogolpe* of President Fujimori." *Bulletin of Latin American Research.*

Wood, Michael

2000 *Conquistadors.* Berkeley: University of California Press.

Yañez Boularte, Carlos

1997 "Retos y posibilidades de los pueblos indígenas amazónicos ante el tercer milenio." In *Desarrollo y Participación de las Comunidades Nativas: Retos y Posibilidades.* Lima: CAAAP and La Defensoría del Pueblo. Pp. 31–35.

Youngers, Coletta

2000   "Cocaine Madness: Counternarcotics and Militarization in the Andes." NACLA: *Report on the Americas.* 34(3):16–23.

Youngers, Coletta, and Jo-Marie Burt

2000   "Defending Rights in a Hostile Environment." *NACLA: Report on the Americas.* 34(1):43–53.

Zirnite, Peter

1997   *Reluctant Recruits: The U.S. Military and the War on Drugs.* Washington, D.C.: The Washington Office on Latin America.

Acronyms

AIDESEP	Asociación Interétnica de Desarrollo de la Selva Peruana, Inter-Ethnic Association for the Development of the Peruvian Amazon
CIDOB	*Confederación de Pueblos Indígenas de Bolivia*
COICA	*Coordinadora de Organizaciones Indígenas de la Cuenca Amazónica*
CONAIE	*La Confederación de Nacionalidades Indígenas del Ecuador*
CONAP	*Confederación de Nacionalidades Amazónicas del Perú,* Confederation of Amazonian Nationalities of Peru
FENAMAD	*Federación Nativa Madre de Dios*
ILO	International Labor Organization
MRTA	*Movimiento Revolucionario Túpac Amaru,* Tupac Amaru Revolutionary Movement
PBC	*pasta básica de cocaína*
PETT	*"Proyecto Especial de Titulación de Tierras,"* "Special Project for Land Titling"
PFMB AIDESEP	*Programa de Formación de Maestros Bilingües de la Amazonia Peruana,* Bilingual Teachers' Training Program
PROMUDEH	*Ministerio de Promoción de la Mujer y del Desarrollo Humano,* Ministry for Promotion of Women and Human Development
SETAI	*Secretaría Técnica de Asuntos Indígenas,* Secretariat for Indigenous Affairs
SIN	National Intelligence Service
SINAMOS	*Sistema Nacional de Apoyo a la Movilización Social*

8

Andean Culture, Indigenous Identity, and the State in Peru

Paul H. Gelles

Major changes in cultural production are taking place in the communities and cities of Peru and in the other Andean nations. These are being transformed by transnational migration, the introduction of new information technologies, and neoliberal economic reforms. However, Andean cultural orientations, social mores, and communal politics condition these transnational and international processes in important ways. I argue for the importance of factoring these orientations in any discussion of indigenous peoples and the state in Peru. At the same time I wish to evoke the historical and cultural-political reasons why Andean cultural orientations have not had much of an impact on Peruvian nation-building.

This chapter approaches these issues by examining the changing understandings of Andean culture, the politics of "indigenous" vs. "peasant" identity, transnationalism, and state intervention in highland Peru. I start by providing an overview of Andean culture and the politics of representation in Andean studies. Here, in stressing the relationship among people, place, and production, I briefly review the history and cultural makeup of rural highland communities. I also sketch some very general differences among Peru, Bolivia, and Ecuador before turning to the particularities of the Peruvian nation-state and its cultural politics.

I then illustrate these particularities in a case study, which looks at two different processes found in the highland community of Cabanaconde in southern Peru. Here I examine the cultural politics of resource management in the community, as well as transnationalism and the way that new media and information technologies are transforming rural life there. On the one hand, I show that maintenance of ethnic identity and resistance to secularization, monetarization, and control by the state are expressed in the continued use of Andean cultural orientations. On the other, we see that Andean culture is shifting, as expressed in the transformations in community life brought about by transnational migration and new cultural imports. My paper argues that a dynamic and processual understanding of "Andean culture" and the highland community—one that views enduring patterns of belief and ritual as compatible with the porous, and even transnational, character of many Andean communities—has a role to play in the formation of Peruvian national identity.

Andean Culture: People, Place, and Production

The central Andean highlands, covering the better part of the largest mountain chain in the world (map 8-1), gave rise to the Inca,[1] the largest indigenous empire to develop in the Americas; today the Andes are home to the largest indigenous peasant population on the continent.[2] Indigenous peasant communities control vast territories in the highlands of Ecuador, Peru, and Bolivia, and one out of every three indigenous people of the Americas is Andean. There are 15 to 20 million Quechua, 3 to 5 million Aymara, and hundreds of thousands, if not millions, of monolingual Spanish-speakers who follow indigenous cultural orientations (such as in the highland regions near Lima).

The major cities of these countries are also populated in large part by people of Andean descent. In Peru, for example, twenty percent of the population lives in the more than 4,500 recognized "peasant communities." At the same time, Ossio (1992) estimates that more than 45 percent of the overall Peruvian population traces its immediate origins to these communities. It is no exaggeration to state that indigenous highlanders and their urban relatives constitute "cultural majorities" in the Andean nations (see Murra 1982). For this reason, and because Andean peoples coexist with Amazonian indigenous people, who inhabit "native" as opposed to "peasant" communities and who have a very different history of relations with the state in Peru, Bolivia, and Ecuador (see Macdonald, Dean, and Gustafson, this volume), it is crucial that we define indigenous "Andean" culture, and its relationship to nation-building in these countries.

The concept of Andean culture, *lo andino*, has recently come under attack from different quarters, especially in Peruvian studies (see Montoya 1987, Poole 1990, Urbano 1992, Starn 1991); the critique is that Andean studies often exhibit what can be called "ethnic primordialism" (see, e.g., Dean 2002). As Abercrombie puts it, "to suggest the existence of a rural/indigenous culture in the Andes, what is often called

Map 8-1

in the literature 'the Andean,' is usually to fall victim to non-Indians' essentializing stereotype of 'the Indian.' In other words, the 'Andean' is only rightly studied as a [usually utopian] image projected by various urban groups" (1991, 97). Questioning "Andeanism" has been salutary for the field, forcing anthropologists to examine the dynamic movement and plural identities of highlanders (see Starn 1991). So, too, greater attention has been directed to the ways that the indigenous peoples of highland Ecuador, Peru, and Bolivia are firmly tied to, and greatly affected by, national and international political and economic forces.

Yet I believe that the critique and subsequent devaluation of all things "Andean" can also play into the dominant cultural discourses of Peru that effectively deny the validity of highland ways of life. Given the relative success of ethnicity-based mobilization in Ecuador and Bolivia, dismissal of lo andino seems premature in Peruvian studies. The fact is that, while they participate in, and are affected by, diverse social, political, economic, and cultural worlds, millions of indigenous highlanders also have similar beliefs and ritual practices that are distinctly Andean, and that are tied to fundamental notions of community and ethnic identity. These beliefs and practices, forged in a colonial context, are today ignored or denigrated by dominant cultural discourses and by policy makers in the Andean nations.

As I have shown elsewhere (Gelles 2000), Andean culture is best viewed as having been created from a hybrid mix of local mores with the political forms and ideological forces of hegemonic states, both indigenous and Iberian. Some native institutions are with us today, albeit in a thoroughly revised form, because they were appropriated and used as a means of extracting goods and labor by Spanish colonial authorities and those of the Peruvian state after independence; others were used to resist colonial and postcolonial regimes. These institutions, reproduced and transformed through the everyday practices of millions of people, today vary greatly from one locality to the next. Andean cultural production is dynamic and adaptable, providing orientations and identity for villagers as well as for migrants who transit different national and international frontiers.

To understand Andean cultural production, and the definition of lo andino that I wish to advance here, we must understand the highland community, "the principal source for the reproduction of Andean identity" (Ossio 1992b, 249). This is not to say that Andean cultural production does not take place in the cities of Peru; it most certainly does. But the relationships, social and spiritual, that have come to define lo andino take place in rural community settings. Let us first review the material base that these relationships rest upon.

Andean communities make up the agropastoral productive units that provide most of Peru's production of cattle (62 percent), potatoes (99 percent), and corn (79 percent) (Ossio 1992b). A good part of the foraged foods and crops that are cultivated in the highlands are grown on terraced fields fed by irrigation. In contrast to the neighboring Amazon basin (see Bunker 1985, Hecht and Cockburn 1990, Dean 2002, this volume), extractive industries in the Andes and on the coast, such as those based on silver, guano, oil, and other resources (see Thorp and Bertram 1978), have drawn on highland communities that possess well-established territories and relatively stable systems of agricultural and pastoral production. These productive systems have been the material basis for maintaining a large peasantry and cheap labor force, and for extracting foodstuffs, tribute, and taxes over the last 500 years.

Perhaps most importantly, the political economy of extraction in the Andes has been bolstered by an extensive and long-standing agricultural infrastructure. Covering countless thousands of mountain slopes, the canals and terraces that indigenous states and local polities built are truly monumental structures, which represent millions of days of human labor. Unlike the pyramids, palaces, and fortresses that pre-Columbian polities also built, the congealed labor found in terraces and canals has reproduced their investment in this form of "humanized nature."

With the great population decline that followed the Spanish invasion, close to three quarters of the pre-Columbian terraces were abandoned (Masson 1987), as were countless thousands of irrigation canals. While the 4,500 recognized highland peasant communities in Peru control well over a third of the nation's vast highlands, only a tiny percentage of this land is arable. Over the last century, the rapidly growing highland population has put pressure on communal resources and has engendered attempts to recover some of the lost infrastructure. However, because of Peru's coastal-oriented political economy of development and the negative stereotypes of highland peoples and their resources that predominate in Peru, the productive potential of this infrastructure is far from realized.

While this infrastructure constitutes the material basis for the thousands of communities and villages found throughout the highlands of

Peru, Bolivia, and Ecuador today, we must also understand these rural settlements historically and culturally. The Andean community is clearly the product of Peru's "colonial matrix" (Fuenzalida 1970), which brought together indigenous and European social, cultural, and political forms to constitute a new and unique entity.[3] Many of the thousands of highland communities that dot the Andean landscape and control vast territories were established as locally dispersed populations and resettled by the Spaniards into *reducciónes* (nucleated settlements) for the purposes of tribute assessment, social control, and religious indoctrination in the late sixteenth century. Since that time, successive national governments have see-sawed between "emancipating," that is, severing, indigenous populations from their communal identities and collective forms of organization, and providing official recognition and legal protection to their communities.

In the early Republican period, "progressive" thought in Latin America held that "Indians" should be incorporated as individual citizens into the country and intermediary forms of association—such as ethnic groups and communal identities—should be done away with. By the same token, communal ownership and organization were seen as obstacles to progress. This mindset led to reforms that often took away the only safeguards peasants had against predatory haciendas, mines, etc. But in the 1920s, under the Leguia government, several hundred communities gained title to their lands and became incorporated as legally recognized *Comunidades Indígenas* (Indigenous Communities). This number steadily increased through the century, receiving an even larger push in 1969, through the massive land reforms and reorganization of rural life by the Military Radicals; it was at this time that they were renamed *Comunidades Campesinas* (Peasant Communities).

Today, with the neoliberal reforms that are sweeping the Andean nations and the rest of Latin America, we see the pendulum swinging back to the policies of the early Republican period, with these economic reforms threatening again to bring back the concentration of land, the removal of communal safeguards, and attacks by different industries, private citizens, and government agencies on indigenous highland communities, their common property regimes, and their cultural identity.

These communities, and the ways in which Andean cultural identity is threatened, denied, or marginalized by current and past regimes, must also be understood in terms of a cultural orientation that links people, place, and production within particular communities. During pre-Columbian times, and well into the Spanish colonial period, Andean peoples and polities throughout the Central Andes traced their origins to sacred features of the landscape, such as mountains, lakes, and springs. Salomon (1991), for example, shows how in the early colonial period the use of the term *llaqta*, which can be understood as "town," expressed a strong bond between what he calls a "place-deity" or "deity-locale," the territory it was believed to control, and the group of people that depended on this territory and who were favored by the local deity. Fuenzalida (1970) has shown how such an identity was reconfigured through the colonial period and through the fusion of Andean and Iberian beliefs, practices, and institutions in the reducciones or "Indian towns." The way in which the Catholic saints were incorporated into this communal dynamic is important: today, towns are represented by a patron saint and other, lesser saints, and these play an important role in defining personal and communal identities in the highlands.

As providers of fertility and life for crops, livestock, and people, as well as of disease, death, and destruction, these different protector spirits and emblems of communal identity must be placated by ritual offerings, libations, and religious celebrations (e.g., fiestas). The prosperity of each family, village, and community is to a large degree seen as depending on frequent gifts to local mountain deities, the Earthmother, and assorted figures in the Catholic pantheon. This is a key feature of life in the Andes, defining ritual practice and social life, as well as cultural and ethnic identity. These beliefs and ritual practices have also long been a fundamental component of local systems of agricultural and pastoral production, of those activities that sustain life.

Clearly, then, there is a strong material and spiritual basis to the Andean ways of life and cultural orientations, one that has a firm foundation in a long-standing infrastructure and in well developed understandings that join sacred landscapes to production, community, and cultural identity. Before illustrating this cultural dynamic in the case of a particular community, let us first examine the larger political context that also conditions Andean cultural understandings and identity.

Indigenous Mobilization and Cultural Politics in Peru

Against the common historical, political, and cultural processes that I have outlined above—an indigenous empire that further developed an already extensive infrastructure, the loss of much of this infrastructure and the resettlement of rural populations in reduccíones during the Spanish colonial period, and the "Andean" type of identity that conceptually links people, place, and production to local deities (both native Andean and Catholic)—we have the separate nation-states or "imagined communities" (Anderson 1983) of Peru, Bolivia, and Ecuador that developed since independence in the early nineteenth century. Each country has its own complex history of nation building, cultural politics, and ways of dealing with its indigenous inhabitants. Here I will only signal major differences in indigenous ethnicity-based mobilization in these different national contexts before turning to the particularities of Peru.[4]

In the Andean nations of Ecuador and Bolivia, indigenous peoples from both the Andes and the Amazon have made significant political gains (see Macdonald, Gustafson, this volume). While we must not exaggerate these gains—indigenous resources, leaders, and organizations are still very much under attack—the way that activists have organized along ethnic-based lines in these nations is virtually inconceivable in Peru (see, e.g., Remy 1994).

In the case of Bolivia, the importance of ethnicity-based mobilization is best exemplified by the rise of the Aymaran Katarista party, which used indigenous Aymaran symbols, denounced ethnic discrimination, and called for the formation of a plurinational state. Yet Víctor Hugo Cárdenas, the former Katarista leader turned vice-president in 1992, gained his position only by forging a series of unlikely alliances with neoliberal political interests. Indeed, while Bolivia is currently one of the nations most attuned to bilingual education and other cultural issues concerning its indigenous majority, the tension between neoliberal and indigenous political interests is great, and there is a wide breach between official rhetoric and practice (Albo 1994, Gustafson, this volume).

In Ecuador, as in Bolivia, indigenous movements have made a political space for themselves, at first receiving a lot of impetus from their class-based counterparts, but eventually formulating their own demands. Unlike in Bolivia, however, in Ecuador indigenous organizing grew out of Amazonian groups (Macdonald, this volume). In the Andes, a federation of *comunas*, or peasant communities, followed later. Since 1980, a national federation of indigenous people united these groups. With its nation-paralyzing strikes and demands for bilingual education and legal reform, it is now "the most prominent social movement in the country" (Selverston, 1994, 150). Yet indigenous leaders continue to be assassinated, the constitution does little to protect indigenous rights, and recent governments have worked to undermine the federation.

In contrast to Ecuador and Bolivia, indigenous organizations in Peru have only recently begun to have some impact on national politics, and most of these represent the interests of Amazonian "native" communities (see Dean, this volume) as opposed to the large concentration of indigenous people found in Andean "peasant" communities. Indeed, as Remy shows, although the Peruvian state has generated organizations and policies for indigenous peoples, "most of the sectors to which such policies are directed do not identify, organize, or mobilize as indigenous peoples, nor do they raise ethnic grievances" (1994, 108). And despite the fact that, for several million people, Quechua has been the "language of struggle" in peasant movements, "no one fought for Quechua" (1994, 115).[5] Like the Ecuadorian comunas, the 4,500 officially recognized Peasant Communities enjoy official status as legal entities and have jurisdiction over natural resources and customary law on their territories. Unlike in Ecuador, peasant communities in Peru have not organized into ethnic-based indigenous federations, but rather into peasant federations.

The reasons for this have in great part to do with the fact that the Velasco regime (1968–1975) largely "peasantized" the highlands of Peru (see, e.g., Mayer 1994), that is, made the class-based term of campesino the predominant idiom for discussing rural dwellers; the regime replaced an ethnic designation, *indígena* (as in Comunidades Indígenas) with a socioeconomic one, *campesina* (as in Comunidades Campesinas).

This is part of the mixed legacy of the Velasco regime. On the one hand, the greater state intervention in the highlands that began with the Velasco reforms of the late 1960s and early 1970s broke the concentrated power of local elites in rural areas, power that was already being challenged from within communities (see also Guillet 1992, Long and Roberts 1978, Seligmann 1995). The regime carried out massive land reform, made Quechua a national language, and ruptured Peru's colonial past. However, the "democratically" elected regimes since that time have rolled back many of the gains of the early Velasco years, and there has been great political upheaval and a steady decline in the standard of living since that time.[6]

But what is important for our discussion of ethnicity- versus class-based mobilization in Peru is the fact that the Velasco regime, largely because of its class-based orientations, also sidelined any recognition of indigenous cultural orientations (except in extremely romanticized portrayals of Inca socialism) and the potential for ethnicity-based mobilization. Through its reorganization of rural life in class-based (i.e., "peasant") terms, the Velasco government determined in large part the discourse through which rural dwellers were organized and organized themselves (i.e. peasant federations) in the years that followed.

The 1980s in Latin America were generally a time of transition from authoritarian to "democratic" rule, where the fall of socialism and the decline of the Latin American left cleared a space among popular organizations for ethnic-based mobilization (Van Cott 1994). This was not the case in Peru, where the change from military to "democratic" rule was accompanied by the rise of the Shining Path revolutionary movement. More than 27,000 people, mostly Andean peasants, died in the war between Peru's brutal military and Shining Path, which took up armed struggle in 1980. Hundreds of thousands of people were displaced from their Andean homelands, human rights abuses were carried out on both sides, and the military carried out thousands of extrajudicial executions (see Dean, this volume).

Shining Path used Quechua as a language of recruitment and its rank and file was largely made up of individuals from an indigenous peasant background, yet it eschewed indigenous politics and used the Chinese peasantist model and class-based language to characterize its revolution and the cause of rural dwellers. The language of peasantism and class-based revolution and social change was once again reinforced.

Yet there are other reasons that go beyond the use of class-based terms which explain the almost total lack of indigenous mobilization and the defense of Andean cultural rights, and which explain why Peru has been compared to apartheid South Africa in terms of the "differential incorporation" (Smith 1982) of its indigenous Andean majority. The strong cultural and geographic divide between the coast and highlands in Peru is unique among the Andean nations in its intensity, and it is reflected in language, music, dance, dress, food, education, and many other cultural and social arenas. The reasons for this are complex and many; they include but are not limited to: the fact that Lima was the capital of the viceroyalty of Peru and the center of political and cultural production in the Spanish colonial regime in the Andean nations; and the fact that Lima and the bureaucracies of the state are on the coast, in contrast to the capitals of Ecuador and Bolivia.

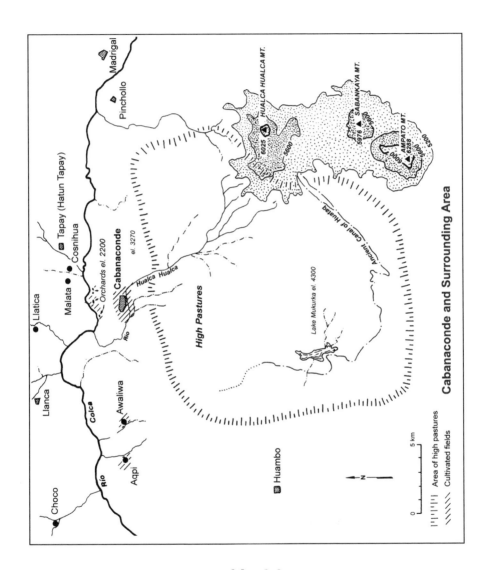

Map 8-2

Although there is a constant and dynamic interaction, melding, and transference between the highlands and coast (see Paerregaard 1997), they are spoken of and conceptualized as iconic of different cultures, the *cultura criolla* (criollo culture) of the coast and *cultura andina* or *lo andino* (Andean culture) of the highlands; the inhabitants of these two areas are often referred to as *costeños* (coastal-dwellers) and *serranos* (highlanders), respectively. While Andean migrants, as well as urban criollos, often restrict their movement to their own particular cultural enclaves in these two regions, their plural identities are conditioned by the radically different cultures associated with each region.

Both geographic and cultural spaces are recognized as forming part of the larger imagined community. But it is criollo culture and coastal society that holds center stage in Peruvian nation-building. The term criollo, which was originally used to designate people of Spanish descent born in the Americas, refers to the "social unit defined in cultural and class terms . . . that has directed state operations since the birth of the republic" (Turino 1991, 260).[7] Today, popular and national cultural discourses present the Spanish-speaking, white, West-leaning minority as the model of modernity, the embodiment of legitimate national culture, and the key to Peru's future.

Just as the coastal cities are iconic of criollo culture in popular national discourse, highland communities are iconic of indigenous culture. Many of the negative stereotypes directed toward the people of the Andes, who are referred to as serranos or *indios* (Indians)—that they are backward and unproductive—are extended to the mountains and their systems of production. In sum, Peru is a nation in which a dominant cultural minority deploys its world view throughout the provinces by means of its educational system, civic ceremonies, language, water and land policies, and through its vision of development. Let me illustrate these cultural politics, and the previous discussion of Andean culture, with a case study from southern Peru.

Cabanaconde: Tradition, Transnationalism, and Cultural Transformation

Cabanaconde, located at 3270 meters above sea level in the Colca Valley (Province of Caylloma, Department of Arequipa) and founded as a reducción in the 1570s, is the largest community of the Colca Valley (map 8-2). The people of Cabanaconde, numbering upwards of 5,000 at present, are bilingual Quechua and Spanish speakers. The Cabaneños distinguish themselves ethnically from other groups in the southern Peruvian Andes, and even from other groups of the Colca Valley. Although Cabanaconde has not been brutalized by the Peruvian military or by Shining Path, the reverberations of the dirty war have been felt there, as have many other foreign political and economic forces.

There has been a considerable amount of seasonal and permanent outmigration in Cabanaconde since at least the early part of this century, perhaps best evidenced by the Provincial Clubs of Cabanaconde operating in both Lima and Arequipa by the 1940s. Since 1965, when a road reached the community, Cabanaconde has experienced greatly increased rates of outmigration. Today, there are large migrant colonies of Cabaneños in Arequipa, Lima, and Washington, D.C., estimated to have 1,000, 3,000, and 600 members, respectively. The provincial clubs formed by migrants in these cities are very much a part of the life of the community and have intervened decisively in conflicts between the community and outside interests. We will soon return to issues of migration, transnationalism, and cultural transformation; let us first look at the cultural politics of resource management and local identity.

Land, Water, and Cultural Identity

Officially, all water in the highlands belongs to the state, which ostensibly has the right to decide not only the uses and allocation of water, but also the organizational models by which it is managed. But highland communities dispute the state's control over "their" water and often refuse to allow the state to determine local irrigation practices. Local and state models of resource management embody fundamentally different historical processes, as well as distinct, competing cultural rationales concerning resources, power, efficiency, equity, and ethnic identity. Irrigation water can thus provide a window into wider cultural and political processes affecting nation-building and society in Peru.

One hundred percent of Cabanaconde's agriculture is irrigated, the water coming from the Majes Canal and the snow melt of Hualca-Hualca, a 6,000-meter-high peak. Twenty-four hours a day for several months a year, irrigation water descends the Hualca-Hualca River and passes directly through a series of canals to the more than 1,200 hectares (3,000 acres) of agricultural terraces found in Cabanaconde's main fields. Hualca-Hualca Mountain, alongside "Earthmother" and figures in the Catholic pantheon, is a principal deity and the object of much worship.

The cult of Hualca-Hualca Mountain is ancient. In 1586, the ethnic lords of the ancient Cavana polity told a Spanish crown official that their ancestors emerged from Hualca-Hualca Mountain, the source of their irrigation water. The same document states that the Cavana people dutifully worshiped her (Ulloa Mogollon [1586] 1965). Beliefs about origins in, and worship of, mountains and other sources of water (Sherbondy 1982; Reinhard 1985) are very much part and parcel of the Andean notions of identity that link people, place, and production.

Today, the irrigation and ritual practices associated with the cult of Hualca-Hualca Mountain are exemplified in the "local model" of irrigation. During most of the yearly distribution cycle, water management is in the hands of two men who carry snake-headed staffs of authority and often have flowers adorning their hats. They alternate, each spending four consecutive days and nights in the fields "together with the water." These are the *yaku alcaldes* (water mayors), the men responsible for the distribution of irrigation water. They are at the center of the local model of dual organization and distribute water to the land classified as belonging to their moiety, either "anansaya" or "urinsaya."

The water mayors are ritual actors and carry out countless rituals throughout the irrigation cycle. The ritual attainment of fertility and the symbolic control over the sources of water through worship of mountain deities and the earth are crucial aspects of the local model, and its rationale and practice must be understood in terms of these. Water, however, can also bewitch, and can even be deadly to those who do not carry out the proper rituals. Dual organization, which involves alternation and an overriding conceptual dualism that seeks equilibrium through the complementary nature of opposites (see Maybury-Lewis 1989), is another fundamental part of this cosmology. Historical evidence demonstrates the great time depth of these different conceptual domains. They continue to inform many other activities besides irrigation, such as herding and health care, as well as communal, family, and gender ideologies.

While the Peruvian state has declared that all water in Peru is the property of the state since the early twentieth century (Andaluz and Valdez 1987), it is only since the 1960s that the state has centered its energies on extending its control to highland irrigation systems by imposing water-user associations and new forms of distribution. This is what Lynch (1988) has called the "bureaucratic transition." Since the 1970s, the state has consistently attempted to intervene in the distribution practices of Cabanaconde. Today, for a brief but important period during the yearly agricultural cycle, there is a different type of "repartitioner," or person in charge of distribution. These individuals, who are community members like the water mayors, implement the state's model of distribution. They are called *controladores* (controllers), and distribute water to the fields sequentially from "one end to the other," ignoring the dual classification of the plots found in the local model.

A whole series of cultural norms, different from those of the local model, accompany the state model of distribution. The controllers, for example, do not receive coca and liquor from the irrigators as the water mayors do. Rather, they receive money. They are not fulfilling a major *cargo*, as are the water mayors, but rather a minor civic duty. Instead of a snake-headed staff to legitimate their authority, the controllers have an official decree from the local Irrigators Commission. They neither perform elaborate rituals nor sponsor large social events, as do the water mayors.

In short, state and local models of irrigation represent two extremely different ways of conceptualizing and implementing water management. One takes a secular and bureaucratic view of water management, while the other is focused on ritual assurance, and views water as part of a larger social and symbolic universe, which is part and parcel of larger Andean cultural orientations that join people, place, and production to identity. Today and over the last fifty years, there have been attempts to completely supplant the local model of distribution with that of the state model. Although the state model has gained ground over the years, key elements of the local model remain firmly entrenched (see Gelles 2000 for more details).

We must understand the adherence to the local model of irrigation in Cabanaconde and elsewhere in terms of the cultural politics of coast and highlands reviewed above, where state policies reflect and deploy the political will and cultural hegemony of a dominant ethnic group. As Herzfeld, (in a different context) puts it, "Nationalist ideologies usually lay claim to some kind of constructed 'national character.' Their bureaucracies have the task of calibrating personal and local identity to this construct" (1992, 3). As such, bureaucracies are directly tied "to long-established forms of social, cultural, and racial exclusion in everyday life" (Herzfeld 1992, 13). They treat particular individuals and groups differently, depending on whether they are seen as sharing the bureaucrats' social world and cultural orientations; this is often expressed with metaphors of race and blood lines. Thus, the institutional cultures generated within irrigation bureaucracies are inevitably shaped by the particular kind of "imagined community" (Anderson 1983) to which they belong.[8]

The ideology of nation-building in Peru, in irrigation matters and otherwise, is shot through with racism; it is built upon the assumption that indigenous people and their cultural orientations (including their languages, mountain rituals, agricultural systems, as well as general ways of life involving food, music, etc.) are backward and that coastal criollo culture is "modern" and thus superior, by virtue of being more rational and efficient. One of the key tenets of modernism is that Western science constantly produces more efficient technologies and ways of organizing and that "cultural differences will fade away as people discover the effectiveness of rational Western culture" (Norgaard 1994, 7). Irrigation politics in Peru and the imposition of state models of development in highland communities must thus be understood in terms of a "long tradition of Western thought which holds that ethnic attachments are irrational and archaic and ought therefore to evaporate as the world moves toward greater modernization and rationality in the conduct of its affairs" (Maybury-Lewis 1982, 220). In sum, the clash between state and local models of irrigation, furthered by post-Velasco irrigation bureaucracies in Peru, is conditioned by a racist colonial legacy and by larger cultural politics in Peruvian society today.

Transnationalism and Andean Culture in Transition

Let us now turn to a very different cultural and political dynamic in Cabanaconde, one that has to do with the longstanding pattern of outmigration of people from the community to cities in Peru, and, over the last thirty years, to the United States. It must be emphasized that Cabanaconde has always been connected to larger economic and political forces,[9] and that the Washington-based colony of Cabaneños is the culmination of a long and much larger process of outmigration by the people of Cabanaconde. By the 1930s, there were already colonies of Cabaneños in Arequipa and Lima, and during the 1940s a migrant association called the Center for Cabanaconde's Progress was established in these cities. The Cabaneño diaspora gained a foothold in the United States in the early 1970s. A small handful of Cabaneños then grew into a colony of more than 250 in the Washington area by 1992. Today that number has more than doubled. The transnational colony of Cabaneños is exceptional in that the basis for affiliation is not a region or series of communities in Peru, *but a single community*. What is key here is that many of these migrants, once established in their new nation and stateside jobs, frequently return to their native communities to invest their earnings and to renew personal and cultural identities.

Transnationalism, and the mountain rituals and other Andean cultural orientations found in the local model of irrigation examined above, would seem to be at opposite ends of the anthropological spectrum. The first evokes world systems and the postmodern condition, with migrants on the move, plural identities, and hybrid cultural borderlands,[10] while mountain ritual conjures the image of an older modernist anthropology concerned with discrete social entities, fixed identities, and enduring social structures. Such a divide, I believe, reflects more on the discipline than on the cultural reality of the Andean nations or contemporary indigenous peasant communities. Even in a phenomenon such as transnational migration, we find that communally based forms of understanding and Andean cultural orientations continue to exert a strong hold over all Cabaneños, even those in far off Washington.

For example, the annual fiesta of the Virgin of Carmen is a key event in the continual production and reproduction of this transnational community (Gelles 2000). During the second week in July, the population of Cabanaconde doubles, as migrants from Arequipa, Lima, and Washington, D.C., return to pay tribute to their patron saint. As reviewed in the first part of this essay, local celebrations of patron saints—as with the worship of local mountain and earth deities—are a key component of the Andean cultural orientation that joins people, place, and production. The Virgin of Carmen is an intimate part of what it means to be a Cabaneño: she is an emblem of ethnic identity, and she must be properly feted each year to insure the fertility and well-being of the populace and its crops and livestock. And even during this Catholic fiesta, offerings are also made by the sponsors and ritual specialists to local mountain deities.

It should not surprise us, then, that this is the key moment in the annual fiesta cycle when migrants return from Peruvian cities and from the United States to visit their homeland. At the core of local identity formation, the fiesta has now become the core ritual in the annual reproduction of this transnational community. For example, in 1991, more than 35 transmigrants returned for the fiesta, and a transmigrant living in Washington sponsored the fiesta, spending more than $20,000 in this sponsorship (Gelles and Martínez 1993).[11] In 2000, another family with a number of its members in Washington sponsored the fiesta, and more than 125 transmigrants from the United States attended. The fiesta tradition continues, with a different U.S.-based transmigrant family sponsor each time.

An increasing number of the Cabaneño transmigrants in Washington use video technology to record *la costumbre* (local customs) on their return visits. Television, which only became available with the installation of a parabolic antenna in 1993, is now found in the majority of homes in Cabanaconde. Four radio stations have sprung up in town over the last few years, and these broadcast important information in Cabanaconde and to other nearby towns and hamlets. And in July 1998 a telephone was installed in the town. Other information technologies are waiting in the wings. Cabanaconde will soon be connected to the Internet and may well become a pilot site for a "telematics network" for improving communications to highland communities. If this project comes to fruition, it will link Cabanaconde with its colonies in Peru and in the United States, as well as with the University of California, the University of London, and the University of Barcelona.

Contrary to what one might expect, these new technologies are not just being used to spread the cultural images and products of the dominant society, but also to reproduce Andean culture. There is a voluminous flow of cultural goods between Washington and Cabanaconde that includes the latest musical exports from the United States as well as videos of the latest fiestas in Cabanaconde. Many of the Washington-based Cabaneños have video libraries of these fiestas and other local rituals, and there are several video versions of the Virgin of Carmen patron saint fiesta circulating throughout households in Maryland, Virginia, and Washington, D.C., as well as in Cabanaconde itself.

Cabanaconde, then, is both "transnational" and "traditional." On the one hand, it must be understood in terms of the larger Cabaneño diaspora and the plural identities produced there. On the other, certain religious and political structures that are hundreds of years old—as seen in both the mountain rituals of the local model of irrigation and in the fiesta of the patron saint—still have a strong sway over community life, and these are dutifully recorded and diffused through the latest technology.

Conclusions

My study has argued that there are a broad number of "indigenous" "Andean" cultural orientations that are fundamental to rural life in the highlands. The perspective advanced here challenges those who would trivialize indigenous ways of life; it underlines the strengths of Andean culture by examining its production and reproduction in relation to transnational migration and larger political and economic forces. On the one hand, the religious beliefs and practices tied to production are just one piece of the Andean community's cultural mosaic—Andean people use many different cultural frameworks as they move to communities, towns, and cities in Peru and other countries. But, on the other hand, my analysis has also insisted that the cultural orientations found in local production and fiesta sponsorship remain an important and vital framework within highland society, and that an examination of these orientations is necessary for understanding important cultural dynamics within the highland community. Indeed, the orientation that joins people, place, and production transcends the boundaries of community and lies at the heart of a culture that extends to urban and transnational spheres.

Implicit in most ideologies of national development in Peru and throughout the Americas is the assumption that indigenous peoples must renounce their cultural orientations and identities in favor of progress. The secular, bureaucratic, monetary, and supposedly more rational and efficient state model of resource management that I reviewed above, today increasingly works hand in hand with neoliberalism and the privatization of land and water. It supposedly does so for the benefit of all, but in fact it extends state control and the cultural orientations of national and international power holders. Here we saw that, in the case of Peru, this involves the cultural politics of the coast and the highlands, in which the relationship between the two areas is completely infused with a colonial mindset that views the human and natural resources of the Andean highlands as inferior to the criollo coast. Such an ideology blinds Peruvian state officials to the instrumental nature of indigenous ritual practices in local irrigation. But state officials and models of resource management have a hard time displacing local models, tied as they are not just to resource management and production, but also to Andean cultural frameworks that inform local and ethnic identities.

On a broader scale, as the materials on transnational migration from Cabanaconde demonstrate, things are changing. While the Cabaneños and other indigenous people increasingly transit regional, national, and international frontiers, discovering new worlds, adopting new technologies, and prospering, they do so without necessarily having to sacrifice their cultural orientations. Rather, indigenous peoples in the Andes and elsewhere are demonstrating that their cultural distinctiveness is entirely compatible with "modernity," urban spaces, transnational migration, and social mobility. Indeed, as we saw above, new technologies are not just being used to spread the cultural images and products of the dominant society, but also to reproduce Andean culture and communal identity.

In sum, Andean culture—just like an abstract notion of Iberian or Latin American culture—must be understood as historically and socially constituted, something that is both transformed and reproduced through the everyday practices of millions of people. Andean cultural production is dynamic and adaptive, providing orientations and identity for villagers as well as for migrants who transit different national and international frontiers. But unfortunately, indigenous identities, Andean and otherwise, are inextricably linked—by representations in popular media, nationalist doctrine, and scholarship alike—to images of poverty and marginality, the implicit message being that to achieve social mobility, indigenous peoples must renounce their identities. The definitions and images generated by the dominant society allow for little else, viewing their cultures as archaic, static, and part of nature, far removed from the cultural mainstream of the modernizing nation. Until native peoples and their advocates succeed in reshaping and resignifying the constraining terms "Indian" and "indigenous people," this situation will likely remain unchanged.

Notes

1   While "Inca" is the established usage in English, the correct spelling, in terms of the officially recognized Quechua alphabet, is "Inka" (see, e.g., Mannheim 1991).

2   While "indigenous" and "peasant" do not encompass all of the diverse cultural, economic, and political processes and identities found among rural peoples in the Andean nations, these terms do highlight important features of highland society. The ways in which these two terms have been used for political mobilization, reviewed below, requires us to further define these. The United Nations defines "indigenous people" in the following way: "Indigenous communities, peoples, and nations are those which, having a historical continuity with pre-invasion and pre-colonial societies that developed on their own territories, considered themselves distinct from other sectors of the societies now prevailing in those territories, or parts of them. They form at present non-dominant sectors of society and are determined to preserve, develop, and transmit to future generations their ancestral territories, and their ethnic identity, as the

basis of their continued existence as peoples, in accordance with their own cultural patterns, social institutions, and legal systems" (in Van Cott 1994, 23). There are more than 40 million indigenous peoples in Latin America, and they constitute over half of the population in some countries (e.g., Peru, Bolivia, Guatemala) and less than one percent in others (e.g., Brazil). I use the term "peasant" to highlight the following relationships: "[the] peasant family as the basic multidimensional unit of social organization, land husbandry as the main means of livelihood, specific cultural patterns linked to the way of life a small rural community/neighborhood, and the underdog position, the domination of the peasantry by outsiders" (Outhwaite and Bottomore 1993, 454–455). This does *not* mean that peasants are economically undifferentiated, that their communities are isolated or there are not other economic processes occurring in them, or that rural dwellers do not transit many other social worlds in which they assume other identities; it is quite the opposite (see, e.g. Colloredo-Mansfeld 1999, Gelles and Martínez 1993, Kearney 1996, Starn 1991). Nevertheless, the term does link identity with the key form of livelihood (land husbandry) and its economic domination by relatively powerful outsiders.

3   As Abercrombie says, "centuries of colonial domination (and resistance to it) have produced many hundreds of small, community sized 'ethnic groups,' centered on 'county seats,' towns in which pre-Columbian populations were forced to settle . . . [They] generally define themselves as members of a local group, coterminous with town-territory, and beyond it, as citizens of the province and department defined by the nation-state to which they also pertain" (1991, 95,96). The Peasant Communities in Peru are similar in many respects to the "comunas" of Ecuador (see Selverston 1994), and the "resguardos" of Colombia (see Rappaport 1994).

4   Indeed, in Bolivia and Ecuador, it is clear that, with indigenous, ethnicity-based mobilization and state recognition of these countries as multiethnic and pluricultural, there are emerging options for thinking outside of the criollo and neoliberal envelope in state building and in empowering indigenous cultural rights. There are also more highly placed bureaucrats of indigenous extraction and some of them are open to the idea of taking indigenous cultural orientations seriously.

5   Quechua, a language that is spoken today by over 15 million people in Peru, Bolivia, Chile, Ecuador, and Argentina, was the *lingua franca* of the Inca empire. While Quechua is one of the only growing indigenous languages in the Americas today, it remains very much an "oppressed" and "fenced in" language. Despite the fact that the current Peruvian constitution recognizes the country as a bilingual nation, the native language receives little institutional support. Indeed, Quechua remains a spoken and generally unwritten language, in spite of the fact that it is increas-

ingly diffused through radio and that a good many of its speakers live in fairly urban areas and also speak, read, and write Spanish (Gelles 1996). With a few important exceptions, lengthy works are rarely found in print. There are important exceptions to this in the Andean countries. In the case of Peru, the Centro de Estudios Rurales Andinos "Bartolomé de las Casas" has produced a number of works in Quechua and is actively promoting indigenous literacy in the native language. And in the Peruvian Amazon, indigenous federations and advocacy groups have promoted bilingual education as a means of cultural survival (Dean 1999, this volume).

6   While the standard of living has steadily declined since that time, the years 1985–1988 saw even greater economic deterioration. To give just one indicator of the disintegration of the Peruvian economy, the cumulative inflation between 1985 and 1990 was over 2 million percent. Half of all deaths in Peru are children under 5 years of age.

7   Criollo is a marked cultural style clearly identified in music, food, and dance. Criollo and its derivatives are often applied to cultural literacy and the ability to move in certain social spaces. If one is "bien criollo" or *acriollado* (criolized), one has adopted clever city ways. But these terms can have both positive and negative connotations. For example, *una criollada* and *la viveza criolla* signify behaviors which can be seen as both clever and treacherous, witty yet duplicitous. The Peruvian system of stratification racializes class and ethnicity, and is quite fluid (Bourricaud 1975). As Fuenzalida (1971, 20) puts it, "The higher one is on the social ladder, the whiter one appears; the lower one is, the darker." As an individual moves from rural to urban areas or ascends socially, different racial classifications will be applied. Unfortunately, such a system has traditionally meant that indigenous persons must sacrifice their cultural identity to gain social mobility (see also Maybury-Lewis 1997, Gelles 1992, Urban and Sherzer 1991).

8   Of course we also have to take into consideration the ways in which the U.S. training of repressive militaries and support of authoritarian governments, and the neoliberal economic policies it exports to these countries, undermines indigenous mobilization and plurinational initiatives.

9   This fact was brought home with the discovery in 1995 of the frozen remains of the "Ice Maiden," a girl sacrificed to Ampato, one of Cabanaconde's sacred peaks, by the Inca state 500 years ago. Several months after her discovery, she was presented to the public at the National Geographic Society in Washington, D.C. In attendance were First Lady Hillary Clinton, Peruvian President Alberto Fujimori, and several Cabaneño migrants. The latter were a small fraction of the several hundred migrants from Cabanaconde now living in Washington, D.C. The event underscored the fact that the Cabaneños and their ancestors have always

been firmly tied into larger political processes, be it the Inca's use of mountain worship to legitimate state power in the fifteenth century or the United States' exoticizing gaze and transnational migrant circuits in the late twentieth.

10   In the last decade, transnationalism has emerged as a vital and important new research focus. The epistemology of the social sciences and humanities has to a large degree been conditioned by the dualism of the nation-state whereby it differentiates between citizen and non-citizen and between its 'modern' Self and 'traditional' Others (Kearney 1996). Members of dominated ethnic groups who constantly and insistently crisscross national borders have tended, until recently, to fall outside the categories of historical, anthropological, and literary analysis. This appears to be especially true, to borrow a phrase from Clifford (1990, 110), of those "diasporic ethnicities unevenly assimilated to dominant nation states." Such is the case of indigenous peoples from the Andean nations who emigrate to the United States.

11   This is documented in the film, *Transnational Fiesta: 1992* (Gelles and Martínez 1993). To date, as mentioned above, the Virgin of Carmen celebration has been sponsored on at least two occasions by migrants now living in Washington. The fiesta of Candelaria in February, another key fiesta when many migrants return to the community, has also been sponsored by Washington-based Cabaneños. One year during this fiesta, a conflict broke out between the transmigrant sponsors and some local residents—this culminated in a protest in the central plaza where these residents burned the transmigrants in effigy (wearing a jacket that had "U.S.A." written on it). Such an event signals new tensions, disjunctions as well as conjunctions, between the traditional and the transnational in highland society.

Works Cited

Abercrombie, Thomas

1991   "To Be Indian, to Be Bolivian." In Greg Urban and Joel Sherzer, eds., *Nation-States and Indians in Latin America*. Austin: University of Texas Press. 95–130.

Albó, Xavier

1994   "And From Kataristas to MNRistas? The Surprising and Bold Alliance Between Aymaras and Neoliberals in Bolivia." In Donna Lee Van Cott, ed., *Indigenous Peoples and Democracy in Latin America*. New York: St. Martin's Press. 55–82.

Andaluz, Antonio, and Walter Valdez

1987   *Derecho ecológico peruano: inventario normativo.* Lima: Editorial Gredes.

Anderson, Benedict

1983   *Imagined Communities: Reflections on the Origin and Spread of Nationalism.* London: Verso.

Bourricaud, Francois

1975   "Indian, Mestizo, and Cholo as Symbols in the Peruvian System of Stratification." In Nathan Glazer and Daniel P. Moynihan, eds., *Ethnicity: Theory and Practice.* Cambridge: Harvard University Press. 350–387.

Brysk, Alison

1994   "Acting Globally: Indian Rights and International Politics in Latin America." In Donna Lee Van Cott, ed., *Indigenous Peoples and Democracy in Latin America.* New York: St. Martin's Press. 29–54.

Bunker, Stephen

1985   *Underdeveloping the Amazon.* Chicago: University of Illinois Press.

Clifford, James

1992   "Travelling Cultures." *Cultural Studies.* L. Grossberg, C. Nelson, and P. Treichler eds., New York: Routledge.

Colloredo-Mansfeld, Rudy

1999   *The Native Leisure Class: Consumption and Cultural Creativity in the Andes.* Chicago: University of Chicago Press.

Dean, Bartholomew

2002   At the Margins of Power: Gender Hierarchy and the Politics of Ethnic Mobilization Among the Urarin. In *At the Risk of Being Heard: Identity, Indigenous Rights, and Postcolonial States.* B. Dean and J. Levi, eds. Ann Arbor: University of Michigan Press.

1999   "Language, Culture, and Power: Intercultural Bilingual Education Among the Urarina of the Peruvian Amazonia." In *Practicing Anthropology,* Vol. 20, No. 2.

Fuenzalida, Fernando

1970   "La matriz colonial." Revista del Museo Nacional 35:91–123.

1971   "Poder, etnia y estratificación en Perú rural." In *Perú: Hoy.* Madrid: Siglo XXI: 8–86.

Gelles, Paul H.

2000   *Water and Power in Highland Peru: The Cultural Politics of Irrigation and Development.* New Brunswick: Rutgers University Press.

1996   "Introduction." In *Andean Lives: Gregorio Condori Mamani and Asunta Quispe Huamán.* Austin: University of Texas Press.

1992   "'Caballeritos' and Maíz Cabanita: Colonial Categories and Andean Ethnicity in the Quincentennial Year." *Kroeber Anthropological Society Papers* 75–76:14–27. Oakland:GRT Press.

Gelles, Paul H., and Wilton Martínez

1993   *Transnational Fiesta: 1992.* Berkeley: Center for Media and Independent Learning.

Guillet, David

1992   *Covering Ground: Communal Water Management and the State in the Peruvian Highlands.* Ann Arbor: University of Michigan Press.

Hecht, Susanna, and Alexander Cockburn

1990   *The Fate of the Forest: Developers, Destroyers, and Defenders of the Amazon.* New York: Harper.

Herzfeld, Michael

1992   *The Social Production of Indifference: Exploring the Symbolic Roots of Western Bureaucracy.* Chicago: University of Chicago Press.

Kearney, Michael

1996   *Reconceptualizing the Peasantry: Anthropology in Global Perspective.* Boulder: Westview Press.

Long, Norman, and Bryan Roberts, eds.

1978   *Peasant Cooperation and Capitalist Expansion in Central Peru.* Austin: University of Texas Press.

Lynch, Barbara

1988   "The Bureaucratic Transition: Peruvian Government Intervention in Sierra Small Scale Irrigation." Ph.D. dissertation, Cornell University.

Masson, Luis

1987   "La ocupación de andenes en Perú." *Pensamiento Iberoamericano* 12.

Maybury-Lewis, David

1997   *Indigenous Peoples, Ethnic Groups, and the State*. Boston: Allyn and Bacon.

1989   "The Quest for Harmony." In David Maybury-Lewis and Uri Almagor, eds., *The Attraction of Opposites: Thought and Society in the Dualistic Mode*. Ann Arbor: University of Michigan Press.

1982   "Living in Leviathan: Ethnic Groups and the State." In David Maybury-Lewis, ed., *The Prospects for Plural Societies*, pp.220–232. Washington: American Ethnological Society.

Mayer, Enrique

1994   "Recursos naturales, medio ambiente, tecnología y desarrollo." In Oscar Dancourt, Enrique Mayer, and Carlos Monge, eds., *Perú: El problema agrario en debate Sepia V*:479–534. Lima: Sepia.

Montoya, Rodrigo

1987   *La cultura quechua hoy*. Lima: Hueso Húmero Ediciones.

Murra, John

1982   "The Cultural Future of the Andean Majority." In David Maybury-Lewis, ed., *The Prospects for Plural Societies*. Washington, D.C.: The American Ethnological Society.

Norgaard, Richard B.

1994   *Development Betrayed: The End of Progress and the Coevolutionary Revisioning of the Future*. New York: Routledge.

Ossio, Juan M.

1992   *Los Indios del Perú*. S.A. Editorial MAPFRE.

Outhwaite, William and Tom Bottomore, eds.

1993   *The Blackwell Dictionary of 20th-Century Social Thought*. Oxford: Blackwell Publishers.

Paerregaard, Karsten

1997   *Linking Separate Worlds: Urban Migrants and Rural Lives in Peru*. New York: Berg.

Poole, Deborah

1990   "Ciencia, peligrosidad y represión en la criminología indigenista peruana." In Carlos Aguirre and Charles Walker, eds., *Bandoleros, abigeos y montoneros*, pp. 335–368. Lima: Instituto de Apoyo Agrario.

Rappaport, Joanne

1994   *Cumbe Reborn: An Andean Ethnography of History.* Chicago: The University of Chicago Press.

Rasnake, Roger

1988   *Domination and Cultural Resistance: Authority and Power among an Andean People.* Durham: Duke University Press.

Reinhard, Johan

1985   "Chavin and Tiahuanaco: A New Look at Two Andean Ceremonial Centers." *National Geographic Research Reports.* 1(3):395–422.

Remy, María Isabel

1994   "The Indigenous Population and the Construction of Democracy in Peru." In Donna Lee Van Cott, ed., *Indigenous Peoples and Democracy in Latin America.*, pp. 107–132. New York: St. Martin's Press.

Salomon, Frank

1991   "Introduction." In Frank Salomon and George Urioste, eds., *The Huarochirí Manuscript. A Testament of Ancient and Colonial Andean Religion*, pp.1–38. Austin: University of Texas Press.

Seligmann, Linda J.

1995   *Between Reform and Revolution: Political Struggles in the Peruvian Andes, 1969–1991.* Stanford: Stanford University Press.

Selverston, Melina H.

1994   "The Politics of Culture: Indigenous Peoples and the State in Ecuador." In Donna Lee Van Cott, ed., *Indigenous Peoples and Democracy in Latin America*, pp. 131–154. New York: St. Martin's Press.

Sherbondy, Jeanette E.

1982   "El regadío, los lagos y los mitos de origen." *Allpanchis* 17 (20):3–32.

Smith, M.G.

1982   "The Nature and Variety of Plural Units." In David Maybury-Lewis, ed., *The Prospects for Plural Societies*, pp.146–186, Washington: American Ethnological Society.

Starn, Orin

1991   "Missing the Revolution: Anthropologists and the War in Peru." *Cultural Anthropology*, 6 (1): 13–38.

Thorp, Rosemary, and Geoffrey Bertram

1978   *Peru 1890–1977: Growth and Policy in an Open Economy*. New York: Columbia University Press.

Turino, Thomas

1991   "The State and Andean Musical Production in Peru." In Greg Urban and Joel Sherzer, eds., *Nation-States and Indians in Latin America*, pp.259–285. Austin: University of Texas Press.

Ulloa Mogollón, Juan de

1965 [1586] "Relación de la Provincia de los Collaguas para la descripción de las Indias que su majestad manda hacer." In Marcos Jiménez de la Espada, ed., *Relaciones Geográficas de Indias*. Vol.1, pp.326–333, Madrid: Biblioteca de Autores Españoles.

Urban, Greg, and Joel Sherzer

1991   "Introduction: Indians, Nation-State, and Culture." In Greg Urban and Joel Sherzer, eds., *Nation-States and Indians in Latin America*, pp.1–18. Austin: University of Texas Press.

Urbano, Henrique

1992   *Modernidad en los Andes*. Cuzco: Centro de Estudios Regionales Andinos "Bartolomé de las Casas."

Van Cott, Donna Lee

1994   "Indigenous Peoples and Democracy: Issues for Policymakers." In Donna Lee Van Cott, ed., *Indigenous Peoples and Democracy in Latin America*, pp. 1–28. New York: St. Martin's Press.

9

Paradoxes of Liberal Indigenism: Indigenous Movements, State Processes, and Intercultural Reform in Bolivia[1]

Bret Gustafson

The enraged horde shouts and lifts machetes on high. [They are] drunken, demented, thirsty for blood and vengeance. [W]ith mouths green with coca, they sack and burn, they rape our girls fleeing terrified through the streets of Calacoto. [. . .] The *indios* (Indians) are descending from the hills and they've taken over San Miguel. They are not here to beg for coins or to clutter the streets for our Sunday afternoon drives. Now nothing holds back these ignorant Indians, these dirty Indians, these *indios de mierda* (shitty indios). They have surrounded the city and they have triumphed. What Julián Apaza and Zárate Willka could not do in years, the Mallku and Evo Morales have done in three weeks.

Luckily it was all a nightmare. [. . .] But in these three weeks the middle classes forgot their democratic, modern, and progressive exterior and asked for bullets against these miserable barbarians. . . . In September we found out that these dirty and repulsive characters that inhabit our nightmares, these beasts of burden . . . are infinitely more numerous than the whites. [. . .] In September the Indians lifted their head and touched our shoulder. It is a shame that it was accompanied by violence. In this bloody September, the Indians have sent us a message.

S. Monasterios, "Sound the Attack"
La Prensa (La Paz), October 8, 2000[2]

Liberal Indigenism

Through the mid-1990s, neoliberal economic reforms in Bolivia were accompanied by legislative measures that "recognized" indigenous identities, languages, and organizations and ascribed to them new categories for participation within formal institutions of state governance

(Van Cott 2000a). Liberal indigenism even took a highly visible form in the personae of the president and vice president of the most active reformist regime of the MNR (National Revolutionary Movement, 1993–1997), represented in the alliance between a wealthy mining entrepreneur and an indigenous Aymara intellectual (Albó 1994, 1999). In a dramatic shift from prior "official" discourse, in 1994 the Constitution was changed to declare Bolivia a "multiethnic and pluricultural" nation. The old Ministry of Peasant and Agrarian Affairs was dissolved and a new Secretariat (now Ministry) of Ethnic and Indigenous Affairs was created (Healy and Paulson 2000). Reforms blending "liberal" and "pro-indigenous" tenets launched during this period include *Reforma Educativa* (Education Reform) in 1994, with a bilingual and intercultural curriculum adapted to cultural and linguistic diversity (Gustafson 2002); *Ley de Participación Popular* (municipal decentralization) in 1994, granting special status to "traditional" authorities and indigenous organizations (Albó and CIPCA 1999); and *Ley INRA* (land reform) in 1996, seeking rational and efficient land markets but also providing for the establishment of collectively titled indigenous territories and some land redistribution in the eastern lowlands (Assies 2000; Muñoz and Lavadenz 1997). In a country historically marked by apartheid-like race and class hierarchies, this blend of "neoliberal" and "intercultural" reformism seemed remarkable. One optimistic observer referred to the changes as the "friendly liquidation of the past" (Van Cott 2000a).

However, recent indigenous and *cocalero* (coca farmer) mobilizations have been accompanied by increasing military violence and a resurgence of racism in the public sphere. This suggests that all is not so friendly—nor has the past been liquidated—in this new period of liberal indigenism. In September 2000, Aymara farmers' unions from the altiplano region near La Paz cut off ground transportation in and out of the capital city for three weeks. Mostly rural Aymara representing part of the national CSUTCB indigenous and peasant union *(Confederación Sindical Única de Trabajadores Campesinos de Bolivia)* were led by an ex-guerrilla named Felipe "the Mallku" Quispe. In the midst of these conflicts, the powerful coca farmers led by Evo Morales were also sporadically closing transportation routes along more than a dozen points in the Chapare region between La Paz and Santa Cruz, largely in response to coca-eradication measures pushed by the United States government. In June and July of 2000, constituent groups of the lowland indigenous federation CIDOB *(Confederación Indígena de*

Bolivia) had also confronted the government with their own set of demands, including the acceleration of slow-moving land reform. Temporarily allied with lowland mestizo peasant and colonist unions, they initiated another march on La Paz like those of 1991 and 1996. As cited in the epigraph, the Aymara Mallku would be associated with historical icons of Aymara rebellion (Julián 'Tupak Katari' Apaza and the 'Fearful' Zárate Willka) and was excoriated as a racial monster.[3] Cocalero leader Morales was similarly cast as a subversive, terrorist, indomestizo. While the response to the lowland indigenous mobilization of CIDOB would not be the same military violence or vitriolic racism, the combination of the three movements was lumped together in public writings lamenting the "anti-systemic" and quite often anti-modern resurgence of these "Indian" masses.

Has neoliberal interculturalism thus run its course? In economic terms, even the World Bank acknowledges that macro-economic stabilization has done little to reduce poverty or narrow the gap between rich and poor (World Bank 1999). In political terms, while some indigenous organizations have embraced land reform and municipal participation, neither appears to have muted indigenous protest. Nor does it seem that Bolivians who consider themselves as other than *indios* have taken rhetorics of "interculturalism" very seriously. Editorial responses to these events—fueled by Evo and the Mallku's own fiery statements—would lead a casual observer to think that Bolivia was on the verge of a caste war. How might we interpret these events in light of the wider aura of indigenous resurgence in the region and particular manifestations of intercultural reformism in Bolivia?

In this chapter I juxtapose indigenous movements, state reforms, and recent events. My purpose is not to judge whether or not indigenous participation has been secured or whether reforms have succeeded or failed. Rather I want to point out how conjunctural political conflicts and reform processes reveal gradual changes in regional and national politics, which are variegated across state terrain. I am interested in problematizing dualist perspectives that assume the existence of a hegemonic state project like "neoliberalism" pitted clearly against "indigenous" peoples, identities, and demands. Nor does the notion of unilinear movement toward "citizenship" or "democracy" totally encapsulate or exhaust the logics of either the state or indigenous peoples. Contrary to its own rhetoric, neoliberal interculturalism is not a uniform process of 'inclusion' of previously excluded Indians, but rather a set of uneven, contradictory shifts of political languages and institutions that seek to reorder and legitimate changing expressions of social difference, citizen identity, and hierarchical forms of participation. These new tactics of governance represent a transformative renewal of discourses and institutions through which elites seek to insulate centralized power (spatially, conceptually, and institutionally) from various forms of "indigenous" and other "popular" forms of political engagement. Certainly laudable for a reformist sensibility, interculturalist reforms do not, however, pursue robust versions of indigenous rights or overhaul structures of economic inequality. Nonetheless, new forms of social mobilization and paradoxes of the reforms themselves suggest that, as in the past, governmental projects are hardly guaranteed to obtain that which they seek and may in fact produce new and unexpected outcomes.

In Part One I describe two organizations usually cast as Bolivian indigenous movements: the multiethnic CSUTCB peasant union of the Andes and the indigenous confederation CIDOB of the eastern lowlands. Internal complexities and relations between these movements and the coca-growers and colonist farmers' unions complicate our understanding of diverse indigenous positions vis-à-vis the state. In Part Two, I describe three key reforms that one might place under the rubric of liberal indigenism: bilingual education, municipal decentralization, and land reform. I sketch the logic and substance of the reforms and point out varied local responses that further highlight divergent regional histories of state-indigenous relations. In Part Three I return to recent mobilizations (the CIDOB march, the Aymara blockade, and cocalero resistance) to consider the relationship between conjunctural events, organized movements, and state reformism. The highly racialized public discourse surrounding these conflicts is highlighted to consider how and why both liberalism and the new interculturalism are far from settled in Bolivia.

I. Indigenous Peoples and Movements in the Andes and the Lowlands

According to the 1992 census, 57 percent of Bolivia's population are native speakers of one of thirty-four Amerindian languages (Albó 1995). The Andean Aymara (1.6 million) and Quechua (2.4 million) generally capture the most attention because of their demographic and historic centrality vis-à-vis state formation processes centered in the highlands (Albó 1995). Aymara and Quechua symbols, languages, and cultural substrates pervade Bolivian identity formations of all types and contribute to the wider imaginary of Bolivia as an "Andean" country. Far from being pristine rural natives, Aymara and Quechua might be farmers, miners, urban intellectuals, schoolteachers, market women, truck drivers, urban merchants, or lest we forget, vice presidents and members of Congress.[4] Those seen as Aymara or Quechua by observers may or may not consider themselves to be part of such a broader ethnic identity. Multiple local and regional histories have generated heterogeneous expressions of Aymara and Quechua heritages—and multiple forms of *mestizaje* and migration—across the Andes and beyond (Abercrombie 1991).

Thirty-two indigenous peoples or *pueblos* also occupy territories now absorbed within the borders of the eastern Bolivian lowlands or *Oriente*. They were called "savages" in the 1900 census when their numbers were estimated at 90,000; the indigenous census of 1995 states that lowland peoples number 260,000 today. These diverse communities that have survived colonialism and neocolonial state formation number from 50 to 200 (Araona, Paikoneka, Yukɨ); to 2,000–3,000 (Canichana, Chácobo, Esse Ejja) to 5,000–10,000 (Guarayu, Ts'iman, Movima) to 40,000–60,000 (Moxeño, Chiquitano [Besɨro], Guarani).[5] By no means isolated tribes or hunter-gatherers, lowland peoples generally live in agrarian regions intertwined with multiple forms of state power, Hispanic latifundist elites, extractive markets for natural resources, and forms of Catholic and Protestant tutelage and mission activity. As with the Aymara and Quechua, there are also lowland indigenous teachers, artisans, merchants, rural politicians, evangelical preachers, and national bureaucrats. One Guarani leader was recently named vice minister of ethnic affairs and a Moxeño leader was vice presidential candidate for the MBL party in the elections of 1997.

Running parallel to this highland-lowland distinction, two of the primary organizations usually referred to as "indigenous" are the Andean CSUTCB *(Confederación Sindical Única de Trabajadores Campesinos de Bolivia,* founded in 1979) and the lowland CIDOB *(Confederación Indígena de Bolivia,* founded 1982). Amidst intercultural reforms and recent conflicts, these two organizations usually take center stage as key subjects and objects of neoliberal interculturalism.

With roots in histories of syndicalism connected to corporatist state-building that began in 1952, the CSUTCB emerged as an autonomous national union in 1979. Though also representing non-indigenous peasantries of Tarija, Beni and Pando departments, the CSUTCB is often considered to be a Quechua-Aymara organization. It is built on pyramidal hierarchies of local, regional, and departmental syndical organizations and has a long history of direct political engagement within and against the centralized state.[6] Having emerged out of the land reforms following the 1952 revolution, today the organization makes periodic demands on the state that cover issues such as prices, agricultural credits, access to higher education, and water rights and control. The CSUTCB maintains alliances with other national unions—primarily schoolteachers and urban workers—though these organizations have been weakened with privatization and the dismantling of the statist economy. Having been labeled *campesinos* (peasants) following the 1952 revolution, CSUTCB leaders maintain this term of self-definition along with the more recent ethnic label *pueblos originarios* (original peoples). Several decades of Andean migration to the lowlands have also generated colonists' unions *(Confederación Sindical de Colonizadores)* independent from the CSUTCB, yet often closely engaged with its political maneuvers vis-à-vis the state.

CIDOB, with offices in the lowland city of Santa Cruz, has a more recent institutional history emerging out of pro-indigenous development and solidarity movements of the 1980s (Riester 1985; Albó 1991). CIDOB voices political demands centered largely on territorial rights (over natural resources and political participation) for the pueblos that make up its membership. It is an affiliate of the transnational Amazonian indigenous organization COICA *(Confederación Indígena de la Cuenca Amazónica)*. Though at times unified with the CSUTCB, CIDOB has generally chosen a less confrontational path of strategic negotiation with the state in pursuit of selective gains. Leaders of the CSUTCB have attacked CIDOB for this more conciliatory approach to state power, especially given the latter's somewhat more energetic appropriation of certain aspects of "intercultural" reformism. CIDOB leaders and observers suggest in reply that their conciliatory tactics are more pragmatic means of dismantling centralist hierarchies—whether of the state or those reproduced within the structures of the CSUTCB movement itself (anonymous interviews, c.f. Urioste and Baldemar 1998; Yashar 1999). While some lowland groups are in fact organized in the structure of rural syndicates, public discourses about native peoples of the lowland generally use the label *pueblos indígenas* (indigenous peoples) in contradistinction to the Andean "original peoples" or the more generic class label of peasant.[7]

Both the CSUTCB and the CIDOB are regionally heterogeneous, multiethnic federations entangled with political parties, NGOs, other popular organizations, and the state. Nonetheless, both generally represent themselves as largely defined by the indigenous or ethnic identity of their constituents. The CSUTCB, for example, is quite frequently allied with the rural teachers' union and the COB labor federation engaging political questions that are often tinged with conjunctural sectoral and regional demands more than the generation of a sustained "indigenous" project. However, CSUTCB's most public rhetoric is the discourse of Aymara-centric *katarismo* (Albó 1994) and the symbol of the colorful *wiphala* flag that marks wider "Andean" pluralism. The organization is shaped in dialogue with advisors from leftist intelligentsia and European labor solidarity actors, and permanently interwoven with political party attempts to co-opt leaders. Sometimes tense factional divisions (which resulted in one death at the last CSUTCB congress) are recurring features of CSUTCB political cycles. During 2000 this division emerged between the Aymara following Quispe and those sectors more aligned with coca grower Morales. Emergence of new movement foci like the *Movimiento Sin Tierra* (borrowing from the Brazilian landless movement), and the Council of Markas and Ayllus (CONAMAQ) further complicates any notion of the CSUTCB as "the" Andean indigenous movement.

CIDOB is an equally heterogeneous movement that has more recently emerged on the national stage, although its constituent members have a long historical relationship with state formation. Lowland peoples are organized in various ways: as federations and "centrals" (*federaciones* and *centrales* are syndical terms), captaincies (*capitanías*, from the pre-Republican practice of labeling indigenous leaders captains), and *cabildos* (a colonial and mission structure parallel to the municipality). Others take their names from ethno-linguistic labels (the Ts'iman Council, the Guarayu Native Confederation, the Ayoreo Council) as well as state provincial jurisdictions (the Indigenous Confederation of Beni). Most of CIDOB's constituent members are dependent on national or international NGOs working in "development." Foreign missionaries still maintain tutelary influence over some of the smaller indigenous populations in the Amazon region. The boom in official cultural policy has created new modes of articulation with the state, especially in development-related projects aimed at 'training' Indians to be healthy, democratic, gender-conscious, environmentally conscious, administratively skilled, non-violent, etc.[8] Within CIDOB, the more numerous Guarani, Guarayo, and Chiquitano often vie for leadership with Trinitario (Moxeño) leaders of the

Beni. Strategic alliances with colonist unions and some NGO influence have also intersected internal CIDOB differences—some of which manifest themselves in the events I describe below. Despite organizational complexity, CIDOB has maintained its position as a unifying confederation, although the possibility for emergence of alternative foci of mobilization is always present.

II. Neoliberal Interculturalism in Three Dimensions

Organizations like CIDOB and the CSUTCB grew in significance and in the "indigenization" of their public demands and connections to international indigenous rights movements during the 1980s and 1990s (Brysk 2000). Across Latin America, states like Bolivia, Ecuador, Colombia, and Mexico responded by adopting constitutions that proclaimed themselves "multiethnic" and granted some "recognition" to indigenous peoples (see other chapters in this volume). While certain aspects of Bolivia's pluralist reforms are certainly improvements on prior histories of violent assimilation or paternalistic indigenismo, the new liberal indigenism is not the sign of recent inclusion of heretofore excluded indigenous peoples. The notion of inclusion generates an illusion of unilinear movement toward citizenship, obscures other politics at work, and masks prior histories of indigenous inclusion in Bolivian state formation—through labor, tribute, clientelism, and centuries of violence. In tension with demands of multiple indigenous actors themselves, this new liberal indigenism in Bolivia seeks to engage and politically (and geographically) reconceptualize entities like the CSUTCB and CIDOB, while gradually dismantling prior idioms and forms of corporatist statecraft—including most significantly the idiom of class, centralized national unions, and discourses linked to "revolutionary" nationalism.

Multicultural neoliberalism emerged during the second of two phases of neoliberal reform in Bolivia. The first was the "stabilization" phase of structural adjustment (1985–1989). During this era the MNR (1985–1989) launched the now popularly satanized "Decree 21060" which freed the exchange rate, drastically cut state spending, and legislated the gradual privatization of state industries. In the face of widespread protests and unemployment, this "adjustment" was achieved with not insignificant use of state force and a gentleman's agreement for pacted governance between the center-right MNR and ex-dictator Banzer's right-wing ADN party (Conaghan et al. 1990; Malloy 1991; Nash 1992). As the interventionist state was reshaped, a boom in development aid aimed at absorbing the shocks of adjustment found fertile ground during this period through discourses linking "indigenous" identity with "poverty reduction" (Gustafson 2002).

This period—one of gradual democratic opening—also saw the emergence of multiple indigenous mobilizations (Yashar 1998), including the massive lowland indigenous march on La Paz (1991) and the indigenous anti-Quincentenary movement (1992) which began to generate more public discussion about indigenous rights (Albó 1994). From 1989 to 1993 an alliance between the ADN (Democratic Nationalist Action) and the MIR (Revolutionary Leftist Movement) occupied power. Though this was a time of energetic effervescence among grassroots indigenous organizations, the state regime was marked by corruption and drug-trafficking scandals and the period was one of little substantive change in either the liberal advance or the cultural opening. The MNR returned in 1993 and launched the second wave of reforms (1993–1998) partially defined by the "cultural" opening. Among accelerated privatization of state industries and attempts to restructure the judiciary, public health, and pension systems, most significant of these second-generation reforms in relation to indigenous peoples were reforms in education, municipal decentralization, and land tenure.

These changes must be understood in reference to parallel transformations that occurred forty years earlier after the 1952 revolution. Then, as now, the state sought to "modernize" political identities and forms of participation to legitimate centralized authority and accommodate changing models of governance. After the 1952 revolution, middle-class reformers (also of the MNR party), launched an era of state capitalism in which a pact among miners, workers, and the party (with the peasants as subordinates) served as the foundation of state power. Indians were offered mass education (1955) to transform them from illiterate non-citizens into Spanish-speaking rural Bolivians. A national peasant syndicate was created and the extension of suffrage to Indians merged corporatist with clientelist structures—pursuing inclusion and "participation" in the form of centralized peasant unions. With agrarian reform in the Andean highlands and valleys (1953), many Aymara and Quechua indigenous communities were granted collective titles. Pre-revolutionary categories of race aimed at "indios" were here reshaped to notions of class aimed at forming a Spanish-speaking citizen reinscribed as inferior in terms of space and occupation: the *campesino rural* (rural peasant). Most of these transformations had little effect on lowland peoples then still subject to feudal hacienda subjugation or marginal existence on violent frontiers of resource extraction. On the other hand, the boom in rural-urban migration spurred by land consolidation and access to education in the Andes would generate a core of urban Aymara and Indianist intellectuals in La Paz, as well as a large contingent of rural Andean sons and daughters who moved through the state schools to occupy posts in the national rural teachers' union. Both have some bearing on current engagements with liberal indigenism.

Considering this earlier legacy of attempts to re-engineer public identities and participation structures, the contemporary phase of neoliberal multiculturalism in the 1990s becomes less of a novelty. Indians—now as much protagonists as objects—are being redefined from class subjects into "intercultural" citizens. With liberal indigenism of the 1990s, the educational system no longer supposes that Indians will be assimilated as Spanish-speaking peasants. They now have the right to maintain their languages as bilingual and intercultural citizens *(Educational Reform, 1994)*. Indigenous collectivities are being reimagined as localized entities and are granted new arenas of participation, no longer as corporatist peasant unions but as differentiated communities engaging a uniform national template of municipal politics *(Law of Popular Participation, 1994)*. A limited land reform now provides for indigenous communal territories—only in the demographically and politically weaker lowlands—seeking legitimacy for a wider plan to rationalize land markets and create a juridical template for resource extraction while dismantling radical agrarianism and national syndicalism *(INRA Land Reform, 1996)*.

This new liberal indigenism may sound like Machiavellian statecraft. It is apparent that cultural openings are secondary—and instrumental—to wider logics of managerial governance. It is also clear that differences between Andean and lowland populations have been consciously manipulated through these changes, accompanied by more and less subtle attempts to weaken the protagonism of centralized union structures (like the CSUTCB and the teachers, for example). However, to conclude merely that interculturalism represents an emergent strategy of liberal governance obscures complexity, reifies these transformations, and is in any case a foregone conclusion—states are defined by the fact that they seek control through hegemonic governance. On the other hand, neither neoliberalism nor interculturalism have the support of all elites or all indigenous and popular sectors.

Though the above paragraph hints at a wider calculated logic, these reforms—like the state itself—are regionally fragmented in their implementation, meanings, and effects. In what follows I sketch in broad strokes the differential, sometimes contradictory articulations between these reforms and diverse settings of indigenous mobilization in the Andes and lowlands regions.

Education as "Bilingual and Intercultural"

In the 1990s, basic public education survived within pro-market reforms as an arena of state intervention necessary for improving human capital and governability (World Bank 1995). Though access to schooling has been a popular demand seen as potentially "liberatory" and "revolutionary" by activists and radical intellectuals in Bolivia, education in the neoliberal paradigm is considered to be a key to creating a literate, flexible labor supply. The pro-market approach favors localized school administration and basic skills learning, positions not altogether contradictory to platforms of international agencies or moderate calls for social equity and equality of opportunity (Reimers, ed. 2000). Along these lines proposals for Educational Reform in Bolivia, gestated during the MIR-ADN government, were nurtured by UNICEF and World Bank support, and would eventually enlist indigenous allies with the inclusion of a quite progressive proposal for bilingual intercultural education (Gustafson 2002). The MNR regime inherited the project and incorporated it into its broader package of transformation launched with decentralization in 1994.

Bilingual intercultural education (EIB) is not part of a standard liberal school reform plan. It emerged out of Latin American histories in indigenist and indigenous political proposals dating back to early expressions of indigenism from the 1950s and beyond. Its most significant precedent in Bolivia was the UNICEF-supported experiment in Aymara, Quechua, and Guarani regions that began in 1989 and that was subsumed into the state's 1994 Educational Reform. As a curricular proposal bilingual education is composed of eight years of schooling in both indigenous languages and Spanish, with administrative provisions for indigenous participation in school administration, curricular design, and teacher training. To meet these objectives, new participatory structures, *Consejo Educativo de los Pueblos Originarios* (CEPO: Original People's Educational Councils) were legislated by reform and have been set up in collaboration between the CSUTCB, CIDOB, the state Education Ministry, and European donors. Now the

Aymara and Quechua "nations," the Guarani (via the Assembly of Guarani People), and the "multiethnic" Amazon (CIDOB), currently make up four such educational councils. While school reform aims at localizing participation to municipal levels, the symbolic legitimacy granted to native languages as markers of regional political territory complicates tenets of municipal governance. For example, Aymara and Quechua CEPOs are to have putative jurisdiction over a range of departmental and municipal boundaries, as do the Guarani, facts that in both cases legitimate and do not dissolve extant supra-local indigenous organizations.

This new proposal for schooling faces a variety of political responses. Bilingualism and educational reform have faced the most opposition from teachers' unions who see it—in some ways accurately—as part of a wider strategy to weaken the national teachers' union (Berríos 1998; R. Calla 1999; Gill 2000). Bilingual education is also attacked by conservative elites as anti-national and atavistic. Both CIDOB and the CSUTCB demanded bilingual education in position statements as early as 1989 (CSUTCB 1991), but these organizations have responded differently in practice. Because the CSUTCB has a history of strategic alliance with the rural teachers' union (CONMERB), Andean responses to education reform have been tepid if not hostile because of teacher opposition to reform. Many Aymara and Quechua also fill the ranks of the rural teachers union and see the reform as a threat to gains they have struggled to achieve (R. Calla 1999), or as "neoliberal assimilation" now dressed in native languages (e.g. Patzi 1999). Tense state-local relations in regions like the Aymara provinces around La Paz also shape a sometimes hostile response to state education. On the other hand, there has been more support for EIB in some Quechua regions of Sucre and Chuquisaca (López, personal communication). Bilingual education has been most actively appropriated by the Assembly of Guarani People (APG), a constituent organization of CIDOB (Gustafson 2002). Lowland peoples like the Guarani were marginal to the 1955 school reform and never benefited from the limited mobility provided by public schooling. New opportunities for accessing teaching jobs and school resources via bilingual school reform have made the Guarani key allies of educational change. The Guarani engagement with state bilingual education reform today also emerges during a period of indigenous revitalization—rather than state corporatism. In Guarani country bilingual education generated a revival of ideas about language and culture that under state and NGO tutelage legitimated the growth of the Guarani movement itself. However, class and liberatory discourses are not so easily effaced, as textbooks, public events defending "education," and increasing Guarani protagonism in rural politics have been marked by claims for land, equality, and an end to feudal systems of debt peonage (Gustafson 2002). CIDOB's other constituent organizations in the lowlands have had less access to bilingual education (due to administrative obstacles, lack of materials, and the difficulty of working with thirty distinct languages).

Decentralization as "Popular Participation"

In April of 1994, MNR President "Goni" Sánchez de Lozada also implemented a dramatic municipal decentralization plan—reportedly his personal favorite—called the "Popular Participation Law" *(Ley de Participación Popular,* LPP). The devolution of certain forms of decision-making and administrative control from centralized regimes to local (municipal) and regional (departmental) levels is broadly referred to as decentralization. In the terms of liberal modernization, decentralization is cast as a means of moving control over the allocation of state "services"—primarily basic health, education, and infrastructure seen as necessary for growth—closer to the "consumers" of these services.[9] For supporters like the World Bank, decentralization promises efficiency and local accountability in the administration of public goods. With "Popular Participation" the central state treasury literally makes periodic deposits into 311 new bank accounts for the 311 municipalities across the country. Decisions about use of these monies have some state stipulations, but are managed by locally elected municipal councils, replacing the old departmental development corporations.

Along with neighborhood groups, civic committees, and other types of local community organizations, "traditional" indigenous organizations like the ayllus, captaincies, and cabildos can now be officially granted juridical status as "territorial base organizations" *(organizaciones territoriales de base,* OTBs*)*. As representatives of juridical entities attached to a certain municipality, indigenous authorities can participate on oversight committees watching over municipal councils. If vetted by a national-level party, indigenous individuals can run for office on the municipal council itself.[10] This intercultural "recognition" was imagined in official public rhetoric as a reconciliation of the modern Western state with the Indian substrate of Bolivia. As President Sánchez de Lozada said in a speech at Harvard's Kennedy School of Government in 1995, "we've taken a Western model of governance and overlaid it onto an Oriental base." Notwithstanding this rhetorical simplification,[11] decentralization indeed emerges within myriad local and regional mosaics of identity and power as state reform seeks to re-shape political energies through electoral cycles (Bigenho 1999). Popular participation is thus a regulated form of limited democratization that attempts to decenter national opposition movements and unions while seeking to relegitimate national political parties managed in quite undemocratic fashion by urban elites. Nonetheless, decentralization planners in Bolivia argue that their plan goes beyond the mere transfer of administrative responsibilities and generates a radical process of citizen participation (Van Cott 2000a). Even those who oppose neoliberal orthodoxies in other sectors concur that Bolivian decentralization promises democratic participation at the grassroots and may transform top-down corruption and prebendalist [this word refers to patron-client systems for distributing economic patronage] party systems (Albó and CIPCA 1999; Andersson 1999). Agrarian activists such as Miguel Urioste (2000) have even suggested that this fledgling "democracy" at the grassroots is preferable to the "old-style" union protagonism pursued by leaders like the 'Mallku' Quispe.

Openings to local participation also respond to pressure from indigenous movements and have been eagerly engaged in the lowlands and the highlands. Overall more than 50 percent of the country's municipalities had some kind of indigenous or "peasant" representation after 1996 (Albó and CIPCA 2000).[12] Because smaller and larger parties qualify for federal funds based on their success in local and national elections, decentralization launched a fever of recruiting indigenous candidates by parties across the ideological spectrum (K. O'Neill, personal communication). Smaller left-leaning parties such as the Free Bolivia Movement (MBL) are now trying to make advances and build constituencies from the ground up. As party politics in Bolivia is rarely an ideological issue, much less a template for ethnic block voting, large parties like the ADN, MNR, and MIR have also sought out indigenous candidates—complicating other modes of indigenous mobilization, dispersing political energies, and dividing leadership networks. In the lowlands, the Guarani, Besɨro (Chiquitano), and Guarayu have had notable successes because they had prior organizational solidity and could muster rural majorities in some municipalities. In the late 1999 elections, municipalities such as San Antonio de Lomerío had nearly all seats on the council occupied by Besɨro representing four separate parties. In the Andes, local level syndicates have also engaged municipal politics (Albó and CIPCA 2000; Urioste and Baldemar 1998). Nonetheless, supra-local leaders and organizations have not all been weakened by decentralization. The coca growers mobilized voters by borrowing the affiliation of a near-defunct party called the Movement to Socialism (MAS). In party clothing the coca-growers' union then took control of nearly every municipality in the Chapare region and put leader Evo Morales in the national Congress with more votes than any politician in the country. As the MAS expands its influence beyond the coca issue, Amazonian indigenous leaders with few explicit ties to coca have also borrowed the jersey of the MAS party to become local candidates, moves that create alliances and factions across mestizo, colonist, coca-grower, and indigenous groups. How these inter-party and intra-ethnic relations work themselves out in relation to formalized indigenous organizational politics is an unfolding question for future research.

The INRA Land Reform and Indigenous Territoriality

The issue of land reform and land tenure is perhaps the most conflictive of this trio of transformations. Liberal prescriptions for efficient market-led growth require land tenure regimes based on private property and efficient land markets. This requires an orderly land registry free of overlapping claims, fraudulent titles, and massive corruption (Muñoz and Lavadenz 1997). Beyond the suppositions of this position, one would also hope for a more equitable distribution of opportunities and land ownership that doesn't reflect years of elite land-grabbing and violent dispossession of the poor—as does Bolivia's current situation. After several years of engagement and struggle among the government, business elites, and indigenous and peasant movements, one set of answers to this land question came in the form of the INRA Law *(Instituto Nacional de Reforma Agraria)* passed in 1996.

As with education and decentralization, Bolivia's version of land reform acknowledges some "indigenous" rights to collective ownership as a means of legitimating *certain* exceptions to a wider market-based model. The INRA law provides for the establishment of *Tierras Comunitarias de Origen* (TCOs: Originary Communal Lands).[13] Private holdings over a certain acreage that do not fulfill a social objective or generate tax revenue for the state can be expropriated for these indigenous territories. Supporters of the law emphasize that the provisions for lowland indigenous territories and stipulations for redistribution to migrants and landless peasants balance "equity and efficiency" and make this more than an "orthodox land market liberalization measure" (Muñoz and Lavadenz 1997, 19). Even radical observers have somewhat generously called the INRA law an "unusual combination of neoliberal and social justice measures" (Deere and León 2001, 37). However, policy analysts suggest that the reform program will have little effect on rural poverty in Bolivia, especially in the Andes where poverty is widespread (Muñoz and Lavadenz 1997, 22).

This was not a generous gift to indigenous peoples. In 1995 CIDOB and the CSUTCB unified to march on La Paz in defense of a more radical version of the law—a march that led to eleven deaths and an eventual division between the two organizations. CIDOB and the lowlanders won favor while the Andean indigenous farmers gained little. Andean communal lands—some held in collective title since the 1953 reform—remained largely unaffected (Muñoz and Lavadenz 1997). Nonetheless, as lowland peoples began to make claims for TCOs, Andean communities have followed. Out of 113 demands for TCOs pending in November of 2001, 32 were demands made by "ayllus" of the Quechua and Aymara highlands (www.inra.gov.bo, February 2002). Colonist unions and lowland peasants can also use the INRA law to apply for both individual and collective (cooperative) holdings—sometimes conflicting with lowland indigenous territorial claims. For their part, lowland indigenous organizations have laid claim to some 14 percent of national territory (15 million hectares), although these TCOs have yet to be completely demarcated (ibid.; Muñoz and Lavadenz 1997, 20). The limited provisions for land titling have been stalled and blockaded during the Banzer regime, as each demand generates scores of complaints and political maneuvers by 'third-party' landowners in indigenous regions. Localized violence in response to the demarcation is erupting between indigenous peoples and cattle ranchers in different sites (Assies 2000; infra.). In addition, indigenous peoples are rarely granted unitary collective holdings, more often regions are divided into several polygonal plots crisscrossed with superposition of 'third-parties' (ranchers, large farms, towns, and public works). Unless coupled with some kind of municipality-like ascription of political power, territoriality promises little in the way of self-governance, control over natural (especially subsoil) resources, or guaranteed access to quality public services. The land reform has, however, generated a new set of identity politics, as diverse communities attempt to redefine collective properties through expression of "indigenous" identity as well as recuperation of traditional areas of use (e.g. Lema 2000, Roper 2000).

These reforms in education, decentralization, and land tenure simultaneously produce standardization and variegation in their logics and their effects. If there are unifying logics behind Bolivian versions of neoliberal interculturalism, they might include the overarching divide (strategically exploited by the state) between lowland and highland indigenous histories, entities, and juridical status; the regulated and technocrat-controlled modes of reform decision making and inculcation of subjects with new "knowledge" for participation; the reproduction of state legitimacy through idioms, laws, and entities for bureaucratically channeling grassroots action; and the attempted respatialization of politics away from state-centric categories of "class" and confrontation with the central government. However, despite this apparent unity, each reform also invokes, legitimizes, and instrumentalizes distinct political imaginaries of the "indigenous" (as supra-local linguistic territory or "nation," as a municipal-level "traditional" authority; or as a potential regional "territorial" collective). Each also seeks to channel indigenous political energies—and diverse levels of indigenous organizations—into distinct state entities shaped by very different kinds of power (schools, parties, bureaucratic structures) and distinct temporal and spatial frames and cycles. Each reform also puts into a play a different, sometimes contradictory set of material and political resources linking Bolivian state legitimacy with European and North American development aid. While there are certainly identifiable substrates that bring these changes into something we can label "liberal indigenism" or "neoliberal interculturalism," contradictions and redirections abound. Case studies of local (Bigenho 1999; Andersson 1999; Roper 2000); sectoral (Assies 2000; Gustafson 2002); and institutional (Van Cott 2000b) issues must be considered to grasp the complexity of state change as it intersects multiple sites and levels. One might also consider the significance of these reforms in light of ongoing social conflicts, as I attempt in what follows.

III. "Bloody September": Reformism and Mobilization

Three sets of what would be framed as "indigenous" protests erupted in the Bolivian national arena in mid-2000. These include the CIDOB mobilization of June and July 2000 in Santa Cruz; the Aymara-dominated CSUTCB mobilizations of April and September of 2000 in the La Paz region; and the ongoing coca growers' struggles in the Chapare region near Cochabamba. The Aymara-CSUTCB and the CIDOB marches were clearly self-ascribed indigenous mobilizations. Both evoked claims of indigeneity to make their demands legitimate and both were labeled as indigenous by the press and government. While the "ethnic" identity of the coca growers as both individuals and as a collective movement is somewhat more complex, I include them here because they were portrayed as part of the wider "Indian" masses by the urban press, because coca-grower politics are inseparable from wider peasant-indigenous issues, and because cocalero leader Evo Morales would also take up the label of "indigenous" during the conflicts.[14] In what follows I will briefly describe each mobilization and conclude with some observations on how these events are linked both to intercultural reformism and to other political processes.

The Context: Political and Economic Crisis

Bolivia in 2000 and 2001 was in a political and economic crisis heightened by the fact that the country was entering into the pre-electoral period for the 2002 presidential elections. Political parties and movement leaders began staking out positions and constructing alliances for national elections. Opposition parties began to attack the government as did a number of movements, sectors, and regional interests. Privatization plans generated a violent conflict over water in Cochabamba in April 2000. The struggle unified urban Cochabamba civic groups with the coca growers and nearly brought down Banzer. The Aymara mobilized in April and again in September, and an array of other public and private sector interests made unrelated demands on the government. Strikes by state employees included the teachers, health workers, and riot police. Truck drivers called a stoppage against rising gas prices and even business elites demanding credit relief threatened a hunger strike. On top of it all, the U.S.-sponsored "drug war" was pushing for complete eradication of "illegal" coca—sparking yet another year of violence in the Chapare region. President Banzer was rather weak in his responses. Determined to cleanse his image as an ex-dictator, he was somewhat unwilling to use the kind of force traditionally practiced by the Bolivian state in the face of significant protests. Despite the regime's feeble attempt at holding conciliatory "National Dialogues,"[15] diverse social protests continued and peaked in September of that year.

CIDOB: Public Negotiations and Backstage Politics

The CIDOB march began and ended with less drama on the national scene than the Aymara and cocalero mobilizations. CIDOB had organized a Grand National Assembly of Indigenous Peoples in June of 2000 as a means of getting their demands on the agenda of Banzer's national "dialogue." After preparatory meetings in seven sub-regions, CIDOB called for its constituent organizations to gather in Santa Cruz to present a set of unified demands to the government. A *pliego petitorio* (list of demands) was drawn up by various CIDOB committees on land, education, health, housing, and natural resources. These included the acceleration of the INRA land reform and the reversion of certain new provisions,[16] the immediate granting of collective titles stalled in the bureaucracy, the reversion of recent timber concessions in indigenous territories, and increased social investment in health and bilingual education. Other more specific demands included those seeking use of debt relief monies for improved housing for the Guarani and Ween-hayek regions and yellow fever vaccination and anti-malarial campaigns in the Amazonian Pando and Beni departments. The political wish list also included radical calls for the granting of municipal status to indigenous territories (the TCOs) and for indigenous control over subsoil resources.[17] The right to elect its own indigenous minister at the national level topped the CIDOB list.

Around 500 indigenous leaders gathered in Santa Cruz in the early days of July. While all were constituents of CIDOB, a portion were aligned with the leadership of one influential CIDOB constituent called CPESC, the Coordinator of Ethnic Peoples of Santa Cruz, representing primarily Chiquitano communities. CIDOB was also joined by two components of "peasant" unions that were more closely aligned with CPESC. One was the Santa Cruz Department affiliate of the national CSUTCB movement (FSUTC-Santa Cruz). The other included provincial and departmental branches of colonists' unions from the northern parts of Santa Cruz and the Amazon area. Each had specific demands somewhat overlapping with those of CIDOB—most clearly the more rapid implementation of the INRA law—though neither of these peasant entities claimed "indigenous" identity. These inter-ethnic alliances had roots in political party connections (through the MAS) and certain NGO agrarian positions promoting alliances across ethnic lines.

Under surveillance from plainclothes police, and rapidly tiring from cold rains, sickness, and lack of logistical support, the indigenous and peasant representatives weakened as government negotiators stalled for time. As the CIDOB-led coalition spoke of initiating a march on La Paz, government ministers finally arrived to negotiate in Santa Cruz. The government would try to sectorialize demands (negotiating separately for health, education, and land), leveraging relatively easy delivery of schools and homes against more contentious points. Some ministers reportedly attempted to bribe individual indigenous leaders to withdraw from the march.[18]

CIDOB reached an initial accord for investment in the areas of health, education, and housing, and declared victory on July 4. However, this agreement was disputed by some of the Amazonian indigenous and northern Santa Cruz-based colonists and peasants as it made no specific agreements on land demarcation processes. CIDOB members CPESC and CIRABO (*Central Indígena Regional de la Amazonia Boliviana*, representing nine northern Amazonian ethnic groups) and the peasant-colonists maintained the plan to march. CIDOB issued a public international statement supporting CPESC and the colonists, although they declared their interests resolved (Amazon Coalition e-mail). The CPESC-colonist-peasant faction went on to achieve the signing of another agreement several days later. This included the promise to move forward with the titling of territories (TCOs) in Chiquitano lands, a promise to grant land titles for colonists' parcels, the reversion of the timber concessions, and even an agreement to establish the Chiquitano Academy of the Besɨro Language.

While I am not prepared to speculate on the backstage politics behind the agreements reached, this outcome highlights the difficulties of speaking of clearly unified indigenous movements and interests. Here party politics, state sectorialized reformism, NGO-dependence, and regional alliances serve to complicate the indigenous position. The institutionalization of "cultural difference" by sectors (education, land, health) here came into play as state agents dismantled wider political positions through selective and separate negotiations. External resources from NGOs continue to be instrumental to the shaping of indigenous tactics and alliances across regions and ethnic boundaries. However, most significant in these events is perhaps the fact that neither the state's liberal indigenism nor indigenous identity-based mobilization precludes the formation of cross-ethnic alliances. The emergence of new connections between entities of national unions and local movements now fragmenting and recombining in new spaces is a process that responds neither to the objectives of official reform nor to a clearly "indigenous" political project.

CSUTCB: Between the Aymara and the Cocaleros

As the CIDOB protest faded from the scene, the Aymara and coca growers struggles would shake the country with road stoppages beginning in April 2000 and continuing through much of the following two years. Judging by the press commentary, the deployment of state violence, and the effective paralysis of the country for twenty days in September, the Aymara and coca growers brought significantly more consternation to the government than did CIDOB. This has much to do with geopolitics. Aymara communities of the CSUTCB are geographically positioned around La Paz and have long been cast as the Bolivian elites' prototypical ethnic foil, garnering much of the intimate racial prejudice expressed against "indigenous" peoples in the national arena.[19] The coca growers are also conveniently positioned along the main highway between La Paz and Santa Cruz. Demographic weight and geographic position grant relative power to these sectors through their use of the nonviolent *bloqueo* (blockade) of the country's main highway. Plan Colombia and the U.S.-backed militarization of the drug war also made of the coca growers' movement an international "security" issue. Internal movement cycles and the upcoming elections further contributed to the events. Both Aymara leader Quispe and *cocalero* leader Evo Morales were engaged in their own competition for prominence within the CSUTCB movement—shaken up by its connections with national political parties and maneuvers for support. All of these factors—geographic centrality, international security, and electoral junctures of both states and movement—gave these events national prominence.

CSUTCB leader Felipe Quispe mobilized several thousand Aymara in his area of influence near La Paz.[20] Blockades were set up around La Paz in April and then again in September. Quite distinct from CIDOB, Quispe and the Aymara proposed a complete overhaul of the INRA law, demanding the implementation of an older CSUTCB proposal, the aptly named INDIO Law *(Instituto Nacional de Desarrollo Indígena y Originario)*. This sought indigenous control over land reform, distribution of titles and territories, and control over subsoil, soil, and water rights for Andean communities. The Aymara also asked for significant state investment in their region and one thousand new tractors—even as the Mallku Quispe simultaneously announced the coming formation of an autonomous Aymara state and Aymara military high command.

The coca growers blocked a score of points along the country's principal highway and shut off all movement between Santa Cruz, Cochabamba, and La Paz. The leader Evo Morales, like many of the coca growers, is a migrant of indigenous (Quechua and Aymara) descent from those regions who migrated to the tropics as a result of mine closings and poverty in the Andes. Morales is also an old rival of the Aymara Quispe and was disputing CSUTCB leadership with him (via his brother, Hugo). A national congressman and charismatic leader fighting U.S.-backed coca eradication, Morales had been named the media "Man of the Year" for his defense of coca as Bolivian national patrimony during the Paz Zamora regime (1992). These days the press increasingly labels him a "narco-terrorist" defending cocaine in an environment polarized by U.S. anti-drug policies. Responding to U.S. pressure, Banzer had pledged to achieve "zero coca" by year's end and violence against coca growers had increased. Morales demanded that farmers have the right to keep small plots of coca and rejected the U.S. plan to build another military base in the Chapare.

Responses: Escalation and Violence

In September 2000 the country was paralyzed. Press accounts and editorials decrying indigenous subversion and imminent racial violence escalated with the conflicts. As violence between the army and protestors escalated, urban commentators called for government action, and the press adopted a language of "we" the urban, modern, Spanish-speaking Bolivia against "them," the anti-systemic, anti-modern, violent, racial other. The reading of La Paz and Santa Cruz-based papers that follows is certainly only a partial lens on these events, but suggests that government violence found some sympathy among urban readers who spoke of events in terms of a modern, ordered, Bolivia against the primitive, unruly, Indian other. Talk of "two Bolivias" returned to the press, creating dichotomies which dehumanized protesters and facilitated justifications for army violence. Urban non-indigenous ideas about the 'Indians' are still mired in colonialist discourses, seemingly incapable of processing the reality of new indigenous protagonisms.[21] Outside of descriptive interest, I comment on press accounts to point out the distance between "interculturalism" as an official policy and the idioms through which indigenous politics are still (mis)interpreted in one segment of the public sphere. These dualisms should also serve as a warning against academic simplifications as well.

The Aymara Felipe Quispe was described as an anti-national "Nazi without boots" (Oliva 2000) seeking a "communitarian guerrilla war" (LR 10/3/00), a return to the "premodern world" of "superstitions and cultural backwardness," and the expulsion of the whites from the country (LP 10/5/00; LR 10/3/00,10/4/00). As meetings with government officials were played out on TV, the Mallku's fiery discourses earned him the label of *cacique lenguaraz* (slick-tongued chief), a "fundamentalist like the Ayatollah Khomeini, the Khmer Rouge, and the Taliban" who all share "discourses petrified in time" (LR 10/3/00). His Aymara supporters were called a "sad demonstration of the result of low levels of nutrition, lack of education, and the excess of alcohol … all of which creates *entes* (beings) who have no usefulness to any society" (LR 10/4/00). Despite the fact that Aymara were demanding university education and tractors for agriculture, their protest was labeled as a "violent rejection of modernizing processes" (LR 10/5/00).

Commentators also attacked the legitimacy of coca movement leader Evo Morales in highly racial terms. One urban "humorist" first attacked Morales for not recognizing his real mestizo nature, saying he was "just playing like an Indian" to get European support (Paolovich 2000a). A few weeks later the same writer would lump both the Aymara and the coca growers together in more colonial terms which cast Indians as state or hacienda property: "*our indios* are blocking the roads so that tomorrow we'll be even poorer" (Paolovich 2000b, emphasis added). A few months later, as Santa Cruz high society elected its (mostly blond) queens of carnival, this commentator would joke of seeing pictures of the "*originarios*" (Quispe and Morales), and write "[while] I contemplated the beauty of the Santa Cruz women, I also recognized the ugliness of these autochthonous leaders who are trying to create an Indian nation as if the Aymara were the Aryans of this country" (Paolovich 2000c).

Though complex in their origins and far from united, both sites of mobilization were lumped together as violent anti-state ethno-racial movements. While Aymaras were labeled "Talibans," the coca growers were compared to the Basque ETA—ethnic, separatist, and terrorist (Anonymous 2000a). Conservative former minister of information Mario Rueda Peña added biological undertones to this label with a racist physiognomy familiar in Bolivian stereotypes about indigenous features and rationality (or lack thereof):

> "[Like Spain's problems with the ETA] we also have subjects of deformed craniums with blocked neurons … whose addiction to the blockade is only one of many signs of the *chatismo craneal* (flat-headedness) within our own collectivity … these flatheads should see their days ended like bugs, targets of a heavy hand" (Rueda Peña 2000a).

These leaders and their constituents were further attacked because of their supposedly determinative linguistic identity (arguments that returned in later attacks against bilingual education), and dependence on outsiders (a sign that any powerful indigenous leader is certainly incapable of autonomous political agency):

> "the word democracy does not exist in either Aymara or Quechua, the languages of the Mallku [the Aymara leader] and Evo [Morales, the *cocalero* leader]. Neither they, nor the external forces who are controlling and financing them even know how to pronounce it" (Rueda Peña 2000c).

An anonymous writer in *El Diario* further merged language and subversion, complaining that the "Mallku and Evo have become integrated—both speaking the *same language of sedition and subversion, though one is Aymarist and the other is Quechuist*—with suspicious links to narco-terrorism [. . .]. It appears that they are in serious negotiations to convert Bolivia into another Colombia" (ED 10/3/2000).[22]

With such commentaries, all that was seen as indigenous was cast as an anti-modern threat with biological and racial undertones. Fortunately Bolivia was not in the midst of a racial war. Nonetheless, the movements would cost the lives (at the hands of the military) of more than fifteen coca growers and Aymara protesters and over 100 wounded. Peasants defending themselves with sticks and slings would inflict wounds on some troops as well. Two or three military officers were killed.[23] Rightist elites in Santa Cruz—including the neo-fascist Santa Cruz Youth Union—began what looks to be the roots of paramilitarism, declaring their intention to violently break the coca growers' blockade and resist the invasion of the Aymara *"kollas."* The U.S. government even stoked the flames by declaring via State Department spokesman Peter Romero that there was evidence that Venezuelan president Chávez was supporting "violent indigenous movements" in Bolivia and in Ecuador (*Miami Herald,* December 8, 2000).

Temporary Resolutions

Both leaders eventually reached separate agreements with the government—though both agreements went unfulfilled and each would mobilize again in the following months. On the Aymara side, the state promised significant investments in infrastructure and investment in the Mallku's Omasuyos region in the form of a 26-million-dollar project funded by Japan, including one thousand new tractors (a populistic demand, as yet undelivered). The state also promised to grant new lands in the lowlands for Andean colonization and to revise the INRA law, both of which sparked protest from CIDOB. Rearranging (or reacknowledging) the continued salience of the "peasants," the Vice Ministry of Indigenous and Original Peoples' Affairs (VAIPO) was reformed into a ministry (MACPIO) with the return of the 'C'-word, campesino. Attempting to assuage CIDOB as well, a Guarani leader from the lowlands was named to the position of vice minister. For his part, Quispe announced the formation of a new indigenous party called the 'Pachakuti Indigenous Movement' (MIP).

The coca growers appeared to receive much less. The eradication continued as planned, although construction of the new military base was postponed. The government suggested that with coca eradicated, there was no need to speak to Morales and that there were no longer any "legal" coca-growers' movements in the Chapare. Morales and the Cochabamba civic committees sought to rejuvenate their protest with another march on La Paz the following year and intermittent conflicts continue. The surprise resignation of Banzer and his imminent death see new tensions arise. In February 2002 the government ceded to cocaleros' defense of regional coca markets (against U.S. wishes), though Evo Morales was removed from Congress under accusations of sedition and instigation of violence. Morales would eventually announce his candidacy for president under the MAS banner.

Conclusions: Interpreting Indigenous Politics

What might be the deeper relationships between these events and the sectoral reforms that have characterized neoliberal interculturalism in Bolivia? With respect to bilingual education, it would appear that these regional movements have little relation. In the midst of these conflicts, leaders of the Educational Councils of the Quechua and Aymara "nations" continued meeting with educational experts to work on curricular development and language standardization. Nonetheless, editorialists turned their racially charged pens against bilingual education as well. Rueda Peña argued that bilingual education was a waste of time since languages like Aymara were "without grammar" and "notably inferior to Spanish" (Rueda Peña 2001). "As in Chiapas" it would only serve to disintegrate a "national unity" built on the Spanish language (Rueda Peña 2001b).

In relation to municipal decentralization these mobilizations could be seen in various perspectives. Were the movements led by Quispe and Morales desperate attempts to maintain supra-local legitimacy in the face of an increasing localization of politics? Quispe himself blamed "popular participation" for the weakening of *katarismo* and the resegregation of power. In his terms decentralization meant the "national level for the whites" and the "local level for the Indians" (LR 10/4/00). Nonetheless, Quispe's regional MIP party may make its strongest move via the electoral process at both municipal and national levels. The coca growers had already used municipal elections to their advantage while maintaining a supra-local unity, albeit one dependent on a crop destined for eradication. In the lowlands, indigenous leaders with more localized constituencies continue to contest municipal offices, many now under the MAS banner of Morales. It is clear that decentralized municipal governance is not leading to the end of pan-local movements.

The INRA law and the issue of land were directly linked to the shaping of these conflicts and will continue to be a source of contention in the foreseeable future. A "Land Summit" in November 2001 was attended by key actors in this milieu, marking older and newer organizations indigenous and peasant movements: the CSUTCB, CIDOB, the new Landless Movement (MST), and the Council of Markas and Ayllus (CONAMAQ) (www.inra.gov.bo).

One might argue that these events were merely side effects of cyclical electoral gambits and the U.S.-backed drug war. This is certainly a possibility, although I have pointed out shifting foci of mobilization and alliances that are leading to new configurations of "indigenous" and inter-ethnic politics within and beyond official interculturalism. As the 1990s development boom fades, indigenous movements are seeking new forms of sustaining their institutionality that do not signal mere acquiescence to state models. This will entail engaging party politics, acquiescing to some dependence on state, Church, or NGO projects, or seeking some benefit from from multinational resource extraction. For example, the Guarani are in the midst of bilateral negotiations with the gas transport consortium Transredes, whose pipelines move gas from Bolivia to Brazil across Guarani country. On the other hand, the Chiquitanos, with the help of environmental NGOs, have been struggling against the pipeline crossing their lands—now embroiled in the Enron debacle.

I have argued that we pursue interpretations of indigenous issues and state reformism through consideration of historical patterns of variegated statecraft and current variations in "indigenous" political locations. This decenters our discussions and problematizes dualist notions of "states versus Indians." This also means interrogating official interculturalism (or 'liberal indigenism') at different levels and sites, and also means questioning our use of the overarching term neoliberal for defining state processes. I use the term with some reluctance. It signals, yet also reifies, an imagined hegemony that is only part of what defines Bolivian statecraft. International financial regimes (and the U.S. military apparatus) have significant sway in shaping Bolivian politics and cultural idioms—and the respatializing effects of neoliberalism on contestatory politics are certainly real—we should neither cast neoliberalism as all-powerful hegemony, nor reduce Bolivian politics to the expression of the "Washington Consensus." Contradictory institutional processes and political agency disputed across multiple fields must be understood as sites wherein power is disputed both regionally and nationally. Resuscitating the cry of neoliberalism has been useful to indigenous movements and has framed several analyses of the nature of the indigenous challenge (Yashar 1998; Nash 2001). However, indigenous movements do not represent any uniform response to neoliberalism as a set of governing logics, logics in any case far from seamless in their manifestations. Rather, indigenous movements are sophisticated, multi-layered actors simultaneously engaging an array of international, national, and regional processes.[24] Our analyses should steer clear of dualistic framings which find echoes in popular racial discourse. Neoliberalism itself may have its days numbered in Bolivia. Notwithstanding the multiple sites of contestation discussed here, events like the rise of natural gas as the newly imagined "tin" of Bolivia may signal a new era of dependency and clamor for rebuilding the patronage state. The technocrats' utopia of "free" markets, "good" (party-mediated) governance, and trickle-down equity is far from a reality in Bolivia. This utopia is unsettled by highly visible crises like that of Enron (entangled in Bolivian gas) and Argentina (the failed "model" right next door), the specter of a re-militarization of politics, and other utopias still circulating in the country. In terms of the highly fragmented state and the multiple sites of indigenous and other forms of social mobilization I discuss here, Bolivia's experiment with the new era of interculturalism is only beginning to hint at some of its possible outcomes, one of which emerged in the presidential elections of 2002.

The 2002 Elections

As this volume went to press, Bolivia went to the polls. Following another series of coca-grower protests, and yet another divided CIDOB march on La Paz in mid-2002, indigenous and peasant movements have definitively staked a claim on national political power. In the elections, coca-grower leader Evo Morales and his MAS party gained stunning support, taking second place with 20.92 percent of the vote, edging out millionaire newcomer Manfred Reyes (20.91 percent), and only slightly trailing the center-right MNR (22.45 percent). The Aymara leader Felipe Quispe and the new MIP party took fifth place with 6 percent—even beating the now decaying party of General Banzer which polled a little over 3 percent. Banzer himself passed away with little fanfare as his party squabbled itself into deterioriation. It appears that the MNR and Gonzalo Sánchez de Lozada will retake the presidency, guaranteeing some continuity of liberal and neo-indigenist reformism. Nonetheless, the presence of indigenous and peasant leaders in congress is overwhelming. MAS and the MIP together polled more votes than any other party, and MAS will have eight out of twenty-seven senators (including a number of long-time radical miners' and coca-growers' leaders), and 27 out of 130 deputies (including Evo Morales himself). Quispe's MIP will also have six deputies. Andean surnames like Auca, Huanca, Mamani, Condori, and Colque now find themselves occupying space among the Macleans, Sánchez, Paz, and Justinianos. Chiquitano leader José Bailaba Parapaino, who followed the more radical line during the CIDOB march, will also take a deputy-ship under the MAS party. CIDOB leaders who allied with the MIR party may also make inroads into state posts. Though taking fourth place, the MIR will surely gain positions in any ruling alliance, likely maintaining forms of indigenist patronage in the ethnic ministries. Most significantly, the success of the MAS signals defiance of the neo-imperialist U.S. anti-drug war, the tenacious protagonism of Bolivian popular and indigenous movements, and the quite tenuous hegemony of the so-called neoliberals. Our analytical frameworks—and the anachronistic discourses of the Bolivian press—should be struggling to keep up.

Notes

1   The analysis of events in this chapter draws on Bolivian newspaper sources collected between April 2000 and January 2002. Background information on state reforms draws on recent research by anthropologists

and policy analysts as well as the author's fieldwork (1993–1999) on indigenous politics and bilingual education in the Guarani region and in
Bolivian policy-making arenas. Analysis of the CIDOB event draws on
recent conversations with indigenous leaders of CIDOB and CPESC. My
thanks to Jordi Beneria and Derrick Hindery for their dispatches on the
CIDOB march, and to Jordi Beneria for his first-hand insights. Discussion with the other authors in this volume and with María Elena García,
Luis Enrique López, Tony Lucero, Kathleen O'Neill, and Claret Vargas
was helpful. The interpretations are the author's responsibility and
should not be taken as representative of indigenous positions nor of
those consulted during the writing of this chapter.

2   *Toque de a degüello,* figuratively "sound the attack," refers to the down-
ward swoop of a sword, i.e., "signal the beheading." This and following
translations by the author.

3   *Mallku* means "condor" in Aymara and Quechua. It is also a designation
of traditional ceremonial leadership. Apaza led a failed siege of La Paz
following the Tupac Amaru rebellion in the late 18th century; Aymara
caudillo Zárate Willka supported liberal elites during Bolivia's turn of
the century civil-war, but was later executed when he began to demand
rights for the Aymara who followed him.

4   For example, former Aymara vice-president Victor Hugo Cárdenas, con-
gresswoman Remedio Lozas, and the congressman Evo Morales, among
others. In a wider sphere of cultural politics Aymara and Quechua are
also taken up in spheres of debate as varied as native language education,
where the idea of "nationalities" is circulated (infra); in music and folklore, where hybrid expressions of indigenousness are invented and reshaped through spectacle and performance (Gustafson 1992); in urban
indigenous intellectual networks (Albó 1994, THOA 1998, Chachaki
2000); and in populist politics, where a range of raced and gendered substrates intersect public performances of cholo and indigenous identities
as broadly 'popular' (Albro 2000). At the risk of reproducing an erroneous stereotype that seeks to contain the "indigenous" in "rural" places,
in this chapter I will focus primarily on expressions of the indigenous as
they relate to regional, mostly agrarian-based mobilizations.

5   VAIPO (2000).

6   The classic history of Andean peasant struggles is Rivera (1984); see also
Albó (1982, 1991; 1994); Lavaud (1993); Calla (1993); Ströbele-Gregor
(1996). For recent self-representation: www.puebloindio.org/CSUTCB3.
html. Aymara and Quechua cultural and political organizations outside of the CSUTCB structure are proliferating. See, for example, www.
aymaranet.org and the ayllu movement centering around CONAMAQ
described by Choque and Mamani (2001).

7   The terms "indígena" and "indio" are seen as derogatory by some An-

dean leaders who consider that the heritage of the Inka empire marks a higher level of political organization than that historically obtained by the lowland "chunchos" or savages (Chumira, personal communication). On the other hand, the term "campesino" is taken as a marker of contrarian syndicalism and party tutelage by some CIDOB leaders, who prefer the territorial imaginary and autonomy evoked by the notion of "indigenous people." "Original peoples" is somewhat of a mid-point. As pointed out by numerous observers and the other authors in this volume, the tug-of-war between "class" and "ethnicity" is central to the indigenous question in Latin America. It most often leads to agglomerations of terms which all seek to contain indigenous identities within a space defined by rural agrarianism, albeit for different interests. The most recent manifestation of this was the 2000 transformation of the Ethnic Affairs ministry into the "Ministry of Peasant, Indigenous, and Original Peoples' Affairs." Activist attempts to unify indigenous with syndical organizations have also pursued this "rural agrarian" unity through usage of phrases like "peasant-indigenous" in their research and manifestos (e.g., Albó and CIPCA 1999).

8   This boom in indigenous-centered development is spreading across the Andes and lowlands in other countries as well (cf. Ramos 1998). The spread of *talleres* (training workshops) has led some of my Guarani colleagues to jokingly complain of *talleritis*, "workshop-itis" and contributes to a mode of conflict as leaders compete through "per-diem politics" and invitations to national and international events. Nonetheless, NGO and state meetings and workshops indirectly subsidize movement reproduction (by bringing leaders together) and directly reproduce movement legitimacy in the wider public sphere. This dependence on transnational resources runs parallel to the foreign dependence of the Bolivian state political system itself, and should not be taken as a sign of inauthenticity or artificiality of the indigenous movement.

9   See Willis et al. (1999) for a review. There has been a boom in research on Bolivian decentralization too immense to cite here (see citations below).

10   The technocrat reformers rejected proposals to allow for independent candidates to run for local office. Thus any candidate—indigenous or otherwise—would have to seek the support (or be sought out) by one of the nationally approved parties. See Van Cott (2000a) for a rich narrative description of these discussions. The carefully managed opening to local "participation" reflects a substrate of technocrat discourses wary of the loss of "authority" *(autoridad)*—a fear constructed at least partly on ideas about the indigenous "racial" threat and natural proclivities toward disorder held by uneducated masses. Decentralization was cast as a process of "educating" and "capacitating" the people. The restriction on participation to nationally controlled parties also aids in the reproduction of centralized "authority." Thus Bolivian municipal politics is tech-

nically less democratic than notoriously authoritarian Guatemala, where local civic groups and indigenous networks can organize independent committees to run for municipal office, (e.g., Maya-dominated *Xel-Ju* in Quetzaltenango). This political party monopoly on local politics is currently under debate in Bolivia.

11   Policy makers and political analysts (and some indigenous leaders as well) reproduce this dichotomous language of cleavage between "Western liberalism" and "indigenous communitarianism" in their official documents and their empirical research (R. Calla 1993; Van Cott 2000a). Like other binaristic framings, this is a reductionist political position rather than a reflection of anything empirically discernible at the ground level where the state and indigenous peoples have long centuries of interdependent existence.

12   O'Neill reports (personal communication) that 18 municipalities out of 311 elected "indigenous" leaders in 1995. Albó and CIPCA (2000) use a broader category which lumps together "indigenous" and "peasant" (campesino).

13   Government avoidance of the more politically charged term "territory" is not coincidental, though I have heard indigenous leaders use the term territory when describing TCOs.

14   The coca-growers' longer heritage as descendants of highland miners (mestizo, Quechua, and Aymara) and the highly multiethnic shaping of the coca region complicate ascription of any one ethno-linguistic identity to the coca-growers. Compare with the discussion of the cocalero movement in Colombia, where the identity of colonos is somewhat more sharply opposed to that of the indigenous (Ramírez, this volume). Although they are usually labeled "Quechua" by urban commentators, the coca-growers are a heterogeneous population, and, like the followers of Quispe, do not represent all Quechua or Aymara subjects. Evo Morales was labeled "Quechua" by the press—a convenient way of lumping both labels into the wider mass seen as "violent" and "Indian"— though he is in fact also often labeled Aymara (www.aymaranet.org). In any case he hails from Challapata, Oruro, a Quechua-Aymara bilingual region. These facts further suggest the need to consider critically the political meanings of deployment of one or another label. It is not my intention to ascribe (or question) the "indigenous" identity of the coca-growers or other protagonists, but rather to consider how and why these issues are spoken of in certain ways in public politics.

15   The dialogues were partially linked to the debt-relief granted to Bolivia as an HIPC (Highly Indebted Poor Country) in 2000, through which the monies were to be distributed to favor the poorest municipalities of the country.

16   The INRA law deems land unproductive if it does not fulfill a social and

economic function (or if no taxes are paid on it). Such lands are then available for appropriation with and without indemnification, for redistribution as indigenous TCOs. INRA bureaucrats had sought to introduce a loophole—with no public consensus—which would exempt properties of less than 500 hectares (thus potentially allowing large landowners the opportunity to divide ownership among individual family members and avoid expropriation). CIDOB's demands opposed this change.

17   Throughout Latin America the state is the self-proclaimed owner of subsoil resources (oil, gas, minerals), a fundamental obstacle to indigenous territorial claims (and potential economic, hence political, autonomy).

18   While this is hearsay I have gathered from indigenous participants and the press, it is well within the realm of imaginable practice.

19   While a specifically Andean, and especially La Pazean phenomenon, the intimate racisms between the Aymara and the *q'ara* (mestizo or criollo) tend to predominate in highly centralized "Bolivian" politics. Aymara women largely constitute the urban domestic labor force in mestizo households, Aymara-descended "cholos and cholas" control much of the market in basic goods and contraband, and the ever-growing city of El Alto near La Paz is largely viewed as an "Aymara" threat to urban Hispanic La Paz (cf. Gill 1994; 2000). Even lowland Hispanics of Santa Cruz have made comments to me such as, "I can put up with a Quechua, but the Aymara I can't stand" (anonymous). Such proximity to the centralized state and the racist imaginary explains, I believe, the intensely felt fear of Aymara leaders like Felipe Quispe, as well as complexly negotiated *rapprochements* between such leaders and the white political class. This is a long historical relationship between the Aymara and the Hispano-Bolivian state which is by no means new to the multicultural era. This centralization of both Andean Aymara intelligentsia and peasantist movements at the heart of state power certainly contributes to the deceptive success of "Bolivian" indigenous movements (compare with Gelles' discussion of Peru in this volume), but is in fact a highly regionalized Aymara phenomenon of ten provinces near La Paz.

20   These are not the poorest nor most culturally "traditional" Andean regions. Quispe's Omasuyos area is relatively prosperous and thoroughly integrated with international trade, urban migration, schools, and national party politics.

21   For a comparative case of racial and gender ideologies mediating anti-indigenous violence, see Stephen (1999).

22   The tenuous support for bilingual education by some progressive-minded elites takes on new significance in such a highly anti-indigenous context.

23   Aymara protesters beat one military officer to death in revenge for the

shooting deaths of two Aymara in April. As the urban press reacted against these "violent Indians," Quispe would respond, "it's a crime to kill a white or a mestizo, but killing an Indian is like killing a bird here. There is no justice." (LR 4/17/00). In the Chapare two soldiers were kidnapped and killed, although it is unclear who was responsible. One army sergeant killed in the Chapare (allegedly by coca-growers) was an Aymara from Achacachi, the Mallku Quispe's center of support (compare here Schirmer's description of military strategy and inter-indigenous violence from the Guatemalan case).

24 As Abercrombie (1991) emphasized in a review of Bolivian indigenous politics a decade ago, local heterogeneity belies any attempt to conclude that "Indians" and "Indianness" is any one identity in the country (cf. Bigenho 1999). Gelles (this volume) discusses perspectives on "Andeanism" and the limitations of the category "indigenous."

Works Cited

Newspapers and Periodicals Consulted

LP. *La Prensa (La Paz)* (www.laprensa-bolivia.com)
LR. *La Razón (La Paz)* (www.la-razon.com)
ED. *El Diario (La Paz)* (www.eldiario.net)
LO. *La Opinión (Cochabamba)* (opinion-bo.com)
El Deber (Santa Cruz) (www.eldeber.com.bo)
BoliviaPress (La Paz) (www.cedib.org)

Other Works Cited

Abercrombie, Thomas

1991 "To Be Indian, to Be Bolivian: 'Ethnic' and 'National' Discourses of Identity." In *Nation-States and Indians in Latin America*. Greg Urban and Joel Sherzer, eds. Austin: University of Texas Press. Pp. 95–130.

Albó, Xavier

1982 "De los mataindios al poder indio." *América Indígena* 42(3):505–511.

1991 "El retorno del indio." *Revista Andina* 9(2):299–366.

1994 "And From Kataristas to MNRistas? The Surprising and Bold Alliance between Aymaras and Neoliberals in Bolivia." In Van Cott, Donna Lee, ed. *Indigenous Peoples and Democracy in Latin America*. Washington: Inter-American Dialogue. Pp. 55–81.

1996 "Nación de muchas naciones: nuevas corrientes políticas en Bolivia." In González Casanova, Pablo, and Marcos Roitman Rosenmann, eds. *Democracia y Estado multiétnico en América Latina*. Mexico, DF: CIICH/UNAM. Pp. 321–366.

1999   *Iguales aunque diferentes: hacia unas políticas interculturales y lingüísticas para Bolivia.* (CIPCA Cuadernos de Investigación 52). La Paz: CIPCA /UNICEF.

Albó, Xavier, comp.

1995   *Bolivia Plurilingüe: Guía para planificadores y educadores* (2 tomos). La Paz: CIPCA/UNICEF.

Albó, Xavier, and Equipo CIPCA

1999   *Ojotas en el poder local: cuatro años después.* Cuadernos de Investigación CIPCA (53). La Paz:CIPCA/PADER.

Albro, Robert

2000   "The Populist Chola: Cultural Mediation and the Political Imagination in Quillacollo, Bolivia." *Journal of Latin American Anthropology* 5(2):30–88.

Almaraz, Alejandro

1998   "Bolivia: Los pueblos indígenas de la Amazonia, el Oriente y el Chaco." In *Comunidades: Tierra, instituciones, identidad.* Carlos Ivan Degregori, ed. Pp. 171–190. Lima: CEPES/Arariwa.

Andersson, Vibeke

1999   "Popular Participation in Bolivia: Does the Law "Participación Popular" Secure Participation of the Rural Bolivian Population?" CDR Working Paper 99.6. Copenhagen: Centre for Development Research.

Anonymous

2000a   "Nuestra propia ETA." *La Razón*, May 18.

2000c   "La cultura del bloqueo." *La Razón*, September 22.

2000d   Editorial: "El gobierno está obligado a pacificar el país." *El Diario*, September 29.

Assies, Willem

2000   *Lands, Territories, and Indigenous Rights.* Mimeo.

Berríos Gosalvez, Marlene

1995   *¿Quién le teme a la reforma educativa?* La Paz: CEDOIN.

Bigenho, Michelle

1999   "Sensing Locality in Yura: Rituals of Carnival and of the Bolivian State." *American Ethnologist* 26(4):957–980.

Brysk, Alison

2000   *From Tribal Village to Global Village: Indian Rights and International Relations in Latin America.* Stanford: Stanford University Press.

Calla, Ricardo

1993   "Hallu hayllis huti. Identificación étnica y procesos políticos en Bolivia." In *Democracia, etnicidad y violencia política en los países andinos.* Pp. 57– . Lima: IFEA/IEF.

1999   "Educación intercultural y bilingüe y flexibilización magisterial: temas de la Reforma Educativa en Bolivia." *Bulletin de l'Institut Français d'Études Andines* 28(3):561–570.

Chachaki, Waskar Ari

n.d.   *ARUSKIPASIPXAÑASATAKI: El siglo XXI y el Futuro del Pueblo Aymara.* La Paz: Editorial Amuyañataki.

Choque, María Eugenia, and Carlos Mamani

2001   "Reconstitución del ayllu y derechos de los pueblos indígenas: el movimiento indio en los Andes de Bolivia." *Journal of Latin American Anthropology* 6(1):202–224.

Conaghan, Catherine, J. Malloy, and Luis Abugattas.

1990   "Business and the Boys. The origins of neoliberalism in the central Andes." *Latin American Research Review* 25(2)3–30.

CSUTCB

1991   "Hacia una educación intercultural bilingüe." *Raymi* 15.

Deere, Carmen Diana, and Magdalena León

2001   "Institutional Reform of Agriculture under Neoliberalism: The Impact of the Women's and Indigenous Movements." *Latin American Research Review* 36(2):31–64.

Gill, Lesley

1994   *Precarious Dependencies: Gender, Class, and Domestic Service in Bolivia.* New York: Columbia University Press.

2000   *Teetering on the Rim: Global Restructuring, Daily Life, and the Armed Retreat of the Bolivian State.* New York: Columbia University Press.

Gustafson, Bret

1992   *La Festividad de Nuestro Señor del Gran Poder: Apuntes Etnográficos.* Unpublished ms.

2002   "Native Languages and Hybrid States: A Political Ethnography of Guarani Engagement with Bilingual Education Reform in Bolivia, 1989–1999." Unpublished doctoral dissertation, Harvard University, Department of Anthropology.

Hale, Charles

1997   "Cultural Politics of Identity in Latin America." *Annual Review of Anthropology* 26:567–590.

Healy, Kevin

1986   "The Boom Within the Crisis: Some Recent Effects of Foreign Cocaine Markets on Bolivian Rural Society and Economy." In Deborah Pacini and Christine Franquemont, eds. *Coca and Cocaine: Effects on People and Policy In Latin America*. Cambridge, MA:Cultural Survival and Latin American Studies Program, Cornell University. Pp. 101–143.

Healy, Kevin, and Susan Paulson

2000   "Political Economies of Identity in Bolivia, 1952–1998." *Latin American Anthropology* 5(2):2–29.

Klein, Herbert

1982   *Bolivia: The Evolution of a Multi-Ethnic Society*. New York: Oxford University Press.

Larson, Brooke

1999   "Andean Highland Peasants and the Trials of Nation-Making during the Nineteenth Century." In *Cambridge History of the Native Peoples of the Americas*, v. III, Part 2. South America. Frank Salomon and Stuart Schwartz, eds. Cambridge: Cambridge University Press. Pp. 558–703.

Lavaud, Jean Pierre

1993   "Conflictos sociales y democracia en Bolivia." In *Democracia, etnicidad y violencia política en los países andinos*. Pp. 43–53. Lima: IFEA/IEP.

Lema, Ana María (coordinator)

2001   *De la huella al impacto: la participación popular en municipios con población indígena*. La Paz: PIEB.

Malloy, James M.

1991   "Democracy, Economic Crisis and the Problem of Governance: The Case of Bolivia." *Studies in Comparative International Development* 26(2):37–57.

Martínez, José A.

2000   "International Cooperation and the Rationalization and Titling of Indigenous Territories in Bolivia." (Santa Cruz). IWGIA document (www.iwgia.org).

Monasterios, Sergio Molina

2000   "El toque de a degüello." *La Prensa*, October 8.

Muñoz, Jorge A. and Isabel Lavadenz

1997   "Reforming the Agrarian Reform in Bolivia." Development Discussion Paper No. 589 (June 1997). Cambridge: Harvard Institute for International Development.

Nash, June

1992   "Interpreting Social Movements: Bolivian Resistance to the Economic Conditions Imposed by the International Monetary Fund." *American Ethnologist* 19(2):275–293.

2001   *Mayan Visions: The Quest for Autonomy in an Age of Globalization.* New York: Routledge.

Oliva Alcázar, Hugo

2000a   "El racismo al revés sigue siendo racismo: también hay nazis en el Tercer Mundo." La *Razón*, October 3.

Paolovich

2000a   "En el Día del Indio." *La Razón*, August 2.

2000b   "Esto es el colmo." *La Razón*, September 22.

2000c   n.t. *La Razón*, March.

Patzi, Félix

1999   "Etnofagia estatal. Modernas formas de violencia simbólica (una aproximación al análisis de la Reforma Educativa)." *Bulletin de l'Institut Français d'Études Andines* 28(3):535–559.

Paulson, Susan, and Pamela Calla

2000   "Gender and Ethnicity in Bolivian Politics: Transformation or Paternalism?" *Journal of Latin American Anthropology* 5(2):112–149.

Ramos, Alcida R.

1998   *Indigenism: Ethnic Politics in Brazil.* Madison: University of Wisconsin Press.

Reimers, Fernando, ed.

2000 *Unequal Schools, Unequal Chances: the Challenges to Equal Opportunity in the Americas.* Cambridge: Harvard University Press.

Riester, J.

1985 CIDOB's Role in the Self-Determination of the Eastern Bolivian Indians. In Macdonald, Ted, ed. *Native Peoples and Economic Development.* Cambridge: Cultural Survival.

Rivera Cusicanqui, Silvia

1984 *Oprimidos pero no vencidos: luchas del campesinado aymara y qhechwa de Bolivia, 1900–1980.* La Paz: HISBOL/CSUTCB.

Roper, J. Montgomery

2000 "Whose Territory Is It? Resource Contestation and Organizational Chaos in Bolivia's Multiethnic Indigenous Territory." Paper presented at the 2000 Meeting of the Latin American Studies Association. March 16–18.

Rueda Peña, Mario

2000a Untitled. *La Razón*, August 15.

2000b "Y después, ¿qué?" *La Razón*, October 2.

2001a "Educación bilingüe en duda." *La Razón*, March 19.

2001b "De ida al cementerio." *La Razón*, April 10.

Stephen, Lynn

1999 "The Construction of Indigenous Subjects: Militarization and the Gendered and Ethnic Dynamics of Human Rights Abuses in Southern Mexico." *American Ethnologist* 26(4):822–842.

Ströbele-Gregor, Juliana

1996 "Culture and Political Practice of the Aymara and Quechua in Bolivia: Autonomous Forms of Modernity in the Andes." *Latin American Perspectives* 23(2):72–90.

Suárez Ávila, Manuel

2000 "Yo que nunca les he comprendido." *La Prensa*, October 8.

Ticona, Esteben, Gonzalo Rojas Ortuste and Xavier, Albó

1995 *Votos y wiphalas.* La Paz: Fundación Milenio/CIPCA.

Urioste, Miguel

2000 "¿Para qué representantes comunales, si existe el MIP?" *La Razón* (La Paz), November 25.

Urioste, Miguel, and Luis Baldomar

1998 "Bolivia campesina en 1997." In *Comunidades: Tierra, instituciones, identidad.* Carlos Iván Degregori, editor. Pp. 147–170. Lima: CEPES/Arariwa.

Vacaflor, Jorge

1995 "Problemes d'interpretation des disposition de la Convention 169 en Bolivie." *Recherches amerindiennes au Quebec* 25(3):72–79.

VAIPO

2000 *VAIPO: Política nacional indígena y originaria (aspectos principales).* La Paz: VAIPO.

Van Cott, Donna L.

2000a *The Friendly Liquidation of the Past: The Politics of Diversity in Latin America.* Pittsburgh: University of Pittsburgh Press.

2000b Party System Development and Indigenous Populations in Latin America: The Bolivian Case. *Party Politics* 6(2):155–174.

Willis, Eliza, Christopher da C.B. Garman, and Stephen Haggard

1999 "The Politics of Decentralization in Latin America." *Latin American Research Review* 34(1).

World Bank

1995 "Priorities and Strategies in Education: a World Bank Review." Washington, D.C.: World Bank Publications.

1999 "Bolivia: Implementing the Comprehensive Development Framework." World Bank Document (Report 19326-BO).

Yashar, Deborah

1998 "Contesting Citizenship: Indigenous Movements and Democracy in Latin America." *Comparative Politics* 31(1):23–42.

1999 "Democracy, Indigenous Movements, and the Postliberal Challenge in Latin America." *World Politics* 52(1):76–104.

Acronyms

ADN   *Acción Democrática Nacionalista,* Nationalist Democratic Action
APG   *Asamblea del Pueblo Guaraní,* Guarani People's Assembly
CSUTCB   *Confederación Sindical Única de Trabajadores Campesinos de Bolivia,* Unified Syndical Confederation of Peasant Workers of Bolivia
CIDOB   *Confederación Indígena de Bolivia,* Indigenous Confederation of Bolivia
COB   *Confederación Obrera Boliviana,* Bolivian Workers' Federation
CONMERB   *Confederación Nacional del Magisterio de la Educación Rural de Bolivia,* National Teachers' Confederation of Bolivian Rural Education
CPESC   *Coordinadora de Pueblos Étnicos de Santa Cruz,* Coordinator of Ethnic Peoples of Santa Cruz
EIB   *Educación Intercultural Bilingüe,* Bilingual Intercultural Education
FSC   *Federación Sindical de Colonizadores,* Syndical Federation of Colonists
INRA   *Instituto Nacional de Reforma Agraría,* National Agrarian Reform Institute
LPP   *Ley de Participación Popular,* Popular Participation Law
MAS   *Movimiento al Socialismo,* Movement to Socialism
MIP   *Movimiento Indígena Pachakuti,* Pachakuti Indigenous Movement
MIR   *Movimiento Izquierdista Revolucionario,* Leftist Revolutionary Movement
MNR   *Movimiento Nacionalista Revolucionario,* Nationalist Revolutionary Movement
VAIPO   *Viceministerio de Asuntos Indígenas y de Pueblos Originarios,* Vice-Ministry of Indigenous and Originary People's Affairs. Replaced the Secretariat of Ethnic Affairs (SAE, *Sub-secretaría de Asuntos Étnicos, 1993–1997*) when ADN came to power in 1998. Would be converted to Ministry level and renamed Ministry of Peasant, Originary Peoples' and Indigenous Affairs (MACPIO, *Ministerio de Asuntos Campesinos, de Pueblos Indígenas y Originarios*), after the September conflicts of 2000.

SECTION

IV

Lowland South American Countries

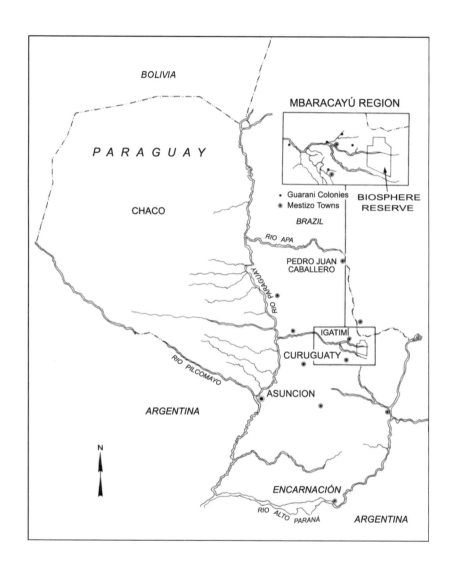

BOLIVIA

P A R A G U A Y

CHACO

MBARACAYÚ REGION

• Guaraní Colonies
⊛ Mestizo Towns

BIOSPHERE
RESERVE

BRAZIL

RIO APA

RIO PARAGUAY

PEDRO JUAN
CABALLERO

RIO PILCOMAYO

IGATIMÍ

CURUGUATY

ASUNCION

ARGENTINA

N

ENCARNACIÓN

RIO ALTO PARANÁ

ARGENTINA

Map 10-1

10

New Rules for the Game: Paraguayan Indigenous Groups and the Transition to Democracy

Richard Reed

In February 1989, Paraguay's dictator was deposed by his own troops. The thirty-four year reign of General Alfredo Stroessner ended with surprisingly little bloodshed and, as the iron-fisted ruler boarded the plane for exile in Brazil, Paraguay began the long and difficult road toward democracy. After a decade the institutions of government are still weak, but political dialogue and popular elections are becoming a reality. Political parties, labor unions, peasant organizations and business groups are flexing their muscles in a world without Stroessner. New parties have formed, fresh issues (such as the environment) are discussed and novel voices assert themselves in the new political arena. Women's groups, religious organizations and, of special interest here, indigenous minorities struggle to be heard in the cacophony of political debate.

More than 50,000 indigenous peoples of diverse ethnic groups survived the Stroessner era. Having struggled for power and resources under the authoritarian system, the indigenous minority has reason to both strive for and fear political change. During the decades of Stroessner's rule, Indians asserted themselves as an ethnic minority in the Paraguayan nation. They developed powerful patrons in the highly stratified, personalist system of caudillo politics and won political protection that was denied the mass of peasants. The rhetoric of democracy promises political power to all, but challenges established political certainties. Always outsiders, indigenous groups are strangers in an ever-stranger land.

How have Paraguayan indigenous groups been affected by the transition to democracy; and how have they reacted? Democratic change promises increased political participation and, through that, access to power. But the experiences of Paraguayan indigenous groups in the new, more democratic elections raise concerns. As political bosses lose their authority, it is not clear that indigenous groups are finding representative voices in the new political dialogue.

Paraguayan indigenous groups are losing the political position afforded by ethnicity and hoping to gain new power as independent voters. Rather than networks of patrons and clients, indigenous peoples find themselves in long lines on election day, standing next to faceless peasants as they struggle to assert political power.

The experience of Paraguayan indigenous groups calls attention to more general issues in the increasingly democratic world of Latin America. The indigenous societies of the New World developed outside the realm of liberal or authoritarian systems and often retain a fundamentally different concept of power and leadership. These societies adapted to colonialism, dictatorship, and authoritarian governments. Recent democratic reforms offer to complete the liberal project that Bolivar first promoted, making each individual an independent actor on the national stage. But the democratic opportunities bring new pressures. After centuries of struggling to fend off dictators, indigenous political organizations and leadership must find new tactics to articulate with the structures of national governance.

The indigenous population is only a small portion of the Paraguayan nation. Of the 4.1 million people counted in the 1992 national census, only about one percent is native (Censo nacional de poblacion y viviendas, 1992). Despite being only a small minority, the population includes great diversity. There are five distinct language families, from which seventeen distinct ethnic groups can be identified. And even these groups show important cultural variations among regions and communities.

More than simple cultural variation, there is social conflict. Many indigenous languages are mutually unintelligible and interethnic relations are often as problematic as those with non-Indians. Even before the arrival of the Spanish, differences bred antipathy and contact caused violence. While this social conflict between indigenous ethnic groups has declined with the growth of the mestizo population, there hasn't been a commensurate development of a common ethnic indigenous identity.

Stroessner's Authoritarian Regime

If control of the population is a measure of success, General Alfredo Stroessner was extremely successful. From the first weeks after he assumed power in 1954, his political apparatus insinuated itself into all aspects of Paraguayan national life, assuring loyalty of his subjects through the careful allocation of all state resources. Politicians received smuggling contracts for drugs, alcohol, and tobacco; military officers acquired fiefdoms for cattle and timber; and businessmen were allowed to launder money with impunity. Peasants (and Indians) were allowed to stay on their land and largely ignored. Critical voices that could not be co-opted were suppressed. Peasant organizations, labor unions, and opposition political parties that refused to play the game were destroyed with bureaucratic harassment and police violence.

This authoritarian state was both extremely hierarchical and highly personal. As a classic caudillo system, it transformed personal ties into powerful client relations. Functionaries of Stroessner's Asociación Nacional Republicana (ANR), better known as the *Colorados,* dispensed the resources of the state as favors, to be repaid with loyalty or a portion of the profits. It was popular mythology that anyone, no matter how lowly, who appeared at Stroessner's office at 6:30 on Thursday morning would be given an audience, and a stroke of the dictator's pen might grant the subject his appeal. The system applied to indigenous peoples as it did to peasants.[1]

For the indigenous population, the authoritarian system was both a blessing and a curse. On one hand, it created a set of dependency relations that allowed them direct access to state functionaries and state resources. On the other, there was no means or incentive for the various ethnic groups to act together. In fact, by granting only individual favors, the state undermined the solidarity of pan-ethnic indigenous organizations that fought for all native peoples' rights.

Throughout the Stroessner years, the indigenous population was administered through the Departmento de Asuntos Indígenas (DAI) of the Defense Ministry, much as the Bureau of Indian Affairs was established under the United States War Department. Native communities needed to make personal requests to the defense minister for land, medicine, or schools. Throughout most of the Stroessner years, the minister received requests directly in the ministry. The applicant was expected to show himself in the antechamber of the office, wait his turn among the other supplicants, and place his request personally to the minister. Few requests were rejected out of hand; many were granted—but with strings attached. A road was built or a parcel of land protected, but loyalty or logs or land was extracted in the process.

Native groups had a low profile in Stroessner's early years; the state quietly adopted a program of assimilation. In the Chaco, Stroessner looked to Anglican and Mennonite missionaries to "civilize" indigenous groups. In eastern Paraguay, the Guaraní were expected to acculturate into the peasant population, becoming tobacco or cotton farmers (Bejarano 1977).

The system mollified demands, but did not solve basic problems. Caudillo politics, commercial agriculture, and ranching undermined the self-sufficiency of indigenous communities. Although individual appeals to the government resulted in small parcels, there was little legislation or infrastructure to deal with the more general problems of indigenous groups. Rather than assimilate, indigenous groups saw their standard of living sink even below that of poor peasants.

In the 1970s, urban and peasant unions made demands for better conditions. Among indigenous groups this took the form of a pan-native movement and a non-governmental agency called "Proyecto Marandu," fighting for health, education, and land rights of the indigenous population.[2] Marandu began as a small indigenista agency, dedicated to indigenous culture and rights. It gained considerable momentum from peasant activists and international funding and became a political center for a wide variety of efforts to help indigenous communities.

These growing social movements stimulated a widespread and violent repression by Stroessner. Peasants were shot, unions were closed, and activist indigenistas in Marandu were jailed. As the general repression attracted international attention, the plight of indigenous people became a potent symbol of the violence used against all political actors in this small country. Specifically, the conditions of the Ache, many of whom were forced from the forest in the early 1970s, became an international cause and a rallying point for criticism of Stroessner's brutality (Munzel 1973).

It was with surprise, we can assume, that the Stroessner government found itself vilified for "genocide" against its Indian population (most violence was directed at others). Seeking to regain international respect, and unwilling to ameliorate the problems of peasants and laborers, Stroessner began to respond to Indians, indigenistas, and anthropologists who were requesting reservation status for indigenous communities. Although Stroessner was unwilling to defend indigenous communities against *latifundistas*, as was the case in much of the Chaco, the government lost little time in setting aside land in areas with available *tierras fiscales*. By 1978, roughly 80 percent of the communities in eastern Paraguay (at least those identified at that time) were provided some legal protection for their lands.[3]

A centerpiece of the new relations with indigenous groups was an office named the Instituto Nacional del Indígena, which was soon renamed the Instituto Paraguayo del Indígena (INDI). INDI was charged with identifying indigenous communities and providing state services, such as land titles and legal recognition. A citizen board was established, made up of missionaries, Indians, and indigenistas, to oversee and advise the agency. To regularize land, funds were allocated from congress for the indemnification of latifundistas who held title to contested areas. Despite these changes, the administration of Indian affairs remained under the direct control of the defense minister. He or a trusted aide held court each morning to receive indigenous leaders to hear and respond to their requests.

One of the most fought-for laws to assist indigenous groups in the Stroessnista decades was the Ley Indígena 904/81, which guaranteed land to indigenous communities. Before that time, Indian resources were protected only through a 1930 law allocating land to individual peasant households. The new law sanctioned communal ownership of land and mandated that it be titled directly to indigenous groups.

New laws did not alleviate most problems of indigenous groups. In many cases, government rhetoric hid an unwillingness to take direct action. The law was fitfully applied and useless to counter the inequities of Paraguayan land tenure. Without power or funds, the citizen committee remained simply advisory to a military bureaucracy that had little interest in listening. Not even the government functionaries within INDI had the means to acquire the land that indigenous groups were due. Despite liberal legislation, INDI could only offer vague assurances and little action.

Where institutions failed, the minister or the dictator could take swift unilateral action. Even in the worst years of Stroessner's repression, indigenous groups could request and maybe win a portion of the lands they needed, even as the mass of the peasant population went begging. Where bureaucracy failed, the caudillo system worked effectively. International pressure to defend indigenous peoples was satisfied; the pockets of bureaucrats were lined with a portion of indigenous peoples' land or timber; and the native population received some assurance of their rights to land. And in the manner of patronage politics, the indigenous communities were expected to remain staunch supporters of the status quo. Most did.

In spite of the modest gains, the end of the Stroessner period found indigenous people to be the poorest of the poor in one of the world's poorest nations. Most remained on land that was titled to others (even the lands that were protected remained in the name of the INDI). Although there had been gifts of schoolhouses, few communities had teachers. Where INDI built clinics, medicine remained in critically short supply, most provided by missionaries and the Red Cross. Notwithstanding the government's economic development programs, indigenous workers were increasingly forced to leave native communities and seek the patronage of ranchers and farmers.

The Transition to Democracy

Stroessner's political regime, in the final analysis, was felled by economic diversification. As new sources of wealth overshadowed traditional commodities, Stroessner lost control of the resources that greased state machinery. In the private sector, commodities (such as cement, electricity, and textiles) created political entrepreneurs who were not dependent on Stroessner's largesse. Among the military, cocaine trafficking replaced rum running and provided uncountable fortunes for officers to purchase and arm their own loyal troops.

When the tanks deposed Stroessner in 1989, the country held its breath. The coup could have gone two ways: either initiating a transition to democracy or bringing in a new caudillo. The ambiguity was maintained as power was assumed by Stroessner's right-hand man (and the country's principal drug smuggler), General Andrés Rodríguez. Rodríguez declared marshal law and suspended the constitution. Then, when the semblance of peace was instated, he called for elections and a transition to democratic rule. Rodríguez's leadership was quickly ratified in a popular election that left the basic question unanswered: was Paraguay under the old or a new order?

Rather than cause for celebration, political change has always been viewed with concern by the Paraguayan population. After all, new leaders usually arrived with empty pockets, looking to line them with the spoils of victory. Political change was remembered only in the stories of the civil wars of 1947–1948, when internecine fighting between the two political parties destroyed much of the national infrastructure. Like peasants and city dwellers, indigenous groups were left in a state of confusion by the 1989 overthrow. All official activities ground to a halt, as bureaucrats waited to find out the ground rules of the new state. New military leaders might offer resources and opportunity to Indians, but might also strip them of their special status. Rodríguez offered few clues as neither his speeches nor press releases made mention of indigenous peoples. (Although his patrician sympathies were evident in newspaper photos of his wife distributing food and clothing on reservations.)

While the president offered little information, there were early signs that the democratic process could work for indigenous peoples. As soon as the new Congress was elected, a coalition of missionaries and indigenistas pressured the new democratic body, which approved legislation supporting indigenous communities. Ley 1989/43 was quickly passed to defend to Mbya communities in precarious conditions on contested land in Caaguazu. It eviscerated previous pro-farmer legislation by restricting development, clearing, or sale of land under legal claim by indigenous communities. And Rodríguez's early actions reformed INDI. First, he appointed a civilian as president of the agency, Numa Mallorquin. This, coupled with a new advisory board of Indians and indigenistas, provided the first civilian administration in the agency's history. Second, the budget of the institution was almost doubled to $730,000 in the first year, with a 160 percent increase in the monies allocated for the indemnification of landowners (DIM 1990, 12–14). This financial gain was increased in the subsequent year, when INDI's budget was increased by another 243 percent.[4]

A new constitution, passed in 1992, made explicit statements about the government's intentions for native peoples. It recognized the special status of indigenous peoples, exonerating men from military service and public works. The constitution also identified Indians' right to distinct cultural and social groups. More than simply hold land in common, each group had right to territory sufficient to maintain this cultural and social integrity. (Despite requests by indigenous peoples, the new constitution stopped short of allocating representation to native groups in constitutional assemblies. It offered a voice, but not a vote, to indigenous delegates.)

Other legislation quickly strengthened the constitutional recognition. In 1993, the senate ratified the International Labor Organization's statement on the rights of indigenous communities. Ley 234/93 stated that the government assumes "the responsibility of developing, with the participation of the groups affected, a coordinated and systematic means to protect the rights of those groups to guarantee their integrity." The Paraguayan law specifically demanded that the Paraguayan government safeguard the right "of groups to use lands that have not been exclusively occupied by those groups, but to which they have had traditional access for their traditional and subsistence activities" (author's translation).

Despite bureaucratic reorganization, these early policies offered little real aid to indigenous communities. Rather than structural improvement, changes at INDI created a bloated bureaucracy. Almost half of the budget in the 1990–1991 fiscal year went into salaries, and the paid staff climbed from 47 in 1989 to 140 in 1993 (Kidd 1997, 33). More than wasted funds, the change created distance between indigenous leaders and INDI. Few of the new officials were indigenous or were experienced in Indian affairs, nor did they have incentive to visit indigenous communities. Where the previous minister met leaders and community members in an unassuming office on the ground floor of the INDI headquarters, Mallorquin's office was moved onto the second floor of a dramatically refurbished office space. Few Indians were welcome up the narrow staircase that separated the mass of indigenous visitors on the ground floor from the INDI officials above.

After positive early policies, the rhetoric of the Rodríguez government quickly adapted to the demands of Paraguay's traditional vested interests. Despite early assurances that the new government would guarantee "tierras para todos" (land for all), by 1990 the government rhetoric changed to that of "propiedad privada" (private property). In a time of social uncertainty, this subtle but powerful shift won approval from investors abroad and local elites, and had an immediate and direct impact on indigenous lands in contest.

INDI responded to the signals of the new president. Peasants, loggers, farmers, and ranchers moved with impunity onto Indian land. Although the government responded swiftly to squatters on the vast estates of the wealthy, it turned a blind eye to those who settled on government or native lands (DIM 1990). Only the lobbying of NGOs and international agencies could win the eviction of squatters, and then, only after the land had been stripped of valuable timber and fertile soils had been degraded. The forests that remained in these contested areas disappeared at an increasingly alarming rate. The rate of deforestation rose from 200,000 hectares a year under Stroessner (already the highest proportional rate in the Americas) to almost 500,000 hectares annually (OAS 2001, 23).

Going beyond inefficiency and insensitivity, INDI actively undermined efforts to secure land. Rather than fight for the petitions of Indians against titleholders, functionaries negotiated compromises. Settlements often gave substantial ground to illegitimate land claims by non-Indians. In some cases, INDI defended farmers and ranchers from the requests of indigenous communities. For example, INDI officials helped evict the community of Ykua Pora from land colonized by farmers and tried to pay Mbya of Caazapa to abandon their homesteads to Mennonites. The Dialogo Indígena Misionero, published by the Equipo Nacional del Misiones, documents the ongoing complicity of INDI, and specifically Numa Mallorquin, in this usurpation of native lands.[5] Even when lands were purchased for native communities, prices were inflated for land that was usually of little value.

The final blow to the hopes offered by the new INDI came quickly. In late 1992 the budget was reduced by 60 percent. Idle staff was protected as money for land purchases was slashed almost 75 percent. Kidd points out that despite continuous and intense work for indigenous lands in the Chaco, no gains were made under the administration of Rodríguez (Kidd 1997, 23). The only significant lands acquired were in eastern Paraguay, where the Nature Conservancy purchased land on the open market for the Ache. In sum, the first years of democracy offered little to indigenous communities.

Democratic Action and Indigenous Communities

The movement toward democracy took a major step forward with each of the civilian elections of 1991, 1993, and 1998. Although elections in 1989 ratified Rodríguez as president, there was little to distinguish them from the electoral charades of Stroessner. Municipal elections in May of 1991 and those of the constitutional assembly later that year increased popular participation. The elections of 1993 and 1998 offered the first times since 1951 that the military did not dominate the process or predominate in the candidates. Moreover, the steady decline of the social influence of the Colorado Party between 1989 and 1998 created a true *apertura* for political debate and dialogue. The return of exiled groups and the formation of new parties, such as the Encuentro Nacional, broke the decades-long deadlock between the Colorados and the Liberal parties. Popular support for these groups signaled new political vitality; third party candidates first won regional elections and then the mayor's office in Asunción.

With real reform in popular elections, indigenous groups were called upon to join the rest of the nation in democratic action. The past was defined by decades, even centuries, of caudillo politics, where they were beholden to individual patrons for any rights and resources. Rural political bosses provided indigenous communities with a measure of security, in exchange for Indian labor in the forest (cutting timber and *yerba mate*) and civil projects, such as building roads and bridges. The future was in free voting and political dialogue, in which each person would make individual and personal choices from a range of political options.

But my own research in rural Paraguay points out two problems that impede democratic solutions from answering indigenous peoples' problems. First, it is not clear that indigenous peoples' voting patterns reflect their individual choices. Despite the continued transformation of the electoral structure, natives have little introduction into participatory elections. Second, it is not clear that neo-liberal politics are in the best interests of ethnic minorities. Indigenous peoples are a national minority and, more specifically, are being outnumbered in areas where they used to predominate. There is little evidence that the democratic process is any more capable of defending their rights in the to and fro of representative decision-making.

The experience of Guaraní voters near the mestizo town of Igatimi illustrates the complexities of ethnic minorities' involvement in the democratic transition. Despite widespread and enthusiastic involvement in the last two elections, no candidates visited the Guaraní communities or included the Guaraní in their platforms; Guaraní rarely cast their vote on the basis of candidates' qualifications or party platform; and their needs are rarely considered in the policies that derive from these democratic elections. After almost a decade of democracy, the communities are more confused and cynical than even under the politics of Stroessner.

These communities are in the department of Canindeyu, in Paraguay's eastern forests, about 50 kilometers from the Brazilian border. It is perhaps helpful at the outset to note that there is a direct link, yet a profound difference, between political relations in the capital city and those in rural areas. Over the last century, political parties have exerted themselves in rural regions through caudillos. Local officials and police held offices through direct ties to local party bosses, who were usually the largest landowners. Since 1890, justice and resources in Igatimi have been controlled by political bosses who, in turn, depended on the power and beneficence of the party's national political machine. Since they first came to power over fifty years ago, Colorado bosses in Asunción maintained their ties to local bosses who guaranteed social order and electoral votes in return for total control over the region and its population.

Like the peasants of Igatimi, Guaraní leaders of the area have been beholden to local party bosses. Party leaders helped solve conflicts with local landowners, fixed criminal charges, and even paid Guaraní debts to local merchants. In return, Guaraní provided workers for municipal projects and votes in elections. Unlike peasants, however, Guaraní leaders had direct access to the Minister of Defense. When national power was useful, indigenous leaders could travel to Asunción, sit hat-in-hand in the minister's antechamber and appeal for help. Consequently, Guaraní leaders were familiar (if not common) faces in the corridors of power and in the offices of INDI. National contacts had limited currency against local Colorado leaders, but if used judiciously, could provide access to military support, international funds, and government land.

The Guaraní repaid with loyalty. The vast majority cast their lot with the ruling Colorado party. Within the Guaraní communities, this political affiliation was usually insignificant, but each September 11, the Guaraní from around Igatimi would don whatever red clothes they owned and traipse off to the Colorado Party *asado*, an open fiesta where local officials would harvest several of their ranch cattle to feed the townspeople. In Igatimi this was held at the home of the local judge. The small bands of Guaraní would stand at the edge of the yard, looking and feeling vaguely out of place among townspeople and peasants, until called over to have their fill of some of the less than prime cuts of beef.

Not all the Guaraní cast their lot with the Colorados. One small (but committed) kin group held determinedly to Liberal party affiliation. These attended the opposition party's fiesta on July 10th. With blue hats or kerchiefs, they went off to the home of their patron, an aging Liberal whose father had been the principal caudillo under the previous regime. Like the smattering of Liberal peasants, these Guaraní recognized allegiance to patronage relations that predated the Liberal loss in 1947.

Although bitter opponents at the national level, the Colorado and Liberal factions of the local township had longstanding modes of mutual accommodation. Liberal leaders could never expect favors, but nor did the local Colorado leaders take undue advantage of their political position. Therefore, elections in Igatimi during Stroessner's reign were a quiet and contained affair. Voting was mandated and stamps on the backs of voters' identity cards proved that they had performed their national duty. Like most peasants, the Guaraní quietly paid their political debt. Each election day would find a stream of men and women walking the seven kilometers into town to vote, then over to the Colorado or Liberal party headquarters in hopes of being offered a bite to eat and a *trago* of cheap cane liquor. (The more enthusiastic voters would make their way to both party headquarters on election day, hoping to double their share of the post-election revelry.)

The elections held by Rodríguez in 1989 to ratify his presidency were unchanged from those of Stroessner. There was no debate and little suspense. Guaraní and peasants alike trooped to vote, then removed themselves to the headquarters to celebrate. The Colorado victory was a foregone conclusion.

Things changed significantly in 1993. In an important step toward democracy, General Rodríguez removed himself from the ballot. Factions within ANR fell to fighting and the conflict cost them considerable support. The best they could do for a candidate was Juan Carlos Wasmosy, a lackluster businessman who had acquired a fortune in the construction industry. While the Colorados were divided, Liberals played on the popularity of their long-time leader, Domingo Laino, who was recently returned from exile. Finally, a new party entered the fray, the Encuentro Nacional, breaking the simple dichotomy between the Liberals and the Colorados. And, for a population who defined politics by color, a ballot with stripes cast a note of visual uncertainty into what was previously a predictable process.

Electioneering in the capital city was intense, and rallies in the streets showed the popular enthusiasm and the state acceptance of political action. Things were more placid in the region of Igatimi. Posters of Liberal candidates sprung up at the expected places, but there was little of the partisan debate. Although the political dialogue never reached the Guaraní communities, beef did. On the Saturday before elections, people gathered at the house of the Guaraní political leader, explaining they had come to the Colorado political rally. By the time the blue pickup of the Colorado Party boss bounced up the dirt track, most of the community was waiting. With the flourish of a caudillo, the boss stepped out and officiated as his men unloaded a recently butchered steer. Even before the Guaraní had begun to carve up the carcass, the boss and his helpers were back on the road, presumably to take another steer to another "rally."

As most of the community gathered for their portion of the Colorado beef, a smaller and more doleful group of Liberal party loyalists watched from some distance off. Only after the steer had been divvied up and hauled off, did a second truck arrive in the community, making a turn through the field to stop in front of the waiting Liberals. The group went out and received a small front quarter of beef. Then, with obvious displeasure and a good deal of grumbling, they observed to themselves that the Liberals could never hope to win with such a small *asado*.

Election day was predictable. As in previous elections, the Guaraní walked to town, stood in line and, after casting their votes, retreated to a party headquarters to celebrate. When Wasmosy had been announced the winner for the Colorados, they claimed their *trago* and returned home. In experience, and in local effects, the democratic transition had little importance for the Guaraní. The Colorado officials returned to their sinecures.

Although Colorados claimed all seats in the regional offices in Canindeyu in 1993, the opposition parties made important progress at the national level. In the Chamber of Deputies, the ANR earned 44 percent of the popular vote, winning 40 out of 80 representatives to the national congress. The Liberals garnered 35 percent, 32 seats, and the Encuentro Nacional made an impressive first showing with 17 percent of the vote and receiving 8 representatives to the national assembly. In the Chamber of Senators, the Colorados did not even retain half the seats, winning only 20 seats compared to the 17 won by the Liberals and the 8 of the Encuentro Nacional.

The bifurcation of the political landscape became even more apparent with the municipal elections in Asunción in 1996. The opposition alliance won that election with 52 percent of the votes, taking control of the political machinery of the capital city.

The elections of 1998 were preceded by a vigorous political debate, stimulated by a profound division in the ruling Colorado Party. The ruling party officials did not back the winner of primary elections; he was nominated from a prison cell in Asunción, where he had been sent for conspiring to overthrow the government. He proposed that his chosen vice president, Raúl Cubas Grau, run for president. Both the Liberales and the Encuentro sought to capitalize on the disintegration of the ruling coalition and elect their own candidates.

By the time of the 1998 elections, the country had changed dramatically. Political movement toward political freedom in the cities was accompanied by dramatic demographic change in the country. Paraguayan state policy has always promoted population growth, and declining infant mortality rates of the 1980s had an immediate effect. The national population grew by over a third between 1982 and 1992, adding more than a million people to bring the population to

4,123,000. The population of Canindeyu grew by more than 50 percent as roads were cut into the forests and bridges built over the rivers. The changes increased dramatically after 1992. Between 1992 and 2001 the total national population increased by over 40 percent, to more than 5 million people. Due to massive land distribution programs between 1992 and 2001, excess population near Asunción was relocated into the country's remaining forests along the Brazilian border. While the population of the departments near the capital dropped by almost 50 percent, the population of Amambay increased by 54 percent; Canindeyu grew by 64 percent; and the population of Alto Paraná by more than 90 percent. Population growth allowed each of the three departments a new representative in the national congress, political capital that was, as yet, uncontrolled.

In Igatimi, the problems within the dominant party began to show up in the local political machine. While the older *patrones* and storeowners held firm to Colorado loyalties, the younger men began to hang posters for the third party on the walls of the sawmill and the dentist office. Political changes were even more apparent in the minibuses that showed up in the months before the elections. Megaphones on the rooftops of aged Volkswagens proclaimed the promises of the various candidates. This in itself was notable, as previous electioneering had been accomplished with mundane posters that made no promises and promoted no specific agenda. (The excitement was heightened by the fact that the minivans that spread the propaganda were the same ones that the circus hired when it came to town, inserting the note of a carnival into this first political debate in memory.)

Much of the political activity in the months leading up to the election in 1998 was in new colonies that had sprung up in the forests surrounding Guaraní communities. Straight roads had been cut into the forests and thousands of families had been located onto the fifty-hectare parcels. The land around the Guaraní reservations was now densely settled by farmers, each intent on forging a new life in this frontier region. These new communities had only weak ties to the local power structure. Few of the new settlers spent any time in Igatimi and, having acquired rights to land through the national land reform office, had few debts and loyalties to local power brokers. In short, they were political loose cannons, whose votes could not be easily controlled.

Soon the small roads to these colonization schemes were being traversed by the muddy vans, pamphlets were distributed that exhorted the peasants to vote for Laino or Cubas or one of the various other candidates. But while electioneering was intense in the colonization areas, the minivans never made it down the track into the Guaraní communities. Residents soon were aware that something was afoot, but it wasn't clear that they were a part of it.

As the free-wheeling propaganda attempted to sway new colonists, the Colorado machine moved to guarantee its traditional voting base. In Guaraní communities, this political apparatus was evident in schoolteachers who arrived to prepare residents to vote. Early one day in the week before the elections, a teacher from a nearby grade school arrived in Itanaramí. Tied to the back of his bicycle was a voting box stuffed with mock ballots. A meeting was called and, after most of the community was assembled, the teacher began to introduce the Guaraní to the meaning of elections and voting. The training consisted of explaining to the Indians the importance of voting and how to use the ballot box. Most importantly, they were taught to vote with the red ballots for the Colorado candidates, rather than the blue, green, or striped ballots. Then after reviewing the documents of all those who were ready to vote Colorado, and assuring that they were registered on the voting list, the teacher hopped back on his bicycle to do voter education at the next town. The machine had inserted itself so thoroughly into the functioning of the apparatus of the government that it wasn't even considered ironic that the most respected employee of the local government was exploiting his position to "teach" the Guaraní the proper way to vote—for the Colorados.

On the day of elections in 1998, there was a new air of uncertainty. National polls showed the election could go to either presidential candidate and, without rural surveys, the local races were anybody's (and everybody's) guess. In Igatimí, the steady stream of voters soon filled the school courtyard where the election was held and, after checking their names, people waited in long lines to drop their marked ballots in the wooden boxes. The outcomes were so uncertain, in fact, that a great many people chose to wait outside the voting station and watch the excitement, rather than retire to the respective party's headquarters. The atmosphere in the new colonies was even more politicized. The rhetoric was bombastic and the tension almost palpable. These voters had few of the political ties that determine voting in more established rural outposts, and both the opposition and the Colorado activists hoped to see them as cogs in future political machines.

It was the next day before results were announced from the capital city. Although the Colorado party was not thrown out of power, radio broadcasts showed a country almost evenly divided. Cubas won a narrow victory, and the Colorados also held onto their majority in congress. But the political machine in the Igatimi region was dealt a serious blow as the Liberals won the new seat in the *Camara de Diputados,* the national senate, creating parity between the two parties.

Moreover, political activists immediately began a campaign to facilitate the candidates' responsiveness to local concerns. Internationally funded and carried out by progressives from Asunción, they held meetings in each of the local settlements reviewing the promises that had been made by the winning candidates, and the mechanisms to request action without recourse to local caudillos. Whether by chance or design, they never scheduled a meeting among the Guaraní to explain the promised changes and how to fight for them, and the effects of the political change were felt almost immediately. The new Liberal senator actively and aggressively moved to expropriate land from local latifundistas, not for Guaraní, but to settle new colonists from outside the region.

For the Guaraní, the democratization of political activity in Igatimi accompanies a decline in the traditional caudillo power. As the balance shifts from party machines to party ballots, Colorado patrons lose power and privilege. Guaraní are forced to exchange the modicum of protection from these caudillos, for the tug and fray of participatory politics. And it is not clear that the indigenous block has the power to enter the game.

Minority Populations and Local Power

The rise of democratic institutions has created new arenas for the contestation of power in Paraguay. In the ideal, indigenous minorities have been offered a new means of voicing demands and fulfilling their needs. But in practice, the changes do not result in a greater voice for indigenous affairs, nor greater resources to satisfying indigenous peoples' needs.

According to a report of the Organization of American States Inter-American Commission on Human Rights, published in 2001, the last decade of democracy has seen little change from the Stroessner years. Of the 47 communities that appealed for land between 1994 and 1998, only one received title, half have acquired vague assurance of their land claims through INDI, and the rest have nothing to show for their effort.[6] As a final blow, the 2000 budget for land expropriation was cut 58 percent from that of 1998, bringing the national land acquisition program to a virtual standstill.

The response of the democratic government to indigenous peoples' needs and the effectiveness of Guaraní voting makes it clear that the tug and pull of the new democracy is transforming the established power structure in rural areas and forcing indigenous minorities to contend with a widening field of new political actors.

A decade of events in rural Paraguay suggests that indigenous voices may be drowned out in the cacophony of political dialogue. Despite being a small minority of the national population, indigenous peoples have comprised a larger and highly visible portion of several rural departments. But for the same reasons that indigenous groups have found refuge in the forests of the government, new colonists desire them for new settlement schemes. Land settlement schemes and spontaneous colonization had dramatically increased the proportion of non-Indians in these areas, diminishing the importance of Indians' votes, ironically, just as votes began to have political power. In 1982, there was a population of 4,100 Guaraní in the department of Canindeyu, scattered in small colonias indígenas. As the entire population of the region was 66,000 individuals, indigenous peoples constituted about 6 percent of the total population. Today, with the total population of more than 160,000 in the department, the indigenous population is less than 3 percent. The same is the case in the other departments with large Guaraní populations: in both Amambay and Alto Paraná, the portion of total residents who are indigenous has declined by more than 50 percent (Helders 2001).

In the dry western Chaco, where settlement is sparse and indigenous residents comprise a greater portion of the population, the change has been even more dramatic. In the department of Boquerón, the indigenous portion of the population has dropped from 86 percent to 30 percent, while in the department of Presidente Hayes indigenous residents dropped from 39 percent to 14 percent. In all but one of the departments with over 1,000 Indians, the total population has more than doubled in the last two decades, with an average growth rate of 260 percent. In the remaining departments, those with less than 1,000 Indians, the average population growth in the last two decades has been half that, only 130 percent (Helders 2001). Consequently, those regions in which the traditional political machines are most disrupted, and those areas in which massive new unaligned populations are forming, are those areas in which indigenous peoples have historically found political and economic refuge from the state.

In sum, the democratic transition creates two distinct problems for the indigenous populations of Paraguay. First, representative institutions undermine patronage relations, the traditional means of power for Guaraní. As representatives replace caudillos, indigenous people find they must struggle against a wide variety of other interest groups. Rather than having a personal claim on powerful patrons, indigenous leaders find they represent a minority that is despised or ignored by majority and powerful sectors, including peasants, ranchers, lumber companies, and agro-industries.

Second, the democratic government's effort to win popular support by distributing land to peasants has further diminished the power of indigenous peoples' votes. With the sparse populations of previous eras, indigenous groups had a significant block of votes to deliver to the local Colorado machine. Today, indigenous communities are over-shadowed by massive land settlement schemes in the surrounding forests. The importance of their votes is greatly reduced, and they are forced to cast them into increasingly unpredictable waters.

Recent political events in South America's southern cone will exac-erbate the problems of indigenous groups. Paraguay, its government, and indigenous peoples face the difficult task of creating a new politi-cal structure as the state becomes less important in regional affairs. Mi-gration from Brazil has changed the ethnic character of many border regions. As it works to create representative institutions in eastern ru-ral areas, the government is faced with what has become an unregis-tered Brazilian majority. Massive influxes of small farmers from west-ern Brazil have overwhelmed the small Paraguayan population, shifting the language on the street from Guaraní to Portuguese and the currency from the Guaraní to the Real.

The demographic shifts are accompanied by economic changes. As commercial soybean farming increases, the agricultural power of the national economy moves from small cotton and tobacco farmers to multinational corporations. Moreover, the production is destined for Brazilian feedlots and, like Brazilian migrants, avoids official purview as it crosses the border. These issues became even more difficult as Paraguay integrates into the Mercosur common market. On one hand, the new trade agreements greatly reduce the problem of smuggling; on the other, they deprive Paraguay of the wealth (both legitimate and not) earned by the massive import and export sector.

The greatest threat to the new democracy, however, comes from within the nation. Disgruntled military officers and disaffected Col-orado Party power brokers wait impatiently on the sidelines, waiting to seize power from the country's weak presidency. The reality of this danger became bitterly apparent in 1999 when one of these dissenting generals, Lino Oviedo, assassinated Vice President Luis María Argaña and attempted to seize power. Despite being the subject of an international manhunt, already sentenced to jail for a 1996 coup attempt, Oviedo continues to declare his intent to become the next president.

As the country struggles to maintain its fragile democracy, indigenous rights are far from the immediate concern of most people. In this new system, native peoples must stand beside other disenfranchised poor in fighting for a modicum of power. But it is a struggle that is unique neither to Paraguay nor to the current political situation. Since the time of Bolívar, indigenous peoples have been faced with the difficult choice between ethnicity and nationalism. As we enter the twenty-first century, there is renewed awareness of the choice. Throughout Latin America, from Chiapas to Chile, native struggles are garnering political space in new democracies. In this strange new world, ethnic affiliation and individual national identity provide alternate means to achieve political power. Whichever they choose, the fight to regain access to the machinery of state will take time and determination. One can only hope that indigenous communities prove as resilient under democracy as they were adaptive under dictatorship.

Notes

1 It is common knowledge, and may be true, that the first colonia indígena, Fortuna, was a personal request granted to the Guaraní leader, Don Knuto Sales, who cured Stroessner of a painful skin disease.

2 In fact, indigenous peoples were allowed a level of political organizing and political action that was prohibited among laborers or peasant. The indigenous population never threatened the state, and specific leaders learned to play the patronage game. Consequently, personal pleas by individual leaders often yielded a modicum of results.

3 This, however, represents less than half the total population, as was subsequently enumerated in the national census conducted in 1991.

4 This money was provided from funds that were generated by taxes imposed in Ley 904/81, but which previously had never been extricated from the government's general operating budgets.

5 The problems of funding and action were covered in a series of articles in *Dialogo Indígena Misionero* (volumes 35–37), published by the Equipo Nacional de Misiones of the Centro Episcopal Paraguayo in Asunción. 1989–1991.

6 The single group to have received land, the Enxet-Sanapana of the Chaco, did so only after considerable international pressure was placed on the government. The remaining Enxet groups remain as dislocated refugees with little hope.

Works Cited

Censo nacional de población y viviendas

1992   Asunción: Dirección general de estadística, encuestas y censos.

Bejarano, Ramón César

1997   "Solucionemos Nuestro Problema Indígena con el INDI." Series Estudios Antropológicos (No. 6). Asunción, Paraguay.

Diálogo Indígena Misionero

1990   Equipo Nacional de Misiones of the Centro Episcopal Paraguayo. Asunción. Volume 30.

Diálogo Indígena Misionero

1991   Equipo Nacional de Misiones del Centro Episcopal Paraguayo. Asunción. Volume 31.

Helders, Stefan

2001   http://www.world-gazetteer.com/fr/fr_py.htm. *The World Gazetteer.* 26 May.

Kid, Stephen

1997   "Tierra, política y chamanismo benévolo. Los indígenas Enxet en un Paraguay democrático." *Suplemento Antropológico* (Centro de Estudios Antropológicos UCA). Asunción. December.

Munzel, Mark

1976   *Genocide in Paraguay.* Philadelphia: Temple University Press.

Organization of American States, Inter-American Commission on Human Rights

2001   County Report—Paraguay: Pueblos Indígenas.

Acronyms

ANR   *Asociación Nacional Republicana*
DAI   *Departmento de Asuntos Indígenas*
INDI   *Instituto Paraguayo del Indígena*

11

For Reasons of State: Paradoxes of Indigenist Policy in Brazil[1]

David Maybury-Lewis

The indigenous peoples of Brazil have attracted a great deal of attention in the world's press ever since the 1960s, when they were the victims of a kind of "winning of the West" Brazilian-style. Given this attention, people are often surprised to learn that there are fewer Indians in Brazil than in most other countries of the Americas and that they make up less than a quarter of one percent of the national population. This is not because the indigenous population of Brazil has been more drastically reduced than the native populations of other comparable countries, but rather because Amazonian populations have always been relatively small and sparse. It is true that Brazil's indigenous population, like native populations throughout the Americas, declined dramatically after the arrival of the Portuguese and only started to pick up again in the twentieth century, but similar declines were registered in the United States, Argentina, and Chile, all countries with sparse indigenous populations that were conquered and later pushed aside by states intent on realizing what each considered to be its "manifest destiny." Yet Brazil has fewer Indians in its population and a much smaller indigenous percentage in[2] its national population than any of these other three nations.

Historically, Brazil's indigenous peoples have, for the most part, been marginal to the life of the nation. At the time of the conquest, the Indian peoples living near the Atlantic coast were courted as allies by the various European nations that warred with each other as they tried to establish colonies in South America, but this period did not last long (see Hemming 1972). The contrast with North America is striking. At the end of the eighteenth century the Iroquois were still a force to be reckoned with in North America. The French, English, and Americans competed with each other for their alliance (see Calloway 1995). By that time, the coastal Indians of Brazil had long since been defeated and subjugated or annihilated. They were not, in any case, numerous enough to do the work of the sugar plantations that produced the wealth of colonial Brazil. Black slaves were therefore imported for that purpose.

By the nineteenth century, Brazil had become a country of blacks, whites and mulattos, with Indians playing a marginal role, both economically and socially. The "Indian question" simply was not on the national agenda. Instead, the major social issues being debated were the future of black slavery (not abolished until 1888), the future of the monarchy (overthrown in 1889), republicanism (the Republic was proclaimed in 1889), regionalism, and the rights of the rural oligarchs who intended to control the new republic (Maybury-Lewis 1994).

Rondón and the SPI

At the end of the nineteenth century there was concern in Brazil about the demarcation of the nation's borders and the means of travel and communication within its vast and sparsely settled territories. This led to renewed discussion of what the nation's policy should be with regard to the indigenous peoples who were coming into renewed contact with fresh waves of settlers. This discussion came into national prominence as a result of debates and denunciations in scientific circles, both in Brazil and in Germany.

German immigrants to Brazil were settling in substantial numbers in the southern state of Santa Catarina. As they cleared new land for agriculture, they clashed with indigenous peoples who fought to defend their traditional territories. The Germans hired Indian hunters to get rid of the Indians who were bothering them. The murderous activities of these men were denounced in the International Congress of Americanists, held in Vienna in 1908 (Frič 1910). The denunciation added fuel to the fire of a debate that was already raging in Brazil about what should be the proper way to deal with "wild" Indians.[3]

Professor Hermann von Ihering, a German-born anthropologist who was director of the São Paulo state museum, one of Brazil's prestigious research institutions, defended the colonists, arguing that they had the right to defend themselves against "savage" Indians who were bound to disappear anyway as they made way for civilization. This view was challenged by other scientists, particularly those from a rival institution, the National Museum in Rio de Janeiro. These scholars rejected von Ihering's pessimism about the future of indigenous peoples in Brazil, arguing that it was unscientific, inhumane, and un-Brazilian to condemn indigenous peoples to extinction. Their view prevailed, thanks to the efforts of two remarkable men, Colonel Cândido Mariano da Silva Rondón and the minister of agriculture, Rodolfo Nogueira da Rocha Miranda. Rondón, himself part Indian, was a deeply religious positivist who believed that all human societies, including the indigenous ones in Brazil, possessed the capacity to climb the ladder of progress and participate in the unfolding of civilization. In his view, the indigenous societies of Brazil should be protected, assisted, and educated until they blended into the national civilization. Meanwhile he gave a remarkable demonstration of his convictions when he was placed in command of expeditions responsible for establishing telegraph services in "Indian country" in the hinterlands of Brazil. Rondón's motto for his men was an extraordinary one for the times. He told his men that they should live by the precept "Die if need be, but never kill." In fact his expeditions never did kill any of the Indians whom they met. His views and his personal demonstration that it was possible to establish friendly relations with indigenous peoples, however hostile they might seem to be at first, established him as a Brazilian hero and as the leading exponent of what came to be thought of as a peculiarly Brazilian way of dealing with the native peoples of their nation. It was Rondón's knowledge of the interior and his prestige as a returned explorer that enabled him to persuade the Brazilian government to set up the SPI (Service for the Protection of Indians) in 1910. The government, for its part, favored the idea of an Indian service and also Rondón's ideas about what kind of a service it should be, thanks to the strong support Rondón received from Rodolfo Miranda, the minister of agriculture.[4] The service was inaugurated on September 7 (Brazil's Independence Day), 1910, with Rondón as its director.

The policy of the service was to concentrate on four main objectives:

1) to increase the state's knowledge about indigenous peoples within its boundaries

2) to protect indigenous peoples from massacre and exploitation

3) to protect indigenous lands

4) to provide indigenous peoples with education to enable them eventually to enter Brazilian society.

This was a huge task in a country of continental size, whose sparse indigenous populations lived in its least accessible regions. From the start, the perennially underfunded SPI had great difficulty in carrying it out. Indigenous peoples continued therefore to be protected as much by their remoteness as by the SPI. True to the spirit of Rondón, however, the SPI developed and perfected techniques of making friendly contact with indigenous groups that had not previously had dealings with the outside world. These techniques of "attraction" involved traveling through the jungle, locating trails used by uncontacted groups and leaving presents for them until they were willing to show themselves in face-to-face encounters. This is still the most romantic work that the Indian service does and is currently the responsibility of the Department of Isolated Indians, a branch of the service directed by Sydney Possuelo. This department has identified 16 areas in the Amazon forests where there are uncontacted peoples, i.e., peoples who fight or flee when they meet outsiders. Possuelo's department believes there are 29 more such areas, but the presence of uncontacted people in these areas has not yet been confirmed.[5] Possuelo and his department are correct when they stress that these uncontacted peoples are especially vulnerable and that the Indian service should therefore make especial efforts to contact and protect them. Yet Possuelo and his work are largely irrelevant these days to the task of defending the majority of Brazil's indigenous peoples, who have all too much contact with the society that surrounds them.

This contact resulted from the steady movement of population into the Brazilian interior during the first half of the twentieth century. The "opening up" of the interior was given an enormous boost by the transfer of the nation's capital from Rio de Janeiro to Brasília in 1960, which moved the center of gravity of the country away from the Atlantic coast for the first time in Brazilian history. This process was given a further boost by the policies of the military regime that seized power in 1964. The military claimed to have seized power in order to forestall a revolution that would have imposed leftist solutions for the problems of poverty and land hunger that bedeviled the country. The military rejected the leftist remedies, especially insofar as they involved redistribution of land and resources, and decided instead to solve the nation's problems by, among other things, encouraging the development of the interior. They therefore offered cheap loans to agribusinesses and cattle ranchers in the Amazonian regions (see Hecht and Cockburn 1990). As the minister of the interior put it at the time: "Cattle are the pioneers of our decade." As a result, indigenous peoples found themselves being overwhelmed by large enterprises and streams of would-be smallholders as they flooded into the backlands. If the natives tried to protect themselves, they were considered "anti-development" and therefore, in the logic of the times, subversive. Since the regime was so strongly in favor of its own model of development, it did little to protect indigenous people from the assault on their lands and their lives that accompanied it. The shocking result was that Brazil found itself accused of genocide in the world's press (see Jobim 1970), and Rondón's proud and humanitarian agency, the SPI, found itself accused of collusion with the very people who were harming the Indians. The government reacted by disbanding the SPI and replacing it in 1967 by FUNAI, the National Indian Foundation. It also carried out an inquiry that was ostensibly intended to punish those, both within the SPI and without, who had harmed indigenous people. The inquiry, however, was perfunctory and inconclusive and ended with little action being taken against anybody.

FUNAI and the Military Regime, 1964–85

Since its inception, FUNAI has been caught on the horns of a dilemma. It is an agency whose mandate is supposed to continue the traditions of Rondón and the SPI, namely to protect the indigenous peoples of Brazil, their rights, and their lands. At the same time, FUNAI was launched by a government that firmly believed in development and felt that indigenous peoples should not be allowed to "stand in the way of development." FUNAI's protection of Brazil's Indians has therefore always been ambivalent and somewhat ineffective. Under the military regime, FUNAI could not mount a strong defense of indigenous rights and lands. Instead, it was instructed to campaign for the "emancipation" of its indigenous wards. Rangel Reis, when he was minister of the interior, presented the policy of emancipating the Indians as a progressive measure, similar to the abolition of slavery in 1888. Indians and their allies were, however, quick to point out that this was a bad analogy. The indigenous peoples of Brazil were not slaves and could not therefore be emancipated from their servile status. Instead, it was clear that the government wished to relieve them of their very Indianness. "Emancipated" Indians would cease to be Indian, and eventually, so the government hoped and believed, there would be no more Indians in Brazil and hence no more Indian service and no more Indian question. Indian spokesmen immediately pointed out that this was quite unacceptable to them. They had no wish to be freed from their identities, which they prized. What they did wish for was that the government would carry out its responsibilities to them under the constitution; in particular that it would demarcate and protect their lands.[6]

The battle over emancipation mobilized indigenous and pro-indigenous opinion and helped to launch a pro-indigenous movement in Brazil (see Conselho Pro-Indio 1979 and Cultural Survival 1979). Indigenous groups began to meet to discuss how they should mobilize against the government. They were supported by non-indigenous associations and especially by CIMI, the Indianist Missionary Council, a Catholic organization devoted to the Indianist cause. CIMI helped indigenous groups to come together for meetings, no small matter in a country the size of Brazil in which indigenous peoples live widely scattered. FUNAI opposed such meetings, arguing that indigenous people were wards of the state and were not therefore permitted to hold meetings without the authorization of FUNAI itself.

FUNAI lost this battle as it did other high profile battles in which it attempted to assert its right to control the lives and the comings and goings of Indians in Brazil. Yet it continued to insist that indigenous individuals should either be subject to its authority or should be considered emancipated and no longer Indian.[7] Meanwhile the pressure on indigenous lands increased. There were gold rushes in various places. Reserves of tin, bauxite, and cassiterite were discovered, so that mining companies as well as agribusinesses and smallholders invaded what were ostensibly "Indian" lands. Meanwhile a process of *abertura* (political opening) had been set in motion by the military in preparation for a return to civilian government. During the phase of this political opening, the pressures on indigenous lands and peoples were regularly discussed in the national press as a way of alluding to the burdens placed by the Brazilian model of development, which the military had championed, not only on the Indians but also on the rural poor.

Civilian Government and the Constitution of 1988

When Brazil returned to civilian government in 1985 the (mal)treatment of its indigenous population was being intensively debated both nationally and internationally. Meanwhile, as the nation summoned parliamentarians to Brasília to draft a new constitution, there was hope that this constitution would emphasize strengthened protections for indigenous peoples; but the indigenous scandals continued.

The case of the gold rush into the territory of the Yanomami was particularly striking. The Yanomami live on both sides of the border between Brazil and Venezuela. Their supporters had been urging the government for years to demarcate and protect one contiguous area for the approximately 10,000 Indians in this region. This was not done. Instead, nineteen small areas were recognized as "Yanomami territory," but even these were not protected. Gold miners invaded this territory and nobody could or would eject them. The police in the remote northern state of Roraima claimed that they were not strong enough to evict thousands of miners, all armed to the teeth. The army was unwilling to take on the job. It was clear that the sympathies of the authorities lay with the gold miners and not with the "wild" Indians. Meanwhile, the Yanomami were attacked and brutalized, their environment was poisoned by the chemicals used in the mining operations, and they were afflicted with epidemics of malaria against which they had no resistance. In addition, over a period of three years, the Brazilian authorities not only failed to assist the Yanomami, but they forbade doctors, health workers, and others who wished to assist them to enter Yanomami territory. Access to it was in this way reserved for gold miners, the military, and FUNAI (Ramos 1991). When reporters at length succeeded in gaining access to the Yanomami region, what they saw horrified them. One quarter of the Yanomami in the region were dead. The majority of the rest were desperately sick and many of them (especially the women and children) were starving and emaciated (Ramos 1995).

Indigenous affairs had been progressively militarized under the dictatorship, and this trend continued after the end of military government. The process of formally demarcating indigenous lands, which Brazil was required to do under its own constitution, had always been exceedingly slow. FUNAI regularly claimed that it lacked the funds to carry out the task, and successive administrations showed little eagerness to allocate the funds necessary to do it. On the contrary, the task was made even more difficult by the government's decision that issues of indigenous land demarcation should be initiated by FUNAI but brought later before a body known as the National Security Council, which was dominated by the armed forces. This further slowed down the whole process of demarcation and officially made it a matter of national security.

The mere fact that the affairs of such a small, remote, and comparatively weak segment of the Brazilian population are considered matters of national security calls for some explanation. It has to do in part with the security of Brazil's frontiers, which is a perennial preoccupation of the Brazilian military; likewise, as we saw above, this issue was very much on people's minds in the days when Rondón was exploring the backlands and suggesting that the nation should have a policy and an agency to deal with its indigenous peoples.

Furthermore, Brazil borders on seven other countries in the Amazonian region.[8] Some of these are quite unstable, involved in civil wars, drug wars, and guerilla uprisings. The military worried about the possibility of indigenous peoples in remote areas getting caught up in these kinds of subversive activities. At the same time, international concern over the deforestation of the Amazon and occasional calls for international measures to prevent it both alarm and irritate Brazilian elites and the Brazilian military. They feel that the policies to be pursued in the region are a strictly Brazilian affair. These policies were set out in the *calha norte* (northern drainage) plan, developed in secret by the military at the behest of the newly installed civilian administration after the end of the dictatorship (Pacheco de Oliveira 1990). The plan called for the military to establish an effective presence throughout the Amazon, to develop it, to guarantee the nation's frontiers within it, and to develop new policies with regard to its Indians. The plan noted that much of the mineral wealth of the region lay in indigenous lands and proposed therefore that ways be found either to permit mining on indigenous lands or to redefine mineral-rich areas as lying outside the boundaries of indigenous lands. This attack on indigenous rights, which were held once again to impede the nation's development, came to a head during the debates concerning Brazil's new constitution in 1988.

During those deliberations, Indians from various tribes, but notably the Kaiapó, dressed in their ceremonial paint and feathers and maintained a constant vigil in the antechambers of parliament, where the constitutional convention was meeting. Pro-indigenous advocates meanwhile urged that various measures protective of indigenous rights be included in the new constitution, including a declaration that Brazil was a multiethnic nation that recognized the rights of indigenous peoples to maintain their own cultures.

A backlash was already setting in, however. Brazilian newspapers, using data supplied by FUNAI itself, argued that the concern for protecting indigenous lands was exaggerated and that Indians had more land per capita than non-Indians in Brazil. A study of these allegations by Brazilian anthropologists showed that they were based on erroneous and misleading interpretations of statistics that were themselves suspect (CEDI 1987). First, the categories listed by FUNAI as "Indian lands" were inflated in order to make the agency's record on land de-marcation look better. A closer analysis of the data showed that only 7.9 percent of these lands had actually been registered as indigenous territories. The process of demarcation had not even been initiated for over half of the lands listed as Indian lands. Second, many of the lands listed as Indian lands had been invaded by outsiders and were neither occupied nor controlled by indigenous peoples. Third, FUNAI and the newspapers compared the inflated figures of land per head supposedly controlled by Indians with a figure obtained by dividing the territory of Brazil by the number of its inhabitants, including its large urban populations. A proper comparison would have compared lands actually controlled by indigenous peoples with lands actually controlled by others who lived in rural areas. Such a comparison would have shown that there is severe maldistribution of land in Brazil, leaving not only the Indians but the rural population as a whole controlling very little land.

Although this maldistribution is well known and has led to the growing strength of a social movement known as the MST (The Move-ment of the Landless), it is noteworthy that the statistical slanders against indigenous populations were so widely disseminated and that people were so willing to believe that Indians in Brazil controlled a su-perabundance of land. Nor were these the only anti-indigenous slan-ders that received wide currency. In 1987, as the delegates in Brasília were getting ready to vote on a new constitution, the *Estado de São Paulo*, Brazil's largest newspaper, ran a series of front page articles every day for a week (from August 9 until August 15) denouncing sup-porters of the Indian cause for being engaged in what they called a "conspiracy against Brazil." This conspiracy was allegedly coordinated by a body called the Christian Church World Council. The body did not in fact exist and was presumably mentioned in a clumsy attempt to implicate the World Council of Churches, which was accused of work-ing together with environmentalists and supporters of indigenous rights to prevent Brazil from extracting its own mineral resources and developing its own Amazonian regions. The evidence for these allega-tions turned out to be a mixture of forgeries and suspect documents provided to the press by Brazil's largest tin-mining company, whose mining rights on indigenous lands were being challenged in the courts. The Brazilian Catholic Church sued the newspaper for slander and de-manded (and received) a parliamentary commission of inquiry to look into the whole matter. But the damage had been done. The "conspiracy" was widely reported in the press and the supporters of the indigenous cause were put on the defensive just as indigenous rights were being debated in the constitutional convention. In the end the article of the constitution proclaiming Brazil to be a multiethnic society was voted down. Indian lands were not granted constitutional protection against mining, though the constitution stipulated that they could only be mined with special authorization from the government. The new constitution did, however, continue to offer de jure protection of indigenous rights to their lands and their ways of life. What the whole debate made clear was that the growing national support for indigenous rights was matched by a growing backlash among conservatives against these rights, arguing that they were harmful to the vital interests of the nation.

Brazil's Indians Today

The romantic indigenism that Rondón championed, according to which Brazil could and should protect its indigenous peoples and bring them through education into the national society, is now out of date. It is true that, as noted above, FUNAI still maintains a department that specializes in bringing virtually uncontacted tribes into Brazilian society, and it is equally true that the services of this department continue to be urgently needed. As a woman of the Ykunsu people, contacted in 1995, put it: "White man comes, killing, killing. Us fleeing, fleeing. Why white man not live with us? Country big. Room for all of us" (Felipini-Bia 1998).[9] The fact is that indigenous affairs in Brazil are, for the most part, no longer a matter of bringing remote peoples into Brazilian society. They are rather a matter of what place not-so-remote indigenous groups are to be permitted to occupy in that society.

The early liberalism of Brazil's indigenous policies that guaranteed the protection of indigenous lands and cultures is now increasingly seen by influential sectors of Brazilian opinion as contrary to the national interest. Yet it is difficult for Brazil to abandon its official protection of indigenous rights. When the military took no action to protect indigenous peoples against the advancing frontiers of settlement in the 1960s and 1970s, Brazil found itself accused internationally of genocide. Later, when the military tried to resolve the "Indian question" by emancipating the Indians and thus abolishing them as a category of people with special rights, this fueled the growth of a strong pro-indigenous movement. Since the return of civilian rule and the passage of the new constitution, the Brazilian government has returned to the strategy of paying lip service to indigenous rights without doing what is necessary to protect them effectively.

The whole process of demarcating indigenous lands shows this very clearly. FUNAI regularly complains that it does not receive sufficient funds to demarcate the lands that it should, yet its budget requests are regularly cut back drastically. Another measure, introduced in the administration of the current president, Fernando Henrique Cardoso, appeared to hand a new weapon to the opponents of indigenous land demarcation. This was decree 1775, which established a procedure and a timetable for people to challenge demarcations of indigenous lands that FUNAI was undertaking. Fortunately for the Indians, these challenges were thrown out in the courts and it seemed as if the demarcations were at last proceeding apace. The problem was, and still is, that the demarcations themselves are of limited use unless the indigenous beneficiaries are protected from land invasions. Yet violence is endemic in the Brazilian countryside, particularly against the landless and against the Indians. This violence is not only unleashed on remote peoples like the recently contacted Ykunsu mentioned above. It is more especially directed against peoples whose lands or resources are in dispute.

For instance, state or local authorities frequently sabotage the federal government's efforts to demarcate and guarantee lands for indigenous peoples by issuing titles to those lands to local ranchers or businessmen. The possessors of these local titles then go to court and contest the process of guaranteeing indigenous lands. In the meantime, they employ gunmen to threaten or expel the indigenous peoples whose lands are not yet legally guaranteed. Neither FUNAI nor the local police have been effective in dealing with such coercion. Death threats against indigenous or peasant leaders are routinely ignored by the local authorities, who covertly or sometimes quite openly side with the threateners. This contributes to the culture of impunity that is endemic in the rural areas of Brazil. This impunity is shown all too clearly when indigenous or peasant leaders are actually gunned down. Those who threatened them are rarely brought to book. On the rare occasions when they are arrested, they routinely "escape" from detention.

A dramatic demonstration of this culture of impunity and the context in which it flourishes occurred in Brasília in August 1997. Galdino, a leader of the Pataxó Indians, had journeyed to the capital to press the case for the land rights of his people. At the end of the day, he was sleeping on a bench in the bus station when five young men "of good family" set fire to him. He died later of his burns and his killers stated in their own defense that his death was a prank gone wrong. They had never intended to kill him. The judge who heard the case appeared to accept the defense and did not convict the young men of murder but only of causing bodily harm that resulted in accidental death. This outraged public opinion throughout the country[10] and prompted newspaper comment on the fact that the Galdino case was one of many similar ones. Sleeping indigents are regularly harmed or set on fire in the streets of Brazil's major cities. In fact, the Galdino case, though it did not lead to major punishment for the perpetrators of such cruelty, at least attracted publicity and attention. So many other victims of the violence visited by the elites on the poor die in obscurity.

It was outrage against such impunities that prompted the Catholic Church to sponsor a march on Brasília, with demonstrations in the nation's capital on Brazil's Independence Day (September 7) in 1997. These demonstrations brought together indigenous peoples, landless rural workers, and others in an event that was billed as the Cry of the Excluded. Nor was this the only event of its kind. By the end of the century, the social movements representing the poor were gathering strength, as was the movement in favor of indigenous rights. This movement was receiving support both nationally and internationally. Nationally, there was a dramatic proliferation of indigenous organizations in the 1990s. This was due to the constitution of 1988, which made it easier to found indigenous organizations, and also to the eagerness of national and international NGOs to fund environmentalist projects together with indigenous groups. By the end of the decade, there were hundreds of properly constituted indigenous organizations in Brazil and the number was growing into the thousands. Some of these organizations were small associations representing single communities. Others represented (or claimed to represent) indigenous tribes or regions or intertribal alliances or, as in the case of the Alliance of Forest Peoples, an alliance that brought together Indians and non-Indians engaged in a common struggle. These associations have learned from working with international organizations and are becoming more skilled in defending their peoples, both inside and outside of Brazil. As we have seen, though, the protests and demonstrations of the indigenous movement and the rural poor have not only called attention to their grievances but have also provoked a backlash against the protesters, who are held in conservative circles to pose a serious threat to the nation.

There are many aspects to this supposed threat. The principal one is that the demarcation and protection of indigenous lands interferes with development. Mining operations on indigenous land are not forbidden outright, but they can be challenged and delayed. The same can be said of logging or large-scale agriculture. It is much easier if the lands in question are not designated as indigenous lands or, failing that, if the indigenous claimants to the land can be forced to vacate it. That is where violence against indigenous peoples plays an important role. Indigenous groups thus threatened can expect little protection from the authorities, who normally side with those encouraging "development" rather than with the indigenous peoples who are "interfering" with it. This perpetual pressure on indigenous peoples and their lands not only leads to a climate of violence against indigenous groups but sometimes leads them to despair, resulting in epidemics of suicide in certain areas. It is true that some indigenous groups, backed by CIMI, NGOs, and/or FUNAI, have succeeded in fighting back. The campaigns waged by the Kaiapó and the Xavante of Central Brazil are a case in point. A single contiguous area of land was also eventually set aside for the Yanomami, but these are relatively rare successes. It is more usual for indigenous insistence to be met with unpunished violence.

This was brought home embarrassingly clearly during the celebrations to mark the quincentenary of the arrival of the Portuguese in Brazil in 1500. Indigenous representatives from all over the country, together with delegates from the Black Movement and the Movement of the Landless planned to converge on Pôrto Seguro, where the Portuguese first landed and where an international cast of dignitaries had been invited to come and celebrate the event. There the Blacks, the Indians, and the Landless intended to hold a conference focusing on the rights of the excluded and a demonstration indicating that the Indians of Brazil saw nothing to celebrate in the Portuguese invasion. The conference and demonstration were, however, prevented by the army and the police, who used considerable force to break them up. Reports and pictures of Indians being beaten up by the authorities, who were celebrating the Portuguese invasion of Brazil, appeared in the world's press as embarrassing testimony to the way in which the nation still treats its native peoples. The whole affair led to the resignation of the president of FUNAI. He was accompanying the indigenous delegates and had planned to attend their conference. In his opinion the authorities over-reacted to a pointed but peaceful demonstration of opposition to the official celebration, and he resigned in protest.

The demonstration at Pôrto Seguro underlined another reason why Brazilian conservatives oppose the indigenous rights movement. That is because the movement has gathered strength and begun to ally itself with other movements, such as those representing Blacks and the Landless. The idea of a unified social movement of the excluded, capa-ble of challenging the government or at least embarrassing it interna-tionally, is exactly what conservatives consider to be a threat to devel-opment and the social order in Brazil. This goes some way to explaining why the indigenous movement, which necessarily repre-sents only a small fraction of the country's population, is treated in government circles as a matter of national security.

It also explains why there are continuing efforts to abolish the cate-gory "Indian" and therefore the "Indian question" in Brazil. The efforts made under the dictatorship to abolish the Indians by emancipating them failed. They not only failed but actually strengthened the pro-in-digenous movement. The constitution of 1988 finally eliminated the expectation that Indians should abandon their cultures and become assimilated into Brazilian society. Yet efforts are still being made to challenge the Indianness of indigenous peoples. A CPI (parliamentary commission of inquiry) in the Brazilian congress has been appointed to try to revise the limits of indigenous territories that have already been demarcated. In 1999 it demanded that FUNAI should study the degree of acculturation of certain indigenous groups whose lands were in dispute, with the idea of declaring these peoples no longer Indian if they had adopted too many customs that were not part of their imme-morial traditions.

This demand is part of a policy that successive Brazilian administra-tions have been trying unsuccessfully to put into effect. FUNAI under the military was expected to determine whether indigenous groups and even indigenous individuals were truly indigenous. When Brazil-ian anthropologists pointed out that there was no scientific way of making such determinations, FUNAI fell back on other indicators. In-dians who completed courses entitling them to licenses, diplomas, or degrees were told that these qualifications indicated that they were no longer indigenous. Meanwhile the documents describing the *Calha Norte* program made it clear that it would offer protection only to unacculturated Indians. Acculturated Indians would be emancipated, would lose their rights to their traditional lands, and would be treated like any other segment of the rural poor.

These anomalies were further compounded by the constitution of 1988. This document did not declare Brazil to be a multiethnic country, but it did recognize indigenous peoples' rights to their social organization, customs, languages, beliefs, traditions, and traditional lands. The state no longer sought to integrate them into Brazilian society and no longer insisted that they were wards of the state, with FUNAI as their guardian, entitled to speak and act on their behalf. Where did this leave the Indians? Their lands and their cultures were constitutionally guaranteed, but there was little tradition of enforcing such guarantees and little political will to do so. On the contrary, there was a sustained effort, both in parliament and in the backlands, to vitiate such guarantees wherever possible. Meanwhile there was no agreement even on how indigenous peoples should be referred to. The state refused to call them *nações indígenas* (indigenous nations), as the Indians themselves requested. The Indians rejected the state's counter proposal that they be designated as *comunidades indígenas* (indigenous communities). The current compromise is to refer to them as *povos indígenas* (indigenous peoples).

This debate over how to refer to indigenous groups parallels a similar debate that has become a live political issue in Mexico.[11] The significance of the disagreement derives from its reference to the role of indigenous peoples within the state. Mexico has, in its latest constitution, declared itself multiethnic, yet there are still powerful people and interests within that country who oppose the idea of accepting indigenous peoples as nations, separate but equal within the state. The Brazilian government will not call indigenous peoples—especially indigenous peoples who have their lands and cultures guaranteed by the constitution—indigenous nations, because that implies that they too are separate and equal within the state. Since the days of the military regime, the Brazilian government has resolutely affirmed its opposition to allowing "ethnic cysts" (as one minister of the interior called them) within the state. This, it is claimed, would undermine the state itself, weakening it through formally tolerated pluriethnicity or through separatism and threats of secession.

Separatism is regularly cited as a pressing danger if ever and whenever the rights of indigenous peoples to maintain their separate cultures are recognized. Yet the evidence from all over the world shows that indigenous peoples normally fight for local autonomy within the states where they live, not separation from those states. In fact secession only becomes an issue when local autonomy is denied (Maybury-Lewis 1997, chapter 1).

It is, however, the effects of pluriethnicity, more than the possibilities of secession, that appear to trouble the Brazilian authorities, who believe that the formal recognition of indigenous cultures would undermine the state. This leaves us with a paradox: Indigenous cultures have been recognized in the Brazilian constitution, yet powerful interests within the state are fighting to minimize the effects of such recognition. Meanwhile the Indians are engaged in a constant battle to enjoy rights that are constitutionally guaranteed to them.

Notes

1 I wish to thank Roque de Barros Laraia and Jô Cardoso de Oliveira for their invaluable help to me as I was preparing this article.

2 The comparable figures are, approximately, as follows:

Country	National Population	Indigenous Population	Indigenous Percentage
Argentina	36 million	0.18 million	0.5 %
Chile	15.3 million	1.3 million	8.5 %
USA	278 million	1.9 million	0.7 %
Brazil	174.5 million	0.3 million	0.17 %

3 This debate is fully discussed in Stauffer 1955.

4 The service was originally, and briefly, called the Service for the Protection of Indians and the Settlement of National Workers, since it was expected to "pacify" and protect the indigenous peoples of the interior and also to arrange for the settlement of rural workers on the lands that would become available in the process. That is why the Indian agency was located in the ministry of agriculture. The debates and maneuvers that led up to the launching of the Indian service are fully described and analyzed in Stauffer 1955.

5 This information is taken from a personal communication from Adrian Cowell, who is collaborating with Sydney Possuelo.

6 For contemporary discussions of the emancipation issue see Comissão Pro Indio/SP 1979 and Cultural Survival 1979.

7   In spite of FUNAI's constant efforts during the military regime, I know of no Indian who agreed to declare him- or herself emancipated.

8   They are French Guyana, Surinam, Guyana, Venezuela, Colombia, Peru, and Bolivia. Other countries that share a border with Brazil, namely Paraguay, Argentina and Uruguay, lie outside the Amazon region.

9   This is my translation of the speaker's broken Portuguese.

10 However, not everyone was incensed on Galdino Pataxó's behalf. A colleague of mine reported a chilling incident that she had witnessed in a remote town in northern Brazil. An Indian was waiting in line with other local people who started to joke out loud about him, to the effect that they had the gasoline for him. Others chimed in saying that they had the matches so that between them they could take care of the situation.

11 See Jerome Levi, this volume.

Works Cited

Calloway, Colin G.

1995   *The American Revolution in Indian Country: Crisis and Diversity in Native American Communities.* New York: The Cambridge University Press.

Comissão Pro-Indio/SP

1979   *A Questão da Emancipação.* São Paulo: Editora Global.

Cultural Survival

1979   *Brazil: Special Report No. 1.* Cambridge: Cultural Survival.

Felipine-Bia, María Cecilia

1998   "Falta política para índios 'isolados.'" In *Porantim* XX No. 205, May.

Frič, Alberto

1910   "Völkerwanderungen, Ethnographie und Geschichte der Conquista in Südbrasilien" in *Verhandlungen des XVI Internationalen Amerikanisten-Kongresses.* Vienna and Leipzig.

Hecht, Susanna, and Alexander Cockburn

1990   *The Fate of the Forest: Developers, Destroyers and Defenders of the Amazon.* New York: The Penguin Group.

Hemming, John

1972   *Red Gold: The Conquest of the Brazilian Indians.* London: Macmillan.

Jobim, Danton

1970   *O Problema do Indio e a Acusação de Genocidio.* Ministry of Justice: Conselho de Defesa dos Direitos da Pessoa Humana, Bulletin No. 2.

Maybury-Lewis, David

1997   *Indigenous Peoples, Ethnic Groups and the State.* Boston: Allyn and Bacon.

1994   "From savages to security risks: The Indian question in Brazil." In Mendelsohn, Oliver and Upendra Baxi, eds., *The Rights of Subordinated Peoples.* Delhi and New York: The Oxford University Press.

Pacheco de Oliveira, João

1990   "Projeto Calha Norte: Militares, Indios e Fronteiras." *Serie Antropología e Indigenismo #1.* Rio de Janeiro: Editora UFR.

1987   *Terras Indígenas no Brasil.* São Paulo: CEDI (Centro Ecuménico de Documentação Indígena).

Ramos, Alcida Rita

1991   "Os Direitos do Indio no Brasil: Na Encruzilhada da Cidadanía." *Serie Antropologia 116.* Brasília: Universidade de Brasília.

1995   *Sanuma Memories: Yanomami Ethnography in Times of Crisis.* Madison, The University of Wisconsin Press.

Stauffer, David H.

1955   "The Origin and Establishment of Brazil's Indian Service 1889–1910." Ph.D. Dissertation, Department of History, University of Texas at Austin.

Acronyms

SPI	*Serviço de Proteçao aos Indios,* Indian Protection Service
FUNAI	*Fundação Nacional do Indio,* National Indian Foundation
CIMI	*Conselho Indigenista Missionario,* Missionary Indigenist Council
MST	*Movimento dos Sem Terra,* The Movement of the Landless
CEDI	*Centro Ecuménico de Documentacao Indígena,* Ecumenical Center for Indigenous Documentation

Conclusion[1]

David Maybury-Lewis

The Indian Question in the Americas was posed in colonial times with brutal frankness. The European invaders of the New World asked themselves what they needed the indigenous inhabitants of their conquered territories for, and how, depending on the answer, they should be treated. If the invaders concluded that they had no use for the indigenous peoples, they needed to decide how they were to get rid of them.[2]

Initially the invaders wanted two things from the native peoples. They wanted them to show the way to gold, silver, and other treasures. They also wanted them to work for their conquerors. The invading Europeans therefore established slavery wherever they could. Contingents of slaves were even sent back to Spain from the Caribbean only a few years after the arrival of the conquistadors, but such shipments soon ceased because the indigenous populations of the Caribbean were rapidly annihilated by a combination of disease and harsh working conditions. Slavery and forced labor of various kinds were, however, institutionalized in those regions that possessed indigenous populations sufficiently dense that enough of them could survive to work for their overlords. Elaborate systems were put in place to compel indigenous labor in what are now Mexico, Central America, and the Andean regions. These systems of forced labor were later replaced by ingenious systems of debt peonage, whereby Indians were enmeshed in debts that they spent their lives unsuccessfully trying to work off. In the nineteenth century, Guatemala and El Salvador instituted nationwide forced labor by setting up passbook systems. Indians were required by law to perform a certain number of days of labor at very low wages, and they had to carry passbooks, signed by their employers, showing that they were up to date in their work schedules. Through most of its history, Peru levied a special tax on Indians which provided an important part of the national budget. It also required Indians to work without pay to build and maintain the nation's roads—a requirement that was maintained until the 1930s.

In those areas of the Americas that possessed sparse indigenous populations, such as the United States, Brazil, Argentina, and Chile, the invaders faced the problem of who was to do the work of the colonies and how the scattered indigenous populations were to be driven off their lands. The labor problem was dealt with by the importation of slaves from Africa, a solution that dramatically affected the nature of society in the United States and Brazil. Meanwhile, the Indians were driven off their lands in campaigns that were referred to as "the conquest of the desert" in Argentina or the "winning of the West" in the United States. Brazil moved comparatively late to "open up" its backlands and carried out its own version of the "winning of the west" in mid-twentieth century, when it was no longer politically correct to do so, with the result that it found itself accused of genocide.

The point is that, whether the indigenous peoples of the Americas were forced to become the laboring masses or whether they were treated as marginalized "savages," there was no place for them *as Indians* in the countries where they lived. In the centuries since the European invasions, the only future assigned to them was to become "civilized," to abandon their Indianness as the price of being accepted as fellow citizens of the nations in which they lived, even though such acceptance was by no means guaranteed, even if they did try to assimilate.

The history of the Americas since the European invasions is that of a 500-year attempt to abolish indigenous cultures. Indigenous societies were decapitated, their religions prohibited, their customs banned, their children taken away, their lands confiscated, and their communities broken up. First the category of "Indian" was imposed on the distinct peoples and cultures of the hemisphere, and then systematic efforts were made (and continue to be made) to abolish that category.

Simón Bolívar tried unsuccessfully to abolish the use of the term *indio*, which he considered pejorative and offensive. He was only the first of many to have tried to abolish Indianness with a stroke of the pen. Centuries later (in the 1960s) General Velasco Alvarado tried to abolish Indianness in Peru by legislating that there would be no more indios in that country, only *campesinos* (peasants). Brazil has likewise been trying to "emancipate" its Indians ever since the 1960s. Even the Alaska Native Claims Settlement Act, which is often considered one of the more generous settlements to be reached with an indigenous population, extinguishes indigenous rights and undermines indigenous identities in the process of indemnifying the native peoples of Alaska.

It is remarkable that the indigenous peoples of the hemisphere have resisted and have fought to maintain their cultural identities in the face of this 500-year-long assault. During all this time, the authorities in the Americas have insisted for a variety of reasons that the toleration of indigenous societies and cultures would undermine their states. In recent years, however, the nations of the Americas have started to reverse themselves. They are altering their constitutions and proclaiming themselves multiethnic. Why is this happening now? Are the authorities now less concerned about the threat they have always claimed that pluriethnicity would pose to the state, or are they willing to risk the threat for other reasons?

Consider Mexico, a nation which has since its revolution in 1910–20 been a hemispheric leader in *indigenismo* or the development of pro-indigenous policies. Mexican indigenismo was launched immediately after the revolution by major figures like Manuel Gamio, José Vasconcelos, and Moises Saenz. It flourished during the presidency of Lázaro Cárdenas (1934–40), when the nation's official policy became one of educating its indigenous populations so that they could join the Mexican mainstream. Mexican indigenismo was remarkable for its insistence that indigenous peoples could be helped to assimilate into Mexican civilization by showing a proper understanding of and respect for their own cultures. The appreciation of indigenous cultures and their eventual disappearance, as indigenous peoples blended into the national mestizo civilization, were not thought to contradict each other. Meanwhile *ejido* lands were made available to many (but not all) indigenous communities under the terms of the post-revolutionary land reforms.[3] At the same time, Mexican indigenists set up the III (International Indigenous Institute) and the INI (National Indigenous Institute), both located in Mexico City and both directed by Mexicans. It is noteworthy that the International Indigenous Institute was launched before the National Indigenous Institute, making it clear that Mexico intended these institutes to spearhead an international movement on behalf of the indigenous peoples of the Americas.

The high-water mark of Mexican indigenismo came in 1940, when Mexico hosted the Congress of Pátzcuaro, the first hemispheric conference to focus on indigenous affairs and to attempt to develop pro-indigenous policies. The contrast at Pátzcuaro was striking between the Mexicans, who took the lead in efforts to develop indigenist policies, and delegates from some of the other countries attending, who argued that there was nothing to discuss or even that there were no Indians in their own countries.

By the 1970s, however, Mexicans were beginning to wonder whether their brand of indigenismo was working. President Echevarría asked in one of his speeches whether indigenismo had failed, and Mexican anthropologists and intellectuals were beginning to think that it had. Certainly the agrarian reform that had been an important element of Mexico's indigenist policies had run out of steam. By the 1980s, no more ejido lands were being distributed, and the government was insisting that Mexico could no longer afford to support a large and economically uncompetitive peasantry. This undermined the livelihood of most indigenous peoples in Mexico.

The announcement that no more ejido lands would be distributed had a devastating effect on states like Chiapas, which had never been reached by the land reform and where many had clung to the hope that it was soon to be their turn. However, it was not merely the unavailability of ejido lands that caused the Zapatista revolt. As Levi (this volume) points out, summarizing the recent scholarship on Chiapas and the Zapatistas, a blend of pressures and possibilities had already prepared the way for an uprising in this part of Mexico. Yet Chiapas is by no means the only place that is in revolt. Indigenous movements in other Mexican states, notably Oaxaca and Guerrero, have announced that they are in a "state of resistance," with some of their members pressing for armed uprising. This serves to emphasize the extraordinary nature of the Zapatista movement. Its insistence that it would not resort to arms, and its skillful handling of the media have captured public imagination, both nationally and internationally. Above all, the Zapatistas' insistence that they wish neither to secede from Mexico, nor to overthrow its government, but rather to change the nature of the Mexican state and the way it conducts its dialogue with its own citizens, has elicited sympathetic agreement from broad sectors of the Mexican public.

A remarkable result of this was that indigenous issues were hotly debated during the last national elections. The government, going into the elections, was from the PRI. It had signed the San Andrés Accords, an agreement concerning the recognition and guarantees that it would extend to Mexico's indigenous peoples, but had subsequently reneged on it and offered a different proposal. Meanwhile, the new president, Vicente Fox, was from the PAN party, which offered yet another proposal. Much of the debate turned on (and still revolves around) the kind of recognition that the state is willing to grant to indigenous peoples. If they are to receive formal recognition, will it be as *pueblos,* meaning "communities," or meaning "towns" or meaning "peoples"? The issue was not resolved, since all of the proposals were gutted in congress. Nevertheless, the Zapatistas traveled to Mexico City and succeeded in obtaining permission to address an unsympathetic and sparsely attended meeting of congress on the issue. The result to date is a stalemate with extremists on both sides demanding the use of force.

From one point of view, it is dismaying to note that Mexico's current efforts to include its indigenous populations in its national life are being undermined by a conservative backlash. That backlash can be put in perspective, however, if we compare Mexico's indigenist policies with the radically different strategies of nation building employed in Central America.

In Central America, particularly in Guatemala and El Salvador, it was decided to force indigenous peoples to assimilate into the national culture or face the prospect of annihilation. In El Salvador, in the 1930s, the government decided that it was threatened by a communist insurrection and that the insurrection was supported by the nation's indigenous population. The army therefore set out to massacre Indians in the name of anti-communism. The high point of the killings came in 1932, during the grim period that is known in El Salvador simply as *La Matanza* (The Killing). The killing campaign so traumatized the indigenous population of El Salvador that the majority of them ceased wearing their traditional clothes or speaking indigenous languages in public. They tried, in effect, to conceal their indigenous identities, with the result that El Salvador became one of the American nations that for decades reported that it had no more Indians in its population.

A variation of this strategy was used more recently in Guatemala. Jennifer Schirmer describes in this volume how the repressive government of Guatemala and its army were faced with an insurgency that was having some success in recruiting indigenous peoples. The army therefore decided to massacre the indigenous populations it could not control and to forcibly control the rest by making them over into what Schirmer calls "the Sanctioned Maya." These were the Maya who had been forced to collaborate in military atrocities and who had become the kind of Maya that the military had co-opted and of whom they therefore approved.

Compared with these genocidal extremes in Central America, the hesitations and occasional brutalities of Mexico's treatment of its Indians appear more benign. Indeed, the wars and massacres in Central America are the bitter price that the countries of the region have paid for their reluctance to include their indigenous populations in the process of nation building. Instead they were determined to maintain the rule of the traditional oligarchies, by whatever force it took, and the massacres were the result.

The Andean nations of South America are, by contrast, experimenting with new relationships between states and their indigenous populations. Ironically, this process is least advanced in Peru, which has a long tradition of indigenous mobilization together with an equally long tradition of indigenismo. Over the years, these traditions have tended to fuel a conservative backlash that has succeeded in maintaining the subordination of the Indians. Indigenous mobilization, for example, led to a history of indigenous uprisings in the highlands, which were regularly and ferociously suppressed. Meanwhile the advocates of Peru's brand of indigenismo were traditionally held at bay by the nation's dominant conservatives. When Florinda Matto de Turner published her book *Aves sin Nido* (Birds without Nests) in 1889, its effect on the Peruvian public was similar to that of *Uncle Tom's Cabin* in the United States. It raised people's consciousness of the cruelty and injustice that was routinely visited on the nation's Indians; but those who tried to remedy these injustices politically were branded revolutionaries by the conservatives and repressed. José Carlos Mariátegui, Peru's great socialist thinker, argued in the 1920s that "Without the Indian, Peruvianness is not possible." At the same time, Víctor Raúl Haya de la Torre, who founded APRA (the Popular Revolutionary American Alliance) was insisting that "Revolution in our America will be an Indian revolution." This led to Mariátegui and his followers being branded dangerous revolutionaries and Haya de la Torre and his APRA party being fought by the conservatives and kept out of power until 1985.

The watershed event in Peru's treatment of its indigenous populations was the coming to power of General Velasco Alvarado at the head of a reformist military regime in 1968. Velasco sponsored land reform and broke the power of the rural elites that had rested on the backs of the Indians, but his policy sought to abolish the Indianness of the Indians, to recognize them and improve their lot certainly, but as peasants. In any case, Velasco's indigenist policies were soon interrupted. Peru's economy collapsed in the 1970s. Velasco himself fell sick and his regime was replaced. APRA was finally brought to power by the landslide electoral victory of Alan Garcia in 1985, but it was too late. The conservatives had fought for decades to prevent APRA from taking office. When it finally took over the government, it did so in Peru's darkest hour. The country was mired in economic crisis. It was being undermined by drug traffickers and torn apart by revolutionaries of the Shining Path movement. Shining Path capitalized on the economic crisis and profited from the drug trade that filled its coffers at the same time as it demoralized the army that was trying to fight it.

By the late 1980s serious commentators feared that Shining Path might emerge victorious, especially since the Peruvian army had become corrupt and inefficient and antagonized its own citizenry as much as it fought the revolutionaries. Thousands of ordinary Peruvians, especially Peruvian Indians, found themselves in the classic dilemma, caught between contending forces who demanded their allegiance but did not protect them or their interests. So began the mass exodus of refugees from the rural areas to the shanty towns of Lima and other smaller cities, where they hoped to escape the horrors of the war. The indigenous refugees referred to this grim period as "the time of Chakwa," using a Quechua word that refers to the dismantling of the universal order of things by the clash of two diametrically opposed forces.

The authoritarian regime of President Fujimori has to be seen against the backdrop of these desperate circumstances. He succeeded in defeating the Shining Path and bringing Peru's inflation under control. He might have been hailed for these accomplishments, in spite of his dictatorial style of government, if he had been willing or able to curb his own authoritarianism and its consequences, but he was not. He could not eliminate the corruption over which he had presided, nor could he produce a clean slate for Peru out of the dirty political process that he had instituted.

In the midst of these conflicts, Peru's indigenous peoples could not organize to defend themselves. The Amazonian lowlanders could not take the lead as they did in other Andean countries. They were too busy fighting to defend their resources, which were being seized and distributed by President Fujimori and his cronies. The highlanders were likewise fighting to defend their community lands in the midst of civil war. The result is that there has not been, up till now, any lowland-highland indigenous alliance; nor has there been a florescence of ethnic politics as part of the rethinking of the Peruvian state. Indeed there has not been any systematic rethinking of that state and of its relationship to its indigenous populations. It is possible that such a rethinking may be on the agenda of Peru's newly elected president, Alejandro Toledo, who is of Indian descent and proud of it, but it is too early to tell.

The battle between indigenists and conservatives in Peru has traditionally produced a stalemate that prevented the adoption of policies that would ameliorate indigenous subordination. It is the other Andean countries that have recently begun to experiment with establishing new relationships between their indigenous populations and their states. Colombia, for example, took the lead in redefining the rights of its indigenous populations. In the constitution of 1991, indigenous peoples were granted a place in the nation that did not require them to abandon their own cultures. Their indigenous identities were recognized and guaranteed, and these in turn provided the official rationale for their land rights. Were the policy to be fully implemented it would transfer very large tracts of land to indigenous control. Moreover, these territories would be integrated into the table of organization of the Colombian state, in the same way that counties and municipalities are incorporated in the state in other countries.

This new policy toward minorities has been put forward as symbolizing the new Colombia, but it has led to complex negotiations over identities and minority rights. Rural populations of *colonos* or settlers have claimed that they too have distinct cultures that deserve recognition on a par with indigenous cultures. Minority populations are thus competing with each other over the right to have rights. Even coca growers are demanding the right to be granted government assistance to move out of coca cultivation (at present their only viable option) and into other economic activities. All this is taking place in the midst of the most virulent and longest-running civil war in the hemisphere. It is a civil war in which the government has ceded and in some cases lost control over much of its territory. It is a war that involves government forces, paramilitaries, various groups of revolutionaries, and drug traffickers, who may be any or all of the above. Under the circumstances it is exceedingly difficult to reorganize the state and to bring its indigenous populations into the new Colombia that has not yet been born. The significance of the Colombian initiatives has therefore been largely symbolic so far.

The situation is different in neighboring Ecuador, where indigenous peoples have recently instigated a national dialogue concerning their role in the nation. It should come as no surprise that Ecuadorian Indians have played this pioneering role, for indigenous federations were established in Amazonian Ecuador early in the 1970s, and they have played an active part in national and international discussions of indigenous rights ever since. The indigenous federations of lowland Ecuador also developed the technique of getting their nation's attention by means of *levantamientos* or uprisings. "Uprising" is however a misnomer for their protests. They were, properly speaking, stoppages during which roads were barred peacefully and the country was obliged to choose between using force to remove the demonstrators and stopping to listen to their grievances. Remarkably, the stoppages were not met with force. Instead they elicited some public sympathy and newspaper commentary to the effect that perhaps it was high time that the nation listened to its indigenous peoples.

The Amazonian federations, with their experience of participating in the international indigenous movement, raised regional and national issues concerning ethnic minorities. They did not focus on resolving local problems as the highland Indians tended to do. Very soon, however, the lowlanders and highlanders made common cause and argued for a new vision of Ecuador as a multiethnic state bringing together its different peoples—Hispano-Ecuadorians, Indo-Ecuadorians, Afro-Ecuadorians—into some kind of federation. This new vision of an Ecuador of all its ethnicities would be in the spirit of *Pachakutik*, a Quichua word indicating the remaking of the world as well as the rethinking of the state.

In the course of these discussions, indigenous and non-indigenous Ecuadorians discovered that they were equally outraged by the actions of then president Jamil Mahuad, who had authorized repeated government bailouts of his cronies, and their failing banks. Accordingly, when Mahuad was ousted and a junta took over the government, it set up a three-man presidency, including one military officer and one indigenous leader. The junta resigned after a few hours, but Mahuad's departure was final, and a point had been made about the willingness of the army and the indigenous peoples to support each other in the national interest.

Perhaps the most remarkable changes of all are those that have taken place in Bolivia, the most Indian country in the hemisphere, in terms of the indigenous proportion of its national population. Bolivia too has proclaimed itself a multiethnic country, thus departing from the direction of its watershed revolution of 1952, which improved the lot of the nation's highland Indians by helping them to become a prosperous peasantry. The focus on Indians as peasants is seen in the name of the militant organization that has represented them. It is the CSUTCB or the Sole Syndical Confederation of Rural Workers of Bolivia. In recent years, however, there has been a tendency in Bolivia for *asuntos campesinos* (peasant affairs) to be thought of as *asuntos etnicos* (ethnic affairs). Meanwhile there is a tendency for ethnic affairs to be referred to as indigenous affairs in the Bolivian Amazon, whereas they are referred to as having to do with Bolivia's *pueblos originarios* (first nations) in the highlands. The highland organizations have traditionally acted like trade unions, taking a militant stance on local bread-and-butter issues. The lowlanders, on the other hand, have been more willing to enter into negotiations, especially concerning regional and national issues. Meanwhile, organizations of coca growers who were not Indian at all have claimed, like their Colombian counterparts, to have the right to have rights—to be considered as groups deserving recognition and support because of their separate identities. In fact such groups are sometimes even referred to as indios, indicating that they occupy, or at least aspire to, a position analogous to that of indigenous peoples.

In recent years the lowland/highland divide has been bridged by indigenous marches on La Paz that involved meetings in the capital between highland and lowland representatives to present their grievances jointly to the government. The first of these marches took place in 1991, anticipating even the ones in Ecuador and making Bolivian Indians pioneers in this type of protest. These demonstrations succeeded in drawing the government into lengthy negotiations, the results of which have been quite modest up until now. Nevertheless, the negotiations in themselves are a real step forward, for they have been peaceful and they have included hitherto marginalized populations in a dialogue concerning the future of the nation. Unfortunately, even this cautious inclusion of indigenous peoples as partners in the national project has already caused a virulent backlash. The newspaper excerpts that Bret Gustafson cites in his paper for this volume show that there is a body of middle- and upper-class opinion in Bolivia that thinks of indigenous peoples as being something less than human and is outraged if they are treated any differently—and this in spite of the fact that the vice president of the country between 1993 and 1997 was Víctor Hugo Cárdenas, an Aymara Indian.

This evidence of enduring prejudice is tragic, but it should not blind us to the remarkable story of the past decade, which is that, after 500 years of denial, the countries of the hemisphere with large indigenous populations have decided to incorporate them into their respective nations while recognizing their distinctiveness. The exceptions to this trend are in Central America, where repressive regimes, backed by the United States, have chosen to see indigenous protests as leftist insurgencies, to be defeated by whatever force it takes. These repressive regimes have one thing in common with the new multiethnic ones that emphasize tolerance and dialogue. Both kinds of regime assume that the relationship with indigenous peoples and their manner of incorporation into the nation are central aspects of nation building. The states that now seek to recognize indigenous identities within themselves are trying to redefine themselves and are admitting that their previous policies did not work. The states that refuse such recognition are trying to continue in the traditional way of incorporating indigenous peoples into the nation by forcing them to assimilate.

But what of countries with small indigenous populations? Do they feel much need to incorporate them into the state or at least into the national dialogue about the nature of the state, or are they content to leave them marginalized? The examples discussed in this volume are inconclusive. They show that in two instances indigenous peoples are marginal to the states in which they live, while in a third they are treated as a central issue.

The Kuna, discussed by James Howe, are not the only indigenous group in Panama, but they are the most prominent. Their independence and tenacious defense of their rights have made them famous. They have been helped in this by the special circumstances of Panama's independence, when the country was wrested from Colombia in a process that took place under the aegis of the United States. The Kuna have subsequently benefited from their remote location close to Panama's border with Colombia and from their tenacity and skill in managing their own affairs. Now the marginality that they have traditionally turned to their advantage has become problematic for them. Their territory is being invaded by Panamanian peasants and also by the groups involved in Colombia's civil war, which is spilling over into Panama. The relative weakness of the Panamanian state, which has traditionally been an advantage for the Kuna, now means that the Kuna cannot hope to receive effective support from the state in protecting their interests. In any case, the parties that compete with each other in the Panamanian political system have little interest in defending the Kuna, who are thus left exposed in the midst of forces that they are having difficulty in combating.

The indigenous peoples of Paraguay, who are discussed in Richard Reed's chapter, face similar problems, though their circumstances are very different. They have never achieved the kind of local independence that has made the Kuna famous. On the contrary, they have always been economically and politically weak and have sought to protect themselves by attaching themselves to powerful patrons. These would defend them in exchange for their services and for the resources that they would otherwise have controlled. Since the fall of General Stroessner and Paraguay's move to a more democratic system of party politics, the old patronage system has evaporated. There are no longer powerful agencies, ministers or *caudillos* (political bosses) to whom indigenous groups can attach themselves as clients. Meanwhile politicians find the votes of relatively small indigenous groups, scattered throughout the country, to be of limited value. Above all, they see little political advantage in defending indigenous rights against those of non-Indians who seek to claim or seize indigenous resources. At least the native peoples of Paraguay are not being sucked into any of the civil wars on the continent, but they are being affected by the turmoil in the Paraguayan countryside resulting from the fact that it has been invaded by a massive influx of land hungry Brazilians from across the border.

Paraguay has proclaimed itself multiethnic, which Panama has not, but this appears to make little practical difference. The recognition of indigenous identities by the state has done little to protect the native peoples of Paraguay. Meanwhile the local self-determination of the Kuna did not stem from government policies or any national declaration of multiethnicity, but resulted rather from the Kuna's ability to seize the geographical and political opportunities that were offered to them.

Brazil is the third example, discussed by Maybury-Lewis in his chapter entitled "For Reasons of State." It is perhaps the most paradoxical case, because the indigenous population of Brazil is tiny, yet indigenous policy looms large in Brazilian discussions about the future of the nation. This is because Brazil's treatment of its native peoples unexpectedly became an issue at the beginning of the twentieth century and has remained so ever since. The issue seemed to have been laid to rest by the benevolent policies of Candido Rondón and the Indian Service that he founded; but it was revived again in the 1960s, when the brutal effects of the advancing frontier made headlines throughout the world, accompanied by fresh accusations of genocide against Brazil. This was all the more shocking since Rondón had made a name for himself by demonstrating that it was possible to establish friendly relations with even the "wildest" Indians and had founded a government agency whose task it was to protect Brazil's indigenous populations and bring them into the national civilization. Rondón's indigenism was very similar in theory to the indigenism advocated by the Mexicans after their revolution. It advocated a policy of respect for the persons and cultures of indigenous peoples. Meanwhile they would be protected and educated in such a way that they would be drawn into and eventually assimilated into the national mainstream. The assimilationist aspect of these policies would be criticized by indigenous rights advocates today, but in Rondón's day they did not appear coercive. Instead it was assumed that such policies would protect and benefit indigenous peoples until their cultures were absorbed into the dominant civilization.

When the military took over the state in 1964, they soon wished to discard the Rondonian approach. It was too respectful of peoples who were in military circles considered "savages." It was too slow, for it soon became clear that if the "savages" were to be assimilated into Brazilian society following Rondón's methods, it would take a long time, if it ever happened. Above all, it was too generous. The guarantees that Rondón offered to the Indians in terms of their lands and cultures would leave them in control of valuable resources and planted squarely "in the path of development." This the military would not tolerate. On the other hand, it was reluctant simply to abandon the Rondonian guarantees, which would embarrass the government both nationally and internationally. The solution invented by the military regime was "emancipation." It proposed to do away with the category "Indian" altogether. Only truly "wild" Indians, minimally affected by civilization, would in future be entitled to the protection of the state. Others would be released from their Indianness. This would ensure the disappearance of minorities having special status that entitled them to lands and resources that could, in the opinion of the generals, be more profitably used by others in the service of development.

It was clear to indigenous and pro-indigenous people alike that the emancipation proposals were intended to legalize the seizure of native resources with the excuse that this would enhance development. The result was the growth of the indigenous movement and of a lively pro-indigenous movement dedicated to protecting indigenous rights. These movements soon made common cause with the Movement of the Landless, another category of people who were also being made to suffer in the name of development.

Neither the military nor the conservatives who took up their policies after the military regime were able to get the emancipation decree through the Brazilian congress; but, as we saw above, some congressmen are still trying to demonstrate (or force the FUNAI to demonstrate) that certain indigenous groups are not really indigenous at all. This would terminate the protection of their lands and cultures to which they are entitled at present.

The result of these battles over indigenous rights was that the framers of the constitution of 1988 upheld the guarantees of indigenous lands and cultures, but refused to declare Brazil a multiethnic state. This, it was and still is argued, would lead to separatism that would undermine the state. Yet this is hardly a realistic concern. As the U.N.-sponsored draft declaration of indigenous rights makes clear, indigenous peoples rarely demand the right to secede from the state. Rather they ask for the right of self-determination and limited local autonomy within the state. This is especially true in Brazil, whose small indigenous groups have never shown any sign of wishing to secede. It could be argued of course that if Brazil proclaimed itself multiethnic, this might encourage other non-indigenous separatist movements, in the northeast, for example, or the far south, both areas that have flirted with separatism at one time or another in Brazilian history. Yet such an argument also strains credulity. The slight flickerings of separatism in these regions had little to do with any notion of Brazil's being multiethnic. If Brazil were to proclaim itself multiethnic, this would entail that the state should maintain a dialogue with the minorities in its midst. Many people might think that was a good thing, though governments might prefer not to have to do it. In fact, if such a dialogue were to serve as a model for citizens disaffected enough to consider separatism in the northeast or the south, then that might be a good thing too.

All this is in the realm of wild speculation. What the Brazilian case does show, however, is that discussions of indigenous policy in that country entail discussions of the nature of the state, of its model of development, and above all of its treatment of the have-nots within the country. Such discussions in their turn entail a possible rethinking of the nature of the state, which is exactly what the proponents of multi-ethnicity in Mexico and the Andean nations have argued for. What we are witnessing, then, throughout the Americas,[4] is a series of debates, conflicts, even wars concerning not merely who controls the state, but the nature of the state itself and the kinds of negotiations and dialogues that take place within it.

Notes

1   This paper summarizes and comments on the other contributions to this volume. They should be consulted for general reference. I only refer to them specifically when citing specific details or arguments.

2   A general overview of the treatment of indigenous peoples in the Americas can be found in Maybury-Lewis 1993.

3   The land reform stipulated that lands known as *ejidos* would be allocated to indigenous communities. *Ejidos* were owned by the state but used by the communities who received them and were responsible for administering them.

4   I think that the argument holds for both the nations discussed in this volume and others that could not be included.

INDEX

(Please note that organizations and entities are referenced under both their full names and their acronyms.)